STUDIES IN BRITISH ART

1. Sir Thomas Lawrence P.R.A. *Joseph Farington.* R.A. 1796 (164). Formerly collection of Miss Susan ffarington.

THE DIARY

OF

JOSEPH FARINGTON

edited by

KENNETH GARLICK and ANGUS MACINTYRE

VOLUME I

JULY 1793 — DECEMBER 1794

Published for the Paul Mellon Centre
for Studies in British Art
by
YALE UNIVERSITY PRESS
NEW HAVEN AND LONDON
1978

Designed by John Nicoll.
Set in AM747 Times by Preface Ltd, Salisbury, Wilts.
Printed in Great Britain by Biddles of Guildford.

Published in Great Britain, Europe, Africa, and Asia (except Japan) by
Yale University Press, Ltd., London. Distributed in Australia and New
Zealand by Book & Film Services, Artarmon, N.S.W., Australia; and in
Japan by Harper & Row, Publishers, Tokyo Office.

Library of Congress Cataloging in Publication Data

Farington, Joseph, 1747–1821
  The diary of Joseph Farington.

  (Studies in British art)
  CONTENTS: v. 1. July 1793–December 1794.--v. 2.
January 1795–August 1796.
  1. Farington, Joseph, 1747-1821. 2. Artists--England--Biography. 3.
Arts, English. 4. England--Civilization--18th century. 5. England--
Civilization--19th century. 6. London. Royal Academy of Art.
I. Garlick, Kenneth, 1916-   II. Macintyre, Angus D.
III. Paul Mellon Centre for Studies in British Art.   IV. Series.

N6797.F37A2 1978   759.2[B]   78-7056
ISBN 0-300-02314-6

PREFACE

The diary of Joseph Farington, running with few interruptions from 13 July 1793 until the day of his death on 30 December 1821, has been known to most readers in the version edited by James Greig and published in eight volumes between 1922 and 1928. Its importance, chiefly as a source for the history of English art and artists but also for the social, political and literary history of the period, has long been recognized. For some years, a transcription of the diary — the Windsor Typescript, made after the diary passed into the possession of King George V — has been available both in the Royal Library at Windsor Castle and in the Department of Prints and Drawings at the British Museum; and this bare typescript has served scholars in the absence of a full printed version.

By gracious permission of Her Majesty the Queen and under the generous auspices of the Paul Mellon Centre, it has been decided to publish the text of the whole diary. It was originally planned that each volume would contain annotation to provide the reader with the information necessary for the understanding and enjoyment of the diary. The steep rise in the costs of printing and publication and the desire to produce as soon as possible an accessible text of the whole diary enforced changes in our original plan. Instead, each volume will comprise the plain text of the diary as established from the original, with our editorial interventions confined to essential corrections and directions and contained throughout the volumes in square brackets. When the complete text has been published, we shall provide a full Index, in one or more volumes, and a further volume, *A Companion to the Farington Diary*, which will incorporate in an encyclopaedic form the editorial materials and commentary collected originally for the purposes of annotation.

The Introduction to this volume is divided into three parts. In the first, we give an account of Farington himself — his family and connections, his work as an artist, his position in the Royal Academy — and a summary of the principal themes which run through his diary, paying particular attention to the years covered by the first two volumes. This is followed by a description of the manuscript of the diary and an account of its transmission. Finally, we describe our editorial approach to the text and the methods which we have adopted in editing it for publication. We shall provide a short introduction to each succeeding pair of volumes.

We have incurred many obligations in the course of our work. In the Index and Companion volumes, we propose to thank those who have already generously helped us on matters of scholarship. Here we wish particularly to thank Sir Robin Mackworth-Young, Librarian of the Royal Library at Windsor Castle, for providing us with unfailing co-operation and ready access to the main text of the diary, and Professor Sir Ellis Waterhouse for his support and encouragement. To John Nicoll of the Yale University Press we owe much for his guidance on the technical problems involved in publishing this edition. Mrs. John Bradford and Mrs. B. B. Parry have given us invaluable assistance at different stages in the preparation of the text. For permission to reproduce Farington's diary of his tour of Kent in 1794, we thank the Trustees of the British Library. For their kind permission to reproduce (in Vols. I and II) works in their possession, we thank Lady Hesketh, the Hon. Robin Neville, the Royal Academy of Arts, the Trustees of the British Museum, the National Maritime Museum and the National Portrait Gallery, and other private owners. We are grateful to the Archaeological Survey of India for providing the photograph of Bacon's statue of Lord Cornwallis, of which they retain the copyright, and for giving us permission to reproduce it.

February 1978   K.J.G.
                                                          A.D.M.

CONTENTS

LIST OF PLATES

INTRODUCTION

I. JOSEPH FARINGTON AND HIS DIARY

Joseph Farington was born on 21 November 1747 at Leigh, near Manchester, in Lancashire. He was the second son of the vicar of Leigh, the Rev. William Farington, and Esther, daughter of Joseph Gilbody of Manchester. His father, the second son of William Farington of Worden and Shaw Hall, Leyland, was educated at Brasenose College, Oxford, where he matriculated on 11 February 1722/3 at the age of eighteen, took his B.A. in 1726 and eventually proceeded to B.D. in 1766. He became vicar of Leigh in 1733. One of the patrons of the parish was his elder brother George (also a Brasenose man), and in 1766 he was instituted rector of Warrington, a living which belonged to his relations, the Athertons of Atherton Hall, and which he held *in commendam* with the vicarage of Leigh. He did not enjoy these combined benefices for long, since he died on 3 August 1767, leaving a widow who long outlived him and died in 1794, and seven sons. His clerical career was as conventional as his whole life seems to have been placid. Vicar of Leigh for thirty-four years, he was the author of some *Sermons* posthumously published at Warrington in 1769, and of a further series of sermons in manuscript which show him to have been an able controversialist against the Papists but which also, according to a local historian, reveal 'that the spirit of the times had absorbed all the old devotional feeling'.[1]

Some account of the family to which Farington belonged is essential if certain important contexts of his life and diary are to be appreciated; in a work written immediately for his own use, he does not trouble to explain relationships and contexts which naturally required no explanation for him. His family was a cadet branch of an ancient and substantial gentry family of Lancashire, the Faringtons (or Faryngton, ffarington or ffaryngton) of Farington, Worden and Ribbleton. In nineteenth-century genealogies, their descent was traced back to Roger de Bussli or Bussel, Baron of Penwortham under William the Conqueror. A later and more

1. Quoted in Edward Baines, *History of the County Palatine and Duchy of Lancaster*, ed. J. Croston (1891), IV, 323.

cautious genealogist listed the family among those which, if not demonstrably Norman, ranked in antiquity little behind the genuine Norman families. The Faringtons were certainly established by early Plantagenet times.[1] From John, the first to be styled de Faryngton, who married Avicia de Bussel and acquired a moiety of the manor of Leyland before he died in 1314, the family in its various branches remained prominent in Lancashire and active in the service of the Crown. John's son William, sub-custodian of the peace for Leylandshire under Edward II, attended the Great Council at Westminster called by Edward III and was knighted by the King. Under the first Tudors, Henry ffaryngton, who succeeded in 1501, was squire of the body to Henry VII and knighted at the coronation of Ann Boleyn in 1533; he served as a knight of the shire in the Parliaments of 1529 and 1536, as a commissioner for dissolving the monasteries, and as steward of the King's manor of Penwortham, acquiring the manor of Worden for himself in 1534 before he died in 1555.[2]

It was from Sir Henry's second marriage, to Dorothy, daughter of Humfrey Okeover and widow of Sir Arthur Eyre, that Joseph Farington's branch of the family was descended. William Farington (1537–1610), the first of Worden, son of Sir Henry by this marriage, was an active justice of the peace who served as steward of the household to three Earls of Derby and also enlarged his own estates; it is said of him that 'in religion he was externally a conformist to the Elizabethan settlement, but reputed to be in secret its bitter enemy'.[3] His descendants remained Protestants in a county which contained much recusancy. His son Thomas served Queen Elizabeth as constable of Lancaster Castle and steward of the Queen's lands in Lonsdale, but he was also apparently 'an irreclaimable spendthrift' whose father settled the family estates away from him and on his son, William.[4]

The career of this William Farington was more noteworthy and more chequered. He served in the difficult office of high sheriff of the county in 1636 and was one of the knights of the shire in the Short Parliament of 1640. As Colonel of the Lancashire militia and as a follower of the Earl of Derby, he rallied to the King at the beginning of the Civil War in 1642 and

1. A. C. Fox-Davies, *Armorial Families* (1910), xli. The main sources for the family's history are *The Victoria History of the County of Lancaster*, ed. W. Farrer and J. Brownbill (1911), VI, 3–14; *Burke's Commoners* (1836), III, 339–42, with necessary corrections; W. D. Pink and A. B. Beavan, *The Parliamentary Representation of Lancashire* (1889); and pedigrees in Baines, op. cit., IV, 170–3; Joseph Foster, *Pedigrees of the County Families of England: Vol. I, Lancashire* (1873).
2. For the line of descent from Sir Henry, see the pedigree at the end of this volume.
3. *VCH Lancs.*, VI, 12.
4. Susan Maria ffarington ed., *The Farington Papers, Chetham Society* (1866), XXXIX, iii.

was appointed a commissioner of array. His activities included ordering
his servant to take possession of the stocks of gunpowder at Preston and
accompanying Lord Strange to the siege of Manchester in 1642, but his
most notable contribution to the King's cause was to act as principal
adviser to the Countess of Derby during the first and successful defence of
Lathom, the seat of the great house of Stanley. His estates had been
sequestered by Parliament at the beginning of the war, and by 1646 he was
a prisoner. His were, as a Victorian member of the family remarked, 'the
ordinary sufferings of an ordinary royalist gentleman'. He compounded in
1647 for his estates for the sum of £536, and again in 1649 for £511, and
died in 1658.[1] His elder son William (1612–72) also served the King as a
captain in Lord Strange's militia regiment, fought at both sieges of
Lathom and was nominated for a knighthood of the Royal Oak — the
order which was projected but never instituted. The family seems to have
retained its loyalties to the house of Stuart for a generation. George, who
died in about 1704, of Shaw Hall, the second son of the royalist Captain
William, was among those challenged by the Crown at the Jacobite trials in
Manchester in 1694 — presumably on suspicion of Jacobite sympathies.[2]
His elder son, William of Shaw Hall, who succeeded his cousin William at
Worden in 1715 and died before 1718, was the father of the Rev. William
Farington and grandfather of Joseph.[3]

   In their various branches, the family produced no figures of particular
distinction or importance unless exceptions are made for Sir Henry, who
played his part in the Henrician Reformation, and for Colonel William
Farington, the royalist. They were substantial middling gentry, justices of
the peace and officers of the militia who occasionally acted as sheriffs of
the county; if they did not aspire to be knights of the shire, they had, as the
principal landowners of the western part of the parish of Leyland, considerable importance and secure standing in their own community. They
married into families of comparable rank, usually of Lancashire, Cheshire
or Westmorland, rarely further afield — ffleetwood of Penwortham,
Whitmore of Thurstaston in Cheshire, Swettenham of Somerford Booths,

1. Susan Maria ffarington, *op. cit.*, vi. Her volume contains, besides letters written
during the Civil War, other family materials of the sixteenth and seventeenth
centuries. For valuations of William Farington's estates and his compounding, see
VCH Lancs., VI, 13; M. A. Green ed., *Calendar of Proceedings of the Committee for Compounding etc., 1643–1660* (1891–2), 2024–5, 2822.
2. William Beaumont ed., *The Jacobite Trials at Manchester in 1694*, Chetham
Society (1853), XXVIII, 64.
3. The arms of Farington of Worden, confirmed in 1560 by Norroy King at Arms,
are described in Bernard Burke, *The General Armory* (1884), 340, and were
painted above the mural tablet in the church at Broxbourne, Herts. commemorating the Rev. William Farington and his family, including Joseph. The family motto
was 'Domat omnia virtus'.

Cheshire, Pricket of Natland Abbey in Westmorland, Atherton of
Atherton, Charnock of Leyland and Astley, Banastre of Bank, Nowell of
Altham and Underley, Wilbraham Bootle of Lathom. William, Joseph
Farington's grandfather, was exceptional in moving outside a local gentry
family to marry in 1694 Elizabeth, the daughter and sole heiress of Dr.
James Rufine of Boulogne, who is said to have been a Huguenot refugee.
Shaw Hall, the main family seat (later called Worden Hall), half a mile
from Leyland, was described in the early nineteenth century as 'a large but
irregular mansion' with some spacious rooms. The house had been altered
and enlarged soon after 1742 by the diarist's first cousin, Sir William
Farington, and contained a museum of 'natural curiosities, busts, marbles
&c. and a collection of paintings, some of them frescoes found in the ruins
of Herculaneum and brought from Italy by Sir William', together with a
Noli me tangere attributed to Titian.[1] When Farington began his diary in
1793, the head of the family was Sir William's nephew, also William, a
J.P., a deputy lieutenant of the county, and, like his royalist ancestor,
lieutenant-colonel of the Lancashire militia.

Farington's connections in Lancashire included the prominent families
of Wilbraham Bootle (now the owners of Lathom which Farington's
ancestors had defended) and Atherton. With Richard Wilbraham Bootle,
M.P. for Chester, whose daughter Sybella Georgiana was the first wife of
the last-mentioned William Farington, Farington was obviously well
acquainted.[2] Henrietta Maria Atherton, 'Miss Atherton' in the diary, the
young heiress of Atherton Hall, near Leigh, was a cousin of Farington's
whom he naturally saw with her sisters and their uncle Lawrence
Rawstorne when they visited London, and whose case against a projected
extension of the Lancaster Canal he followed in person in the House of
Lords.[3] Farington's keen interest in the affairs of noble and gentry families
was not simply snobbish. No doubt he had his share of inquisitiveness
about other people's business, and in his profession it could often be
important to know men's connections, interests and finances. But when he
recounts the vicissitudes of Lancashire families such as the Leghs and
Parkers,[4] he is writing about people long familiar to him, neighbours of his
own family, features of his own past life and of the family in which he took

1. *Burke's Commoners*, III, 342; *VCH Lancs.*, VI, 14. The museum and
collection of paintings, including family portraits, remained *in situ* when a modern
house incorporating parts of the old Shaw Hall was built by Anthony Salvin in
1840-5 for James Nowell Farington (d. 1848). The house has been demolished. The
portraits were dispersed in the sale, by order of the executors of H. Nowell
ffarington, of the contents of Worden Hall by E. J. Reed & Sons, 26-9 July, 1945.
2. See, e.g., 21 June 1794.
3. 8, 10, 11, 15 Mar. 1794. Henrietta Maria Atherton married in 1797 Thomas
Powys, second Baron Lilford. For her and her sisters, see the pedigree.
4. See, e.g., 3 [4], [29] Jan. 1794.

much pride. Nor is his interest in Lancashire confined to the gentry. Through his brothers and through his friends and visitors, he kept himself informed about affairs in Manchester: he followed the political activities of Thomas Walker, the radical cotton manufacturer,[4] and notes the state of trade, taxation and prices there.[2] He was linked to Liverpool, less directly, through his cousin Isabella's marriage to Gill Slater of that city.[3] He regularly records his brother Dick's attendance at the annual dinners in London of members of the Manchester Church and King Society, the body which contributed largely to the crushing of Thomas Walker's movement.

When Farington's father took orders, he was the first Farington to do so since the fifteenth century. The family's connections with the Church had been through their benefactions to Leyland parish church, in which they had their chapel and ancient claims to pews and vaults, and through marriage into clerical families — a tradition maintained both by Farington's aunt Isabella when she married the Rev. Dr. John Woodcock, rector of Byford and vicar of Canon Pyon, Herefordshire, and by Farington himself. The family also had some military links. In the branch descended from Henry, younger brother of the spendthrift Thomas of Queen Elizabeth's time, Thomas Farington (who died in 1712) was commissioned into the Coldstream Guards and rose to lieutenant-general. A closer relation of Farington's, his first cousin Bradshaw, third son of George Farington, was killed at Fontenoy at the age of twenty-two. By the late eighteenth century, the family had also developed strong links with the navy. Two of his first cousins, William and Austin Bissell, the sons of his aunt Margaret by her marriage to William Bissell of Seabourns, Herefordshire, were naval officers.[4] A much more important naval and family connection was with Rear-Admiral Alan Gardner (1742–1809), the son of Colonel William Gardner of Uttoxeter by his wife Elizabeth, elder daughter of Valentine Farington, M.D., of Preston.[5] Admiral Gardner, who proved himself a distinguished fighting sailor despite his nervous temperament, commanded the *Queen* at the Glorious First of June and was given a baronetcy and promotion to vice-admiral for his services.[6] His account of the action was duly recorded by Farington,[7] who was evidently

1. See, e.g., [29] Jan. 1794; 27 Jan. 1795.
2. 6 Oct. 1793.
3. 6 Oct. 1793; see also, e.g., for affairs in Liverpool, 3 Dec. 1795.
4. William, whose career was interrupted by a spell in the Marshalsea, presumably for debt (to which there are frequent references in the diary in 1793 and 1794), never rose above the rank of lieutenant. Austin became a captain.
5. See pedigree.
6. He was created Baron Gardner of Uttoxeter in the Irish peerage in 1800, and of the United Kingdom in 1806.
7. 18 July 1794.

on easy terms with him and his family and who called on the admiral, as recorded in the diary, to help in the reinstatement of William Bissell in the navy.[1]

Farington had an even closer connection with the sea and with the greatest of English imperial interests. No less than four of his brothers entered the sea service of the East India Company.[2] William (1746–1803), the eldest, referred to as 'Will' in the diary, rose from fourth officer in the *Duke of Gloucester* in 1770–1 and first officer of the *General Coote* in 1782–4 to command the *Mars*, a new ship which was lost on Margate Sands on 8 December 1787, after which he lived at Hoddesdon in Hertfordshire with his family. Henry (1750–1827), the third brother, 'Harry' in the diary, served as purser on various East Indiamen between 1772 and 1788. Richard Atherton (1755–1822), the fifth, 'Dick' in the diary, began as third officer of the *Queen* in 1778–80 and on the *Lascelles* in 1780–1, of which he was later captain from 1786 to 1793. His last command, beginning in 1796, was the *Henry Addington*, and Dick retired from the sea in 1798 on his return with his ship from China. Both Harry and Dick were connected with Manchester through their marriages to sisters, the daughters of James Borron of Manchester; and Dick, who seems to have been the most successful in worldly terms of all the brothers, bought Parr's Wood, at Didsbury, near Manchester in 1795,[3] and settled down there as a J.P. for Lancashire and Cheshire. The sixth brother, Edward (1758–90), after serving as purser in several East Indiamen, was lost in the *Foulis* in 1790.

Of the remaining brothers, George (1752–88), the fourth, was a history and portrait painter, a pupil first of his elder brother and then of Benjamin West. He is known to have worked with his brother at Houghton after 1773; nine years later he too went out to India and became a busy painter, his chief work being a large picture of the Nawab's durbar at Murshidabad, where he died suddenly in 1788.[4] Finally, the youngest brother, Robert (1760–1841), 'Bob' in the diary, followed his father first to Brasenose, where he matriculated in 1777 and obtained his B.A. in 1781, and then into the church. A bachelor, he was successively fellow in 1782, vice-principal in 1792–3 and senior bursar of Brasenose in 1796–7, became D.D. in 1803 and served as rector of St. George's-in-the-East in London for thirty-eight years. It is clear from the diary that the five brothers still living in 1793 formed a close-knit and harmonious family and that

1. See 24 Dec. 1793; 11 Jan; 21 June; 16, 22 July 1794.
2. For the brothers, see J. E. Cussans, *History of Hertfordshire: Hundred of Hertford* (1876), 194–5, who records the mural tablet mentioned above (p. xiii n. 3); and *The Farington Diary*, ed. James Greig (1922), I, 346–8. For their families, see the pedigree.
3. See 17 April 1795.
4. Sir William Foster, 'British Artists in India, 1760–1820', *Walpole Society* (1930–1), XIX, 31–2.

JOSEPH FARINGTON AND HIS DIARY

Farington, with no children of his own, was much interested in his brothers' concerns. When, for example, Will's children passed through London on their way to school, Farington did his duty by them; when Will fell into some financial difficulty, he and his brothers came to the rescue.[1] His sense of his family and its interests as well as his patriotism are excellently demonstrated by his arranging a meeting in December 1793 between his brother Will, who must have acquired considerable knowledge of the Indian Ocean, and Admiral Gardner, then a lord of the admiralty, to discuss the situation of the French island of Mauritius — a subject of considerable strategic interest to the navy.[2] Farington's links with India and the East give an additional significance to his interest in the work and experience of the Daniells in India,[3] in matters connected with Lord Macartney's embassy to China[4] and in the impeachment of Warren Hastings.[5] These were matters, along with the more humdrum affairs of the Company, in which no member of a family such as Farington's could fail to be interested.

Norfolk provided another important dimension to his life. He owed this to his wife Susan Mary, the only daughter of the Rev. Dr. Horace Hamond, rector of Harpley and Great Bircham in Norfolk from 1744 to 1786 and prebendary of Norwich for thirty years until his death in 1786. The Hamonds of Wootton were a landed family, lords of the manor of Swaffham, with a seat at High House, Westacre, near Swaffham.[6] Dr. Horace Hamond was a younger son of Anthony Hamond (1685–1743) by his marriage to Susan, youngest daughter of Robert Walpole and sister of Sir Robert, the first Earl of Orford and Prime Minister. By his marriage to Dorothy Walpole Turner (of the Turners of Warham), Dr. Horace Hamond had one son, Horace, who also entered the church, and the daughter who became Farington's wife.

Susan Farington remains a shadowy figure in her husband's diary. They had no children, and her poor health obviously gave Farington much concern. But the measured terms in which this apparently most unemotional man records her death at the age of fifty on 24 February 1800 cannot conceal the depth of his feeling for her:

> This day the greatest calamity that could fall upon me I suffered in the death of the best, the most affectionate, the most amiable of woemen,

1. 19 Nov. 1794.
2. 24, 30 Dec. 1793.
3. See, e.g., 3 Nov. 1793; 28 Dec. 1794.
4. See, e.g., 26 July, 28 Dec. 1794; 10 June 1795.
5. See, e.g., 3, 14, 16, 20 June 1794; 23 April 1795.
6. For High House, which was built before 1756 and refronted in 1829, see N. Pevsner, The *Buildings of England: North-West and North Norfolk* (1973), 372; and J. Chambers, *A General History of the County of Norfolk* (1829), I, 482.

my beloved wife. Unexpected indeed was the blow — long had I reason
to consider her delicate frame with apprehension, but as she had
encountered the severity of many winters so I fondly hoped she might do
this and that a more favorable season would restore her strength . . . at 3
o'clock this day I witnessed the departure of what I held most dear on
earth.[1]

For over five weeks, he was so broken by his loss that he could not keep his
diary — perhaps the most eloquent tribute he could pay his wife. He owed
his recovery to his strength of will and to the rational advice of his
friends, who pointed out that 'mental derangement' would be the consequence of continuing 'in the desponding way' and that Farington's moral
and religious duty was to overcome his grief by 'having recourse to Society
and to exercise and to amusement'. Temporary abstention from church
services and devotional books was also recommended.[2] The cure was
in due course effective. Farington's life and his diary continued.

Through his wife, Farington was drawn into the society of Norfolk,
more particularly into that part of it rooted in the north-west of the
county, a world similar in many ways to that of his own family in
Lancashire. The Hamonds were related to the Walpoles, Cholmondeleys
and Turners, to a number of the lesser gentry families of the country —
Henley of Sandringham, Case of Stradsett — and to the leading merchant
dynasties of Kings Lynn such as the Bagges and the Swanns. The head of
the family at this time, Anthony Hamond (1746–1822), Susan Farington's
first cousin, served as sheriff of the county in 1792–3; his brother, the Rev.
Richard Hamond, who married Elizabeth Bagge, was rector of
Pensthorpe; and the Rev. Horace Hamond, Farington's brother-in-law,
rector of Great Massingham from 1793 until his death in 1815, was
frequently the Faringtons' host in Norfolk and their guest in London. He is
referred to as 'Horace' in the diary. On his visits, Farington moved as an
equal among the Norfolk squires, parsons, merchants, professional men
and their families. In this largely rural society, he found much less to
record in his diary than when he was in London, confining himself often to
lists of those he met, but he noted such important local matters as the Eau
Brink canal project in which the authorities of Kings Lynn and neighbouring landowners were interested,[3] Miss Broderick's murder of Mr.
Errington,[4] and the most recent purchases of land by Thomas Coke of
Holkham, one of the outstanding exemplars of agricultural improvement

1. 24 Feb. 1800.
2. See 3, 11 April 1800.
3. 1 Sept. 1795.
4. 9 Sept. 1795.

in England.[1] In his professional life, it was during a visit to Norfolk that he became the first to hear of Samuel Lane, the deaf son of the collector of customs at Kings Lynn who became his pupil and, later, pupil and assistant to Lawrence.[2] More important for his own work, his wife's relationship to Horace Walpole doubtless smoothed the path to Strawberry Hill and to an apparently comfortable relationship with Walpole, whose conversation Farington records at length and with obvious pleasure. There were other advantages. In 1792, when Farington was engaged on work for the views to illustrate the *History of the River Thames*, Walpole wrote to Lord Harcourt asking him to allow 'Mr Farrington the painter (who married a cousin of mine)' to sketch at Nuneham.[3]

Farington's work as a busy and highly professional topographical artist, his relations with other artists and his close involvement in the affairs of the Royal Academy were the dominant themes of his life outside his immediate family interests; and London was his true centre. Comparatively little work has been done on him as an artist. Until recently, the most useful contribution was by F. Gordon Roe,[4] but the exhibition of watercolours and drawings organized for the Bolton Museum and Art Gallery in 1977 by William Ruddick and Mark Turner has, with its accompanying catalogue, brought the study of this aspect of Farington's art up to date.[5]

He came to London at the age of sixteen in 1763 and entered the studio of Richard Wilson, whose work he probably knew at first hand already. Wilson was, after all, a native of Flintshire. One of his favourite subjects was a stretch of the River Dee near Eaton Hall in Cheshire, no great distance from Farington's own part of Lancashire, and it seem likely that he was working there in the early 1760s. Wilson's picture of Tabley House, also in Cheshire, although not exhibited until 1780, is known to have been painted much earlier and may well belong to the same years.[6] It is in any case characteristic that Farington should have decided so early on landscape as the field in which he wished to specialise. As far as is known he never undertook any other kind of subject, and when he accepted 'historical' commissions from Boydell and Bowyer, he prescribed his own limits, collaborating with Smirke in scenes which required a setting of

1. 15, 16, 27 Oct. 1795. His note, 17 Jan. 1794, on radicalism in Norwich, although written while he was in London, reflects his links with Norfolk.
2. 25 Oct. 1795.
3. Walpole to Harcourt, 4 Oct. 1792, *The Yale Edition of Horace Walpole's Correspondence*, ed. W. S. Lewis, XXXV (1973), 542.
4. F. Gordon Roe, 'Dictator of the Royal Academy: An Account of Joseph Farington, R.A., with some notes on his brother George', *Walker's Quarterly*, No. 5 (Oct. 1921).
5. Bolton Museum and Art Gallery, *Joseph Farington: Watercolours and Drawings* (1977), Exhibition Catalogue.
6. W. G. Constable, *Richard Wilson* (1953), 186.

woodland and boskage, Smirke painting the figures, Farington the back-grounds. Their joint works, such as *Falstaff and Poins at Gadshill* and *Charles II at the Boscobel Oak*, cannot at present be traced. It is very desirable that they should be, for the engravings suggest that Farington's part in them was as good as anything of his we know. His being placed as a pupil with Wilson was appropriate in another way, for Wilson occupied rooms over the north arcade of Covent Garden Piazza which had been previously tenanted by Thornhill, Kneller and Lely. This was a fact which Farington, with his respect for tradition and his historian's temperament, would have fully appreciated.

It would seem (although this can only be surmise) that when Farington came to London he was a very mature sixteen-year-old, clear in his own mind of what he wanted to do, aware of his potential and perhaps aware also of his limitations. In 1764, a year after his arrival, he gained a premium at the Society of Artists for landscape drawing. He repeated this success in 1765 and 1766, and in 1765 was elected a member of the Society. It is significant that these premiums were granted him for drawing because, despite the fact that over the years he must have produced a good many oil-paintings, it was as a landscape draughtsman rather than a landscape painter that he was to make his mark. This again suggests that his personality and predilections were clearly formed at an early stage, for his drawings, which depend for their effect on precise, delicate line, owe little to Wilson, whereas in his painting he sometimes deliberately followed Wilson's style, loading the brush with a rich impasto and spreading the palette with a Wilsonian range of tones. It is difficult to assess the merit of his paintings since so few have entered public collections and compara-tively few have appeared in the sale-rooms. This probably means that a large number pass unrecognised under other names. A Farington drawing, however, almost immediately speaks for itself. His calligraphic style owed a prime debt to a study of the pen-and-ink drawings of Canaletto. At a later stage he worked towards a broader and less broken line. Within their narrowly defined limits, his drawings transmit his personality: accurate, sensitive, but unromantic. Despite the closeness of his association with Wilson and the fact that they went on sketching tours together in the 1760s, Farington's drawings never attain Wilson's breadth and strength. A comparison of Wilson's *Tree Stems*[1] (undated) with Farington's *Study of Trees*[2] (1786), admittedly later than the Wilson, shows that while they used an almost identical calligraphy in the leaf and branch forms, Farington's modelling is relatively tame. It is true that Wilson worked in charcoal, a

1. Coll. Brinsley Ford. See Brinsley Ford, *The Drawings of Richard Wilson* (1951), pl. II.
2. Whitworth Art Gallery, University of Manchester; *Joseph Farington: Watercolours and Drawings* (1977), Exhibition Catalogue, pl. 30.

medium which allows much greater freedom of modelling than the pen-
and-wash of Farington, but it is clear that Farington deliberately went his
own more restricted way — another example of his self-knowledge. The
more restricted method was the one that suited him best. He did of course
lean heavily on Wilson when it came to composition. The arranged
Claudian composing of many of his views of the Thames is Wilsonian in
pattern, if not in effect.

In 1768 the Royal Academy of Arts was established by royal charter.
Wilson and a number of other members of the Society of Artists broke
with that body and became founder members of the new one. Farington,
still only twenty-one, was in no position to attempt such a move, but he
enrolled as a student at the Royal Academy schools in 1769 while
continuing to exhibit at the Society of Artists and becoming one of its
directors in 1772 or 1773. This latter body was to decline in importance
with the years, and Farington then found himself completely free to
associate more closely with the Academy.

Between 1773 and 1776, he was employed with his brother George by
Alderman Boydell (the beginning of a long association) to make water-
colour copies of the collection of paintings at Houghton, most of which
were to be sold to the Empress Catherine of Russia in 1779. These copies
were engraved and published in two volumes in 1788.[1] It is curious but
typical of Farington's unsentimental approach to the events of his busy life
that when some twenty years later he records in his diary a visit to
Houghton on 5 December 1794, he notes methodically the paintings by his
contemporaries — Fuseli, Opie, Garrard, Cipriani and Reinagle — some
of which must have replaced the works by Rubens, Raphael and
Rembrandt he had copied, but makes not even a passing reference to the
fact that the great collection had been dispersed.

At some point in 1776, he left London, returned to the north and worked
for two or three years in Lancashire, Cumberland and Westmorland. It is
a period about which we know little, but he must have spent it actively
making drawings and sketches which served him as stock-in-trade and
memoranda for some years to come. His Academy subjects between 1778
and 1784 and again in 1788 consisted solely of north country views. He
returned to London and settled finally in December 1780 at 35 Upper
Charlotte Street, Fitzroy Square (a house which later belonged to
Constable), where he assumed an established position within his chosen
world, becoming A.R.A. in 1783 and R.A. in 1785, producing his *Views of
the Lakes etc. in Cumberland and Westmorland* in 1789, the first of a series
of topographical works. *Views of Cities and Towns in England and Wales*

1. *Set of Prints engraved after the most capital paintings in the collection of Her
Imperial Majesty, the Empress of Russia, lately in the collection of the Earl of
Orford at Houghton in Norfolk*, pub. J. & J. Boydell, 2 vols. (1788).

followed in 1790, and the illustrations to the two volumes of *An History of the River Thames* in 1794 and 1796. The preparation of the Thames volumes, upon which he is at work when the diary opens, can be followed in sequence in the diary. The commission had come from the two Boydells. Farington was to supply the drawings, William Combe, the raffish writer and journalist who later achieved celebrity as 'Dr. Syntax', the letterpress.[1] Farington's drawings were engraved in aquatint by J. C. Stadler. They accompany a text of no great distinction — Farington records criticisms (one from Horace Walpole) that it is 'too flowery'[2] — a piece of respectable hackwork with few pretensions to originality or thorough knowledge. Whatever Farington may have thought of Combe's part in the collaboration, their personal relations seem to have been smooth and friendly. Today the books are of interest solely for the plates which are beautifully produced and stylistically well-matched to their subjects. The world of the country house and its estate, the river-side villa in its grounds, and the gentle English panoramic landscape vista, was one which he understood intuitively and completely. He lived in London, he was a man of the world, and he was, without holding an official position, an astute administrator; but had he been called to them he would have carried out the duties of a country gentleman with dignity and success.

Farington's work on this commission was interrupted on 11 August 1793 by his journey to the war front at Valenciennes, which he recorded in a note-book kept separately from the main diary. The proposal that he should visit Valenciennes to record 'some of the Scenes, which have done so much honor to the combined Armies'[3] came from William Windham and was conveyed through Nathaniel Marchant, with the Boydells also having an interest in it — no doubt a suggestion that they might publish what Farington, who was accompanied by Stadler, would produce.[4] Windham, a leading Whig politician and formerly a close friend of Charles James Fox, had broken with him over the French Revolution. Now under Burke's influence, he had become a fervent opponent of the Foxite opposition and of the radicals and a strong supporter of the war. He had himself visited Valenciennes during the siege by allied forces, including English troops, under the command of the Duke of York; and it is possible that the sending of Farington on this mission, for which Windham provided a letter of *laissez-passer*, was seen by Windham as part of his campaign to stimulate support at home for the war at a time when the allies

---

1. Farington usually spells Combe's name as 'Coombes', but occasionally 'Combes', in the diary.
2. 10 May, 31 Aug. 1794.
3. William Windham to General George Ainslie, 10 Aug. 1793; see below, [13] Aug. 1793.
4. 8–10 Aug. 1793.

appeared to be achieving successes. When he inspected Farington's Valenciennes sketches in March 1794, Windham thought that they would make 'very interesting prints'.[1]

If Farington knew or even suspected this political motive, he gives no hint of it in his diary, in which he recounts his experiences in his customarily sober and alert way. It is an interesting possibility that he was acting on this expedition as one of the earliest official war artists. Windham had not yet joined Pitt's government, but he was in close touch with it and no doubt obtained official permission for Farington to visit the front. Armed with Windham's letter and with a letter from General George Ainslie, the commandant at Ostend, Farington was working under official auspices. Whatever the exact circumstances, he was some three weeks ahead of that slightly incongruous pair, Philip de Loutherbourg and James Gillray, who also went to Valenciennes to record the siege and who were also furnished with official credentials to execute what began as a private commission.[2] Farington's critical comment in his diary on Loutherbourg's *The Grand Attack on Valenciennes* (Plate 6) that 'The picture of Valenciennes appeared to me much worse than I thought it last year. — When the novelty is over these pictures appear very defficient',[3] should be read in the light of this interesting conjunction. His other official assignment in these years was the execution of two, presumably large, paintings of the dockyards of Chatham and Deptford which were commissioned by the Board of the Admiralty and paid for by the Navy Office. Neither painting can now be traced. It is characteristic that he should record in his diary information about ship-building prices and the wages of shipwrights which he had acquired in the course of his work.[4]

Farington soon established himself as a person of great authority on almost all matters concerned with the visual arts, a man whose judgment could be depended upon; and he used what became a position of considerable influence with tact and with policy, knowing exactly when to speak and when to be silent, when to advance and when to draw back, whom to encourage, whom to keep in his place. The respect in which he was held is nowhere clearer than in his private capacity as an expert adviser to friends who were collectors wishing to make new acquisitions or to dispose of old ones. The names of William Hardman of Manchester, Daniel Daulby of

1. 20 [21] Mar. 1794. His finished drawings of Valenciennes, together with a volume of sketches, appeared in the sale at Puttick and Simpson's in 1921 which included the manuscript of the diary. One of them, possibly the most important, *The Mons Gate*, passed into the collection of Sir Bruce Ingram and came into the London sale-room again in 1965; its present whereabouts is not known to us.
2. For their expedition, see *The Reminiscences of Henry Angelo* (1904), I, 296; and Draper Hill, *Mr. Gillray, The Caricaturist* (1965), 49–53.
3. 3 Mar. 1795.
4. 24 Nov. 1793.

Liverpool, and Joseph Berwick, the banker of London and Worcester, recur frequently in the diary; these collectors kept in touch with him regularly, and when he supervised the despatch of books or paintings to them, he also often advised them what and where to buy. Another instance of his authoritative position is the important part he played in consultations with the Earl and Countess of Inchiquin on the disposal of the print and picture collections of Sir Joshua Reynolds.[1] Lady Inchiquin, Reynolds's niece and heiress, emerges from the diary as a woman of sense and business ability, albeit sometimes grasping and tiresome, with whom Farington did not find it difficult to deal. His records of discussions with her and of the details of the sales are an excellent example of the value of the diary today to the art historian. He was not, it should be noted, a serious collector himself. Some Wilsons, together with three rather minor old masters bought in at the Reynolds sale and given him by Lady Inchiquin,[2] formed the sum total of his pictures as far as this can be deduced from the diary, and he is not apparently mentioned as a collector in any context outside the diary.

He was an industrious artist undertaking numerous small works, sometimes replicas of earlier ones, alongside the occasional more important commission, but he never appears to have been hurried and was careful not to undertake more than he could fulfil. Although he regularly records what the critics have to say about his work in the exhibitions, he does so with no appearance of strain or competition, or of his future depending on professional success or failure. He no doubt owed this self-assurance and self-knowledge to his relatively secure finances, his social position and his stable temperament. What has become of his paintings? Some which have appeared in the sale-room in recent years, *Carnarvon Castle*,[3] for example, are careful, over-conscientious, rather dry works. Others, such as *The Oak Tree* in the Tate Gallery, in which he most clearly studied the methods and effects of Wilson, are much more lively. One suspects that *The Oak Tree*, which seems to relate in sóme details to a drawing in the Victoria and Albert Museum of the Lady Oak near Cressage, Shropshire, is a 'made-up' landscape, and that he allowed himself more technical freedom in this kind of picture than he did in more accurately topographical 'views'. In *Carnarvon Castle*, he approached the subject with the eye of a careful painter in water-colour and the result is stilted. In *The Oak Tree*, where he did not have to record buildings, he allowed himself to enjoy the oil medium. His record of George III's being able to recognise all the buildings in the picture of the *High Street*,

1. See, e.g., 26, 27 Jan.; 1, 4 Feb.; 1, 8 Oct. 1794; 31 Jan. 1795.
2. 20 Mar. 1795.
3. R.A. 1793 (204). Property J. H. McNeil, Christie's sale, 24 Nov. 1972 (91).

Oxford[1] makes one wonder whether, if it comes to light, we shall perhaps be disappointed.

The death of his wife Susan in 1800, as we have seen, was a severe blow to Farington, not least in its effect on his life as a productive artist. A year later, he told William Daniell 'that now it was near 9 months since I used a pencil with colour, and that professional emulation seemed extinct in me, but I wd. try to recover an inclination'.[2] He had twenty years to live, and although he was to pay an exceptionally interesting visit to France in 1802 during the Peace of Amiens and to be occasionally busy with specific commissions, he exhibited at the Academy on only five occasions up to 1813, and not at all after that year. In May 1806, he remarked philosophically in his diary, as to his not having exhibited that year, that he 'must be considered like the *ebbing tide* which while retiring touches the shore only occasionally'.[3] His social life and his active participation in the affairs of the Academy did not however cease, nor did his keeping of the diary. In December 1821, he was staying with his brother Dick at the latter's house, Parr's Wood, at Didsbury. On the last day of the year, he wrote up part of the daily entry of his diary, noting that he had twice attended church that day. At the end of the evening service at Didsbury, in coming down from his brother's pew in the gallery encumbered with hat, umbrella, prayer book and galoshes, he slipped, fell and was killed instantly. His niece, noting that illness affected her uncle greatly and would have embittered his declining life, wrote emphatically that his death was '*doubtless all in Mercy*'.[4]

Farington has been called the 'Dictator of the Royal Academy',[5] though whether the sobriquet was applied to him during his lifetime is uncertain. Beechey was nearer the truth when, in a hostile mood, he called him 'Warwick, the King Maker'.[6] He made the remark in 1796, but it is clear that he might have made it with equal justice in 1793 when the diary opens. 'Dictator' is indeed too strong a word. Farington did not seek power openly or through the holding of office. He never held any of the official positions in the Academy, but his fine presence, his quick and exact mind, and the superiority of his social position to that of the other members — qualities brilliantly conveyed in Lawrence's portrait of him of 1796 (Plate 1) — ensured that his *unofficial* position was one of great strength. Northcote who, like Beechey, disliked Farington, should not be taken too literally when he said that Farington 'cared nothing at all about pictures;

1. 7 July 1794.
2. 4 Mar. 1801.
3. 5 May 1806.
4. In a note following Farington's last entry, 30 Dec. 1821.
5. William Sandby, *The History of the Royal Academy of Arts* (1862), I, 195.
6. See 24 April 1796.

his great passion was love of power — he loved to rule. He did it, of course, with considerable dignity; but he had an untamable spirit, which, I suppose, was due to the fact that he had lost the game as a painter, and that it was too late to mend the matter.'[1] This judgment suggests that in his earlier years Farington had appeared to be ambitious as a painter. If he had 'an untamable spirit' or an obvious 'love of power', these qualities are not evident in the diary. He did, however, possess a natural gift for administration, and he must have known it. This is clear from his ability to sway a meeting or to draft a resolution, and from his frequently-demonstrated skill as an eminence, often behind the scenes, in directing the actions of his fellow academicians. He had qualities that would have made him an outstanding president and which he must have known that Benjamin West lacked. There was however no question of his ever running for that office because his standing as a member of the profession could not possibly warrant it. He would have been the first to recognise this fact, and as far as we know, he never questioned the view that West had a strong claim to succeed Reynolds by virtue of his achievements as a history painter. At the same time, West's weaknesses — in particular, his failure to command the permanent respect of the members of the Academy as a body and an unsureness of touch in his personal relations — undoubtedly strengthened Farington's influence and position. It was to him rather than to the president that many members turned for advice. Farington was a gentleman among artists and an artist among gentlemen. He was in no sense a gentleman amateur like Sir George Beaumont, but he moved in the Beaumont circle as an equal.[2] At the same time, he was accepted by professional artists as one of themselves. It is significant that in Singleton's group portrait, *The Royal Academy in General Assembly, 1795* (Plate 12), the tall and handsome figure of Farington is placed prominently among those in the foreground of the picture.

Like many men who come to exercise influence in a particular group, Farington did so because the conditions enabled him to do so. The death of Reynolds in 1792 removed a completely dominant figure. West, with his American origins (and their liberal political overtones), was a contro-versial figure, and the fact that he was much favoured by the King aroused envy. West was *primus inter pares*, but Farington with his experience, his knowledge of men and the world, and his assiduity was, it might be said, 'more equal than others'. In general, his influence was a steadying and moderating one, inclined towards conservatism; but he undoubtedly had a strong sense that in elections, both to A.R.A. and R.A., the prime consideration must be the candidate's ability and qualifications. His

1. *Conversations of James Northcote R.A. with James Ward on Art and Artists*, ed. Ernest Fletcher (1901), 165.
2. He and Beaumont first met in 1773; see 15 Sept. 1794.

handling of the election of Sawrey Gilpin to A.R.A. is a case in point.[1] His views as to who should or should not be invited to the annual Academy dinner, the weight which his opinion carried in the discussions relating to the twenty-fifth anniversary celebrations in December 1793, and his effective intervention in the debate about the proposed statue of Lord Cornwallis for Madras[2] are all examples of the dominance of his opinion which are related in detail in the diary.

It is equally evident that as well as being strong-minded and to some degree autocratic, Farington was also a kind man. Partly because the demands on his time as a professional artist were relatively light, he was able to give a great deal of attention to other men's concerns, to attendance at meetings at the Academy, or to the informal gatherings of artists in the Royal Academy Club, in his own house in Charlotte Street, in the houses of other artists or in the coffee-houses. The friends he gathered around him were often young and by no means always conventional or established. To the young he was particularly generous with his advice. Lawrence and, later, Constable owed him a great debt; Constable needed his sympathy and encouragement, Lawrence his guidance in practical matters. In different ways, he was a moral tutor to them both. They happened to be men who achieved eminence, and in doing so they grew closer to Farington, not further from him; but they were only two among a large number. He was always clear-headed in matters of finance. In 1809, he was one of the auditors who revised the whole system of Academy book-keeping and finance, and in recognition of his success he was presented with a piece of plate. In many other ways, whether in collecting sub-scriptions for colleagues or their dependents who were ill or in debt, attending to the pensions dispersed by the Academy, or in supervising the domestic arrangements of the housekeeper or the porter at the Academy, Farington showed a goodness of heart and an unflagging devotion to the welfare of the Academy, together with a keen appreciation of its responsi-bilities as an institution.

The chief importance of his diary lies in the quality and quantity of information it provides about artists and their works and on the organization and patronage of the arts. Yet as a chronicler of his time, particularly of London, Farington sets this diverse information within a broad context which gives his material true life and unity. Like every great diarist, Farington achieves a remarkable comprehensiveness and conveys at the same time a clear sense of place and atmosphere, symbolised aptly by his recurring notes of weather and temperature. The whole diary contains a wealth of interesting material on social and political develop-ments and on literary affairs. In this introduction, we confine ourselves to

1. See 4 May 1795, *et seq.*
2. 24 July 1795.

commenting on those themes which predominate in the early years of the diary, principally between 1793 and 1796.

It is clear that he was keenly interested in politics and politicians. He follows proceedings in Parliament in some detail, frequently noting the names of speakers as well as the figures of division lists, and occasionally attending debates. What he could not discover for himself or from newspapers he could learn from friends or acquaintances who were in Parliament or in contact with the world of politics. His pages are full of news, anecdotes and biographical details of politicians: of Fox, Pitt and Burke, Dundas, Windham and Spencer, Pitt's brother Chatham and the Dukes of Portland and Richmond, the Foxites — Sheridan, Erskine, Grey — and Wilberforce. Almost every leading politician is mentioned, often at some length, but so are the less prominent, men like John Blackburne, M.P. for Lancashire, or John Nicholls, who provided Farington with some interesting views of oligarchical Whiggism.[1] The member of Parliament whom Farington knew best was Sir George Beaumont; but Beaumont, in no sense a professional politician, became disillusioned by the bitter debates in the Commons over the government's repressive legislation in 1795 and did not sit again in Parliament after 1796.[2] His retirement made no difference to Farington's appetite for political news and comment. The Westminster election in 1796, when the Pittite Sir Alan Gardner and the Whig Fox beat off the remarkably strong challenge of the Radical Horne Tooke, found Farington in his element. His family connection with Gardner gave him a particular interest in the election, during which he canvassed actively and about which he provides much valuable information concerning the candidates, the conduct of the election and the votes of individuals.[3]

He was plainly as well-informed about the politics of revolutionary France as the war allowed him to be — probably more knowledgeable, through his many contacts in London, than the great majority of private gentlemen of the time. While he shows little or no interest during these early years in living French artists, he records meticulously the series of executions during the Revolution, preserving among his press-cuttings, for example, an account of the death of the Duke of Orleans, Philippe-Egalité,[4] as well as relating news of the war at sea and on land or what he can learn periodically of the internal condition of France. On both Marat's and Brissot's periods in England before the Revolution, he has uniquely valuable information.[5] This degree of concern with politics might be

1. 22, 30 Jan. 1796. Nicholls was M.P. for Bletchingley 1783-7, Tregony 1796-1802.
2. 11, 24 Nov. 1795; see also 18 May 1796.
3. 19, 20, 28, [31] May; 1-17 June 1796.
4. 15, 18 Nov. 1793.
5. 27 Oct. 1793.

expected in a methodical and alert man living in London through years of revolution abroad, war and domestic crisis. But Farington took his interest in politics to lengths surely unusual in a man whose own professional concerns lay elsewhere. The most remarkable illustration of this aspect of his character (as revealed in the opening years of the diary) lies in his persistent interest in the Foxite party and in the radical opponents of Pitt's government — an interest which was not a reflection of his sympathy with these movements. Windham's supposition that Farington was 'a democrat', apparently based on seeing him in the gallery of the House of Commons during a debate on the Bill suspending Habeas Corpus in May 1794, was entirely erroneous. In correcting Windham, Marchant described Farington as 'a violent Aristocrat'[1] The phrase, appropriate enough when dealing with a man of Windham's views and at a time when French labels were temporarily entering the terminology of English politics, should not be taken too literally. It is a striking feature of Farington's accounts of both popular and parliamentary politics that his tone is remarkably cool and impartial. He observes and reports. We receive few positive clues as to his own views. A serious-minded, church-going Anglican (with no leaning towards 'enthusiasm'), he was certainly averse to radicalism in politics and supported the war without qualms. In reporting parliamentary debates, he gives equal treatment to government and opposition without, as a rule, commenting personally on the issues in dispute. It is a mark of his method as a diarist and of his cautious character that he rarely gives his own opinion on matters outside his professional knowledge or competence — and not always then.

Some of his fellow-artists, for example Thomas Banks the sculptor and Robert Smirke, were enthusiastic radicals; and the Royal Academy itself was thought by some alarmists to harbour 'many Democrats'.[2] Banks, a friend of John Horne Tooke, the leading gentleman-radical in London who was among those tried for treason in 1794, was himself arrested on suspicion of treasonable activities and brought for questioning before the Privy Council, although no proceedings were taken against him.[3] The episode led to no breach in Farington's relations with Banks. He continued to see him and to record whatever he could learn from others (including Dr. Batty, his own physician) about Horne Tooke's position and|views.[4] One of Farington's closest private friends, Charles Offley, a port wine merchant, was a member of the Whig Club in London and thus an adherent of Fox; Dick, Farington's brother, was a 'Church and King' man from loyalist Manchester. In these early years of his diary, Farington

1. 29 May 1794.
2. 28 Dec. 1799, referring in particular to the year 1794; see also 16 Dec. 1795.
3. 19 June 1794.
4. See e.g., 17, 22 Dec. 1794; 22 Jan.; 10 May 1796.

shows remarkably little interest in or respect for Pitt, perhaps because Pitt, unlike Fox, took no interest in the Academy or in artistic matters, or because Pitt's political preoccupations kept him isolated behind the increasingly 'dry and rejecting' manner noticed by Beaumont and passed on to Farington.[1] Fox appears much more prominently in the diary of these years. Farington's interest in him, an interest tinged with discerning, almost tolerant disapproval, is well conveyed in the vivid account of Fox 'rolling along . . . among a crowd of low people, and blackguards' near New Palace Yard, Westminster, after the public meeting on 16 November 1795 to protest against the Sedition Bill, accompanied by Sheridan and Tierney and followed by the Duke of Bedford and Charles Grey: 'the whole scene was such as when a drunken fellow is supported along, in the midst of an encouraging mob'. Farington returned home, after listening to the speeches of Fox and his friends, 'well satisfied . . . of the appearance of the people, that their minds are not in a state to create an alarm for the publick peace, and that the [Sedition] Bill may be passed with safety'.[2]

He had not always expressed such confidence. The upsurge of the radical movement, based on the corresponding societies in London and in many provincial centres, the gradual disintegration of the Whig party, marked by the extremism of one section of the Foxites and culminating in the formal coalition of Portland and his followers with Pitt in July 1794, widespread dearth and distress in the winter of 1795, constant uncertainty about the situation in Ireland — these were all symptoms of acute political and social crisis. The war, linked with an increasingly harsh but never entirely effective repression of radicalism at home, blurred the distinctions between opposition and sedition. These developments find their place in Farington's diary, with its undertone of concern at the situation in 1793 and 1794. Yet he remained remarkably calm, perhaps because he took the trouble to see and to hear things for himself. He attended one of the mass meetings called by the London Corresponding Society in the winter of 1795 and gives a closely observed and unique picture of the orators and their speeches; a week later, he went to hear one of John Thelwall's political lectures and records its substance in his diary.[3]

Farington's connections with the scholarly and literary world of London were diverse and interesting. Many such contacts were made and maintained through the Boydells, those extremely active entrepreneurs of the arts, to whose Shakespeare Gallery he was a frequent visitor. His acquaintance with George Steevens, the editor of the Boydell Shakespeare, may well have come about in this way; his collaboration with

1. 11 Nov. 1795; 23 April 1796. See also Farington's record of Nicholls' judgment, distinctly less than adulatory, of Pitt: 30 Jan. 1796.
2. 16 Nov. 1795.
3. 7, 14 Dec. 1795.

Combe arose out of a Boydell-inspired enterprise. He seems to have been on friendly terms with Dr. Alexander Wolcot, 'Peter Pindar', who dined with him on 29 November 1793, discoursed on politics and ranked Young of *Night Thoughts* as 'next in Poetical power to Shakespeare' among English poets. The *cause célèbre* of William Ireland's alleged discovery of lost Shakespeare plays and documents provides matter for numerous entries. Farington, basing himself perhaps unfairly on his knowledge of William Ireland's father, was a sceptic at an early stage; but he was present on 2 April 1796 for the first and only night of *Vortigern* at Drury Lane.

He does not seem to have been at all close to Gibbon, his colleague in the Academy; but on the last visit to England of the Professor of Ancient History, Farington records details of his family, his state of health, his death and his will — the last matter one of the rare instances in which he is in some respects clearly mistaken.[1] With Boswell, the Secretary for Foreign Correspondence, he was on familiar terms, and on Academy business they can be seen working effectively together. Boswell evidently spoke freely to Farington about friends such as Bennet Langton, Windham and Malone, and about Dr. Johnson; they were close enough for Farington to be considered for the 'small society' proposed by Boswell and Humphrey to meet at each other's houses in the winter — a plan which apparently never matured.[2] Farington's attitude to Boswell, 'poor Boswell', was affectionate and sympathetic; perhaps he agreed with Lady Thomond's remark that 'she could have better spared a better man'.[3]

It may have been through Boswell that Farington came to know Edmond Malone, one of his chief sources for political news, for literary matters in general and for Burke in particular. Among Farington's acquaintances were William Hayley, Samuel Rogers and Richard 'Conversation' Sharpe (the last two were members with Farington of the Council of Trent Club); of the blue-stockings, he seems to have known Mrs. Piozzi best, and perhaps because of this friendship would not agree to Hoppner's thoroughgoing condemnation of the Della Cruscans.[4] Naturally, he took a close interest in the controversy over the Picturesque, though without apparently taking sides in it. He was a member of the Society of Antiquaries and regularly attended its meetings. One of his closest friends was the antiquary Samuel Lysons, who kept him informed about the progress of his work, consulted him about reproducing his archaeological discoveries and invited him to provide illustrations to the

1. See 25 Jan. 1794. Cf. the summary of the will in D. M. Low, *Edward Gibbon, 1737–94* (1937), 349–50.
2. 8 Nov. 1793.
3. 28 Sept. 1806.
4. 26 Nov. 1793.

Britannia Depicta.[1] A contact with yet another circle was through the *conversazioni* of Sir Joseph Banks, where he met many members of the Royal Society.

His main link with the worlds of journalism and the stage was through John Taylor, the royal oculist who was also an active journalist with an avid interest in the stage. Mrs. Siddons and Kemble, Mrs. Jordan, Perdita Robinson and Sheridan as well as many less well-known figures appear in the diary in different contexts. Of the journalists apart from Taylor and Combe, he saw the Rev. Charles Este quite regularly; he has interesting and detailed information on James Perry and James Gray, the owners and editors of the *Morning Chronicle*, and on John Heriot of the *Sun* and *True Briton*. His professional concern for criticisms of the work of artists, including his own, must have sharpened this interest in journalism. When the Academy discussed the question of how to prevent the annual exhibition from suffering by 'the general abuse of newspapers', it was decided to engage Taylor to 'manage such a matter'; and Farington's proposal that the *True Briton*, with which Taylor was connected, should be one of the two newspapers to carry the Academy's advertisements, was also adopted.[2]

As a source for the political, social and literary history of his time, as opposed to the history of the arts and the lives of artists, Farington is rarely original; exceptions to this rule are the descriptions of Valenciennes in 1793 and of the various political meetings in 1795, his detailed and consecutive account of the Westminster election of 1796 and his notes (valuable even if, in some cases, they come at second-hand) of the experiences of General O'Hara and others who had been prisoners in France.[3] But he is an invaluable recorder and illustrator; his diary constantly corroborates and amplifies, often graphically (the more so because he does not strive to achieve effects) and always clearly: Fox's *ménage* at St. Anne's Hill,[4] the details of Burke's early life[5] and of the death of his only son;[6] Admiral Gardner's account of the action of the Glorious First of June.[7] Farington is no Pepys; he was not as interesting a man nor so interested in himself and his relationship to his world. But he would perhaps have accepted the tribute that his diary is the product of a true historian.

1. Samuel's brother, the Rev. Daniel Lysons, was also close to Farington and gave him his invaluable work, *The Environs of London* (1792–6).
2. 29 Apr. 1795.
3. See, e.g., 10 May; 29 Oct.; 25 Nov.; 3 Dec. 1795.
4. 4 Nov. 1793.
5. 13 July 1795.
6. 1 Oct. 1794.
7. 18 July 1794.

Why did he keep a diary? In keeping with a work which contains almost no confessional or introspective elements, he makes no explicit statement of his intentions within the diary itself. But in a note to his executors dated 17 April 1809, he directs that the books containing the diary should be given to his brother Dick and desired him, 'if he be so disposed', to read them regularly through and to 'EXPUNGE SUCH PASSAGES . . . which are of too PRIVATE AND PERSONAL A NATURE TO BE SEEN BY ANY OTHER EYE' than his or the other brothers'. There follows a somewhat puzzling direction that Dick is to keep the diary in his possession 'if the contents shall not appear too trifling', in order to give them 'a second inspection and perusal', although with what purpose is not stated. Farington continues:

> The Diaries were written for my amusement and much of them to assist my recollection in matters in which I was engaged, or to enable me to reconsider opinions given, and thereby to strengthen my own judgment. Much also I was induced to put down in writing as being curious anecdote and useful to the Biographer. It will be seen by the great proportion of trifling detail contained in them that they were written for myself only, and it was long my intention to destroy them before my decease, should it please God to give me time to see my fast approaching end, but on further consideration, being happily so situated with respect to my family as to have near relatives in whom I could place all confidence, I have made this disposition respecting my Diaries.

Finally, he directs that Dick shall have the small manuscript diaries written for other purposes (the travel diaries) as well as 'the CABINETS on STANDS and others in which my manuscript books are arranged for the purpose of conveying them and keeping them together'.[1]

This is an apparently clear and full note. Dick did not censor the diary heavily, if he censored it at all; and he apparently took no steps towards publication if that is one possible meaning behind the injunction to 'a

---

1. The note is printed by Greig, *Farington Diary*, I, xi. See also 17 May 1796, where Farington, in communicating the contents of his will of that time to Dick, also mentions showing him 'the annexed note relative to my Diaries and private papers.' His will (P.R.O. Prob. 11/1655, 1822), dated 1 Feb. 1819 and proved at London 19 April 1822, contains no explicit reference to the diary volumes. To Dick, a co-executor with his brother Henry, Farington bequeathed 'whatever property I may die possessed of be it of whatever description . . . in acknowledgment of the great obligation I am under to him for his fraternal kindness . . .' Codicils, dated 2 Feb. 1819, concerned bequests — of paintings, his watch, his Bible etc. — to other members of the family, and of ten guineas each to his two servants. The note to his executors which Greig printed was presumably attached to the diary; if so, it became detached and has since disappeared.

second inspection and perusal'.[1] If Farington was serious about his intention to destroy the diary — and he was not a man who said things lightly — then his confidence in his family prevented him from destroying a work of unique value which must have cost him much time and labour and which, as Pepys did before him, he kept in special cases. The note certainly fits several aspects of Farington's personality: his love of method and order, his caution in giving judgments without having all the facts and without recalling, if necessary, his earlier opinions or those of others. That he was in the habit of using the diary as an *aide-mémoire* is evident from occasional subsequent corrections or additions. His interest in 'anecdote' and biography is proved most forcibly by the diary itself, which would have been extensively used had he ever completed his projected history of the Academy.[2] He published *Memoirs of the Life of Sir Joshua Reynolds* in 1819.[3] He was always interested in other men's historical researches, mentioning, for example, Boswell's 'serious intentions' of writing a life of Reynolds,[4] and Combe's plan to write a history of George III's reign.[5]

Yet Farington's careful note to his executors, written fifteen years after he began his diary, leaves some questions unanswered. Why did he begin to keep a full diary, opening in the first manuscript volume as we have it, on Saturday, 13 July 1793, on the day when he, George Dance and Samuel Lysons breakfasted with Horace Walpole at Strawberry Hill? He had already kept working and travel diaries.[6] Yet these, recording his Scottish tours of 1788 and 1792, while they contain some general passages and anecdotes, were apparently kept for immediate professional purposes. We shall perhaps never know exactly what was in his mind when he started on what was to become the main diary. The first manuscript volume contains an inscription by Farington inside the cover (undated but plainly written *c.* 1793–4) directing his executors to 'burn this Memorandum Book when it falls into their Hands'.[7] This instruction suggests that he envisaged a diary kept strictly for his own 'amusement' and use. Knowing that it would contain material certain to offend others if it became public, he takes care to

1. One word, the name of the poet in the entry of 28 July 1793, and one passage of nineteen lines dealing with Will's financial difficulties in that of 19 Nov. 1794, are the only examples of deletion in the diary, and both could have been Farington's own work.
2. See also below p. xxxvi, n. 3.
3. *Memoirs of the Life of Sir Joshua Reynolds, with some observations on his talents and character* (1819).
4. 27 Mar. 1795.
5. 12 May; 27 Nov. 1795.
6. See below p. xxxvii.
7. A second, undated but much later inscription by his nephew William ffarington notes that this direction was subsequently cancelled by the bequest to Richard Farington of the books containing the diary.

prevent this happening. Like other diarists, he doubtless became addicted to his pastime. His fluency is remarkable. The diary begins as it is to go on, the style clear, relatively unadorned, yet smooth and balanced in its own distinctive way. Judging by his manuscript, he must have been gifted with considerable facility of expression as well as a tenacious memory. One substantial portion of the diary (3 January to 22 June 1798) consists of rough notes kept on loose sheets. It is possible that these notes indicate his regular method of preparing his materials before writing up his entries in his books; on the other hand, they may simply mark a period when, for some unexplained reason, he fell out of his normal routine for writing his diary.

Whatever the immediate origins of the diary, it is certain that by 1809 (and probably much earlier) he had some distant posterity in mind. In this connection, part of his entry for 26 November 1795 is interesting and suggestive. He records dining with Wilton and talking to him about his 'professional life, and of other distinguished artists his contemporaries.'

> Wilton . . . produced books containing a diary of his expences when on his travels, and many particulars relative to himself, and others, of purchases, & expences: but lamented not having extended his Diary to accts. of a different kind, so as to have made up a progressive relation of everything worth recording of himself and those with whom He has lived. He felt this neglect forcibly while he lately read Boswells life of Johnson, which He thinks one of the most fascinating relations He has ever met with.[1]

Farington too had kept working and travel diaries. He was now immersed in keeping a consecutive diary which did indeed constitute 'a progressive relation of everything worth recording of himself' and of others in his world. His silence here and elsewhere as to the possibility of eventual publication in some form of his own work, as Boswell had published his, certainly does not mean that he did not see a parallel between himself and Boswell. He was perhaps beginning by 1795 to see himself as the Boswell of his society — in some respects the most appropriate description of Farington and his diary. His contemporaries, particularly his fellow-artists, must have been aware of his close interest in their lives. None, as far as we can discover, knew or guessed what form this interest was taking.

II. THE MANUSCRIPT OF THE DIARY

The main diary in the Royal Library at Windsor is contained in sixteen substantial vellum-bound books, uniform in their general appearance and each inscribed with its dates by Farington himself. The early books were

1. 26 Nov. 1795.

evidently supplied by Esther Smith, later F. Seaton, of 40 Oxford Street, and all, with their good, strong paper, may have come from that shop.[1] The history of the transmission of the diary may be briefly outlined. From Farington's brother Dick it passed to his nephew Admiral William Farington of Woodvale, Isle of Wight, and after him to his son William who married Cecil Frances Tyrwhitt and built a house, Northwood Lodge, at Wallington, Surrey in 1885. On Mrs. Farington's death intestate, her property passed to her brother Montagu Dymock Tyrwhitt and her two sisters, one of whom, Miss M. L. E. Tyrwhitt, bequeathed her property to her second cousin Miss Jowitt. The diary reappeared in 1921, exactly a century after its author's death, in a mahogany case (perhaps one of the cabinet stands in which Farington kept it) in an attic of Northwood Lodge; and as part of Farington's collection of drawings and papers, it was included in a sale held by Messrs. Puttick and Simpson in London on 9 December 1921. James Greig, the art critic of the *Morning Post*, had already inspected the diary, recognized its importance and advised Lord and Lady Bathurst, the newspaper's owners, and H. E. Gwynne, then editor, to buy the work for publication. In the presence of representatives of the Royal Academy and of other galleries, newspapers and publishers, it was knocked down to Greig (who had been instructed to bid up to £1000) for 110 guineas. The success of its serial publication in the *Morning Post* between January 1922 and October 1923 was considerable. In 1922 the first volume edited by Greig and covering the years 1793 to 1802 was published by Hutchinson and Co.; other volumes followed, the last appearing in 1928. Finally, Lady Bathurst presented the manuscript volumes of the main diary to King George V in 1934.

There are at Windsor various other materials, including three smaller notebooks — those in which Farington recorded his expedition to Valenciennes in 1793, his Scottish tour of 1801–2 and his journey to Paris in 1802.[2] These materials were purchased separately by the Royal Library; the Valenciennes notebook was bought on 9 March 1951 from Thomas Thorp & Co. of 27 Albemarle Street, London, who found it among the books of the late James Greig which they had purchased.[3] Another small notebook in which Farington recorded his tour of Kent in 1794 and which had also belonged to Mr. Greig passed successively through the collections of Mr. J. Ford and Dr. Theodore Besterman, who presented it to the

1. Fourteen of the books measure 9½in. × 7½in., each containing between 250 and 350 pages; two others, of the same size, are considerably thinner.
2. These notebooks measure 8in. × 6⅜in., 8in. × 6½in. and 7in. × 4½in. respectively.
3. Other Faringtonia at Windsor include sundry accounts and correspondence relating to his work for *Britannia Depicta* and *Magna Britannia*, together with notes towards a history of the Royal Academy and short biographical accounts of artists.

British Library in 1973. We have been unable to trace the notebooks which Greig also owned and in which Farington kept his accounts of his tours of the Wye in 1803 and of Devon and Cornwall in 1809. Two other travel and working diaries, those in which Farington recorded his visits to Scotland in 1788 and 1792, are in the Central Public Library, Edinburgh; we shall print selections from these diaries in the *Companion* volume. James Greig's edition of the diary was governed largely by the selections which were originally serialized. No doubt there were good reasons for publishing only selections, but he did not say what these reasons were, or indeed that he had made selections. He printed many of the most obviously interesting passages, although he also frequently abridged them; he omitted most of the references to Farington's family and, in the early years, all the entries made while Farington was in Norfolk; he also omitted the account of the journey to Valenciennes in 1793. His text is generally faithful to the selected original passages, though he does not reproduce Farington's paragraphs and is at times cavalier both about dates and in following Farington's spelling and punctuation. More seriously, Greig's edition fails to do justice to the full range of Farington's interests and to his steady accumulation of significant detail. By presenting the diary as a public and dramatic document, a record, in his words, of 'the sayings and doings of the eminent men and women and the stirring events of a . . . momentous period',[1] Greig created a somewhat misleading impression of it. Within his immediate terms of reference — the presentation of extracts for the large reading public of the *Morning Post* in the 1920s — he was no doubt right to do so. His omissions, in addition to those already mentioned, included some accounts of Royal Academy committee or sub-committee meetings, full particulars of Academy elections and finances, small talk between academicians and less important artists, and similar matters which were not of great interest to the general public at that time. They are however precisely the details which are of value to the historian of British art today. In the fifty years since the appearance of Greig's edition, art historical studies in general have advanced to an unprecedented degree, and in the last twenty-five years this has become true of British art history in particular. Farington's diary is recognised as a major source of information in this field. The growing interest by scholars in the artists, both major and minor, of the period it covers makes the publication of the diary in its entirety desirable, and indeed necessary.

III. EDITORIAL PROBLEMS AND METHODS

The manuscript diary itself presents few serious technical problems. Farington writes up to his margins and frequently crowds his pages, but his bold hand is usually legible. His abbreviations of common words, while

1. Greig, *Farington Diary*, I, viii.

by no means always consistent ('evening' and 'eving', 'morning', 'morng.', and other variants, 'called', 'call'd' and 'calld,' for example), are generally comprehensible and have been retained. Occasionally, in a moment of discretion or through haste, he gives only an initial (or initials) for certain persons; in those cases where positive identification has been possible, these persons' names have been added within square brackets. Some of his spelling is idiosyncratic. For example, he writes 'adress', 'of' for 'off', 'poeple', 'reccomendation', 'woemen', although at times he also reverts to conventional spellings of all these words. In these cases, we have aimed to retain such examples of Farington's persistently idiosyncratic spelling, and have silently corrected only minor obvious slips. His inconsistency in spelling not infrequently affects a surname within a single entry and even extends to the surnames of some persons who were his close friends (for example, he writes 'Salisbury' for 'Salusbury', although again not consistently). We have retained his spelling of such names and will provide the necessary cross-references to these persons in the Index. Similarly, in the case of names which Farington had obviously heard only in conversation and spells incorrectly, we have retained his spelling, adding the correct spelling in square brackets only when Farington's version is seriously wide of the mark or misleadingly incomplete.

We have retained his inconsistent use of capital letters, his emphases (to which he plainly attached importance), and his paragraphs, which significantly indicate the pattern of his thoughts and their expression. His punctuation is, by modern standards, frequently erratic, but we have corrected it only in those relatively rare cases where we have judged that strict fidelity to his punctuation might make it difficult for the reader to follow his meaning. We have retained his frequent use of dashes inside paragraphs and after proper names, but we have eliminated them when they occur at the end of paragraphs, dates or entries. We have not corrected his occasional failure to begin a sentence with a capital letter. He frequently places a comma after a surname, particularly at the beginning of a sentence, thus: 'G. Steevens, told me . . .' (6 Jan. 1795). He may have adopted this practice for his own purposes of reference to the diary, and we have followed him as faithfully as possible. His use of full stops after initials is also inconsistent, but since his inconsistency will cause no difficulty to the reader, we have not regularized it. Where we have judged that his occasional omission of inverted commas (most frequently, at the end of quotations) may be misleading, we have inserted them where they are obviously required.

We have followed both Farington's practice in placing his dates in the centre of his page immediately above his entries, and the differing ways in which he gives his dates. In those few instances in which his dating has obviously erred, we have placed the correct date alongside in square brackets. We have also indicated the remarkably rare occasions on which he failed to make an entry or left an entry uncompleted; and where he has accidentally omitted a word or words, we have placed our insertions (several of which must be based on guesses) in square brackets. He illustrated his diary in four ways: by occasional plans and diagrams, by the insertion of newspaper cuttings, usually pasted into the text, by plans of the seating at dinners and other occasions which he attended, and by sketches. We reproduce all diagrams[1] and those newspaper cuttings which are of direct relevance to matter in the text; where we omit cuttings, we indicate such omissions and summarise the contents of the cuttings in question, with full references wherever possible.[2] There are relatively few examples of Farington's table plans in the early years of the diary, but the habit plainly grew upon him and forms one of his most delightful and useful contributions to the information of posterity — and, indeed, to the art of keeping a diary. The skill of our printers has enabled us to reproduce all the table plans for private dinners, and many of the larger plans for public dinners (chiefly those of the Academy).[3] We have reproduced all his occasional sketches, of which there are considerably more examples in the early years of the diary than in the later.[4]

Our aim has been to reproduce Farington's text as faithfully and as clearly as possible. Fidelity to his text is an editor's first duty. It is also particularly appropriate in the case of Farington, a man of precise habits and methodical cast of mind. We believe that his readers will become as accustomed to those of his idiosyncrasies which we have retained as we have ourselves become. These idiosyncrasies were a part of our diarist, and they convey both his essence and the flavour of his period in ways which would be irrevocably lost if they had been tidied out of existence.

1. See, e.g., the key to the hanging of pictures in the Academy Exhibition, under [26] Apr. 1794; and the diagram of Harrison's building at Lancaster Castle, 20 Dec. 1795.
2. See, e.g., 18 Nov. 1793; 14 Nov. 1797.
3. See, e.g., the table plan of the Academy dinner, 31 Dec. 1793; and, for a private dinner, 3 May 1796. Table plans not reproduced with the text of the diary will be included in the *Companion*.
4. See, e.g., his sketch of Nathaniel Dance's landscape, 28 Jan. 1794; and the sketch of the floating battery, 15 June 1794.

JULY 1793

Went early this morning in company with Mr. George Dance, the architect, and Mr. Saml. Lysons of the Temple, to Lord Orfords at Strawberry Hill, where we breakfasted with his Lordship. — In the forenoon Mr. Dance made a drawing from His Lordships profile, an excellent resemblance. — Lord Orford is now in his 76th year, infirm in his body, but lively & attentive in mind. He went into the different apartments with us, and we were very much pleased with the singularity of the appearance of them as well as with a variety of curious & valuable miniatures, some larger pictures, and sundry articles, particularly with a silver Bell enriched with carving by Benvenuto Cellini. — While Lord Orford was sitting to Mr. Dance the conversation naturally enough turned upon Hereditary personal resemblance. His Lordship carried his opinion much farther, and was decidedly of opinion that even habits and affectations frequently descend. The Cavendish family is a striking instance. A peculiar awkwardness of gait is universally seen in them, and He noticed its having passed to a collateral branch, in the instance of Mr. Walpole, his cousin, eldest Son of Lord Walpole, whose Mother is Aunt to the present Duke of Devonshire. He insisted that if through a window He only saw the legs of Mr. Walpole in motion He should say He was a Cavendish. That affectations descend He produced a strong proof in Miss Hotham daughter of Lady Dorothy Hotham; Her mother was affected in an extraordinary degree. But the likeness of Miss Hotham to her Mother in this respect could not be the effect of imitation, as she went from home an infant, and was brought up by Her [aunt] a Lady of the most simple manners.

Mr. Berry and his two daughters came to dinner at 4 o'clock. They are near neighbours to Lord Orford, and reside in a House in which the late Mrs. Clive the actress dwelt. It belongs to Lord Orford, who gave it to Mrs. Clive during the latter part of her life, and since her death to Mr. Berry to be a country House for him & his daughters. The Misses Berry are esteemed very accomplished women, and have been twice in Italy. They are handsome in their persons and the eldest in particular has an

1

interesting and engaging manner. She appears to be 2 or 3 and thirty. Indifferent health is expressed in her countenance. — These Ladies are the great nieces of a Mr. Ferguson a merchant in the City who died some years since leaving a very large fortune, which He is said to have intended for his eldest nephew Mr. Berry but bequeathed him only £400 a year and made Mr. Berrys younger Brother, Heir to the bulk of his property, who with proper feeling settled £600 or £1000 a year on his elder Brother in consideration of his disappointment. The cause of Mr. Ferguson disinheriting Mr. Berry was his having married a very amiable woman; the mother of the Misses Berry.

In the evening Mr. Dance returned to Town with me. Mr. Lysons crossed over Kew Bridge to visit the Revd. Mr. Peach, his Uncle, at East Sheen. — The weather this day very fine.

Sunday July 14th.

The weather continues very fine. Mr. Dance having only Saturdays & Sundays to command, owing to his business in the City as Architect & Surveyor to the Corporation, my Mother & wife [Susan] sat to him this day for their profiles, which He executed with his usual success.

My Mother is now in her 77th year, but excepting that she does not hear quite so well as formerly, all her faculties are perfect & her health very good. Mr. Dance and his Sons, Tom & George & Charles Webb, drank tea with us. In the evening I went to Wheatleys.

Monday 15th.

Rose at 6, and busily employed in forwarding the examples for the publication of views of the Thames &c. — went to the Shakespeare gallery, where I met Mr. Bulmer, the Printer, who informed me, He had recommenced printing the first volume of the Thames, after a very long cessation, and that it will now go on uninterruptedly as Mr. Coombs has promised to supply him with manuscript as wanted. — Mr. Bulmer advises not to publish till after Christmas when the Town will be filling which He thinks will be a very material advantage. — Mr. Hearne & Mr. Baker dined with me. News of the taking Condé from the French. Mr. Lysons called in the even'g. Sir Jos: Banks is to call on me with him; and to engage Mr. Gibbon who is on a visit to Lord Sheffield, to sit to Mr. Dance.

July 16th. 1793.

Rose at 7. This is the 12th day of uninterrupted fine weather, and generally very hot. At 4 this afternoon the Thermometer stood on my staircase, to the North, at 89; the window open. — employed on the work of the Rivers.

17th.

Rose at ½ past 6. Breakfasted with Mr. Dance, and compared my views of

July 13th 1793

2. George Dance R.A. *Horace Walpole, fourth Earl of Orford*. 13 July 1793.
National Portrait Gallery, London.

POPE'S HOUSE.

3. *Pope's House. An History of the River Thames*, Vol. II (1796), plate 2.

Blenheim with his edition of Campbells Vitruvius, in which I find some variations, in the decorations, from the present state of the building. Probably though originally designed, some decorations which are found in Campbell were never executed. — Mr. Dance made a remarkable likeness, a profile, of Mr. Lysons. — The weather still very fine. The glass at 82 on my staircase.

July 18th. 1793.

Rose at ½ past 6. — Some lightening and a little rain in the night, and today. Regulating views of Oxford. — The weather gloomy, glass fallen to 72. — and in the evening to 68. — Charles & John Offley dined with me.

19th.

Rose at ½ past 6. Breakfasted with Dance at Lysons. — forwarding River drawings. Two young Jodrells dined with me.

20th.

Rose at 6. Went with Dance & Lysons to breakfast at Mr. Piozzis at Streatham. — Mr. Dance made drawings of Mr. & Mrs. Piozzi.

In the library at Streatham, are ¾ portraits by Sir Joshua Reynolds, of Lord Sandys, Lord Westcote, Mr. Murphy, Dr. Goldsmith, Sir Joshua Reynolds, Sir Robert Chambers (Judge in Bengal,) Mr. Garrick, Mr. Thrale, Mr. Barretti, Dr. Burney, Mr. Burke, and Dr. Johnson. — Over the chimney piece whole length portraits of Mrs. Piozzi and Her eldest daugr. Miss Thrale. — Mr. Piozzi obligingly played on the Piano forte & sung in a charming taste. He is a very obliging unaffected Man, and as much English as a foreigner can be in manner and way of thinking. He & Mrs. Piozzi are nearly of the same age, somewhere about 50. Miss Harriet Lee, authoress of a Novel called, Errors of Innocence, was on a visit to them. The youngest Miss Thrale is also with them. A good humoured pleasing girl of 17. — Lord Cahier & his Tutor, the Revd. Mr. Beaver, passed part of the morning at Streatham, also the Revd. Mr. Chappelow. — Mr. Ray of the Temple, and Mr. Jones, Father of Mrs. Mackay, were at dinner. — In the evening we returned to Town. — The weather to day Showery, and the evening rather cool. The glass 66.

Sunday, July 21st. 1793.

Rose at 6. — Went with Mrs. Farington & Mr. Lysons by Putney, & East Sheen, and through Richmond Park, to the Star & Garter to breakfast. — went on to Strawberry Hill. Lord Orford shewed us the House, which we had sufficient time to view at our leisure. — we saw the small room in which are Lady Di Beauclerks designs for Lord Orfords play of the Mysterious Mother, — also his China Closet, neither of which are shewn but seldom. — Lord Orford has the best picture of Paul Brils I have seen. — we dined at 5, and in the afternoon Mr. Berry and the Miss Berrys came.

In the evening we returned to Town. The weather very pleasant. Lord Orford mentioned that at Richmond, and in the neighboroud, there are a great number of French Emigrants, many of them of high fashion. That party spirit rages among them, some being Royalists, others as they call themselves Constitutionalists, which makes it necessary to be cautious not to assemble them together, though they labour under the common grievance of being expelled from their native country.

July 22d.

Rose at ½ past 7. — My mother went this forenoon to Hoddesdon accompanied by Betty. — proceeded with drawings for publication of Rivers. — Will [Farington] returned in the evening with Betty.

23d.

Rose at 7. etched view of Blenheim. Susan [Farington] went off this evening for Oken. — News of the murder of Marat in Paris, a character universally detested.

24th.

Rose at 6. — after some days of Cloudy and moderately cool weather, it is now become again very hot. Letters from Mr. Twining and Mr. Thackeray with invitations to Isleworth. — Supped with Lysons.

Mrs Piozzi recd from Cadell, the Bookseller, £150 for the manuscript of her anecdotes of Dr. Johnson, & £500 for her Letters from Italy. Cadell lost by the publication. — Mrs. Piozzi subscribed 2 guineas towards the Monument proposed to be erected to the memory of Johnson.
Lord Camden a man of singular bad temper in his family. Peevish in particular to his daughters.
Judge Blackstone a man of unpleasant manners.
Glass at 11 at night, 75.

25th.

Rose at 6. — employed in finishing drawings for Mr. Berwick. — weather very warm. — dined alone.

July 26th.

Rose at 6. — Mr. Cartwright called abt. etching — Had some conversation with Nollekens today. — Bacon recd. from the Treasury £6,000 for his monument of Lord Chatham. — Nollekens offered a design during the administration of Lord North, for a monument to be erected to the memory of the three Captains killed on the 12th of April, fighting under Lord Rodney, which he esimated at £4,500. Dance during the administration of Lord Shelburne estimated the design at £3,500. — The monument was not determined on till the administration of Mr. Pitt, when with some alterations, at an estimate given in by Bacon & Wilton, Nollekens design was adopted at £4,000. Horace Hamond came to night from Southampton. — Dr. French Lawrence of the Commons, who had a principal share in composing the Rolliad, a satirical Poem, and two of the Probationary odes, Son of a Jeweller at Bath, where his mother now keeps a boarding House.

Corbets military government of Gloucester, material in making up a history of the Severn. Lysons has it. A scarce Book. — employed on drawings. — Glass 74. — dined alone.

July 27th.

Rose at 6. — employed in outlining the 5 drawings for Mr. Erskine of Mar. — A continued rain through the day. — Charles Offley & John, & Horace Hamond dined with me. — Will returned from Isleworth, where He had been to settle with Bob [Farington] abt. George [Farington]'s going to School, and went to Hoddesdon. Glass. 64.

Sunday July 28th.

Rose at ½ past 6. Breakfasted with Messrs. Hodges, Lysons, and Cockerell, at Mr. Dances. — walked up to dine at Mr. J: Boydells at west-end, Hampstead, to dinner. Alderman Boydell & Mrs. Lloyd, Mr. & Mrs. Broderip, & Mr. Westall, and the Revd. Dr. Steevens, there. — Dr. Steevens married the late Duke of Cumberland. The Attorney of the Duke of Clarence has produced a paper to the Creditors, in which the Duke binds himself to appropriate £6,000 a year, of the £12,000, He receives, for the payment of his debts, which it is reckoned will be discharged, with interest, in 8 years. — This engagement was proposed 10 days since. — Some of the articles which made up the Dukes debt, He pledged himself for the payment of on delivery. Several of them were for Mrs. Jordan, the Actress, — ordered by him in her presence. — Westall at this time supports his Father, Mother, a Brother, and a Sister, who is blind. They now reside at Hampstead. His Father was formerly a Brewer at Norwich.

Woodmason, has been disappointed in Ireland. The Pictures which were painted for him for an Irish edition of Shakespeare, have not been understood, or relished, by the people of Dublin. The work is stopped at present, and probably will not be revived. It is supposed He will lose abt. £3,000 by the speculation.

Lord Grosvenor, & Sir Richd. Symons, two of the most profligate men, of this age, in what relates to women. — They maintain Houses in which persons appear respectably situated, into which young women are decoyed as maid servants &c., and are subjected to the attempts of the employers. [erased and illegible] the Poet, was employed by Lord Grosvenor, in assisting to seduce a young Lady, Miss Baird, from the residence of Her mother near Monmouth.

It has been before observed, that affectation, as well as feature, may be traced occasionally, as passing from generation to generation. Today it was observed that *impudence* came in with a similar claim. A Person was mentioned whose grandfather was sufficiently remarkable for possessing this quality, as to have the addition of *Brass* to his name, given him at Oxford where He resided. The Son of Brass the first preserved the title; and the Grandson, now alluded to, so far excells his progenitors, as to be honored with the title of *Corinthian* Brass, as being of the first order.

When Lord Thurlow proposed to build a House at Norwood, near Dulwich, He told Holland, the architect, He did not mean to exceed £6,000. — Holland, by management, & Lord Thurlows inattention, increased the Plan so as to make up the whole charge about £18,000. The building into the bargain ill executed. An arbitration was settled, and George Dance & Saml. Wyatt, determined that Holland should refund to Lord Thurlow £ [blank]. The weather to day cloudy, but no rain. Glass 63.

Monday July 29th.

Rose at ½ past 5. — weather cool. Proceeding with drawings for Mr. Erskine &c. — Called on G Dance, Lysons came there with an impression of Dances first attempt to draw portraits on Copper by means of the soft ground. Sir William Chambers is much pleased with a visit of the Prince of Wales, who came to him at Whitton, from Hounslow Heath, with some Officers of the 10th Regt. of Dragoons. — Sir Wm. in return dined with the Prince & Officers at Staines, when there was much jollity, & the Prince sung many songs.

George Dance consulted Banks, the statuary, & others before He settled the estimate for Nollekens design for the monument of the three Captains.

Tuesday July 30th.

Rose at ½ past 6. Outlining view of Worcester Bridge &c for Mr. Berwick. Horace Hamond returned from Fanhams & dined with me. — Weather pleasant. Glass 68. — I recd. the 3 pictures which Mackenzie bought for me yesterday at Dalling, the Frame makers sale. One by Wilson — and 2 by Brooking. — Lysons came in the evening & shewed me a new manner of pasting. — He informed me of Hughes having got a Prebend of Westminster, for which He applied to the King, in exchange for his Prebend of Worcester.

July 31st.

Rose at 7. A wet morning. Outlining view of High Street, Oxford, on Canvass. Called at the Shakespeare Gallery. — News of the taking Valenciennes. Dined at the Bedford Coffee House, with Messrs Berwick, D & S. Lysons, and H. Hamond. Excellent Port wine. — Called in the eving with Berwick & S Lysons on G: Dance, to see the profile Heads. — Fine day. Glass rose to 71. — Mason, is the Author of the Ode to Sir William Chambers, which was published more than 20 years ago.

AUGUST 1793

August 1st.

Rose at ½ past 6. Fine morning. tinting drawings of Rivers. — dined with H. Hamond & John Offley at the Bedford Coffee House, went afterwards to Sadlers Wells. Richer, a wonderfull performer on the Tight Rope.

2d.

Rose at 7. — A fine morning. Glass 72. Outlining view of High St. Oxford, on Canvass. — dined alone & evening. Marchi called. He is going to Wales.

3d.

Rose at ¼ past 6. — fine morning. Glass 72. Painters began to paint outside of the House today. — Outlining High St. Oxford. — In the evening went with Battersbee to Beddington Lodge. Much Thunder & Rain at night.

4th.

Rose at ½ past 7. — Colignon at Battersbees. H. Hamond came to dinner. — Weather pleasant. — Battersbee bought Beddington Lodge, with some fixtures for £1,800, of Arthur Blake, who married an heiress that possessed it.

Monday/5th.

Rose at 6. — Returned to Town after breakfast. — Whitwashers began working. — tinting drawings. Will, brought George to go to School. — Evening rainy.

6th.

Rose at ¼ past 7. Fine morning. — Will took George to School at the Revd. Mr. Eccles at Bow near Stratford, 1 mile from Mile end. Outlined view of Buchannan House. — dined alone. — Will, here in the eveng.

7th.

Rose at ½ past 6. — Fine morning. — Thunder & rain in the afternoon. Glass 72. H. Hamond dined with me. — On the Prints of the Rivers. — Will came in the eveng. — G: Dance called on his return from Revd. Mr. Hooles.

8th.

Rose at ¼ past 6. — A wet & dark morning. — Horace Hamond went to Brighton. — washing outlines of Rivers. — C: Offley dined with me. — afternoon fine. About 55,000 pipes of Port wine were imported into England last year (1792). The greatest quantity ever known. — The Port Houses are not responsible for wine when shipped, it then becomes the care of those merchants who have ordered the wine. — There is a probability of a marriage in the Offley family.

Marchant called in the evening with a proposal relative to Valenciennes. Mr. Windham has today described the very picturesque & extraordinary appearance of that place since the seige. — Will, came in the eving.

August 9th.

Rose at ½ past 6. — Fine morning. William[Farington]s Certificate recd from the Navy Office of his having now served 3 years 4 months & 4 days. The remainder of time is 2 years and 9 months.

Called on Messrs. Boydells who are desirous of having the views of Valenciennes undertaken, and that Mr. Stadler shd. accompany me to that place. — Dined with C. Offley.

August 10th.

Rose at ¼ past 6. — Called on Mr. Windham, to have Marchant introduce me. Mr. Windham gave me particular directions for the views of Valenciennes. — got Bills from Hammersleys House on their agents abroad. — fine day. preparing for Journey.

August 11th.

Rose at 5. Fine morning. at ½ past 6 set off for Valenciennes.

[*Farington's journal of his visit to Valenciennes, kept in a separate pocket-book, now follows.*]

At seven this morning left London accompanied by Mr. Stadler. I also took my servant James with me. Passed through Rochester, Canterbury &c to Dover, where we arrived about half past seven in the evening. The weather very pleasant. Mr. Stadler was much pleased with many circumstances of scenery as we passed along, particularly with the very extensive retrospective view of the country we had travelled through, from the high ground about 3 miles before we reached Canterbury. — I think the Poeple at the Inns on this road are civil, but eager to get all they can. — The stage from Canterbury to Dover is in many parts Hilly, with a few distant peeps of the Sea and Dover Castle. We saw the Coast of France from the road very plain; the evening sun illuminating the white cliffs. — When we arrived at Dover, I was much disappointed on finding the Packet for Ostend, had sailed that night (Saturday) and that it only sails on Wednesdays and Saturdays. — The wind also being fair for sailing from hence, consequently prevented the Packets which had sailed before from returning. In this situation the Master of a Decked Boat, a fishing Smack, offered to take our Party over for five guineas, which after making some enquiry I thought it prudent to do, as remaining here at a certain expence and unemployed would double the loss. — The usual price by the regular packets is one guinea each person. — The distance from Dover, to Ostend, is calculated to be 18 or 19 leagues. Though so near the Coast of France no danger is apprehended from any French Vessells or Boats. The English Frigates &c preventing their appearing in this Channel. We found an advantage today in travelling by a line of Houses connected with each other. Commencing with the George at Dartford, we had the privilege of taking the Chaise *through* to Dover, which saves time & the trouble of changing Luggage. — At Eleven at night we went on board our Boat which lay in the Harbour, after paying a very extravagant Bill for trifles at the York Hotel. The Master &c very civil but unconscionable fleecers. — We were joined in our Boat by a Lieutenant of a Cutter which is stationed to cruise off the Coast of France under the direction of Captn. Robinson, of the Brilliant Frigate, stationed at Ostend. The Lieut. had been in London on acct. of an East Indian Imperial Ship which was taken lately near Dunkirk, in consequence of producing false papers. — She is a Ship of full 1200 tons, & Her papers described her as a Vessel of 500, besides other contradictions. — The Smack on board which we now are is abt. 30 Tuns, and carries on such occasions as this 3 men and two Boys. — A small Cabbin containing 4 Bed places held our Party; and in our Cloaths, we laid down from 12 oclock till 7 in the morning. — The tide was in favor but a want of wind prevented our making much way, so that at 7 in the morning we had not proceeded on our passage more than 16 miles, and still discerned the North Foreland. The weather very pleasant, and the day became clear and warm, with a light breeze which carried us at the rate of 2 miles and a half an Hour against tide. Several Vessels passed in various directions within sight of us Colliers &c, and their sailing singly shewed a general confidence that the Coast is well guarded by our Cruisers. — While we were at the Inn at Dover, we were waited upon by a Person belonging to the Customs, who requested we would write down our names, for which & for passing our packages witht. examination as He said, there was a slight fee of Half a Crown, which was paid him. He told me French Emigrants were not on going abroad required to give in their names. He did not take James's name.

About noon we were almost becalmed & when the tide turned in our favor at one oClock, we had no wind to assist us. At three oClock we had a fine breeze, and at half past 4 were brought to by the Brittania cutter, from which a shot was fired for that purpose. The Lieutenant who commanded her came alongside us in his Boat, and after a little conversation with the Lieutenant who was on his passage with us, returned to his Cutter, and we proceeded. — We saw Dunkirk Steeple about this time. — The weather continued extremely pleasant. I could not but observe the importance which these Officers felt, on account of the authority which is vested in them; and I am willing they should have all the gratification which they can derive from it. The fatigues and trouble they are subject to when on such duty, is but slightly recompensed by any feelings raised by a little temporary power.

The East India Ship which I have mentioned as having been taken, was commanded by a Mr. Popham, who is or has been, a Lieutenant in the English Navy.

Towards the evening the wind came more to the East ward and our vessel made but little way being obliged to tack; this continued till 5 oClock in the morning of

Tuesday [13th].

when we arrived of the Harbour of Ostend and landed. The piers which form this Harbour are made of Piles and project in a Curve a considerable way, and appear to render the entrance very safe, but our Boatmen told me accidents often happen and that they had seen a vessel totally lost with the Crew almost close to the Pier. — They began to praise their own Harbour at Dover as superior to everything which is fair & natural enough. — On parting with them I gave them five shillings for themselves with which they seemed satisfied. They carried our Luggage to the Inn, and we were not molested as at Calais & Dover with a Crowd of Helpers, no one coming towards us for that purpose. — We put up at the Imperial Court, an Inn so called, kept by Morisson, an Englishman. I walked through the Town with Stadler and went to Mass in a Church belonging to the Capuchin Friars, where 3 priests performed the service at three different Altars at the same time, dressed in the Mass Cloaths, White with a broad purple red Cross on the back, decorated with Lace. Each was attended by a Friar, of the same Convent, dressed in their Habit of the order, a dark brownish coloured stuff, of thick, wolleny, manufacture, tied with a rope about the middle. Both priests and Friars have long Beards, and some of them wasted countenances. They performed the service with many gestures, and an appearance of great devotion. — A considerable number of poeple were kneeling in the Church against stools in the form of a desk. They were chiefly woemen, with Hoods to their long Capuchin Cloaks, made of

various stuffs, striped &c. — The service only lasted about 20 minutes
when the Priests descended from the Altars, each carrying the Calips,
[Calyx] which is a vessel used in consecrating the wine, covered first with a
small plate in which the Host is consecrated, cloths are also covered over
the top of the Calips so as to make up a square appearance.

We afterwards walked to the guard House. The 37th English Regt. and a
Corps of French Emigrants were now doing duty at Ostend but no
German troops.

After breakfast I waited on General Ainslie, the Commander in Chief
here, and delivered a Letter to him from Mr. Windham, Member for
Norwich. — The General recd. me in a very polite manner, and offered to
give me a Letter to the Governor of Valenciennes, which He observed
would lead to an introduction everywhere that I proposed to go. The Duke
of York with the main British Force is now on his way towards Dunkirk,
and the remainder of the British troops with the Austrians. — The General
said I might be assured of assistance whenever I joined the Army, from the
Officers. — As the General had to go to the Parade, Mr. Stadler walked
with me to the great Church, which is pretty large, but of no regular Architecture, Gothick or Roman, on the outside and very plain within. Three
Altars at the East end of the Center and outer Aisles, were heavily ornamented, to the very Ceiling. Many persons were collected for the purpose
of a service. The Superior of this Church being dead, His Successor
performed duty this day for the first time. — No seats as in the English
Churches, but Chairs placed in Rows, with a ledge to rest a Book, or the
Arms upon, when kneeling. This ledge is on the top of the Back. — Many
Pictures in this Church, but indifferent or very bad. Some upright large
Landscapes with Scriptural Stories. — At small Bye Altars there were
strung offerings, of models in Wax. Legs, eyes, ears &c. alluding to the part
affected which the offering convalescent may have had a complaint in.
These offerings were of a very small size.

We afterwards went into the Chappel of a Nunnery. At an aperture
facing the Altar sat a Nun knitting. Before her on a table was placed a
Glass of a tubical form in which were some relicks of a Saint, which the
devout on coming in or quitting the Chappel, take up and kissing it, drop a
small offering into a plate placed by it.

The woemen in Ostend universally go without Hats. A Short Jacket &
petticoat, with a winged Cap, and an Apron of any kind, make up the
dress. Over these is thrown when going to Church &c a Capuchin, or long
Cloak, with a Hood to cover the Head, made of printed stuff, or Cloth &c.
— They very much resemble the Scotch Woemen, with this advantage in
their favour that they wear Stockings & Shoes & some of the lower order
large wooden Clogs; so that the legs & feet being covered, we are left to
guess at their particular form & state; but their faces from being constantly
exposed lose all delicacy, and they must at an early age look much older
than they are, from the coarseness & hardness of their features &

Price of Wines at Court Imperial, Morisons.

			English				English
Bordeaux {1re. q.	f. 2. 2 }	– 0-3-0		Cherry	f. 2. 2 –	0-3-0	
{2 de.q.	f. 1.15 }	–		Grave	f. 2. 2 –	0-3-0	
Porto	f. 2. 2	– 0-3-0		Malaga	f. 1.15 –		
Bourgogne	f. 2.16 }			Blanc	f. 1. 4 –		
Champagne	f. 3. 3			Porter de }	f. — 10 –	0-0-10½d.	
Madere	f. 3. 3			Londre }			
Rhin	f. 2. 2 }	– 0-3-0			stivers		
	£.s.d.					Demies	

Complexion. The little girls are dressed after the manner of the grown up woemen. — The streets are pretty regularly built; and the Houses generally good. Very few Houses have more than one story above the ground floor. They are mostly built of a light Brick. The windows do not push up like the English, but open like double doors into the room.

On our landing at Ostend we were ordered to go into a Watch House near the landing place, and desired to put down our names, from whence come, profession, and where going. — Soldiers of the 37th regt. were executing this duty, and with them were a few of the Corps of Emigrants.

The weather was very fine but extremely hot.

For drawing waggons, & different working carriages, Ropes are used instead of Leather.

At 4 in the afternoon I wrote a note to General Ainslie, — requesting my Passport & his Letter of introduction, which He obligingly sent.

Copy of General Ainslie's introductory Letter.

Ostend 13th August, 1793

Dear Sir

The Bearer of this Mr. Farington at the desire of many very eminent and respectable persons in Great Britain, having come over in order to employ his eminent talents in describing Scenes and Actions so interesting to Great Britain: I am to solicit your good Offices, towards furthering his views in this laudable undertaking; Mr. Farington will probably require your permission in writing, and to be made known to our military friends all round the different parts or field of actions, which He may be desirous of representing: All which you will be kind enough to procure for him—

I am with true regard (*whoever you may be*) Dear Sir

Your obedt. Hble.servt.

Geo: Ainslie Majr. Genl.

commanding at Ostend.

Inclosed I send a letter from W: Windham Esqr. as this respectable testimony is all that can be required in favor of Mr. Farington.

Copy of Mr. Windham's letter to Genl. Ainslie.

Dear Sir
I hope you will excuse the liberty I take of reccomending to your protection, the Bearer, Mr. Farington, an Artist of eminence and character, who is desirous of making drawings of some of the Scenes, which have done so much honor to the combined Armies. I thought that a line to this effect might not be unsuitable, as a voucher of his being the Person He represents himself to be.

Let me take this opportunity to say, that I delivered your letter myself to Genl. Smith, and sent my servant with that to Lord Leicester; and to assure you, that I am

Dear Sir
Your most obedient
& faithful servant
W: Windham

Hill st. Augst. 10th. 1793
No news as yet that I have heard of the grand fleet.

After dining at Ostend we took a Chaise for the first Post or Stage, which is Thuriot [Thoraut], 15 miles or according to the reckoning here 2 Posts and a half. I was much surprised on arriving at Thuriot,when the Driver demanded A Louis, and half a Crown, (or 23 shillings,) for the Stage, besides pay for himself, which He could *legally* reckon at 1 shilling a Post or half a Crown the Stage; but He said & the Master of the Inn declared He is usually paid 2s a Post, or 5 Shillings the stage. After satisfying myself that I was not imposed upon I paid the whole demand 28 shillings & 6d. for a Stage of 15 miles, which is perhaps the dearest travelling in Europe. — We had 3 Horses to the Carriage, one of the Shaft Horses had Leather harness, the other Ropes. The Man on a Box, who would have obstructed the view had there been any. The Chaise dismal in appearance & the Accoutrements in general of the same cast, including the Driver. But we got on pretty well, about 6 miles an Hour, over a continued Causway from Ostend, and the road so straight, it only curved from a right line in two or three places, the whole way. Trees are planted on each side, which where they are tolerably well grown, fills up very well in a country like this, flat and uninteresting. In most parts an Elm & a Willow are planted alternatively. — For three or 4 miles after we left Ostend the Country is wild & open in appearance, though there is in reality a good deal of cultivation, but being with! Hedge rows or other divisions it does not seem to be so. — The little Cottage or small farm House interspersed are tolerably well built of brick with tiled roofs. As we proceeded to a greater distance from Ostend, Hedge rows started up and fertility, and cultivation were fully expressed. Indeed no difference that I perceived from the common appearance of an English flat country near a road. I must except their farming waggons from this general comparison. They are long & narrow, running on 4 low Wheels, particularly the fore wheels. Ropes they are drawn by instead of Leather. At our Inn at Thuriot our Landlord could speak bad French, but no English. The Landlady only Flemish. — The House very tolerable, and neat enough. The Beds all with tent tops.

About 2 miles frôm Ostend part of the first Regt. of Dragoon Guards were encamped, near the village of Steens, in what seemed a bleak & uncomfortable situation. A mile further another part of the Regt. was encamped, and we passed some on the road marching, each Rider having Provender for his Horse behind him.

Wednesday 14th.

Rose at ½ past 4 and left Thouriout at 5. We now had a Coach. The road still continues paved and little variation from right lines. At certain distances Stone posts are placed on each side the road, & an Iron Bar which would cross the road is left open. These are barriers, and are paid for at the end of each stage being reckoned up with the Carriage expence. It saves the trouble of paying on the road. Several little Chappels are seen near the road erected by devout poeple, they have usually the figure of a Saint in each of them. Frequently a little box is seen nailed to a tree in which is a Crucifix or figure of a Saint.

The Country continues very flat, and Hedge rows grow high, & light trees are interspersed. Many comfortable cottages. A general appearance of comfort & cultivation. We came to a simple House, the first stage from Thourout, situated near a village called Petthun, 9 miles or a Post & a half from Thourout. Here we breakfasted on Coffee and cold Chicken. The Mistress and her Maid spoke French. Our breakfast cost half a Crown. — Butter is her[e] 8d. a pound — Beef 5d. — Mutton 4d½ veal the same. — Partridges 14d. a couple. — Everything much dearer within 12 months. — Only priviledged Gentlemen can kill them, such as have a right of hunting. Poeple are kept by these Lords of Chace, called Chasseurs or Hunters. — Those who kill game being unpriviledged are [punished], for the first offence, their guns are taken & they are confined for a short time, — for a second offence a fine is levied on them, — for a 3d. offence they are imprisoned.

The woemen universally wear Crosses, hanging from a Ribbon round the neck. — The married Woemen wear a ring on the 4th finger of the *right* hand, — the unmarried on the 4th of the *left*.

There were 12 Barriers, (Turnpikes) between Thuriot & Pethuen.

On our quitting Ostend our Baggage was carried into a guard House, opened, & strictly examined, we might, we understood, have avoided this by requesting an examiner to come to our Inn and giving him half a Crown.

The Belgians in the French service behaved worst to the Inhabitants of Pethuen. The Post Houses were particularly alarm'd from being in the service of the Imperial government. — A French Commander in the neighboroud at last protected them.

From Pethuen the road continues in nearly right lines with Trees planted on each side, which was a good effect in a country so flat. We came to Ingminster [Ingelmunster], a clean well built village. At the end of it the first Gentlemans House I have seen. It is large and illshaped, moated round, and the garden plats and clipped Hedges cut in various figures. It belongs to a French Marquiss who usually resided in France. — A considerable time before we reached Courtray the Tower of the Church terminated a long Vista of road & side trees.

I learn'd that for the Barriers from Thourot to Pethuen only 12 sous (or 1 shilling) is charged for these Turnpikes, so that so small a deduction leaves a monstrous charge for the posting only. — When we entered Courtray a Soldier demanded our names, whence come, & where going with great Civility. — At the Post House here we could not be provided with Horses, all being engaged or out. We were therefore necessitated to remain from 10 oClock till 2, to go by the Dilligence to Tournay. The Price for each person in this conveyance is 2s.6d. — It contains if full 12 persons.

The Town of Courtray is not large; Has a handsome market place in which is a large Town Hall of the whimsical architecture of the Country, with a small Tower terminated by little Spires. The Houses are of brick covered with plaister of a grey or white or yellowish Colour. Many Plaister ornaments on the Front. — The Architecture of the large Parish Church is irregular. The great Tower thus

The poeple in this place appear to be idle, numbers for the size of the place lounging in the Market Place or sat before their Houses. — At this time the Dutch Soldiers garrisoned the place, if it may be called a garrison which it is not. However they guard the Town. — Their uniform dark Blue with Red or Yellow Lappels white waistcoat & Breeches and orange Cockades in their Hats. There are also Dutch Hussars with Whiskers, riding small lean Horses, that an English Trooper on an Heavy Horse would crush. — The dress of the Hussars, Red jackets, with Blue Cloaks that hang over their shoulders, these are lined with Fur. — They have high Black Caps. — Certainly the general appearance of these troops & their officers, particularly the *latter,* raise no very respectable opinion in the mind of an Englishman. A want óf neatness is universal, and somehow the accoutrements make a shabby show.

The great Church (Parish Church) is spacious in the inside, but plain and of no stile of Architecture. There are as usual 3 principal altars, one at the East end of each Aisle. The Center one at the end of the Choir is pyramidical in the design. From an Eye in the Center of a triangle issue gilt rays. Below in bad sculpture the ascension. — The Choir gates ornamented with gilding. Many Pictures in different parts of the Church. The subject of each alluding to some Saint; and before each an Altar. No good Pictures, and of them very bad. — Many Confessionals. In a small bye Chappel we thought we perceived through rails a Corpse covered with clean linnen. Supposing it to be so we enquired of two woemen who it might be, & were told a figure of Jesus Christ, was under the linnen, and that the 3 Marys (figures in wood) which were on the other side were weeping over him.

A Procession passed through the Market Place. It was preparatory to the Funeral of a Nun, a French one, who had been recd. into a Convent here.

First Banners were carried on Poles. They were the Ensigns of different Religious Confraternitys.

Next Charity Children in Uniform dresses singing. They are children educated at the expense of that Nunnery.

Then Priests singing accompanied by the instrument called a Serpent.

Then the Corpse laying on a Bier covered with Linnen, and borne by Young Woemen, Novices of the Convent.

Then two Abbe's, followed by a few Woemen as Mourners. We followed them into the Church of St. Michel. It was Eleven oClock. A Requiem was sung. The Body was placed just below the steps of the Choir. It was covered with White Linnen, with a Blue Cross, which signifies a maiden state. — Married woemen have a Black Cover & White Cross. — A Silver Crucifix was placed at the feet. High, lighted, Tapers on each side the Body, of White Wax. Similar ones were on the Great Altar. A Crown of Flowers was placed on the middle of the Corpse, in which is a silver vessel with Holy Water. The Priest who officiated was drest in the Alba, a White dress, with a *Black* Cross over it. The Deacons which administered at the Mass wore a Black velvet dress, bordered with Silver. — This dress is said to be according to the Levitick description of Moses. — Indeed they are called in German (the Deacons) Levites, (Leviten). During the ceremony a

Priest went round the Body throwing from a vessel, suspended by gilt Chains, Incense over the Corpse, also Holy Water. This Priest was preceded by two Boys, who carried wax Tapers, in large Candlesticks. In the Church of Notre Dame, at the East end, behind the Choir, is a very fine Picture of the erection of Christ on the Cross by Vandyke. It is covered with a Curtain.

The Choir of this Church, which is Prebendal, is faced with marble to a certain heigth, but the other parts look very naked.

There are no fortifications at Courtray. I made a sketch of the Bridge of the Towers (Le Pont de Tour,) which is thrown over the Lys. The Towers are of singular forms and are used for magazines of Coals & Grain.

The great mixture of Poeple of different Characters of appearance which are seen in the Market place is interesting to a stranger, particularly at this time when Dutch soldiers & Imperial are blended among them. The Imperial military Colour is White, faced with Red or Yellow &c facings. They look much more military & cleaner than the Dutch.

We dined by ourselves & were served with small dishes of various kinds of fish, salted chiefly, Soup, and fruit & Cheese after dinner. We had some Beer & Brandy, & *including the Servant* the Bill was abt. 5 shillings.

We could not procure a Chaise at the Post House or in the Town, all the horses being engaged in this busy time. We took places.

The road from Courtray to Tournay is paved and continues as before as nearly in a right line as the Country would admit. Abt. 4 miles beyond Courtray, a distance of high country seen, well wooded & cultivated. Indeed the whole country appears to be so, and could a person be removed from England without knowing it He would not discover by any visible sign that he was in a strange one. I mean with the exception of the Inhabitants, the difference of Appearance being very great indeed. — Abt. half way between Courtray & Tournay is a House of Call where stopped. Beyond this place, *French* is the universal Language. Hardly any Flemish, whereas at Courtray little French is spoken. Mr. Stadler says they speak a Patois (provincial) French. I observed that abt. 4 miles from Courtray the country rises, but we soon fell again into the same uniform flat. On the left as we approach Tournay, S͐ Trinity appears a Hilly situation richly woodded & cultivated, and topt with a White Chappel. — We first saw Tournay at 3 miles distance. The situation seems as flat, and not unlike that of Cambridge. The Towers &c of the churches appearing over Bushy trees. — Thick Hedge rows, & Plantations of trees the country is full of. — The French have destroyed all the Gallows which were in this country, and cut down the Rows of trees on each side the road for more than a mile from the entrance to Tournay.

On enquiry I found that the largest Farm in this neighboroud does not exceed £240 a year. Much of the Land belongs to Lords & Convents.

A Verge, is 100 square feet. 700 Verge's make up a Poignée. A Poignée lets here for £4 up to £6.

The payment for the Bureaus or Turnpikes is equal through the
Country. One Sous, for each Horse and one for the Chaise.
We arrived at Tournay at 7 in the evening. Five hours from Courtray, 15
miles.
The weather very fine.
We put up at the Inn called La petite Nef, (The little Vessel). It is
esteemed one of the best Houses in the Town. The Empress is reckoned the
best.
We had this day met a long train of waggons, belonging to the
Hanoverian Bakers, proceeding as we supposed towards Dunkirk.
There appears a general hatred of the French in this Country, but there
is no difference in appearance & manner in the poeple of Tournay from the
French poeple.
Tournay. — The Clubbists of this Town did most harm, robbing the
Churches &c for the French. — These poeple are proscribed, and went
away with the French. They consisted chiefly of Merchants & tradesmen,
no common poeple. The Poor were all against them. — Four of the Houses
of the Clubbists were razed to the ground, the remainder much damaged.
A young man Heir to 10,000 florins a year was a Leader of the Clubbists, &
has since been executed at Mentz.
When we entered Tournay we found we had mistaken the nature of its
situation which is on sloping ground on a side of the River Scheldt which is
here about 75 feet Broad, and much navigated upon if we might judge from
the number of Barges which are very large with rudders of an extraordinary size. A Quay runs alongside and on each side the River to the two
extremities of the Town. It is broad and Trees are planted in a Row along
it. — Boys were bathing in this River, who were tied up about the waist, &
between the Legs, like the poeple of the Sandwich Islands. We concluded
this to be from a motive of decency as the River passes through so publick
a part of the Town. Each boy crossed himself before going into the water.
Young Men bathing were still more generally covered, and one Man had
bathed with his Breeches on. We were after assured it was a custom from a
motive of Decency. I called on Mr. Mee, Deputy to Mr. Brook Watson
Comissary General, as the latter had left Tournay yesterday in consequence of the Army being on the point of moving. He thought Mr. Watson
who went to Ypres would proceed today to Ostend.
If we may judge of the accomodation as to Lod[g]ing in Tournay it is
very bad indeed in one respect. The Bugs & fleas were so troublesome as to
oblige me to rise and lay on the floor in my Cloaths.

August 15th.

We rose at ½ past 5, and walked about the Town, and in the forenoon
went to Mass. It being the Assumption of the Virgin Mary, Mass was
performed in all the Churches with the greatest Splendour of show. St.
Martins is a very spacious lofty building, paved with Marble, in squares of

black & White. It is kept beautifully clean. The Architecture though not regular is more approaching to the Roman than the Gothick, but it is a kind of mixture of both. A Prelate wearing a Mitre, made of gold stuff, with a vestment worn at the Mass of the same materials, performed Mass. He was attended at the Altar by 3 priests, — besides His *Valet de Chambre* in a *Lay dress,* who attended to place a chair for him when He sat down, and held a gold Basin in one hand & an Urn with Water in the other, as the Prelate washed his hands each time before and after touching the Host, — As the Ceremony of the Mass cannot be understood by a Stranger, Stadler described the detail of the Ceremony.

First Ceremony — when He who performs Mass comes to the Altar, He mounts the Altar and puts the Cup in order. — Then He descends to the bottom of the steps before the Altar, and He repeats alternatively with the Deacons attending, verses from the Psalms. He then ascends the Altar again, and on the right hand a Book is open, from which He reads the prayers appointed for the day. He next reads an Epistle for the day — then the Book is carried from the right hand to the left, after which He reads the Collect of the day, during which the Audience stand. He then takes the Host, which is a Wafer about the size & shape of a Crown piece, with an impression of a Crucifix on it on one side, and on the other the name of Jesus. — He puts the Host in a little Plate, and holding it up, says the prayers of oblation. He then takes the Cup, and after wiping it, pours in the wine; then with a little round spoon, which holds about 3 drops of water, He mixes that with the wine. When that is done He repeats another prayer of Oblation, and covers the Cup. He then washes his hands, and turning to the poeple says Orate Fratris — After this a Candick [Canticle] is said or sung in praise of God, which ends with Holy, Holy, be the Lord God of Sabaoth. — Then He prepares for the Consecration, which only consists of these words. "This is my Body", in Latin, "Hoc est, enim Corpus meum". Then He lifts up the Host over his Head that the Poeple may see it and a Deacon attending rings a bell, as a signal of the consecration. This part of the Mass is considered as the most sacred. Afterwards He consecrates the Wine, and says, "This is my Blood" &c and lifts that up as He had done the Host, a Bell is again rung as a signal. — He then says some prayers, and taking up the Host breaks it in two in the middle, and breaks off a small particle of one of the halfs & puts it in the Cup. After this, saying some prayers He prepares for communion, which is in taking up the two pieces of the Host, saying, the Body of our Lord Jesus Christ preserve my soul to the eternal life. He then eats them after this He takes the Cup, saying, the Blood of our Lord, drinks the wine; He then washes the Cup and his hands. And after having covered up the Cup the Book is brought to the right side of the Altar again when He says some more prayers of the day, after which He turns round to the audience & gives them the benediction and the Mass is at an end.

In Tournay Beef is 4d.½ a pd. Veal and Mutton the same. — The year round. Butter varies from 6d. to 8d. a pd. 16 oz. to the pound. — At the Table D'Hote 13d. a head English, — witht. wine, but Beer is included.

The Library which is modern and forms the left wing in the approach to the Cathedral, the La Petite Place, of the Bishops Palace forming the right. It is about 80 feet long, and 31 broad. Wainscoat & floored with Oak. The latter figured.

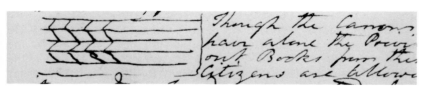

Though the Canons of the Cathedral have alone the Priviledge of taking
out Books from this Library, the Citizens are allowed to read in it every
day, Sundays excepted, from 10 oClock till 12. A Gallery goes round one
side & the ends. Into this Strangers are not admitted at least not witht. a
Canon attending. This restriction is owing as they said to Books having
been taken away. — They told us there were Books in all Languages, but I
could not discover one in the English Language. There are Eleven
windows on one side of the Library. None at the ends. They are divided
into small sashed panes.

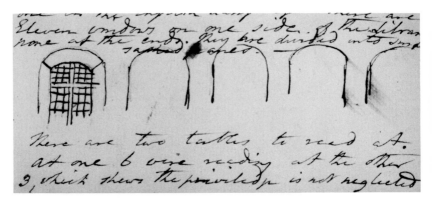

There are two tables to read at. At one 6 were reading at the other 3, which
shews the priviledge is not neglected.
    The Cathedral of Tournay is large. In the inside it is lofty but the Center
& particularly the side Aisles are narrow & dark. It is not regular Gothick,
but the repairs which are modern, are capricious. The Screen before the
Choir is of marble & modern. — The decorations of the Altar what may be
called old-fashioned, heavy, and tasteless.
Manner of sweeping or repairing inside of Cathedral at Tournay. When
He wishes to lower himself he passes down a center rope to a man below,
who prevents precipitancy.

[*See facing page*]

    The Town of Tournay is very amusing taken in a picturesque Sense. The
Houses are built of Brick but after the manner of the Country they are
plastered over or washed with different tints so as to cause a variety
unknown in English Towns. The Architecture of the Houses varies as
much as the Colour. Seldom it happens that 2 which join together are
uniformly alike. Of the Cathedral of Tournay or of the Churches at
Ostend, or Courtray, we can say little, as to consistency of Stile of Architecture or beauty of decoration and finishing. They are not to be compared

west end inside of cathedral of Tournay

manner of sweeping or repairing inside of cathedral at Tournay. When he wishes to lower himself he pushes down by the center rope to a man below, who prevents precipitancy

with the Gothick structures in England, or which were in Scotland. Of the latter we can judge from what remains though in ruins.

Of the Inns in general we can say with truth that they are commonly dirty, unfurnished, and ill attended. An Englishman accustomed to the neatness, & convenience of the Inns in his own Country, and to the civility which is universally found, will require a little time to reconcile himself to those He will find abroad.

Tournay, was formerly esteemed a place of great strength but was dismantled as a fortification by agreement at the Conclusion of the peace of Aix la Chapelle, in 1748.

In the afternoon of August 15th we heard that the British Army had marched from Oschee and was at Basieux a village abt. 6 miles from Tournay and 9 from Lisle. Much firing had been heard in the forenoon which we afterwards found was nothing more than shot fired by parties who were examining the Country while the Army was marching. We proceeded to Basieux, and met several officers, waggons &c on the road. When we arrived at the village we saw the Duke of Yorks carriage & his 6 Cream Coloured Horses, near the House which He had made his Head quarters, close to the Church, belonging to Frontaine, a farmer. We were at this time very much interested with the vast scene of an Army moving. Regiment after Regiment came pouring through the village and in other directions to a very extensive open plain beyond the village. Few Armies have been made up of a greater variety of different Poeple than this was, which we were told consisted of 50000 men. English, Austrians, Hanoverians, Hessians, Bohemians, Hungarians. We passed nearly through the whole Camp which could not cover a space of less than 3 miles in length, and saw the whole process from entering the field to the tents being completely fixed and each Regiment duely arranged. The Army was so large and was made up of so many descriptions, that it was with some difficulty we found out the Scots Greys. That Regiment was in the rear of the Army, and owing to some neglect the tents belonging to it were not brought up, and the Officers were in the field wanting both Tents & food &c. A supply we had carried with us [as] a provision against accident was gratefully recd. by Major Boardman & the other Officers, and seated on a Cloak, and the inside of saddles, we made a very chearful repast. A Watering place was near us, and an Austrian regiment of Horse, returning from it were singing their Vespers. The Orders being given out for the Army to march again at 4 the next morning, At nine Mr Stadler and I got into our Chaise. Major Boardman did the same into his, where we passed the night.

In the morning at half past 4 I went to the Duke of Yorks Head quarters, by appointment with Captn. Hewgill, his R. Highness's Secretary to whom I had delivered a letter from Mr. Windham. Captain Hewgill delivered to me a Passport from the Duke to remove any obstructions in passing through the Conquered Countries. Lord [William] Bentinck & other Officers were at the House.

This morning the breaking up the Camp was a very striking Scene. It was a little before day light. The fires which were blazing in different parts of the Camp added much to the effect, and the appearance of Soldiers of different Countries, their dresses, and savage Aspects, raised an apprehension of danger, during this doubtful light when everything at a little distance was obscure. So well ordered was this Army however, that the Peasants were in a state of perfect security. Whatever was asked for at the little Inns was paid for, and the only priviledge the Army took was to cut forage on or near the spot where the Camp happened to be for the supply of the day. This as was observed to me by an Officer could not eventually distress the farmer much, as no Landlord could expect rent under such circumstances.

Major Boardman spoke particularly of the extraordinary appearance of the Hungarian Grenadiers. Every Man is a Model of form and strength. Indeed we were much surprised at the size and Warlike appearance of most of the foreign Corps. The Imperial Infantry are considered as the most compleat troops in the field, for exactness of discipline and regularity of every kind. The Hanoverian Horse make a very good show but are Heavy. The Hanoverian Infantry seem to be least approved of. Almost all the German troops wear Whiskers which certainly adds much savageness to the look. They are frequently waxed, and are twisted about in long lines.

The Dutch and the Emigrants are looked upon as the most unmilitary Soldiers, and are chiefly made use of to garrison Towns &c but not for field duty.

The Cloth of which the Cloaths of the Austrian & Bohemian Infantry is made is thick & very coarse, and their Shirts like Sack-Cloth. When on a march they wear a Frock, like our Farmers Frocks, which from its coarseness and bad colour, and long wearing, make them look like Felons destined to Botany Bay.

After receiving our Passports we returned to Tournay, where I made a drawing of the Prison House & part of the Cathedral, before breakfast. At Noon we proceeded towards Valenciennes by the way of Fontenoy, Antoine and St. Amand. I had agreed with the owner of a Calash for 15 Shillings a day and half a Crown to the Driver, which if the machine & Tackle &c are considered is dear enough. — But the pretence for charging so high was the great demand for Horses & Carriages on acct. of the Army, so many being required for different purposes.

The road from Tournay towards Fontenoy is very rough & the general appearance of the country the same. There are many lime Pits. It is a cross country road & not paved. The Tower of Antoine [Antoing] appears over the trees of a very singular form. — We passed the little Chappel of Notre Dame in the wood, where Louis 16th. [15th] heard Mass in the morning before the Battle of Fontenoy, and afterwards took his station near it. The House where He had lodged belonged to a Canon of Tournay, and is nearer to that Town. The Village of Fontenoy is abt. 3 miles distant from

Tournay. The Country is open, and unequal. The Battle was fought on the highest ground, from whence is a very extensive view. — At Fontenoy a respectable old Man walked with us over the field of Action and gave us many particulars of it. He was at that time 23 years of Age and resided in the village with his Father. The Regiment of the Dauphine, was quartered in the village & the Coll. of it lodged at his Fathers house 3 days before the Battle and on the morning of it recommended them to get away which they did to Notre dame. The whole Village except his Fathers House & another was destroyed. Trenches were thrown up in and round the Village. — The Coll. sent a Man with him & his Father to a Corps of reserve at a justice or gallows, near Notre Dame, which is abt. ¾ of a mile from Fontenoy. That part of the wood of Barri which the French posessed is cut down. — The Battle began at 4 in the morning on the 11th of May, 1745; and was over about 2 oClock. The Heat of the Action was from 10 to abt. ½ past 12 oClock. — He walked over the field with many other Country Poeple about 4 oClock. None of them durst touch the dead or wounded, the French Soldiers asking them who had gained the Battle? The Soldiers stripped the dead & wounded indiscriminately, and in this naked state they were left in heaps all night. About 6 oClock it began to rain. The day had been fine. This increased the distress of the wounded, who shuddered, and called out Hospital, the only word that could be understood by the Natives. In such fear of the French were the Country poeple, that they durst not bring even water to the wounded to drink. The Soldiers called the English Beasts & bid the Country Poeple not mind them. — After the rain, notwithstanding the Peasants scooped up water in their Hats, and gave it to the wounded. — The French King rode round the Field of Battle abt. 6 oClock. — The next morning the field of Battle was examined and such as were not dead were removed in Carts into tents erected behind the House of our guides Father, in the naked state in which they were, and there their wounds were examined. Such as were not desperately wounded were attended to, those which seemed incurable were buried in the state in which they were in common with the dead in large Holes made for the purpose. — The French carried of their dead, so the Country Poeple could not judge of their loss, and the Soldiers vaunted that they had sustained little. — He said for a long time it was thought the English had gained the Battle, till some Cannon began to fire upon them. — The French King remained here 3 days, and every day rode over the field of Battle. — The English head quarters were at the village of Vaison, about one mile distant in the lower country behind the field. They retreated that night to Ath, 15 miles from the scene of Action. — The Hanoverians behaved well; the Dutch were considered as Cowards. When the French Artillery began to play upon them they fell back & retreated behind a line of Bushes ¾ of a mile distant. — There was no windmill near the Scene of Action at that time. The Mill which now stands on the heigth has not been erected more than 20 years. — The Peasants detested the French, and considered the English as fighting their cause. — While I was taking the above notes a respectable Farmer came up & expressed an Apprehension that I was come to mark out a Camp.

The French have been here lately 3 days, and have cut down the trees on each side the hollow way from Fontenoy to the Plain: They eat up everything & paid for nothing.

From Fontenoy we went to Antonne [Antoing], which is a pretty large irregular built Village, situated on sloping ground which rises from the side of the River Scheldt. It belongs to the Prince of Ligne who has a Castle here which He makes use of as a Hunting Seat, and comes to once in two or 3 years. The form of it is very singular. A round Tower of considerable heigth has united to it several small buildings of such shapes as make up a very fanciful assemblage. If we may conclude from an Old Gateway, & what remains of the foundations of Towers which appertain to this Castle, it must have been a place of considerable strength. Seven villages appertain to this Castle.

From Antonne we crossed the Scheldt at a Ferry. — The Boat lay like a Platform on the Water, so that the Chaise was drove into it with great ease. The River is not wider than it is at Tournay.

At abt. 2 miles dist. we came into the great road, leading from Tournay to Valenciennes, which is paved. At a small Inn we met with some Dutch Officers of the Regiment of La Tour, who had refreshed themselves till they were exceedingly drunk, and very merry, and as we followed them from the place we had noise enough on the road. — About 3 miles short of St. Amand, we passed by the ground on which the Camp of Maulde was formed. It is a rising ground in an open Country, and a windmill is placed in the center of it. On the side trenches were thrown up which remain. It was here that Dumourier arrested the Deputies from the Convention, and sent them to Tournay to Prince Cobourg, & from this place He himself deserted and went to Tournay. His troops immediately quitted this station and fell back towards Valenciennes, & the Austrians took posession of the ground.

It was night when we reached St. Amand. Our Driver passed through the Town to what He called the best House abt. half a mile beyond, where on knocking at the door we were refused admittance for sometime and when we gained it, we were recd. by the Hostess & Her maid Servant with very discontented looks, and two men sat by the fire observing perfect silence. She could not, she said, afford us any accomodation either of eating or lodging, but after a good deal of civility on our side she relaxed and said she wd. make up one Bed and supply us with Bread & Butter & Gin. — We now did very well and were preparing for rest when 4 French Emigrants in the Austrian service came storming into the House, and unpacking some raw meat had the frying pan brought & one of them began to dress it. The Hostess was now very obedient & attended to them readily, while the Men in the House withdrew from the fire place & remained silent. Nothing could exceed the loquacity and rudeness of this set of Fellows. We soon left them in full posession of the room.

Saturday 17th.

Rose at ½ past 5. Walked into the Town, a dull morning. St. Amand is in a miserable state. What were the two principal Inns are only Skeletons. Dirt & neglect everywhere. — The Cathedral a very large pile of Capricious French Architecture, was built as appears from dates on the walls abt. 1647. It is now a magazine for Hay, and a Soldier was placed at the entrance. The Choir, which is ascended to by a high flight of Steps, was locked up and will suffer no further dilapidation. The Abbey House, which is joined to the Cathedral, is very large, but internally as much a Ruin as if it had been uninhabited 100 years. The French when the rage prevailed for abolishing religious establishments, drove the priests from their dwellings here, and destroyed the apartments. Since the Austrians have been victorious the Priests have returned, and reside in the Town & Neigh-boroud, with a full expectation of being restored to their situations.

Across a flat marshy country about half a League from hence is the Abbey of Ano, Benedictines. It is surrounded by water and was occupied by the French 3 months, till they fell back to Famar.

When it is considered how near the Abbeys of St. Amand, Ano, and Vico[i]ng are to each other, & what posessions belonged to them, it cannot be wondered at if the reason of Man decided against supporting such numerous establishments. But in this, as in all their proceedings, the French were not regulated by any moderation, and because these institu-tions were multiplied to an injurious excess destroyed the whole, & nearly their religion into the bargain.

After breakfast we proceeded to the Baths of St. Amand, about ½ a league from the Town. — These Baths are said to have been first discovered by the Romans, but in modern times they have only been famed abt. 100 years. We met an Officer of the English Guards, who was here, for the advantage of bathing, and He obligingly informed us of the quality of the Baths and water.

The *Mud Bath* is that which is probably peculiar to St. Amand. The Colour of it is Black grey, and in consistency the Mud is like watery Pudding. The [bather] steeps [h]is whole Body in this substance up to the Chin or any limb only which may be partially affected. It is usual to remain in the Bath 2 or 3 Hours once a day, during which time the patients may have their Books or converse as the holes in the precipitate themselves are near to each other being only divided by rough rails like Sheep-Pens. — The depth of the mud is about 6 feet & to prevent the Patient from sinking too low, boards are placed across in each of the divisions, on which He rests his shoulders, or Arms, so as to keep His head above the mud. The surface of the mud is Coldish, but below it is warmer, abt. 80 of the Thermometer. It is peculiarly of service in Rheumatick cases, & for such as have Old wounds, and [effects] extraordinary cures in venereal cases. It is asserted as a fact that after a Drummer of a Regt. which the Officer named had bathed here each time there were found 3 grains at least of Mercury, which proves that Mercury will remain in the body. The Officer himself shewed us a Nail of one of his Fingers on which there was a metallick mark that he was fully satisfied was made by an extraction of that quality since He came to St. Amand by bathing.

The Mud Bath is inclosed and the building is in the inside like a very large Barn fronted on one side by Glass Windows similar to a green House, but everything is done in the rudest manner. Neither workmanship in the finishing, nor neatness of any kind.

When Ladies bathe they have a covering over their Sheep-pen.

Whoever bathes, pays by the Body or Limb. For a Limb only put in they payd 7½d. a time; for the whole Body 15d.

The Springs which supply the water Baths produce a great quantity of water and reservoirs are made in that part of the buildings where are the principal Springs. — The Water has a taste like rotten eggs. A Crown piece held in the stream of a spring was changed into a blackish yellow in 3 or 4 minutes. — A little spring in the front of the House is much the strongest.

The Building at St. Amand is of great length and contains not only the Springs & reservoirs, but a great Ball room over them, bathing rooms & Lodging rooms for the Company. Each bathing room has a tub in it in which the patient lays down, and through a Tube with a lock at the end of it, the water is conveyed from the reservoirs and He supplies himself. A Tube fixed below carries of the water which has been used. — Those who come here to bathe hire each one of these rooms which He keeps posession of while He stays. For this they pay 15d. a time.

The water is purgative, and is commonly drank to the quantity of 15 Glasses a day. The Glasses are between ¼ and half a pint. — For drinking the Waters only 2s.6d. is paid for the Season, which commences the beginning of June and lasts 3 months.

The Gallery as it is called above the Bathing and Lodging rooms is abt. 340 feet long, very narrow & dark, with as usual a tiled floor, 22 rooms on one side, 21 on the other, white washed and like garrett Closets in England. In these poeple lodge but particularly Servants.

The Great meeting room has a coarse uneven wooden floor. It is white washed & the little furniture in it is very ordinary. Every Sunday there is a Ball in this room. A Ball was advertised by Papers stuck up, to begin at 2 oClock and end at 7; after which if it was prolonged a fresh expence would be incurred by those who remained.

The Company breakfasts in the Great Room, 6d. a piece.

The Table d'Hote is at a building opposite. The Room equally coarse with the others. Dinner at one oClock. 15d. a head. — Supper 1s. a head. The Lodging Rooms for Gentlemen and Ladies, have tiled floors, bare walls and little and most ordinary furniture. They would in England be considered as bad rooms in an Hospital.

In a good Season they had frequently 60 Gentlemen here, besides Servants, at a time.

The Baths belongs to the Abbey of St. Amand, — It is farmed from them, and including some ground pays 300 Louis a Year.

The present buildings were erected in 1698. It is said they were first dis[covered] by the Romans. — A Bishop of Arras, was cured of the effects of a Venereal Complaint by these Baths, which contributed to make them again known, after having been long neglected.

Inscription on the Front of the Building.

Cette Fontaine

Autre-fois Cultivée par les Romains negligée ensuite, et ignorée jusques a nous, enfin reconnue a ses effects marvellieux, mais presque inaccesible et confondue dans un marais a esté reparée, bastié, et embellie d'avenues, pour l'utillité publique, sous le regne de Louis le Grand, par les ordres du Marechal Duc De Boufflers, Commandeur des Ordres du Roy, Colonel du Regiment des Gardes Francoises, gouvernor general de Flandres &c, — Lan de Grace 1698.

[*See facing page.*]

From the Baths of St. Amand we passed through an extensive wood intersected by walks in right lines. The trees young and very thick. It belongs to the Compte of La Marque, eldest son to the Duke of Arembergh. In another part of this Wood, the Guards made that charge, when they suffered so much from the French Batteries. When we quitted the wood we were at the end of the village of Remes, a long straggling village. Here there was a strong contest between the French & the English & Germans. Genl. Clairfait gained great credit, and a Battery is preserved in which He defended himself and drove of the French though attacked from every quarter. Near the village the Compte La Marque, has a large House and a Park. A German Officer directed us to go down one of the walks which leads to the Abbey of Vicong, in which we should perceive an Offensive smell, which rose from a number of Bodies carelessly buried. What He said we found to be the case. The Abbey church of Vicong is abt. 3 quarters of a mile from the Comptes House. It is a very large Building of Gothic Architecture. The Abbey in which the Abbot &c resided is modern and as handsome as those we see in the quadrangles at Oxford. It has 31 windows in front, and is built of Stone. — The inside of the Church has suffered much in the Choir. All the Prebendal seats are torn away. The

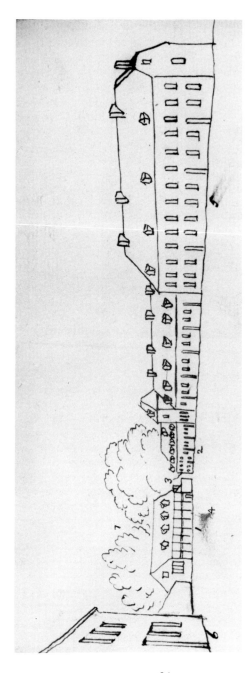

Baths of St Amand — 4 leagues from Tournay, 2 from Valenciennes. They are built of brick with Tiled Roofs.

1 — mud Bath   4 — Bathing Rooms
2 — Water Springs   5 — Lodging Rooms
3 — Great Assembly Room   6 — Table D'Hote
                            7 — Trees among which the Covered walks are made.

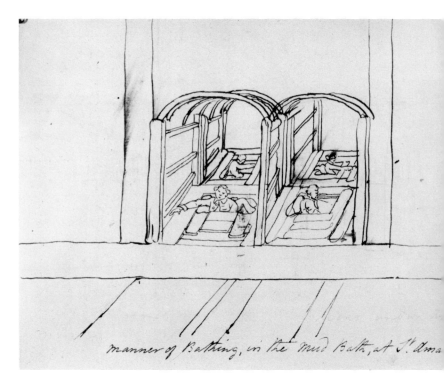

manner of Bathing, in the mud Bath, at S.ᵗ Ama

Manner of Bathing, in the Mud Bath, at St. Amand.

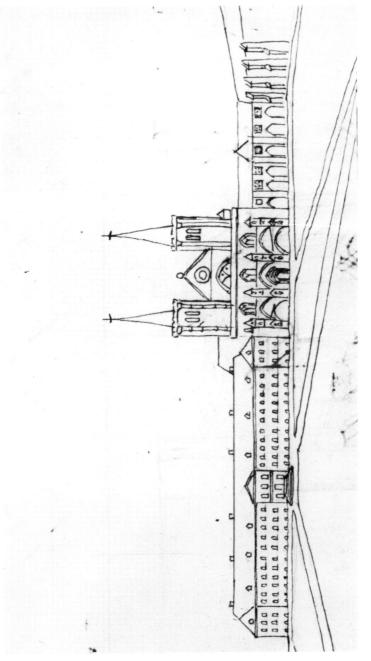

West Front of the Abbey Church of Vicong, and the Convent.

decorations of the Altar are gone. The Pictures were taken away in September last by an order from Valenciennes, and as we understood to preserve them, as they were very fine. As appears by a list of Abbots preserved in the Church there have been 41 in succession and that the Abbey was founded by 1125. The present Abbot is John Grenier, who with his bretheren of this institution fled from the French into Brabant where they subsisted on a territory belonging to their Church. They have returned since the French were drove away, and reside abt. 9 miles from this place, and orders have been given for repairing the damaged parts of the building.

While we were at Vicong, we heard much firing of Cannon, the Austrian Army was now about 15 miles from us, in the neighborood of Bouchaine & Mabeuge. — About 15000 are gone down with the English. We had some refreshment at Remes, and recd. civilities from a gentleman who had a direction of the private provissions for the Prince of Saxe Cobourgh. — There were in Remes and Vicong about 500 Bohemians & Austrians. Inferior troops to guard Baggage &c. — The Prince of Saxe Cobourgh, is abt. 55. A middle sized Man as to heigth & rather corpulent. Very easy of address, but keen in attending to his Soldiers that they shd. do their duty.

The Surrender of Valenciennes was a most striking Spectacle. An Assemblage of the Troops of so many Nations, exhibiting such different characters of appearance produced an effect every way interesting.

Arrangement of the Ceremony of the Surrender of Valenciennes.

[*See facing page.*]

Each regt. had 2 Cannon, its flags and Band of Music, similar to the guards. — The Town lays in a hollow and this line was formed up rising ground. The French came out abt. 10 oClock. The English Flag was thus removed by the English.

First came

Monsr. Ferrand, Commander with 5 Officers. —
Next The infantry
4 a breast.

There were near 5000 infantry. These were followed by abt. 500 Cavalry. When the last regt. of French was out of the Gates, the Princes commanding the Combined Armies rode up to the Gates and entering they were immediately shut. Nobody being allowed to go in till abt. 2 Hours afterwards by which time the Troops in the Town were regulated so as to perform their regular duties. — The Combined Army during this ceremony observed the silence of a parade. The distance from the Gate to

Arrangement of the Ceremony of the Surrender of Valenciennes. —

gate of   Valenciennes

• — English colours very high

Hungarian grenadiers. —

The Prince & Officers of the Staff standing to receive the keys.

Two Cannon Band of musick Company of English guards in 3 lines

Scotch greys 3 lines

Their infantry

Their cavalry

From the gate to the ground about 4 English Infantry on 4 & Cavalry on each side

Prince &

Prince &

The Park

French Grenadiers

French grenadiers

Imperials   English

the opening for the French to go away was near a mile. Behind the ranks were Spectators in Crowds. The whole lasted abt. 3 Hours. — Monsr. Ferrand is a tall Man & lean, with a French face. He was dressed in White with a Brick Coloured facing. — Between the troops Baggage waggons loaded, and on them Woemen & Children passed, & Behind each regt. there were 2 Cannon.

Two Regiments, without Arms, were placed within the Circle called the Park, whose business it was to take care that none of the French went away without grounding their Arms.

Monsr. Ferrand appeared to be a middle sized Man, rather Corpulent. He lookd about him in a fierce, indignant manner, a very plain Man in his countenance.

We proceeded in the afternoon to Valenciennes, about 3 miles from Raimes, and stopt at St. Angin to view the situation from whence the Austrians battered the Town. From a Windmill there is an extensive view of Valenciennes and the principal features of it appear to advantage. It is situated low, the Country to the North & South rising considerably immediately from the Town. To the East and West it is flat and the Scheldt runs in this direction. That River is here about 50 feet broad. The fortifi-cations of Valenciennes appear to be very strong, and the outworks are protected by broad channels of water, — which may be encreased at pleasure. The *Place* as it is called, is very handsomely built of stone. One side regular, the other consists of extensive Publick buildings. There are, for the size of the Town many Churches, but that which we understood to be the principal one, is battered to ruins during the late bombardment. The East part of the Town suffered most during the late Siege. The west end recd. very little injury. — Of the size of the Town I could not judge precisely but from the time it took me to walk from the Gate Cambray, to the Gate of Mons, I think it is abt. [blank] long. — There are 5 Gates to this Town. The Gates of Tournay, of Mons, of Cardon, of Cambray, and of Notre Dame. Three of these only are open at present, and they are guarded very carefully.

The inferior Houses are chiefly of Brick, but the better sort mostly of Stone. — All the Capital buildings have slate Roofs, the others tiled.

The Manufactures of Valenciennes were chiefly Lace, Cambrick and fine Linnen such as Ladies Caps are made of.

We got to the Town abt. 7 oClock, and were much mortified to find we must be contented with very inconvenient accomodation at an inferior Inn. We tried for a better but could find none that was not in a ruined state where we must have slept in rooms that were half broken by Cannon Shot. — At 8 oClock we called at the Lodgings of Baron de Lilien, Commandant of the Town to shew Him our Passport and obtain his permission to make drawings of the place. The Baron was not at home and a servant told us the most certain time to find him would be in the morning towards 12 oClock.

Sunday August 18th.

This morning we walked among the Ruins of the Town, which we found much more extensive than we expected, whole streets crushed as it were to pieces, unlike anything we had ever seen. At 12 we called at the Commandant, and were received by him very civilly. Unfortunately Captn. Hewgill had in making out the Passport made use of the word *Plans,* which struck the Commandant so forcibly that He said He could not possibly grant a permission to us witht. an Order from the Prince of Saxe Cobourgh, and He reccomended to us to go to the Head quarters of the Prince, at Hevin abt. a League distant. — When we came there we found a Young Officer who appeared to be an Aid du Camp, at the Door of the House, a farm House with little more than bare walls, and explained to Him our situation & wishes. He said He would speak to the Prince when He came from dinner, which He did soon after with a General Officer. This was abt. 3 in the Afternoon. The Prince in a few Minutes sent the Officer to us, who carried us to another farm House, where in a long room something better than a Barn, was a long table at which several Officers &c were writing and tracing Plans. — I suppose there were about 17 Persons employed. One of them was directed to make out an Order to be delivered by us to General Lilien, which being carried to the Prince, and signed by him, was sealed up and given to us.

The Prince of Saxe Cobourgh is in height above the middle size or rather a tall man, of a military appearance, yet courteous in his carriage. Manly and roundish features, with a full eye, rather staring. He was dressed in White turned up with red, and a Broad gold Lace on his red waistcoat. — He had Boots on as usual with the Officers.

August 19th.

The morning by appointment we waited on the Commandant Baron de Lilien who favored us with a passport for Valenciennes. The Baron recd. us in his Bedchamber, which was a large lofty room with a Bed in it of Crimson damask. The room covered with flock paper but the furniture so ordinary that a Man accustomed to the goodness & neatness of English furniture must be surprised at such an inequality. The Baron told us the French Convention was going on worse than ever, and that they were worse than Bears & Tiggers, and that mankind was disgraced by them. He told us that a Coll. of the Belgick Legion was taken 2 days ago and was shot this morning at this place. — He also mentioned that the Gulloitine would be burnt in the *Place* this morning at 11 oClock.

Translation from the *German* of the Baron de Lilien's permit.

"The Bearers of this have from me permission to go about within and without the Walls of Valenciennes, also within the works of the Fortifications; and to stop there to take drawings of the Ruins of the Town,

Buildings & Destructions occasioned by the Seige, in small or large: whole, or in parts: and while they are so doing nobody shall hinder them, and they shall pass everywhere: yet this permission only extends to such drawings, but Military Plans, of whatever description, are strictly forbid."

Lilien
Comdt.

Valenciennes, Augst. 19th., 1793 —

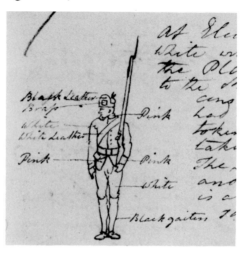

At Eleven the Regt. of Kins[k]y dresst in White with Pink facing was drawn up in the Place, and extended from one end to the other in 3 lines. This regiment consists of [blank] Men. — Each Soldier had a sprig of leaves in his Cap, a token of victory which they wear after taking a Town or gaining a Battle. The Officers of this regt. wear Hats and Coats. — Note, The Sprig of Leaves is also worn by the English on the same occasion.

The Major Commandant of the Town dressed in light Blue Grey, on Horseback commanded the line. I never saw exercise performed like it, it was with an exactness like a well made machine. After the Troops had paraded and a considerable part drawn of to relieve the guards a circle was formed by a few of the remaining troops and mob. The Gulliotine was taken out of a Waggon in which it was laid in pieces, and being placed on some Faggots, the Executioner of the Army set the Whole in a blaze, and this favorite instrument of Democracy was soon consumed. The Regimental Band played Ca Ira.

There were many Officers on the parade this morning, and some of them when they met saluted each other on the Cheek, a custom in this Country as unnoticed as shaking Hands.

After we quitted the Place, we went to the Place Verd, where I begun a drawing of Le Damen de Beaumont, and some of the buildings near it, as specimens of the destructive effects of a bombardment. — We dined at one oClock, and in the Afternoon went in the Calash which I had brought from Tournay, up to Ansin, where I discharged the Calash, and began a drawing of the view of Valenciennes from the Great Battery on Mount Ansin. This situation was posessed by the Austrians during the Seige. — The weather was very fine. — Wrote to Oken.

Tuesday Augst. 20th.

Rose at 6. After Breakfast walked up to the Battery near the bottom of the Avenue, a situation posessed by the English. From this station I began a drawing of the View of Valenciennes, which is directly opposite to that which the Battery on Mount Ansin commands. — Returned to Dinner at one oClock. — In the afternoon I began a drawing in the Place Verd, of the Ruins of St. Nicolas Steeple, &c.: — fine weather. — wrote to Mr. Boydell.

Wednesday 21st.

Rose at 6. After Breakfast began a drawing of the Ruins of the Clarisse's or Urbanisse's, a Convent. At this time many of the poor poeple applied to us for Charity, among them 2 woemen who had lost their Husbands during the Seige. One of them said she had nine Children. In return for something given they willingly sat to me for figures, to put in my drawings. — I afterwards began a drawing of the [blank] one of the most ruined parts of the Town. — Dined at 2 oClock. — In the afternoon went up to Mount Ansin and finished the drawing I had begun from the Battery. — very fine weather.

Thursday 22d.

Rose at 6. — After Breakfast went up to the Battery near the end of the Avenue, and finished the drawing I had begun from thence. — Dined at 2 oClock. — In the afternoon walked to the Abbey of Fontenelle, to see the Communication bridge, made for the use of the Combined Army during the seige, after the flat country near the Scheldt, above the Town was inundated. — weather very fine.

Friday 23d.

Rose at ½ past 5, and before breakfast began a drawing of the view from the road to Briquet, of the Town of Valenciennes and the ground on which the troops of the combined Army were drawn up when Monsr. Ferrand came out with his Garrison. — After breakfast went to a situation near a gravel pit, which commands a view of the Horn works, and that part of the Town which was most battered. Of this view I made a drawing. — Dined at 3 oClock, and in the Evening walked to the Village of St. Sauve below the

Town. Here is an Abbey, from which the Priests were expelled by the French, but since the conquest they are again put in posession, & we met 3 of them who had been superintending some workmen employed in repairing. We found part of a Communication Bridge at this place, and were informed there was one lower down the River but both are in enclosed places & there are no views of distant objects from them. — weather very fine.

Saturday 24th.

Rose at 6. After breakfast went to Briquet and finished the drawing I had begun. — The place where I sat was directly in front of the Camp, yet I was not incommoded by the Men, and very few Officers came near me and they who did were very civil. One of them, Captn. Reichlin, conversed with Stadler and gave us a great deal of information abt. the seige, and situations of the different Corps. — He spoke very favorably of the English troops, and of the good fellowship which subsisted between them & the German troops: but He mentioned laughing their propensity to stealing. This Officer had been constantly in service 7 years & a half and was at the Seige of Belgrade. The Destruction in that Town was much greater than at Valenciennes. The regiment which was encamped here & to which He belongs is Anton Esterhazy; it consists of 24 Companies of 197 Men each. The Uniform is White turned up with Red, long Huzzar breeches of Bluish Grey Cloth, and half Boots laced. The men do not wear Coats but a kind of close jacket. The Officers wear Coats. — The men have leather Caps, with a piece of Brass in the front, the Officers large Hats.

In the afternoon I began a drawing of the Horn work, from the Trenches, which the English had thrown up.

The weather very fine.

Sunday Augst. 25th.

Rose at 6. after breakfast walked to the Communication Bridge at the village of Trit abt. 3 miles above the Town. Before the seige the Sluices which are near this part were opened and the country up to the Bridge, inundated. The Communication Bridge is directly opposite to the Height of Famar[s] where the French had erected the Tree of Liberty, and buried the Body of Genl. Dampierre. — The Bridge is 300 Toises and 4 feet long. (1804 English feet), and abt. 20 feet wide. — This Bridge was constructed by first driving rough piles into the Water, within these fascines were laid, then a layer of earth, then fascines, then earth, and the top made a level surface with sand & gravel. — A number of men were now employed in taking it to pieces and carrying away the Planks which were also used to make the surface level. — Near this Bridge the Abbey of Fontenelle stands. It is a very extensive Building and appears to have been at least well endowed. It was a residence for Nuns, who were expelled by the French near 2 years ago, and the building is now going to ruin. — We had at several times conversations with Farmers and Country Poeple relative to French affairs, in order to collect what we could of the opinions prevailing among that description. Certainly what came to our knowledge proved that they were only interested in the question of the revolution as sufferers by the inconveniences and they consider the Poeple in Towns as the great disturbers of the Publick Peace, & as having made the mischief. A decent young Man who belongs to a village abt. 4 miles from Valenciennes, told us today, that when the General Order was issued by the Convention for raising men out of 42 men in the number fit for service 25 were orderd for service. They *all* went away to St. Amand, a few miles from their village & at that time in the Hands of the Austrians, and avoided the Summons. — He said the Convention were Rogues & Villains, and indeed this is a common way of speaking of them by the Poeple.

We were concerned to hear at the village of Trit, a Country Man in speaking of the different Troops, describe the English Soldiers, as great theives, and that the Orders of the Duke of York, and the activity of the Officers were not sufficient to prevent them. This corroborated what Captn. Reichlin had before mentioned. — We returned to Valenciennes to dinner at 4 oClock. The Day very hot. — In the eving. we walked up to the Camp at Briquet, and not considering our situation, and that the Gates are shut at 8 oClock, we came back too late to be admitted. In this disagreeable predicament we applied ourselves to some persons collected together in a Suttling tent near the Gate and Stadler speaking German soon made them our friends. They told us we had no chance of getting into the Town, unless an Officer happened to have staid beyond his time in the Town, or of a Courier arriving. In this situation we remained till 10 oClock when the loud cracking of a Whip announced a Courier, who hailed the Centinel and said He came from Prince Cobourgh. — One of the Germans with us in the tent, was Musick Master to the Band of the Regt. of Anton Esterhazy, and another Person belonged to the Regt. a party from which was doing duty at the Gate. They undertook to apply to the Lieutenant commanding to request that we might be admitted with the Courier. — It was more than half an Hour before the Officer appeared. He was attended by abt. 8 or 10 Men: On the application being made for us He bid us go on, which we did & found 2 parties more of soldiers at the other Gates, (we had 3 to pass through,) all drawn up in regular array. This proves the Caution which is used to prevent a surprise or improper admission. We reached our Inn at Eleven oClock, heartily Glad to exchange a lodging in a Sutling tent for an indifferent Bed, in a Dirty Inn.

Monday Augst. 26th.

Rose at 7. After Breakfast, went to the trenches opposite the Horn work, and finished my Sketch. — From thence to the Rue de Mons, and proceeded with my drawing of that street. The Dust intollerable, owing to the passing and repassing of Baggage Waggons & Soldiers. My Coat & Hat were as dusty as a Millers before I quitted the place at half past one to go to dinner. In the afternoon I proceeded with my view of the Clarisses's. The day very fine.

Tuesday — Augst. 27th.

Rose at 7. This forenoon employed on my view of the Rue de Mons. Dined at one oClock. Captn. Reichlin, of the Regt. of Anton Esterhazy dined with us & proved a very useful & amusing Companion. — He brought us one piece of information that much concerned us as well as him, of an engagement between the Army under the Duke of York, which went down to Dunkirk, & the French; in which several English Colonels, and the Austrian Field-Marshal Dalton were killed, etc., and that it was an attempt made by that Army to force the French Camp at M[Cassel]. — Further that the Duke of York had sent to Prince Cobourgh for 15000 Men, which He supposed could hardly be spared.

The Captain stated to us exactly the situations of the different Corps of the Combined Army while before Valenciennes.

Situation of the Troops at Valenciennes. —

On the height near Famar, the Hanoverian Cavalry, Infantry and Grenadiers.

Further on the English Cavalry.

Behind them the Camp of the Artillery of reserve.

On the East side of the Ronnelle, a small stream, near Grande Ounlay, Hanoverians.

English Infantry with Grenadiers, then Cavalry and Artillery of reserve. then Grenadiers again upon the road from Valenciennes to Quesnoy. — On the other side of that road, towards St. Sauve, Austrians, English & Hanoverians, mixed; as far as the Scheldt. — On the other side of the Scheldt, by Beuvrage, the Belgian regiments. — Between Rheims, & Anzin, Hanoverians & Austrians.

Near Aubrie, and as far as Trite, all Hanoverians, Infantry & Cavalry. — From Herin, where the Prince of Cobourgh, had his Head Quarters, to Rungries, stood the Armies of reserve, with the Vanguard, by Denain. — Another Corps, of Hessians, Hanoverians, English, and Austrians, laid before Guereain.

Captn. Reichlin said He could make but a rough calculation of the number of Men lost by the Combined Army during the Siege, but He believed they might be averaged at abt. 3000. — He seemed to think this moderate, when the strength and importance of the place was considered. The Siege lasted 44 days. The greatest amity subsisted between the different Corps of the Army, the English & Germans & Hungarians, being constantly Cordial. — He was of opinion that had the Town been stormed a dreadful scene of bloodshed would have been exhibited, the troops having been much exasperated against the Citizens, as well as the Soldiers, owing to many indiscreet insults offered before the bombardment began.

The Captn. was at the siege of Belgrade which was a very bloody affair. It lasted 26 days, and He believes the Austrians lost about 8000 Men. — One part of the Town was stormed, when every person was put to the Sword; and He supposes more than 2000, Citizens, perished. Yet the more populous Town which was immediately under the Garrison was not entered. — When the Garrison Capitulated, and the Officers proceeded to enter it they found it impossible. Heaps of dead bodies, of Men, Horses, Cows, Sheep, Goats, were piled together & obstructed the passage. The stench was also intollerable. Poeple were employed to clear the way which they did by throwing the bodies over the walls into the Danube. It was 8 days before this was effected, and then the stench continued so as to be scarcely supportable. — From what He could learn near 20000 Turks perished during the Seige. — He spoke highly of the Honor & confidence of those Poeple. As soon as a Capitulation had been agreed upon, but before it was signed, many came out of the Town & brought with them Tobacco, Coffee, and other articles, which might be supposed the Austrians wished for. In return they recd. Sheep & rice &c.

During this siege 200 pieces of Cannon played incessantly for 4 days on the Town, and the very ground on which that part of the Austrian Army was placed, shook under them.

After we had drank Coffee, at 4 oClock, we walked to the Citadel, and had the advantage of Captn. Reichlins explanation of many circumstances of military fortification. — The Citadel of Valenciennes, is esteemed very strong. Works within Works, & a great command of water with which they can separate the different divisions of them. They have also Sluices within the works of the Citadel which enable them to overflow the Country to the South of the Town, and the power to do so was fully shewn at the late seige. From the Gate of Notre Dame, which is the South West gate, the suburbs were inundated to the depth of 6 feet above the publick road leading to Paris.

In forming the Communication bridge at Trite, several thousands of the Peasants of the Country were employed. This must be considered a service of necessity as the Peasants were not allowed to refuse their assistance. They were each paid ½ an Austrian florin, abt. 12 or 13 pence English, a day.

At 6 o'Clock the Captain went to his regiment, and I proceeded for an Hour with my drawings on the Place Verd. — One of the Magistrates whose House had suffered greatly stood sometime with me. — It is the custom here for the Magistrates of the Town to wear Black Cloaths when they are dressed. Two genteel Young Men were with me a considerable time, and when I had finished drawing, desired me to walk into their ruined House, which indeed they had a right to call so. They told me they had not any notion when the siege began of the consequences, and everything in the House was standing. Such a Wreck of a building as it was left can hardly be conceived. In a small garden behind the House 3 Bombs had fallen within 6 yards of each other, and there was not a room in the House, which had not been pierced by Cannon Shot or in which a Bomb had not lodged. I asked them if workmen were of opinion that the Walls could be restored or whether they must be entirely taken down. They said that the Walls would bear repairing, and they supposed from such calculations as they were able to make it would cost them £1000 to make their dwelling comfortable. When this Case is considered what must be the amount of private losses in this unfortunate Town.

But the sufferings in this respect extend only to property; it is of more moment to mention the diseases which prevail here and at this [time] carry of numbers. One cannot remain in any street long, witht. seeing a Funeral pass. It appears from the manner in which they are generally attended, as if the poorer sort of poeple were most affected. Several causes have contributed to produce the diseases which are so fatal. Long confinement in Cellars &c under ground, where numbers were crowded together and fed upon a scanty allowance, and the Air of the place may reasonably be supposed to be affected when it is considered what a vast body of stagnant water with which the Country was inundated, must have corrupted, and caused infection. — Both the Inhabitants & Soldiers warned us of the Danger of residing in Valenciennes, as few came who did not suffer more or less from it. The Dysentery was the most common complaint; and our little party felt a portion of the disorder.

The weather today very fine.

Wednesday Augst. 28th.

Rose at 7. In the forenoon I was employed in making a view of the *Place*. It is not a square, but oblong, in form, and makes a very handsome appearance: One side regular and built of Stone: on the opposite side is the Hotel de Ville, (The Town House,) which has an extensive front. Here is a Market every day, for fruit, & garden stuff, and Sutlers who sell Beer, Cheese &c. — Beef is now sold from 3d.½ to 4d. a pound, Mutton and Veal the same. Butter abt. 7d.

It must always strike an Englishman who is travelling in this part of the Continent, and I believe generally, the extreme want of neatness in the Houses, the badness of the finishing, and the wretchedness of the Furniture. — This day I was in a House which promised from the external appearance something above the common accomodation. In the inside it was little better than what would be found in the appearance of a goal. —

Certainly the French do not yet make furniture and cleanliness objects of serious attention.

In the evening Stadler called on Captn. Reichlin at the Camp, hoping to have gained more information of the late affair before Dunkirk, but though the report was confident that after great Slaughter, the French Camp was carried, yet no particulars have been mentioned to the Officers of this Camp. Officially they heard today of the defeat of the French by General Wurmser somewhere near Landau, and that the French had 4000 Men killed & wounded. — The French also lost abt. 400 Men near Lisle on Sunday last in an engagement with 4 Battalions. Fine weather.

Thursday Augst. 29th.

Rose at 7. — A Rainy morning, but cleared up abt. 10 oClock, when I went to the Heights above Trite, to a station where the Hanoverians had thrown up a strong Battery, abt. 2 miles from Valenciennes. — From this point, I made a View of Valenciennes, & the Vale which was inundated during the seige. — The firing at Quesnoy was constant the whole time while I was drawing, and we were informed this morning that the Trenches are extending fast and that it is expected the Besiegers will open their Batteries in 5 or 6 days. — The firing heard to day was from the Garrison to obstruct the Besiegers. — We dined at ½ past 2, and in the afternoon I went to the Verd Place and proceeded with my drawing of the Government House &c.

At the Gate of Cambray, as we returned to our Inn, we met 2 French Deserters, a Dragoon, and an Hussar, who had got away after the engagement off Lisle. I was an eye witness of the appearance which these troops may be fairly supposed to make, and glad of an opportunity of judging for myself. The Dragoon in particular was a tall well looking Young Man, and they were both as well accoutred as a military man could desire.

When a man deserts from the French, He is carried before the Commandant of this place, if He deserts in this neighberoud, who gives him the option as serving as a Soldier or of having his liberty, and doing the best He can for himself. If He chooses to serve He is not permitted to enter into any of the Corps of regular troops of the empire, but must go into what is called a free Corps, such as the Prince of Condes &c.

We were informed this evening by a respectable Young Man that Valenciennes was reckoned to contain abt. 22000 inhabitants. — That number must now be considerably reduced. Many have emigrated; many died during the Seige & since; so that a considerable deduction must be allowed from the above calculation.

The declaration of the Emperor stopping the circulation of Assignats is a heavy blow upon the Inhabitants, and undoubtedly causes many to quit the place; as in France, that paper is current, whereas here it only can be traded in as merchandise. Nobody will accept what cannot be offered in payment. — Yet even here there are speculations on them, which is permitted, and they at present sell at about 20 for one. — Many sales we see every day of the goods of Persons who propose quitting the place, & at these Assignats are paid, as it is understood the sellers are preparing to go into France.

As we propose leaving Valenciennes on Saturday we made enquiry through the whole town for a Calash or Conveyance of some kind to Conde: but found it was not to be had. Many Carriages they told us were broke during the bombardment, and what remained were so engaged it was vain to expect to get one. While in this predicament we learnt that a Diligence would be in town from Conde on Saturday in which if we took places we might return. To be certain which I could not otherways be, I took places & payed the fare *from* & to Conde, 6s.6d. for 3 which set us at rest abt. a conveyance.

Friday August 30th.

Rose at ½ past 6. A fine morning. employed myself in finishing my sketches.

At the commencement of the siege of Valenciennes, the Poor Poeple had a daily allowance each of 5 Sous (2d.½) in Assignats, children were allowed equally with grown up poeple. — There was no fresh meat during the last 3 weeks. — Salt Beef sold for 10d. a pound, — The Cows which were brought into the Town by the milk woemen had been slaughtered, before the 3 last weeks, & milk & Butter were not to be had for any sum. — Before that milk had been sold for 15d. a quart, and the Butter had been sold for 6s. a pound. — Wine & Bread there was a sufficient quantity of to the last, but it gradually became dearer.

It was the interest of the Garrison to keep the lower order of the Poeple in good humour, through fear of their rising upon them, therefore the Assignats were taken witht. any discount, for the salted provission, & Bread.

This afternoon I made a Sketch of a near View of St. Nicholas Church, — which is now in ruins.

The firing at Quesnoy has been very warmly kept up during this day. Thirty men were killed yesterday by the firing from the garrison.

An elderly Austrian Officer talked with us this afternoon of the late action near Dunkirk. He said the English had been too hot, as the Austrians were a few years ago, but that would wear of.

This evening we walked up to the Station where the English Camp was formed beyond Briquet.

A Man came into the Town this afternoon, from Cambray, who says, 15000 Men are expected from Paris today, as a recruit for the garrison, and that the Austrians are within 3 leagues of the place.

The Officer we had conversation with said, if *this* Army could get

Quesnoy, Cambray, and Maubeuge, this season, no further object would be attempted, — Lisle, is so strong as to be alone a work to be taken up at an early period of a Season.

There is a simplicity and civility among the Country Poeple of France, which from the common opinions formed of the Nation, one would hardly expect. Among other customs they have that of pulling of their Hats when they meet persons whom they suppose of a higher degree, and there is no appearance of coxcomry or conceit in their manners.

The Farmers were this day getting in their Crops of Wheat, which grew up to the very lines of the English Camp, which shews how little devastation had been committed beyond what was absolutely necessary.

We cannot yet obtain any information *what* officers & number of Men fell in the late engagement of Dunkirk.

From Valenciennes, to Mons, is 7 leagues

To Tournay	— 7	—
To Lisle	— 12	—
To Cambray	— 7	—
To Mabeuge	— 7	—
To Quesnoy	— 3	—
To Paris	— 43	—

One couple was married during the Seige; but they were violent Patriots: and were determined to be married by the *Constitutional* Preists, who they were convinced would be removed if the Town surrendered.

Saturday August 31st.

Rose at 6. A fine Morning. — walked to the British Camp, and from thence to the high ground at the back of the Austrian Camp stationed before Quesnoy. We had a very commanding view of Quesnoy, and of the Camps which are stationed on different grounds so as to surround the Town. The lines of the trenches appeared to be advanced very near to it. — The firing from the Town was very quick. The flame from the Mouths of the Cannon & Mortars was much more conspicuous than I should have expected it would have appeared by daylight.

The situation of Quesnoy seems to be on rising ground, and the approaches must be made with caution. — The Town has only 3 principal Steeples or Towers, with 3 or 4 smaller ones. From the station from which we viewed it, it does not seem more than half the size of Valenciennes.

It will do credit to the regulations, and exact discipline of the Army now before Quesnoy, when it is mentioned, that on the ground on which we stood to view the situation & operations of the besieging army, 3 labouring Men were employed in cutting Corn, and the Farmer was overlooking them: such was the state of security of the Inhabitants. The contrast is scarcely to be imagined. Looking one way an Harvest was reaping; and the opposite view presented a vast extended Camp, and a Town besieged, with incessant firing. — It will never be conceived by those who have not been witnesses of it, how far habit reconciles Men to situations in which danger is not a consideration. The Military life becomes a business, and the work of it a duty of course. The daily loss of comrades, and companions, does not appear to be received with more than indifference, which is not to be wondered at, when the Men who hear of it, present themselves, when called upon, to the same hazards with apathy.

    The English Camp before Valenciennes was in a very pleasant situation, an open country, high, and very dry, and commanding almost the whole of the vicinity of the Town. I made a drawing from this station.

    At three oClock in the afternoon Mr. Stadler accompanied me to the Commandants, Baron de Lilien, who we found in company with three other Officers, who had dined with him. My object was to return thanks for his civilities, & to shew him a few outlines, which I did partly from propriety and to convince him of the nature of my undertaking. — He received us in a very polite manner, as did the Officers. — They had sat in a large room, at a small square, deal table just large enough for one on each side. They had dined & drank Coffee & the Table was cleared; which shews that Temperance is observed here.

    The Baron mentioned to us the death of Field Marshal Dalton, but had not heard the names of any English Officers who had fallen.

At 4 oClock, we left Valenciennes in the dilligence for Conde. It was made to contain 10 persons & was full. On our way the conversation of the French passengers was on the subject of the present affairs, and they all seemed to detest the proceedings adopted in France. They agreed that the Commissioners appointed by the Convention to attend Armies, & reside in Towns, are particularly to be hated. — They expect a serious business for the *inhabitants, Citizens* of Quesnoy, as their number is too few, and the garrison too strong, to be controuled, whatever the distress may be.

They spoke also of the present unhealthy state of Valenciennes. It is computed 40 die every day. Out of prudence they have desisted from tolling a Bell, as a notice of a Death, that the Inhabitants may not be alarmed by the numbers.

They seemed much diverted at the ill luck of a Merchant of Valenciennes, who has quitted it and carried into France abt. 4000 Livres in Assignats where He expected they would circulate to his advantage. He was scarcely within the lines of France when He was seized upon under the present Order for raising recruits and carried away as a soldier.

The day had been showery and in the evening a heavy rain came on. The situation of Conde as we approach is flat and appears almost surrounded by water.

We got to Conde at ¼ past 6, after having stopt at 2 or 3 dirty Inns on the road: Our Driver was on a footing with an English stage in that respect. — In the Inns men were drinking a Beer, the most miserable Liquor I have met with: small & has a smoky taste but use reconciles for the German Officers seem to relish it as much as the natives.

The Inn at Conde where we stopped was the Post House, and we were accomodated in it with two Beds in a room so narrow that there was just passage enough and nothing to spare. The furniture &c no better than that at Valenciennes.

At the Inn a Table D'Hote was kept for such as chose to come but at present might properly enough be called an Officers Mess, as excepting Mr. Stadler & myself, the rest to the number of 16, were German Officers belonging to Corps in the Town. Among them was an Irishman, who was the most noisy & forward of any present. He left the room in a passion at last because a Young Officer had joked him abt. a Horse. — The Officers in General were very civil. One of them was just come in from Quesnoy. He said that an Austrian Cannoneur had the day before counted the Shot from the Garrison, and that it amounted to 2800, yet only 30 Men were killed.

The expence of this Table D'Hote, was, 14d, for Supper and 1s.9d. for dinner.

SEPTEMBER 1793

Sunday, Septr. 1st.

Rose at 7. — This morning walked through the Town [Valenciennes] which does not appear to be half so large as Conde, but is capable of making a long defence as was shewn in the late blockade. By means of Sluices it can be nearly surrounded by Water to an extent which defys all attack. — There are two Churches, one called Notre Dame & the Parish Church. They are neither of them in the least remarkable for elegance, or any other requisite of Architecture, or finishing. Notre Dame is plain and dirty in the inside. — In it we found a Priest in a Pulpit in the Middle Aisle, exhorting a great number of Poeple, which he did extempore and with much action.

The only views I could find to give a good idea of the situation of Conde, were from the right hand of the road to Brussells, and from the village of Fraine, where I took my station at the foot of a Windmill, in which the miller was very busy grinding & I found by means of Stadler was a violent Democrat. I also perceived that he was a very illnatured fellow, however I mounted his ladder, and looked into his Mill, and was surprised to see a wooden figure of a Crucifix gilt placed against the principal beam.

In the evening it rained, and confined us to the Inn, where we fortunately met with intelligent Poeple who gave us many particulars of the condition of the Garrison & inhabitants during the Blockade.

Conde, was blockaded 3 months and a half and as is understood there upon the representation of Dumourier, who had informed the Austrian General, that it contained no supply of provision. — The fact was, that upon a calculation it contained only *sufficient* food for 17 days, for the Garrison & inhabitants, supposing each person to have a common allowance. From hence it may be concluded what a state of necessity the poeple must have been reduced to when the time is considered that they held out. About 7 weeks before the surrender, the provisions of all kinds were taken from each House and lodged in Magazines, from which *each person* received a daily allowance, which was, an Ounce of Rice, 2 ounces of Horse flesh, and eleven ounces of Bread, for Twenty four hours.

A Mulct of 250 Crowns was decreed against any Person who was

convicted of having kept back provision from the publick contribution.
A list of all the Horses was taken both of the Military & the inhabitants, and it was decided by the Municipality which should be killed first.
Seven Horses a day were allowed for the Garrison, and four for the inhabitants. They eat Horse flesh Seven weeks.
At first, they felt a repugnance to eating Horse flesh, but soon were reconciled to it. The Mistress of our Inn at that time kept a Table D'Hote for the French, as she now does for the German Officers. — She told us she laid the Flesh in Vinegar about 3 days, and boiled it in wine, and larded it with Bacon, and it had much the taste she thought of Deer flesh. Thus the Officers fared luxuriously.
When the Wine in the Town was collected together it proved to be so much that a quantity was left when the Town surrendered.
But solid food was very expensive, and Articles of which regulations took no notice, were purchased at a dear rate. A Cat cost 5 shillings, a Water Rat, half a Crown.
Those who were strong and unemployed bore this strange, and scanty mode of living better than could have been expected. Many of the Soldiers, who were obliged to do regular duty died suddenly on their Posts. Old Poeple & Children also died. A Putrid fever also carried of many.
On that side which looks to the village of Old Conde the Country rises a little and cannot be inundated: but within the fortifications it is admitted even there.
The Garrison fired upon the Austrians to obstruct their Works: but the Austrians never returned it, so the Town did not suffer the least.
A French Officer of the Regt. of Royal Allmande, came today from the Camp near Bouchain. That Regt. was true to the King & deserted from the French. Prince Lambisc, has the command of it. There seems to be a stop put in this quarter to the cruel resolution of the French Convention that every French Man taken prisoner should be put to death. Several prisoners have been taken *from* the French who are kept as Hostages, and lately a Soldier of the Regt. of Allmande was taken by the French, on which the Commander of that Regt. wrote to the French Commander informing him that if that Man was put to death every Prisoner *He had* shd. meet the same fate. He recd. for answer that the Man would not be hurt and was taking care of in the Hospital.
With the Officer came a tall Soldier with remarkably long Beard and Whiskers. He told Mr. Stadler that when He quitted France He vowed never to cut his Beard till He entered it again as a Citizen, and had kept his word faithfully.
In the evening I had some conversation with the Irish officer who I was told spoke French & German fluently, but English imperfectly so far that He did not seem to understand words that were not quite common or what may be called ordinary language. — He mentioned the critical situation of

the Besiegers at Valenciennes, on the night when they sprung their mines near the Horn-work. Had this been delayed half an Hour the French would have sprung them, having so settled their time for doing it. The consequence would have [been] dreadful to the Besiegers, as the Mines of the French extended far under where the English & Austrians were stationed and 20000 weight of powder was lodged in them. The destruction of Men must have been very great, besides the works of the approaches being mined, which would probably have caused, the Siege to be raised.

As we proposed to leave Conde early in the Morning I paid my Bill this evening, and found myself charged about double the regulated price for the Table D'Hote and the same disposition to impose in everything. However I thought it best to submit as the difference did not amount to more than 7 or 8 shillings, and My Companion not at all qualified to contend with them.

Monday Septr. 2d.

Rose at ½ past 5, but was not able to get away till 7. A fresh Scheme of imposition was prepared as the first had been successful. When the things were put into the Chaise I saw there were only 2 Horses instead of 3 which I was to pay for. The Scheme at the bottom was for our Hostess to send us of with a pair of Horses by which she would have passed us as a hired carriage but not as posting, by which she would have cheated the Post as neatly as me. But this was too gross to pass, she had said to Stadler when he remarked there were only 2 Horses, that they were the best, so we had an advantage. I found it was necessary to make an exertion and I did it in *plain English*, saying and acting as I should have done to an English Innskeeper, if He had attempted to impose on me. — It had the desired effect, and I soon saw she was disposed to do what was proper. A third Horse was soon brought, and of we went for Mons.

I think it here necessary to observe that Her Husband took no part in the business, and I did not know she had one till He was pointed out to me, assisting to tie on the Portmanteau. I saw in this Country other instances where the Husband appeared quite a Cypher in what related to Guests.

I should have mentioned before that the Duke De Croiy has a Castle in Conde and that He is proprietor of the Forest & Park of Bonsecoux near it. Happily for him that the War went in this direction as He is already restored to his posessions.

From Conde we went by a road which runs along side a Canal, which forms altogether a high bank raised above the inundation in its present state, but during the seige the water rose to its level. — The first object we saw to call the attention was abt. 3 or 4 miles from Conde, the Abbey of Crepi. Nothing indeed is remarkable abt. it, but it is the only feature, in a very flat country. At Quievran, we came into the Great Road from Valenciennes, to Conde. This Village is situated just within the Barrier which determines the line of the Austrian & French dominions. — We were very civilly questioned as to our having any Merchandise &c but our word was taken witht. examination. — The Country here begins to rise a little. We passed through another long & dirty village called Watteau; and a little beyond it, the Abbey of St. Gilian to the left of the road. — The road in nearly right lines & paved. Many Waggons with Coals were on the road, most of them high & the Coals contained in Basket work within the frame of the Waggon. — We saw at least 4 *small* Carts also laden with Coals, each drawn by Dogs: Two in the Shafts and 5 or 6 in a line before.

The Road as we approached Mons was Arched over with tall trees which has a good [blank]. Flat Meadows on the left, and peeps of the Town.

Mons, is situated on ground which rises considerably in one part, and on the highest point was the Castle. From hence is a view over part of the Town. The *Place*, is pretty large, the Town House in it a Building of strange Architecture. The Town is large, it appears to be equal in size to Tournay. — On entering it we were again examined as to our luggage, but very civilly, and they took our word for our not having Articles of merchandize. — neither here nor at Quievran, was the least hint given of their expecting a douceur, for their moderation. Mons, is no longer considered as a Garrison of defence. It was dismantled by the late Emperor Joseph. What is now called the Chateau, is a high Steeple tower terminated with forms as singular as those which represent the buildings in the East Indies. — On the ramparts is a pleasant walk which looks over a fruitful country, in which are abundance of villages.

Our Postillion drove us to an Inn within a few doors of the Post House where when our things were taken out we found our accomodation as bad as it could have been in a Waggoners Beer House, and a Surly Inn keeper into the bargain. It is necessary to put those who travel on their guard, especially if they have Ladies with them, that they may always direct the Postillion to drive to the principal Auberge in the place to which they are going, & from thence a conveyance may be ordered from the Post House. For it is not in this Country as in England, where accomodation of lodging and travelling go together. — The prayers of the Morning being nearly over we had not time to go into but one Church St. Nicholas, and if one may judge of the piety of the inhabitants from what appeared there it must be great, in every recess was an Altar throughout the Church. The Priest was saying Mass & the Boy behind him who rang the Bell was accompanied by two others, with whom He was laughing & playing tricks the whole time I staid, which was the only instance of want of decorum I ever saw in a Church of this country.

A little after 2oClock we left Mons, and the first Stage was to Castinu — 1 Post — at 15, Skellings a Post, which is the rate at which they charge, Postillion, & Barriers, included. A Skelling, is 7d. english.

		English
From Mons, to Castinu,	1 Poste	8s. 9
Castinu, to Bruine le Compte,	1½ Postes	13. 2
Bruine le Compte – to Attalle,	2 postes	17. 6
Attalle, to Brussells,	1½ Postes	13. 2
A Poste is 6 miles	6 Postes	£2. 12. 7

The road from Mons, to Brussells passes through a rich highly cultivated Country. — extensive woods run in long lines and make up a back ground. It is not a picturesque Country but appears to be very fruitful.

The rate at which we travelled was, changing Horses included, abt. 5 miles and a half an Hour, or rather more. The roads paved, and in their carriages a passenger is pretty well shaken.

The Count of Limbec has a Chateau, near the road between Bruine le Compte and Attalle. It seems large, but is heavy and Old fashioned. If the Woods and Country behind it belong to Him He may boast of his possessions.

Before we reached Attalle we stopt to be Spectators of a Dance by the Road side near an Inn, where some Young Country Poeple were collected to make merry on some occasion. Two of the Young Woemen were pretty and they all were neat and looked modest & danced in a better manner than I should have expected — Here I cannot but observe how much more becoming the appearance of the Woemen is than that of the Men. I mean as to Dress. The Woemens dress is tight & neat, but that of the Men does not at all correspond with it. Their great Hats, and full made Coats, with long skirts, Pocket flaps & number of buttons, makes them appear slouching, loose and heavy.

[*See drawing on facing page.*]

I counted the Waggons which we met between Mons & Brussels going to the Army with supplies. The number was 101.

At nine at night we reached Brussells and found the Gate shut. But there was little difficulty of getting admittance. The Postillion called and a couple of Men, not Soldiers, came out and made a sort of bustle, & took our Names & under pretence of having a permit to go for, demanded a reccompence. I gave them 3 skillings — 1s.9d. and in we went.

The streets of the Town appeared narrow by night, and were lighted with large lamps with reflecting mirrors that threw a strong light. but these are too few.

At Supper time a Waiter came in with a Book in which he desired us to put down our names, that being required by the Governor; a daily return being made of the strangers in Town.

Tuesday Septr. 3d.

Rose at 7. Engaged a man on the reccommendation of the Waiter who makes it a business to attend Strangers abt. this place and Country. His name Armstrong, the Son of a Scotch Man, but born in Brussells. He speaks English as a native. Under his guidance we first went to the *Place* Royal, which is the highest part of the Town. I was struck with the light and chearful appearance of the whole scene. The buildings are handsome and of stone. In front as you enter it, the Church of Cobert [St. Jacques sur Coudenberg] stands, which is a modern building, and very light in the inside.

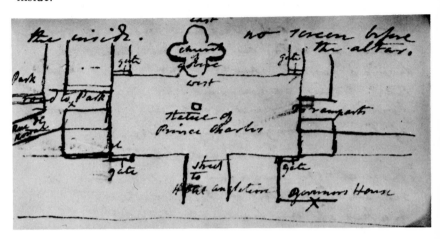

The statue of Prince Charles in Bronze near 14 feet high, was lying near the place where it had stood. The French when here threw it down, and we were told intended to have melted it to make either Money or Cannons of it; but did not effect their purpose; however they left their marks upon it, a great number of bruises on various parts. From our guide we learnt that men, woemen, and Children wept when the French committed this outrage on the statue of their favorite Governor.

On the left of this Square is the Park. Various walks laid out and a number of retired seats for the accomodation of those who choose to rest or read. — It is the most pleasant & singular place that any Town can boast of which I have any knowledge. On the opposite side from the *Place* Royal, a long line of handsome buildings is extended facing the Park, in the Center of which is the States of Brabant, as it is called, being the place in which the Deputies assemble.

We next proceeded to the Principal Church situated on the Slope of the high ground on which the Park is made. It is called St. Gadulle [Gudule], and is the Parish Church. The Architecture of the inside is very heavy and plain; and the eye is distracted among the heaped quantities of loaded decorations. The Pulpit in the Middle Aisle is of carved wood, and is an extraordinary specimen of crowded and ill fashioned forms. There are many Pictures, very bad, and among them several Landscapes, with scriptural Stories, like those at Courtray, in the Artois stile. However, attention will rest on one Picture in this Church, over an Altar, which is painted by Rubens, & is inimitable. Christ delivering the Keys to Peter. It is in the left side Choir.

Three Priests were performing Mass in this side Choir, and one by himself at the Altar, over which is the Picture of Rubens. — A great number of Poeple were attending the Service. I could not help observing that it seems to be very illregulated, when a similar Service is performing by Preists so near to each other. The tinkling of the Bells &c must necessarily one would think divide the attention.

We next went to the Church of the Dominicans, which is large but very coarse & plain in every Architectural sense. A Marble Screen with gilding before the Choir is as heavy as possible. Consistency of finishing, or a ruling taste, to make one part of their Churches correspond with another one may in vain look for. Heaps of marble with gilt absurd decorations abound, where the structure is as plain as possible. I have found no instance where simplicity is attended to. — The Dominicans were performing a Service for a deceased Person, and wore over their habitual dress (White Cloth, with a Black Cope, & two Black stripes, which go over the Shoulders before & behind,) Black velvet dresses, with laced borders. When such Masses are said, the friends of the deceased pay a certain sum.

There were many Pictures in the Church; all very bad.

Our guide next took us to the lower part of the Town, to the side of the Canal, which is kept very clean, and many small Dutch built vessells were upon it. This Canal is extended in different directions, and there is a long vista which is seen from a Bridge through which it passes to Antwerp. — A passage Boat, well built, & covered, goes every day 5 leagues, towards Antwerp, when the Passengers are taken up in a Dilligence &c and carried the remainder of the way. He did not reccommend it as a conveyance.

We walked some way on this part of the Rampart Walk, which is clean & shaded, but there is no view from it here. This brought us to the *Place* St. Michel, a small retired neat Square, desirable for small families. It is regular & built of stone; and small sycamore trees go round the railings of the inside the square.

We next went to the *Grand Place*, which is surrounded by Houses, belonging to *Companies*, and on one side is the Town House. All the

Houses have much odd decoration on the fronts of them, & several of the ornaments are gilt. The French with wanton licentiousness broke down and defaced many of these.

The streets at Brussells are generally speaking too narrow, & many of the houses are brick, but they are all painted White or of a Stone Colour, by which they obviate as much as possible the objection to narrow streets, by the quantity of light which is reflected.

We dined at ½ past 2. In the afternoon walked to the Upper ramparts from whence is a view over the Town. — The Duke of Aremberghs, House & Gardens, make but an indifferent figure, when his great property is considered. That Nobleman is spoken of here with great respect, He is 43 or 4 years of age. About 18 years ago he had the misfortune to lose his sight, in consequence of a shot received from a gun fired at Partridges by Mr. Gordon, the then English Minister. The accident was owing to the Dukes, walking forward behind a Hedge after Mr. Gordon had warned him that He was going to fire. The Duke is married & has 3 Children.

Our guide took us to the Stables of the Governor General, which are long enough to contain some hundreds of Horses, He said. They are very well for the purpose, but are not to be considered as highly finished.

The Governors Palace, near the Place Royal, is a large irregular building. The French stripped it, & committed other outrages, which have not yet been repaired.

We stopped at a Coffee House, and for the first time in three weeks read some English newspapers. We were much surprised at the mistatements in many respects of what we had been eye witnesses of. — But the lying & impudence and scandalous reflections of some deputies of the National Convention when speaking of the Citizens of those two places & the injustice done them after all their sufferings by that detestable Body excited our particular abhorrence.

At 6 oClock we adjourned to the Play House, where we saw performed a Comedy called, La Guerre imprivu or the War Unforseen. — The Musical entertainment was called Le Faux Lord, — The False Lord. — I thought the acting in general very well. One Man in particular, who performed the Lord, supported his part ably.

The Play House is rather large, but not equal in size to Covent Garden or late Drury Lane. — At present it looks smoky & dirty. The decorations are heavy. The Princes Box is stationary, and not placed on the Stage, but is the first Box from the Stage Box, on the right hand, looking *towards* the *stage*. It is lined with Velvet & has many heavy gilt ornaments. Between the Orchestra & the Pit abt. 4 Rows are railed of, and that part is called the Parquet Militaire. The entrance to the Pit is through a wide open passage in the Center of the back part. — There are 4 rows of Boxes, besides a sort of Boxes under the Stage Row, on a level with the Pit. There is no *Gallery* in this Playhouse, the Boxes going all round. — There is a notice given in the Bill of the day that no Servant in Livery can be admitted. — Of course those who are not so may go.

Amidst the variety which assemble in a Playhouse, one may fairly enough judge of any characteristic difference of the aspect and general appearance of the poeple of a Country as it is not concluding from a few Individuals. — Whether the strongly marked distinction between the French & the English had rendered me insensible to one less expressed I cannot at present judge; but at least I can say the Brabantines approach in countenance very near to the English, and their Complexions are much fairer than those of the French. Their Dress also brings them nearer. The better sort of Poeple will soon be a la Angloise.

The Play is usually over abt. 9 oClock to-night, it was half past. There was no dancing. The Prices of admittance are

Boxes	5s.-
Parquet Militaire	5, but they take 2s.6
2d. Boxes	2.6
Boxes on a level with the Pitt	1.9
3d. Heigth of Boxes & the Pit	1.2
4th. Heigth of Boxes	0.7

Mies, is the name of the Comic Actor who performed the La Faux Lord. He is a native of Brussells.

While enumerating the many advantages which Brussells has over most other Towns in what must make it delightful as a residence, it may be mentioned that this, as well as the other Continental Towns we have visited, want the great convenience of a flagged pavement on each side of the streets for the convenience of foot passengers. — In England they are common & the foreigners who have been there acknowledge the advantage.

There are in Brussells, 142 Hackney Coaches.

In regard to living, there can be no better than at Brussells. The Bread is excellent. Plenty of fruit in the Markets. Butter &c as good as can be had anywhere. — By those who reside constantly it will also be found a cheap place, as we were informed.

The situation of the Town is on the side of a Hill, and the Upper part, that is the Park, &c, perhaps too much exposed to a brisk circulation of Air for some Constitutions. — The sudden Change which we experienced from the damps of Conde, to this Climate caused Mr. Stadler & myself sensations in the throat & breast, which we were sensible were only owing to the difference of Air.

[*There follow notes of Farington's expenses and correspondence during his tour.*]

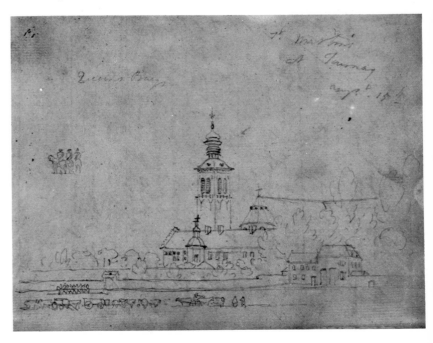

Expences on acct. of Tour to Valenciennes &c.

Saturday
August 10th
Paper	0-13- 4
Memorandum Book	0- 1- 6
3 Maps of Faden	0-18- 6
2 Plans	0- 2- 0

August 11th
Chaise to Dartford	1- 1- 0
Driver & Turnpikes	0- 3- 2
at Dartford	0- 3- 0
To Rochester	0-15- 0
Driver &c.	0- 3- 0

To Sittingbourn	0-11- 0
Driver &c.	0- 2- 9
To Canterbury	0-16- 0
Driver &c.	0- 3- 0
at Canterbury	0- 5- 0
To Dover	0-16- 0
Driver &c.	0- 3- 6
fee at Dover	0- 2- 6
Bill at Dover including what was put on board	0-19- 6

Ostend
August
13th

Paid for passage to Ostend	5- 5- 0
Men of the Boat	0- 5- 0
Paid Banker for letters to be sent me	0- 2- 0
Glass for Camera	0- 2- 0
Expence at Ostend	0-15- 0
Chaise to Thourout 15 miles	1- 8- 6
Expence at Do.	0- 8- 6

August 14

Chaise to Pethuen	0-18- 0
Expence at Do.	0- 3- 0
Chaise to Courtray 12 miles	1- 2- 0
Dinner at Do.	0- 5- 0
Dilligence to Tournay	0- 7- 6
Driver	0- 2- 6

Carried over
£19- 3- 9

Brot over	19- 3- 9
1st Bill at Tournay	0-14- 9
Dinner carried to Camp	0- 5- 0
Chaise to the Camp	1- 1- 0
Do. to Fontenoy & St. Amand	1- 1- 0
2nd Bill at Tournay	0-12- 2½
Waiters in all	0- 5- 6
at St. Amand	0- 6- 3
Hair Ribbon &-	0- 1- 0
at Reimes	0- 1- 6
at Vicong	0- 1- 6
1st Bill at Valenciennes	0-18-10

2 Maps	0- 5- 0
Man for shewing fortifications	0- 1- 0
Calash from Tournay 3 days	2- 5- 0
Driver 4 days	0-10- 0
August 22nd	
2nd Bill at Valenciennes	2- 5- 2
Board for Drawing on	0- 1- 3
Poor Poeple for sitting	0- 2- 6
August 24th	
3rd Bill at Valenciennes	2-13- 9
Paper	0- 2- 0
Expence at Gate of Town	0- 5- 0
Medicines	0- 2- 0
Servant at the *Place*	0- 1- 0
August 29	
3rd Bill at Valenciennes	3-18- 0
Washing for 3	0- 2- 7
30	
Ginger &c.	0- 1- 6
31	
4th Bill Valenciennes	1-11- 0
Septr. 1	
Bill at Conde	1- 5- 0
2	
Breakfast & Maid	0- 3- 6
Chaise to Mons	1- 5- 0
Dinner at Mons	0- 3- 0
Chaise to Castenu	0- 8- 9
Carried over.	42- 4- 3½

Brot over	42- 4- 3½
Chaise to Bruine le Compte	0-13- 2
Biscuits	0- 1- 0
Chaise to Attalle	0-17- 0
Chaise to Brusselles	0-13- 2
Play House for 2	0- 5- 0
Coffee House	0- 1- 0
Bill at Brussells and back to Antwerp	4-15- 0
seeing Laken	0- 5- 0

Coach to Laken & breeches mending	0- 5- 0
expence at Wathem	0- 2- 0
Seeing Churches at Antwerp 1st morning	
8 Skellings	0- 4- 4
Afternoon 4	0- 2- 2
2d. morning — Great Church 6 ⎫	
Jesuits 2 — St. Jaques 2 — Another 2. ⎭	0- 7- 0
Afternoon	
2 Churches — 5, private collection 3	0- 4- 4
Map of Antwerp	0- 1- 2
Washing	0- 2- 7
3rd Morning	
Church of Augustines 2 — St Michel 2 — ⎫	
Abbey room 3 — ⎭	0- 4- 1
Valet de Place, 3 days	0- 7- 6
First Bill at Le Grand Laboureur	2-11- 8
Second Bill at Do.	2- 2- 3
Servants	0- 7- 0
Pint Madeira	0- 2- 6
Chaise to Ghent	1- 5- 0
Driver	0- 3- 0
Bill at Ghent	1- 7- 3½
Valet de Place	0- 2- 4
Seeing a Church	0- 1- 2
Passage in Barge from Ghent to Bruges ⎫	
including dinner ⎭	0-14- 6
Bill at Bruges	0-12- 2
Waiter	0- 1- 2
Passage to Ostend & carrying things	0- 3- 6
	61- 8- 3½

August	*Susan*	Boydell	Will & Harry	Marchant
10	Saturday			
11	Sunday			
13	Tuesday — Ostend			
15	Thursday — Tournay			
19	Monday — Valenciennes			
		Tuesday 20		
			Friday 23	
25	Sunday — do. —	Sunday 25		Sunday 25
28	Wednesday — do. —			

Septr.

   1 Sunday — Conde —

                        Septr. 3d.
                        Will

   7 Thursday — Antwerp

Acct. of Expence

Brot over	61- 8- 3½	Brot. over	71- 8- 3
Bill at Ostend &		Mending instruments	0- 7- 6
Sea Stock	1- 9- 8½	broke	
Passage to		Print of Paris	0- 7- 6
Dover —	2-12- 6	2 Nos. Political	0- 2- 0
Captain Hull	0- 4- 6	Magazine	
Carrying things on board	0- 3- 0		
getting on shore at night	0- 9-		£72- 5- 3
Letter of sufference	0- 1- 6		
Ships steward	0- 2- 6		
Mail coach for 2 to London	2-10- 0		
Coachman & Guard	0- 5- 0		
James outside Expence	0-10- 0		
Bill at Dover	1- 7- 6		
Coach from Blue Bond [?]	0- 1- 6		
	71- 8- 3		

[*Drawing and accompanying comments appear on inside back cover of the notebook: see facing page.*]

Septr. 14.

At Six this morning came to Town in the Mail Coach from Dover. — called at the Shakespeare Gallery. — dined and evening at home.

Sunday 15th.

Rose at 7. called on Mr. Baker, Dances, Lawrences and Wheatleys.
    Sir Gilbert Eliott told Lawrence that He was at School or an Academy with the celebrated Miraubeau. Sir Gilbert introduced him when He

visited England to Mr. Burke. It was very singular to see Mirabeau &
Burke in controversy. Miraubeau could speak little English, Burke,
French imperfectly. Yet these celebrated men argued with as much
earnestness and continuation as if they had been speaking a language
common to both. Mirabeau was astonished at the eloquence and force
with which Burke expressed his meaning, though He could only do it by
uniting words of different languages. — While Miraubeau was in England
Sir Gilbert was often called upon to get him out of scrapes, into which his
irregularities had forced him. — Sir Gilbert lost 4 or 500 pounds by him.

Monday 16th.

Rose at ½ past 7. — working on my Valenciennes outlines. Boydell &
Captn. Westcote dined with me. Batty, Stadler & Smirke in the afternoon.
Captn. Westcote appointed to the Impregnable of 90 Guns, at Plymouth.
Fourth Number of Shakespeare published today.

Tuesday 17th.

Rose at ½ past 7. — Called on Boydell & settled with Stadler for the views of Valenciennes, — which He is to engrave. — Susan returned from Oken.

Wednesday 18th.

Rose at 7. — rainy weather. Dined at Mr. Bakers. — Captn. Westcote, Hearne & Boydell there. Made outline of Buildings at Bruges on Canvass.

Thursday 19th.

Mr. Cary returned — Rose at ½ past 7. rainy, dull weather.

Friday 20th.

Rose at ½ past 7. — dull weather. — Hanging drawings in Anti room.

Saturday 21st.

Rose at 8. — dull, rainy weather. — Chas. Offley & Mr. Carey dined with me. — Guernsey 40 leagues from Southampton.

Sunday 22nd.

Rose at 8. very wet weather. — at home all day.

Monday 23.

Rose at ½ past 8. — dull morning. — Mr. Baker, Mr. Hearne & C Offley dined with me. — H. Hamond came from Brighton. — wet day.

Tuesday 24.

Rose at 8. — showery day. — H. Hamond dined with us.

Wednesday 25th.

Rose at 8. — at Home, recd. parcel from Squire.

Thursday 26th.

Rose at 8. — Dined with Mr. Evans. Mr. & Mrs. Richardson, C & John Offley, H. Hamond & Mr. Harris there. — Mr. Evans gave us Port wine of the vintage of 1773, which He bottled in 1776. — The flavor excellent & the colour full & bright. — Lord Buckinghamshire has left the Blickling House & estate to Lady C Harbord, — another estate of £2,500 a year to Lady Valetort, £70,000 to Lady Emily Hobart & only £5,000 to Lady Ancram, though He was reconciled to her in July last, since which time he had made his will.

Friday 27th.

Rose at ½ past 8. — Beautiful weather. — Dined with C Offley. — Mr.

Evans, H Hamond & John Offley. — Mr. Evans related many particulars of the seizure of the Tavora family at Lisbon. — He was on the spot at the time.

Saturday 28th.

Rose at 8. — Beautiful weather. — Harry came to Town this morning, and went to Battersbees.

Sunday 29th.

Rose at 8. Susan a bad inflammation in her eye. — Mrs. Edge & Mrs. Ravald called. — at Home. — Edwards came in the evening.

Monday 30th.

Rose at 8. — Joe Green called. — Dined at York Hotel with Harry [Farington], Mr. Hill & Green.

OCTOBER 1793

Rose at ½ past 7. — Burch, the enameller called. — Batty went into Lincolnshire. — Harry dined with us. Marchant in the evening.

Wednesday 2nd.

Rose at 8. — George Dance called on his return from Lord Camdens. — Kershaw and Mr. Webb called. — In the evening Hamilton drank tea with me.

Thursday. Octr. 3rd.

Rose at ½ past 7. — Harry sat to Dance this morning. — I dined with Harry, Battersbee, Hall, Green, Allen, Errington, J. Howarth, C & J Offley at York Hotel. — Kershaw came after dinner.

Friday Octr. 4th — 1793.

Rose at ½ past 7. — a fine warm day. Ewen, began to paste for me. — Green & Edwards dined with me. — Storace sold the Song called Captivity, to Dall, the music seller, at the corner of Holles St. Cavendish square, for £50, and in 6 weeks Dall sold 2600 of them for 1 shilling a piece. The Captivity of the Queen of France, the subject. — Sheridan, Kemble, and Storace have the direction of the arrangments in the internal part of the new building of Drury Lane Theatre. Young Tom Sandby called on Edwards to offer him the place of Under drawing master at Woolwich, which his Father Paul Sandby has the disposal of. Edwards declined it.

Saturday 5th.

Rose at 8. — at home.

Sunday 6th.

Rose at 8. — Kershaw came in the Forenoon and staid to dinner. Harry came. Poor rates at Manchester last 3 years 4 shillings in the pound. Land Tax 6d. in the pound.

Principal article of manufacture which sold 3 years ago for 28*s*. now sells for 6*s*. 8*d*. — I think Hanks of Cotton or Yarn. — Profligacy of private expences at Liverpool before the late failures almost incredible. — The expences attending a gala entertainment given by a merchant in his own House *one* evening cost £700. — Gill Slater owed Caldwells Bank £60,000. — Weather very fine and warm — met Boswell, who I think is much altered for the worse in appearance.

Monday Octr. 7.

Rose at ½ past 8. — weather very fine. Harry left Town. — Plott & Marchant drank Tea with us.

Tuesday Octr. 8th.

Rose at ½ past 7. — Hazy weather. — Notice of Candidates for ensuing election of two associates at the Royal Academy.

Charles Peart — Sculptor

Robert Brettingham
W. Fellows
W. Porden   } Architects
Thomas Malton

Saml. Shelley
George Antony Keenan
Gainsborough Dupont
Solomon Polack
James Stewart
William Grimaldi
William Beechey
Martin Shee
John Hoppner   } Painters
Francis Towne
Henry Spicer
Anton Hickel
Richard Livesay
John Graham
Richard Collins
Robert Freebairn
Thomas Whitcombe
Mather Browne
John T. Serres

The election to be on Monday the 4th of November. — Called at Alderman Boydells to look at his Prints of military evolutions. — Met Mr. Berwick.

Wednesday Octr. 9th.

Rose at ½ past 7. — Hazy morning very fine day, the weather is now generally so. — got Prints of Battles from Pallmall. Statement in the papers undoubtedly true of the French Convention having resolved to change the division of the year into 12 months of 30 days, and 5 over; and to change also the names of the months and the days. — The year of our Lord is no more mentioned but the year of Liberty. A further proof of the irreligion of that Poeple or of their rulers. — So extravagant is their conduct in this instance, it was first supposed to be a joke upon them when seen in the papers.

Thursday 10th.

Rose at 8. — Hazy morning, fine day. — Poor rates for Clerkenwell Parish £6000 a year.

Friday October 11th — 1793.

Rose at $\frac{1}{4}$ past 8. — Hazy morning and the weather through the day thick & heavy but no rain. — G. Dance called and showed me a letter which he had recd. from Lord Camden at Brighton, wrote with his own hand, and in so fair and strong a character as surprised me. — The subject was expressing the pleasure which He had in the general admiration of Dances profile drawings, particularly of Miss Vanneck. — The Prince of Wales has desired Dance to paint his Portrait, which has much embarassed the latter who is very unwilling to do it. — I finished today the drawing from Hallow Park for Mr. Berwick, and the outline etching of Broad St. Oxford.

Saturday 12th.

Rose at 8. — Hazy morning. very fine middle of day. — at Home.

Sunday 13th.

Rose at $\frac{1}{2}$ past 7. — very fine morning and day. — Kershaw called and informed us of Battersbees marriage at St. Pauls Covent Garden on Friday the 4th inst. — This Mrs. B acquainted Kershaw with on Friday last. — Mr. Baker called in the evening.

Monday Octr. 14th.

Rose at $\frac{1}{2}$ past 7. Batty returned from Sir Joseph Banks, which is abt. 40 miles from Lynn. — Duke of York left off Dunkirk as one article 400 waggons, which cost abt. £30 each. — made by a man in Edgware road, who is making 600 more. — Sir Joseph deprecates employing so inexperienced a man as the Duke in so critical a situation. — Humphry sent to dine with me & came. — The complaint in his eyes [was] cured bv Mrs. [Marshall] of [blank] Court, Bow street. He was under her care a year & a quarter. — weather very fine.

Tuesday 15th.

Rose at $\frac{1}{2}$ past 7. — Beautiful morning, glass 56. — The Revd. Mr. Lysons called. I went with him at noon to Putney and Wandsworth, and made drawings of that district. — dined with him at 5, and returned to town. — we walked through Mrs. Woods grounds. She talks of letting her House, and asks £1000 a year for the use of it, furniture included. — Gibbon, the Historian, was born in this House. His Father a Citizen of London. He is now in a very indifferent state of Health at Bath. Dr. Milman told Mr. Lysons He thought a recovery doubtful.

Hughes has been very fortunate. A large fine was paid very soon after He was appointed Prebendary of Westminster. His share came to £300.

The Bishop of London does not keep Publick days; but invites 10, or a dozen, of the Clergy of his diocese together, so as to take in most, or all, within the year. — He is a Yorkshire man by Birth. His Father an apothecary I think. When He was a young man He was Esquire Beadle of the University of Cambridge. — He has no Children, but many dependent relations. Mr. Lysons has made up several volumes of selections from newspapers, which He has arranged in the best manner. Advertisements of Giants, — of Dwarfs, — &c. &c. — classing each description together. — Horace Hamond came in the evng from Brighton. They had been much alarmed on Sunday by a report of the coast of Normandy being covered by French Troops meditating an invasion.

The Prince of Wales on Sunday gave a dinner to the officers of his regt. and some others. He sat at the Head of the Table & had three vice presidents, one at the bottom and two in the center of the Table. — He commenced the Jollity after dinner by drinking 10 Bumper toasts, out of Glasses, 6 of which held a Bottle. — This Jolity continued till 12 at night, from 6 when they dined. — The musick playing at the outside the Pavilion. — The French may retort on us for a contempt of Sunday.

Wednesday Octr. 16.

Rose at 7. — a very fine morning. I went over Westminster Bridge and Clapham Common, and through Wandsworth & Putney, to Barn-Elms, I made a drawing of Putney Bridge, seen over part of Wandsworth, from East Wandsworth Hill, — and a drawing of Barn-Elms, including a view of Anspach House, the Margrave of Anspachs. — At 5 I returned to dinner. C & J Offley & H: Hamond came to dine with us.

Thursday Octr. 17th.

Rose at ½ past 7. — morning hazy. — much concerned at an acct. in the newspaper of the death of John Hunter, the excellent surgeon, to whom I was greatly obliged in the course of last summer for his advice &c on acct. of an incested Tumour on my Back, which He removed. — Mr. Hunter was in the Council room at St. Georges Hospital and was suddenly taken ill and being carried home in a close chair, expired about two o'clock. He mentioned to me once, that He had some obstruction or complaint abt. his Heart which He was well assured would cause his death *suddenly*, at some period.

Went in the forenoon to Greenwich, and made a view of the Hospital &c from a situation by the River side to the East of the Hospital. — Returned to dinner at 5 o'clock. — a moist evening.

Friday Octr. 18th.

Rose at ½ past 7. — very thick morning and dull day. — Called on Humphry at his new Lodgings, for which He is to pay 200 guineas a year. — no.13 Old Bond street. — Mr. Heaviside, the Surgeon, had just informed him that John Hunter went on Wednesday forenoon to St. Georges Hospital, and carried a reccomendation of a young man come from the West Indies, who was desirous of attending the Hospital. This was objected to on acct. of some informality and caused a warm debate, in which Mr. Hunter did not join, but suppressed his indignation. A Physician present went into another room, and was followed by Mr. Hunter, who began to speak to him, but suddenly falling forward upon him expired. — The suppression of his passion might probably have caused a suffocation, owing to the weak state of the vessels about his heart. — Mr. Hunter has left a Son and a daughter. The Son abt. 20 years old. The Daughter a very fine girl of [blank] of age.

Hodges & Hamilton called in the evening. Hodges has been to F[arnley], Mr. Fawkes's, in Yorkshire. He went to see Kirkstall Abbey, & Fountains Abbey; the latter He very much admired, and stayed a day there and 6 Hours at Kirkstall. — He also went to Bolton Abbey, where is a waterfall, and admired and thought the situation & Building corresponded beautifully. — Of Pomfret Castle of which little remains He made a sketch. It is near Ferry Bridge.

Hamilton spoke of the ensuing election, and thinks Beechey shd. be one, to which I agreed. He is also anxious that Lawrance should be secured for an Academician's place in February next. I told him Lawrance should have one of my votes. — Paul Sandby has given the place of under Drawing Master at Woolwich to Barney, a young man who is married, and to whom it is most desirable, as He was on the point of going to Birmingham from want of sufficient employ in London.

Saturday Octr. 19th.

Rose at ½ past 7. — a tolerably fine day. — went with Susan & Charles Offley to Fanhams, Mrs. Offleys country House, — very pleasantly situated a mile beyond Ware. — Stopped at Waltham Cross & made some progress in my sketch of the Cross. — Mr. Minet & J Offley came to Fanham.

Sunday [20th].

A fine morning, and day. — Rear Admiral Gardner left his Card in Charlotte St.

Monday [21st].

a Beautiful day. Rode through Ware a circle of abt. 12 miles, and passed Wood-Hall, built by Sir Thos. Rumbold, and since his death sold to Paul Benfield. — Mr. Batty & Mr. T. Proctor came to dinner.

Tuesday Octr. 22d 1793.

Came to Town with C & J Offley, and dined at the Bedford Coffee House. — news of the murder of the Queen of France arrived.

Wednesday [23rd].

This mornings Post brought letters from Mr. Antony Hamond, & Mrs. Dowsing, with acct. of the death of the Revd. Mr. Carey, Rector of Massingham, who died suddenly yesterday morning. — at noon C & J Offley accompanied me to Brightelmstone, to inform Horace Hamond of the above event. — we went by Croydon, Godstone, East Grinstead, Uckfield, & Lewes. It is a longer distance than either of the other two roads, by 6 or 7 miles & the stage from East Grinstead a very heavy road. We were 10 Hours & ½ going. — we put up at the Old Ship, Hicks's at Brighton where H Hamond came to us. — The Country abt. Godstone very fine, and a great command of it from many high points on the road.

Thursday Octr. 24th.

a Beautiful day. — This morning we were much amused at Brighton. The Stein, or Publick walk is very pleasant & airy. we visited the Camp where the militia are stationed. It extends abt. 2 miles along the Coast, on high ground. The Prince of Wales's dragoons at the farthest end of the camp from Brighton.

The great Ball Room at Shergolds is 90 feet long by 45 wide, and lofty in proportion. — The ceiling too plain for the decorations of the other parts.

The Prince of Wales always hands Mrs. Fitzherbert to the top of the room whoever is there.

Brighton affords nothing for the lover of Landscape. It is situated on a very barren Coast.

We dined at the Ship, and with us Captn. Templar of the Princes's Regt. — He married lately a daughter of Sir Frederick Rogers, member for Plymouth.

Friday 25 October.

Left Brighton this morning with Hamond, & C & J Offley, — we took a Post Coach which held 4. We left Brighton at 9 o'clock & were in Town at ½ past 6. — The weather gloomy. we dined at Ryegate. The Country near that place & for some miles is seen extensively from the road, which passes over high and oddly broken ground. We passed Gatton abt 19 or 20 miles from London.

When I came to Town I found a note from Wheatley & went there, where Hamilton had come before me. — Hoppner was there & coming away at the same time with me, we conversed, at his desire, sometime, abt. his situation relative to the Royal Academy.

I passed the evening in Thernaugh St. with Hamond &c.

Saturday 26th.

Horace Hamond went this morning to Strawberry Hill to wait on Lord Orford abt. the living of Massingham.

I called on Hamilton & went with him to the Shakespeare Gallery, relative to Wheatleys Pictures.

I afterwards called at the Admiralty on Admiral Gardner, who was at the Board.

In the afternoon Mr. Randal called. He had recd. a letter from Mr. Hamond relative to Massingham.

C & J Offley, Hamond & Harris dined with me. Minet came. In the eving went with Hamilton to Wheatleys. — Horace brought the Presentation from Lord Orford.

Sunday 27th.

Went with Hamilton to West End, to speak to Boydell abt. Wheatleys Pictures &c.

Hamilton was well acquainted with Marat, and with Brissot when they were in England. Hamilton studied under Zucchi, to whose House Marat came in the most familiar Manner, a Knife & Fork being laid for him every day. He borrowed from Zucchi at different times abt. £500, which He cd. not repay. He professed himself a Physician, and cured Bonomi the architect of severe complaints twice or three times. He had an original way of thinking in his professional capacity as was observed by the Apothecary who made up the medicines, and acted against common rules. He was a little man, abt. the size of Cosway, the Painter; slender, but well made, of a yellow aspect & had a quick eye. He had a great deal of motion, seldom keeping his body or limbs still. He was then discontented, and abused the establishments which existed. This was abt. 18 years ago, when Marat appeared abt. 40 years of age. Zucchi at that time courted Angelica Kauffman, the Artist, & frequently took Marat with him in the evenings when He went to visit her.

Brissot took a House in Newman street and endeavoured to establish a Shop for selling Books & Pamphlets, and He proposed to make his House a sort of meeting place for Literary & Political characters, more particularly of those who were desirous of altering the establishments of the time. — Here He continued abt. a year. His wife was an agreeable woman

& had been a governess to the Children of the Duke of Orleans, and was a favorite of the Dutchess. — Brissot returned to France in company with a Man who had violently attacked the Character of the Queen of France abt. a story of a necklace. — When they landed in France they were immediately arrested & thrown into the Bastile. After a time Brissot obtained an examination & was acquitted; but he held a deep hatred of the family of the King from ever after. — He was a thin man, of a sallow countenance, and carried his head & shoulders in such a way as to appear something deformed though He was not so.

Lawrence allows his Father for the support of his Family near £300 a year. — He pays for his own Lodgings in Bond st. 200 guineas a year. His price for Portraits is 40 guineas for a three quarter; 80 guineas for a half length; & 160 guineas for a whole length.

Proctor, a student of the academy, who has distinguished himself by his ingenious models, called on me to solicit my vote, that He may be sent to Rome, as the Academy Student. — He exhibited his model of Ixion in 1785. The weather has been dull with slight rain two days.

Dined with C. Offley, — Hamond, John Offley & Minet there.

In the eveng went to Wheatleys to meet Hamilton & Mr. Bell.

Monday Octr. 28th.

This forenoon I returned Hoppners visit. Wheatley breakfasted with me this morning on his way to his lodgings. — Horace Hamond went to Norwich to be inducted. — At noon C & J Offley left Town with me. we stopped some time at Twickenham where I crossed the water & made a drawing. — Went to Kingston by Teddington 3 miles to dinner. — The tide rises at Twickenham about 1 foot & a half in common tides, and about 2 feet and a half in high tides. — An Old Boatman at the Ferry gave me this account. — He said the difference between the rising of the tide at Twickenham and Teddington is about 1 foot. The Tide He said seldom reached Kingston. — This was a beautiful day. — The view on the River looking towards Richmond from Twickenham has more of the character of Lake Scenery than of that of a River. The afternoon & evening is the best time for viewing it.

We put up at the Castle (the Post House) at Kingston. Accomodation but moderate, and dear in their charges.

Tuesday Octr. 29th.

Between 8 & 9 this morning rode down the Kingston side of the River towards Ham Common. No circumstance of a picturesque or interesting kind. A few Houses on the opposite side of the River but of no consequence. — Returned back to Kingston & crossed the Bridge. No toll over it. a Wooden Bridge. — Went up by the side of the water to Hampton court between 2 and 3 miles. The Park on the right hand. Thames Ditton, a handsome white House, inhabited by Mr. Solomons, formerly by the Duchess of Gloucester, is situated prettily and quietly, on the Surry side of the River abt. a mile short of Hampton court. — Leaving our Horses at the Toy, we crossed the wooden Bridge, for which Chaises pay one shilling, Horses 2d, foot passengers 1 Halfpenny *each* time of crossing. As I wished to walk down on the other side of the River in order to see what appearance the Palace made when viewed across the River, we were obliged to make a considerable circuit and to pass over a small bridge before we could get into the fields nearest the River, owing to the streams which flowing to the Thames, intersected the Country. The view from the point I chose includes one front of the modern Palace, and a line of that part which was built by Cardinal Wolsey. Of this I made a drawing. — From Hampton Court, we proceeded on the Surry side of the River, and keeping close to it, to Hampton a mile farther. The late Mr. Garricks House & Temple &c make a very pleasing assemblage. Of these I made a sketch. — Immediately beyond Mr. Garricks is the Town of Hampton, a straggling, ill built, exposed, village; which is a very unpleasing contrast to the sheltered, secluded & elegant appearance of Mr. now Mrs. Garricks villa. — Opposite to Hampton is a large Plain or Common called Moulsey Hurst. This we passed over, and went on towards Sunbury. On the side of the River we were now upon there are no Houses but at a considerable distance, but we commanded the whole line built on the opposite Bank. A little short of Sunbury is a very large Brick House, with stone decorations. It formerly belonged to Lord Pomfrets family, & was lately purchased with 100 Acres of land included for £12000, from a Mrs. [blank] by Mr. Richardson, a gentleman who made a fortune in the East Indies. — Sunbury makes a pretty appearance from hence but the view altogether is very flat. — Extensive common, or waste ground, continuing on the Surry side the River. We proceeded on to Walton Bridge, or rather Bridges, there being two distinct from each other. The new one has [four main] arches, the old Bridge [three main]. On the Surry side Lord Tankerville has a villa, and pleasant grounds, which come up to the Bridge, and are only separated from the Park of Oatlands, by the High road leading to the Bridge. At the end of the Bridge, on the other side the River, is a single good looking white House which belongs to a merchant of London. — The Park of Oatlands rises considerably above the flat country through which the River passes, and is very well wooded. The House is not seen from this part, being situated more than a mile from the Bridge and hidden by trees. The Duchess of York resides here almost constantly during the Dukes absence with the army in Flanders. — The Park was open to all the neighbours formerly to ride or walk in, but the Duke has refused this indulgence.

The evening was very wet. The day had been windy and rather bleak. We put up at the Dukes Head, in Walton, a small, but neat House, and good accomodation.

Wednesday Octr. 30th.

A beautiful morning. — Rode to St. Georges Hill about 1 mile and half from Walton Bridge at the back of Oatlands Park. — Sir Henry Fletcher has a House and grounds at the end of Walton. It was formerly Col. Stevensons. It joins Oatlands Park. St. Georges Hill is a considerable rising in a rude and coarse Heath. From this situation there is a most extensive command of the country on every side. St. Anns Hill — Coopers Hill — Windsor, — and sweeping round, also Hampton Court, Richmond Hill, (which intercepts St. Pauls so that it cannot be seen,) — came into the view. But the foreground of this Landscape being barren & brown Heath it is only for an extensive command of distance that it can be pleasing.

From St. Georges Hill we descended to that gate of Oatlands Park which is placed on the Weybridge side. We should not have been admitted, so strict are the orders, but by enquiring for Mr. Duncan, the gardener. On my applying to him, He readily offered to walk along the Terrace with us. I have seen few situations more beautiful than the line of ground which is called the Terrace, and great taste has been shown in whatever has been done by the hand of Art. A large piece of made water, broad as a fine River, is directed in such a way as to appear to be part of the Thames although it has no connexion with it. Above the two ends, where it is lost in wood, the real River appears over the trees, and the imagination readily connects them. In the distance St. Anns Hill, Coopers Hill, & Windsor are distinct objects on one side; on the other side Walton double Bridge, Lord Tankervilles, Sunbury, Harrow, & Highgate. Immediately below the Terrace is an extensive flat country, which is only seen in small proportions, as the Park is well wooded. The water in the Park is about three quarters of a mile long, and was laid out by the present Duke of Newcastle, who had no assistant in designing it. A lofty and well designed Temple is erected on the Terrace but is not finished, which is to be lamented as it would make a fine & proper object in this situation, and the view from it most beautiful & extensive. The Duke of York proposed to finish it since He purchased this place from the Duke of Newcastle but was told by Mr. Holland, the Architect, that it must be taken down & rebuilt as it would not be safe to trust to it as it now is. To an inexperienced Man it appears both solid & sound.

The House at Oatlands makes no appearance equal to the scenery about it, but being in a great measure hidden among trees, it does not become an object of much notice.

Just below the Park the Thames makes a bold sweep, and the point of the angle is called *Cowey Stakes*; this is the place where Julius Caesar forded the River. — It may be half a mile above Walton Bridge. — The village of Hawforth is on the opposite side of the Plain. The Park at Oatlands is about 3 miles round. The long way of it is from Walton to Weybridge which is about a mile & half.

The Duke of York purchased Oatlands from the Duke of Newcastle abt 5 years ago. He became Lord of the manor of Weybridge, and some estate is united to it.

The Duke of Newcastle had a grotto made which is much admired for the beauty of the workmanship and exactness of the imitations. Before it is a small basin of water. The whole is inclosed by trees which make the situation secluded. The grotto contains 2 small rooms, and a bathing room on the ground floor besides passages, and one large room above. All finished in character, with imitations of Icicles, and Shell work. The Stones of which the grotto is composed were brought from Bath & Cirencester. The Spar of which the Icicles are composed, from Derbyshire. The whole was put together by a man of the name of Lane & his son. — They were common Masons by trade, and lived at Westbury, in Wiltshire. They were constantly employed Six years about it. — The Duchess of York in the course of last Summer breakfasted & dined in the Grotto very often.

I made a sketch from the Terrace looking towards Walton Bridge.

Mr. Duncan refused to accept anything for the civility He had shown us, and in every respect appeared a man of a superior kind considering his profession.

We returned to Walton. We were much imposed on by the Landlord, who charged every thing at the dearest rate.

From Walton we proceeded to Weybridge, which is an ordinary ill situated village. Lord Portmore has a House near it. From Weybridge to Wooburn farm, is above a mile, through a flat & Dutch like road.

Wooburn farm belonged to the late Mr. Southcote, who abt 60 years ago began the improvements which have made the place much admired. — When He died abt 10 years ago, He bequeathed it to Lord Petre, who let the place to Lord Loughborough for 5 years. It is now inhabited by Lord Petres eldest Son.

On entering the gate you are directed by the gate keeper to a Path which is made through several small fields. Nothing is remarkable in this part of the farm as it is called, but the hedges which are cut as trim and regular as the old fashioned yew tree rows. — By a circular kind of round you at last approach what appears to be pleasure grounds, and crossing a small stream ascend a sloping Bank to a Summer House, from whence a line of distant country is seen. The summer House is situated at the end of a long high ridge of ground closely planted with trees, between which walks are made and seats are placed at certain points. The extensive view from this high ground includes Chertsey Bridge, — Chertsey Town, and St. Anns Hill, and a considerable tract of flat country through which the Thames passes. As there is a proper quantity of trees planted in the lower grounds, the Landscape has not a naked look, but makes up a very pleasing subject. I made a sketch of that part which includes Chertsey Bridge. — The House is situated in a bottom surrounded by the Farming & pleasure grounds. A piece of made water is carried close to it, and appears so nearly on a level, that one cannot help supposing the situation of the House to be damp; but the gardener told us it was not so. He said the walk round the whole of the grounds was near two miles. — Wooburn farm is two miles from Chertsey, — 1 from Weybridge, — and about 20 from London.

We went on from Wooburn to the Swan at Chertsey, a House of very good accomodation. The mistress a very respectable kind of Woman, Sister, as she told us, of Mr. Daniel, and mother of the younger Mr. Daniel, who have been 9 years in India, and are expected home in the Spring of 1794. They have penetrated into the back parts of India, as far as they could prevail upon guides to conduct them, and were within sight of the snowy mountains of Tartary. — They have compleated 126 views. — They proposed returning over Land through Egypt, and come to England through Italy &c. The elder Mr. Daniel is about 45 years of age, the younger about 25.

This day had been beautiful but the evening was wet.

Thursday, Octr. 31st.

A very fine morning. The ground covered with a hoar frost, so that the Sun had not power to clear the atmosphere till towards 12 o'clock.

We left Chertsey & rode up St. Anns Hill, about a mile from the Town. near the Top of the Hill, Mr. Fox has a House and a small pleasure ground, very pleasingly situated. From the top of St. Anns Hill, which is rough & Heathy, there is a most extensive prospect, not indeed including the whole circle of the horizon, but about two thirds of it. In this range Coopers Hill & the back part of Windsor forest are the boundaries on the left, and the country over Chertsey, St. Georges Hill &c are on the right. In clear weather St. Pauls may be plainly discerned.

We descended from St. Anns Hill, and riding abt 3 or 4 miles passed through Egham, & immediately ascended Coopers Hill by a good carriage road which passes over Englefield green and through Windsor Park. We left the road and turning to right made our way over a field or two to that side of the Hill which commands with some variations the same extensive view as that seen from St. Anns Hill. Windsor Castle is now a more striking object, and we had a command of the River Thames in many places. A little to the right at the foot of the Hill lies Runnymede, so celebrated from its having been the spot where King John met the Barons & signed the Charter, it is now a race ground, and part of it is enclosed. The Town of Staines is seen over the mead, and a line of the River. On the left Windsor with the Forest woods makes a most magnificent assemblage. It is the South East view of the Castle. Ankerwyke, Lord Shuldhams, a large white House in the gothic taste, is situated near the end of the Hill on which we stood and with the line of ground steeply sloping from it, makes up the composition of this landscape of which I made a drawing. In the middle ground below, Beaumont Lodge, the House of Mr. Griffith is seen. A little beyond is Old Windsor but covered with trees. — The front of Lord Shuldham's house looks over Englefield green. We quitted the road which leads to Windsor Park, and descended the Hill by a road on the right and passed through Old Windsor a small, straggling, Shabby village with a very bad cross road through & beyond it. Old Windsor is between 2 & 3 miles from new Windsor. We turned off when we gained the turnpike road, towards Datchet Bridge, which we crossed, & turning to the left went through a field road to Eaton, and saw the north side of the Castle towering over a thick line of high trees. The appearance is very grand, but the River is not seen, till we come near Eaton. The views from hence are very fine. — We passed over Windsor Bridge, and got to the Castle Inn, *Wants*, at ½ past 3.

At Kingston our Bill for three gentlemen, 3 Horses, & a servant, for dinner, Tea, & Breakfast was £2.1.0. Dukes Head, Beds charged, at Walton Bridge for the same 2. 2. — at the Swan, at Chertsey, with better accomodation 1. 18. — at the Castle at Windsor £2. 18. 0. On the whole the expence at Windsor exceeded that of the other places about Ten shillings.

NOVEMBER 1793

Friday, November 1st.

A Cold morning but fair. Left Windsor at ½ past 9, and through Clewer Lane, went to Maidenhead, and forward to Marlow, 12 miles from Windsor. The view of Windsor Castle from Clewer Lane is, I think, equal to any of the various points from which the Castle & Town appear united together. It takes in the North & South parts of the Castle, and the round Tower makes the Apex of the composition. The descent into the vale of Marlow is very striking. After passing through a close lane the wide extended view is suddenly displayed, comprehending the village of Temple, Mr. Williams's House [Temple House], Harleford, Bisham Abbey &c &c. — We changed our Chaise at the Crown at Marlow, a House of but indifferent accomodation. I called on Mr. Davenport at Court Garden, a very pleasing situation, which He has made the most of, and very judiciously managed his improvements so as to make the country and circumstances in his vicinity appear a part of his plan. — Mr. Davenport was formerly a Surgeon in London, and married Miss Sanxay, the daughter of the gentleman under whom He learned his profession. With Her He received eventually a large fortune. She is a sensible and agreeable woman. They have no Children. Mr. Davenport is uncle to Mr. Davenport of Capesthorne, in Cheshire.

From Marlow to Henley is 8 miles. We passed by Harleford, — Danesfield, Mr. Scotts, — Mill end, Mr. Hindes, who married the widow of Mr. Lane, — and abt 1 mile from Henley, Fawley Court, Mr. Freemans. On the left of the road, though but seldom seen, is the Thames; on the right a succession of high swelling ground. Much had been said to me of the views from these heights, and I ascended such as appeared to command the best views. — From one above Mill end, belonging to Mr. Hind, called Ridgwood, there is a beautiful view of Mill end, the River & Culham House & grounds. From another, and higher situation above the Turnpike House, called Pale Hill, is a fine view of Fawley Court & grounds, a long line of the River, and the Town & Bridge of Henley, covered by a high distance. This is the best point I have found below Henley, & here I made a drawing. We went on to Henley where we arrived about ½ past 4. The day had been very favorable, but the afternoon as well as the morning was very cold. — We put up at Marchs at Henley.

At Mr. Davenports, I found a letter from Mr. Coombes, who recommends to me to make a view of Culham, as it may induce a certain set of subscribers.

Culham is now the property of Mr. West, a Brother of Lord Delawarr, who married a coheiress. The other sister married young Mr. Powis of Hardwick, who sold to Mr. West his share of Culham. The Marquiss of Blandford has rented the place. At present Mr. Law, one of the Sons of the late Bishop of Carlisle, and who made a fortune in India, rents it. — Mr. Law married a daughter of the Archbishop of York (Dr. Markham).

Saturday Novr. 2nd.

A very fine morning, but a severe frost and the ground covered with Hoar. Last night remarkably cold.

At Ten o'clock the atmosphere began to clear, and I crossed the Bridge, and went to Culham by a road a little to the right of the River. Culham is situated about two miles below Henley, on the side of steep grounds richly decorated with trees. The park or grounds are confined within a small compass, but are neatly kept; and so advantageously circumstanced as to the surrounding objects, that all which comes into the view makes a characteristic part & gives the appearance of greater extent. — The House is plain in the design; but solid, and spacious. Five windows on each side, yet the House is not a square, the front being wider than the ends. It is built with brick. — The River is of suitable breadth when considered as the Thames, and the Banks are so well cleared that it has the beauty of a made water without the usual formality. In the lower grounds, though very pleasing to ride through, I could find no point from which I could describe, with the pencil, the real situation of Culham; but ascending towards the London road, which leads from Henley to Maidenhead, over the heights; I chose a situation, which commands a view over the House, including the range of hilly ground beyond the river. From hence the Landscape is of a bolder character than would be expected even in this passage of the River. Turning from the view in which the House is included, [there is] another view which varies considerably in the style of the Landscape from the last, [with] more windings of the River than I remember to have seen from any other point. The steep Chalk Bank on which Danes-field is situated limits the vale on the left hand, and a long, but more distant range, sweeping the horizon, describes its extent on the right, the view including Danesfield, [Hurley] and [Temple?]. After having made drawings of these different views, I went into the London road near the two mile stone, and proceeding towards Maidenhead, near the 3 mile stone, turned on the left into a close lane which passes through a thick plantation wood. Abt a quarter of a mile from the road I came to what I thought a Summer House, which I

4. *Scene at Park Place including the Druids' Temple. An History of the River Thames,* Vol. I (1794), plate 28.

5. *Cliefden. An History of the River Thames,* Vol. 1 (1794), plate 37.

find it was intended to have been but is now converted into an Habitation by the Honble. Mr. West, the Owner of Culham, to which this belongs. From the Bank on which it is placed there is a very beautiful view down the River, which includes various windings of it, and more distinctly, several objects, than they can be seen from the last point I had left, with the addition of Harleford, Mr. Vansittarts, which makes an object clearly detached from the chalk cliff of Danes-field.

I returned into the Turnpike road and rode on a mile farther, but it was down Hill, & led into a bottom, from which no object appeared in such a shape as to merit particular notice. In general, I find in riding through this vale, that on both sides of the River, it is necessary to ascend the higher grounds in order to command any striking view. Towards the afternoon the weather changed much. The Landscape was sufficiently distinct, but the frost gave way and it became a little rainy & dull.

I returned to Henley by 4 o'clock. — My companions had passed the day at Park Place. The old gardener who attended them spoke of the amiable disposition of General Conway his master, who is now in his 73d. year.

Many Clergymen have passed through Henley to Oxford & back within two or three days. On the 31st of October an Election came on of a Poetry Professor. Mr. Hurdis, of Magdalen College, author of a Poem called the village curate, was opposed by Mr. Kett, of Trinity College, who lately read the Bampton Lectures. The number of votes were

> For Mr. Hurdis 201
> For Mr. Kett   <u>180</u>
>
>   21

Sunday Novr. 3d.

A beautiful day. Left Henley and returned to Windsor by Braywick. Near Clewer I stopped the Chaise, and made a sketch of Windsor Castle which makes a more beautiful assemblage from this point than from any I have hitherto discovered. What part of the town is seen in this view very happily mixes with the nobler objects and gives additional importance by the contrast of sizes & forms; while the colour of the Brick, which is lowered in its tone by weather & time, and many white buildings interspersed, add greatly to the richness of the colouring and to the spirit of the general effect. No water is seen in this view.

From Henley to Windsor is 16 miles, and from Windsor to Chertsey 10 miles is charged for a chaise, though I do not think it is much more than 8 miles.

We put up at *Mrs. Daniels at the Swan,* where we were before. — *This evening Mrs. Daniells brought me a copy of a letter from Her Son in India, whose tour in that country in company with His Uncle,* has been more extensive than that of any European *Artists* at least.

The following are some of the circumstances mentioned by him. *Mr. Daniels Letter is dated July 30th 1790, Baghulpoor.*

The two Mr. Daniels explored a Country very little known to the Europeans, or even to the natives of Hindostan.

From this excursion they returned about 4 months before the letter was written. Their excursion lasted about 18 months.

They departed from Calcutta about the end of September 1789, soon after the Season of the rains had abated. As the roads at that time were not good they were advised to proceed by water. The eldest Mr. Daniel hired a Pinnace Budgram, roomy and convenient with masts & sails. They were long in getting through the River Cossimbazar, on account of bad winds & strong currents but at last entered the Ganges. The Cossimbazar River is about as wide as the Thames at London Bridge. The Banks decorated with Hindoo Temples and villages.

Much trade is carried on from Cities on the Ganges, by means of this River which makes it alive. When they entered the Ganges they found it from 1 to 3 miles wide. When the rains overflow it, it is double that width. — They were towed by 16 or 20 watermen and went without wind about 2 or 3 miles an Hour; with the wind double that rate. — The Rajimahal Hills appeared in 3 days. Arrived at the City of Rajamahel which 150 or 200 years ago was the Capital of Bengal. — Visited the Ruins of that place and were struck with a new stile of building. — Soon after departing from thence saw a waterfall among the Hills. Abt 3 o'clock in the afternoon fastened the Boat & set of to get a near view. Got to the fall in an Hour & a half. Found it between 30 & 40 feet wide and the precipice over which it dashed abt 220 feet high. Except in the rainy season the water is very inconsiderable but what falls is so clear as to have been called in the Hindoostanie language *Moote Thurna,* or the fall of Pearls. Returned to their boat abt dark.

In a few days reached Baghlepore, situated on the Banks of a small river, which an Island 3 miles wide & 6 long separates from the Ganges. A Resident is here settled to collect the revenues of the district of Rajamahel. Here are a few gentlemens houses with grounds laid out in the English taste. Proceeded to Monghir, a few miles below is a Hot well called Satacoonda, much frequented by the Hindoos who to purify themselves by prayers & oblations, which they Stand in great need of and to pray to the image of Setta the wife of one of their principal Gods.

The water of this well is remarkably good. It is constantly carried to Calcutta for such as are [sick?], there are other wells in the neighborhood but inferior. Mr. Daniels thought the waters of all of them hotter than those at Bath.

Monghir is esteemed the Montpelier of Hindoostan.

Proceeding they in a few days passed Patna, Ghazepoor, & Benares. The 2 former Mussulman Cities of consequence. The latter the first Hindoo City in the world. Idols & Temples of worship very numerous. The numbers who particularly on Holidays go to get purified is incredible. This district is estimated the most fertile in India. From hence in 2 days reached Chunar Ghur, situated on a Rock which juts into the Ganges. Hearing that a party at Cawnpore are about to make the Tour of Agra & Delhi they hired a small boat & pushed forward in 3 weeks reached the place. That party was gone 10 or 12 days before. Heard of another party which was to go from Futty Ghur 80 or 90 miles further up the country in 8 or 10 days. They immediately proceeded to this place in Palankins, & got to Futty Ghur in a day & a night. The Coln. commanding there with 12 or 13 gentlemen were preparing to make the excursion & kindly invited us to be of the Party.

Between Chunar Ghur & Cawnpore about 60 miles from the former place, stands the Fort of Allahabar built by the Emperor Akbar above 200 years ago. It is situated on the Conflux of the Rivers Jumna & Ganges and make a very magnificent appearance. Asoph al Dowla is destroying this noble work and carrying the stones to Lucknow. For a few miles beyond the Fort the Ganges in consequence of a very narrow Channel is so rapid that boats pass it with great danger, and require dextrous management to prevent their upsetting. From hence the Banks of the River begin to be very high, from 20 to 50 feet with wood & villages, all the way to Cawnpore. During the dry Season this celebrated River will scarcely admit a boat that draws 4 feet water to go up it but in the rains is sufficiently deep to float a man of war.

The Party left Futty Ghur and proceeded towards Agra, 15 Europeans whose attendants & Camp followers amounted to near 3000 besides Elephants, Camels, Horses, Bullocks & other beasts of burthen. The usual manner of travelling was to rise about 5 in the morning, to walk till warm, as it is rather cold in Janry & Febry so high up, & then mount Elephants, Horses &c as at hand. Moved about 15 miles which we could do before 9 o'clock & found a breakfast & Tents &c prepared by a guard sent on overnight. In about 6 days arrived at Agra. It is situated on the River Jumna whose Banks for many miles are covered with ruins of Mussulman grandeur. But the principal object is the Tomb of Mumtaza Zemani, or the *most exalted of the age,* the wife of Sha Johan, one of the mogul Emperors who reigned abt 150 years ago. The materials with which this immense octangular building is raised is chiefly marble & the inside inlaid with costly stones. It stands close to the River on a Platform of near 40 feet high & between 2 & 300 feet square. In the 4 corners are placed 4 pyramidical pillars 150 feet high and being open at top were formerly used for assembling people to prayers. In the Center of the building are the tombs of Sha Johan & his Queen. An elegant garden is adjoining to this monument, with fountains. The whole cost £750,000 & was began & finished in 15 years.

There is also a mussulman fort of great magnitude. Between Agra & Delhi the country not long ago was uncommonly beautiful but such destruction has been brought on it by war scarcely a tree or blade of grass is to be seen.

In 14 days from leaving Agra having passed through Muttra where Scindia has had his Camp, reached Delhi, the Capital of Hindostan, but miserably fallen from its former greatness. A Pallace was assigned for their residence but the curiosity of the people to see them obliged them to retire to the skirts of the City.

Delhi is said to be 30 miles in circumference. Of it nothing but ruins of the remains of mosques, pallaces, Tombs & forts which are innumerable. The profusion of marble that is scattered about gives an Idea of its former magnificence. There are still remaining little decayed the Tombs of some of the mogul Emperors. The most mosques which have suffered least are superb beyond description. Black & white marble are the materials with which they are built and the golden Domes that finish their buildings add considerably to their beauty. Handsome gateways & noble flights of steps.

Delhi was the seat of government during the reign of 12 Emperors.

The present inhabited City of Delhi is in tolerable order. They visited a Pillar in the City which measured 242 feet in height from its base. From the top they commanded an extent of 50 miles in circumference, strewed over with heaps of ruins. This pillar has been erected upwards of 750 years yet has suffered from little injury. They staid at Delhi 3 weeks. They got up & breakfasted by sun rise & then went to work.

From Delhi they crossed the Jumna & proceeded to Anopshur the highest settled [place] the English have which they reached in 5 days. They thought they saw the snowy mountains from this neighboroud.

With a guard of 30 Soldiers Mr. Daniel, his nephew, and 4 other gentlemen only, proceeded towards the snowy mountains, 9 days at abt 14 miles a day, and reached Nijiababad, a large City in the country of Rohiland, which Mr. Hastings trial has made well known. The commander a native, shewed them great attention. From hence the first ramp of mountains are distant abt 15 miles & the snowy ones which they saw from Anopshur, abt 10 or 12 days journey, which were just seen from here also.

The commander wrote to the Rajah a prince of Sirinagur, for permission for the party to enter his country. Sirinagur is the capital of a country of that name. As an answer could not arrive in less than 10 or 12 days they visited in the mean time Hurduwar, above 30 miles from Niziibabad, signifying the gate of Heaven in the Hindoo language where the Ganges rushes out of the Hills & enters the plains of Hindostan. Here vast numbers of people assemble from all parts of India to perform ablution & free themselves from impurities, they may have been guilty of.

A great annual fair is held here. It was now a time of one of their festivals when they carry their religious enthusiasm to excess, almost approaching madness. It was supposed 100,000 people were now assembled here. It was attended with some danger to the Europeans, while they were possessed with this Phrenzy.

The Rajahs answer was favorable. Such was the prospect of difficulties to encounter in endeavouring to accomplish this further excursion that 2 of the 4 gentlemen who accompanied Mr. Daniel declined the undertaking. The remainder set of from Nizibabad, and the first day entered a gaut or pass into the mountains and stopped at night at a village called Coajuwar. The difficulties of travelling now appeared so formidable that all their Bengal servants left them, and they hired Hill servants to carry their baggage &c &c. This delayed them some days. A few soldiers are placed at the Gaut to prevent any permissioners from entering the pass without permission from the Rajah.

The 2 first days journey lay up a River course or Nulla, in which fragments of Rocks &c made the passage very difficult. The other 4 days journey over the sides & tops of mountains from which scenes of the grandest kind were exhibited.

They here found the Oak, fir, Beech, willow &c and Rasberry Bush 10 feet high. On their arrival at Sirin[agur] they did not meet with such a reception from the nabob as they expected. He was at war with a neighbouring Prince and seemed desirous of the assistance of the Europeans which they declining He appeared to have an intention of securing their persons, by proposing that they shd cross the River to be removed in case the enemy attacked the City. They saw through the contrivance & finding He cd not obtain his object the Rajah behaved civilly to them 3 days, the time they remained. The inhabitants of the city crowded round their persons to gaze at their novel appearance so as to oblige them to apply to the Rajah for soldiers to keep of the mob. The situation of affairs however prevented their accomplishing the wished for object of visiting the snowy mountains though only 3 or 4 days journey from Sirinaghur, but an enemy so near made it too dangerous. They therefore proceeded on their return towards the plain of Hindostan, by the way of the Gaut which they had entered, after having had the gratification of visiting a Country which no European had ever seen.

After making a circuitous visit to the Cities of [Oudh and Fyzabad] they came down to Lucknow, where the Nabob visited them & expressed his pleasure on seeing the drawings Mr. D. had made & commissioned him to make a set of views about Lucknow, which Mr. D. undertook, & under many disadvantages, it being the rainy season, compleated them, which took him three months. The Nabob recd. them but Mr. D. could never get the smallest retribution for his time & trouble. Mr. D. had not been successful in his endeavours to make a fortune, all admired his works, but little was received from those who expressed it.

Monday, Novr. 4th.

A very wet day. — This morning I read in the paper an account of the death of Mr. Jacob More, Landscape Painter, who died lately at Rome. He went to Italy, I think, in the year 1771. — From his appearance at that time I think He must have been at his death about 54 or 5.

I was informed at Chertsey that Mr. Fox & Mrs. Armstead pass a great deal of their time at St. Anns Hill. Mrs. Armstead is described to be a very agreeable woman, and highly accomplished, and towards 50 years of age. Mr. Fox has a natural Son abt 19 years old, very like him, but unhappily is both deaf and dumb. The Young Man frequently comes to St. Anns Hill to see his Father. Mr. Fox has also a daughter a little girl of 7 or 8 years of age, of whom Mrs. Armstead is very fond though not her daughter. This girl is cross eyed, otherways pretty.

We left Chertsey at 12 o'clock and went by Mr. Woods of Littleton, a clean, pleasant situation, but very flat, to Hounslow, 10 miles. From Hounslow to Charlotte street they charge 13 miles though it is not 10 to Hyde park corner.

I dined with the Offleys at the Percy Coffee House, where George Dance called on me to go to Somerset House, the reception of Sir Francis Bourgeois & Mr. Smirke being fixed for this evening; also the election of two Associates.

There were 25 Academicians present including the new members.
On the first Balot for Associates

Mr. Hoppner	—	13
Beechy	—	13
Gainsborough Dupont	—	3
Hickel	—	1
Malton	—	1
		31

On the second Balot

Beechy	—	13
Hoppner	—	12
		25

On the first Balot to fill the second vacancy

Hoppner	—	23
Dupont	—	4
Graham	—	1
Hickel	—	1
Malton	—	1
		30

On the second Balot

Hoppner	–	23
Dupont	–	4
		27

Two Academicians came in after the first election. — Messrs. Beechy & Hoppner were declared duly elected.

The President read the answer of the Lords of the Treasury relative to Artists being allowed to bring their *own* works Home duty free. The Lords of the Treasury have granted it. Three out of four of the Senior Council of the Royal Academy for the time being, are to inspect at the Custom House, the productions of the artist and to vouch for their appearing to be what He declares them *His own works*. It being expressed that *British subjects* should enjoy this priviledge, Mr. Loutherburgh properly remarked that it ought to be extended to all foreigners, *members of the Royal Academy*. This immediately was concurred in by the Assembly, and will be mentioned to the Lords of the Treasury.

The death of Mr. Serres was declared by the President, — He died this morning, after a very painful illness occasioned by a cancerous complaint in his neck. He was born at Aush in Gascony, and was abt 73 or 4 years of age. Paul Sandby mentioned to me this evening the death of his eldest Son Paul, who died lately at Barbadoes of a fever prevailing there. He was a Lieutenant in one of our Regiments. Mr. Sandby told me his Son had first and last been an expence to him of near £3000. He was a fine young man and well disposed.

I passed the evening at Hamiltons. Lawrence and Mr. Dryander were there.

Tuesday — Novr. 5th.

A very fine morning. — dined with C Offley. — Marchant called on me in the evening.

More, the Landscape painter, had accumulated a fortune of £7000. Part of this was made by buying and selling Pictures. He left Mr. Jenkins, of Rome, Sir James Wright, and Mr. Cooper, the drawing master, of Charles St. St. James's square, his Executors. After providing for some of his relations during their lives He has bequeathed the bulk of his property in reversion to His nephew, Son of his Brother, who keeps a Toy shop in New-street Covent Garden.

Wednesday Novr. 6th.

A fine morning. Rode to Greenwich and made 2 sketches from One tree Hill. Dined at Home. — In the eveng. went with Hamilton to call on Wheatley.

Angelica Kauffman, the Paintress, made abt £14000 while she resided in England. Her application was very constant.

Zucchi made about £8000, while He was in England. — Angelica is abt 48 years of age. Zucchi is near 70 years old.

Mr. Tickel, the celebrated Author of the Pamphlet called Anticipation, published during the American War, and some beautiful pieces of poetry, on Monday last threw himself out of a window of the Attick Story, in the fountain Court of Hampton Court, and dashed the back part of his head to pieces. His Carriage was waiting for him at the time to bring him to the Stamp Office, where He had a place, and Mrs. Tickel, a beautiful woman was in the room. Distressed circumstances and an apprehension of being arrested, it is said was the cause of this momentary phrenzy.

Horace Hamond came from Norfolk.

Hoppner called on me this morning and had a long conversation and He walked with me to Westminster Bridge. I gave him my sentiments abt. the Academy.

Thursday Novr. 7th.

A fine morning. Glass 45. It has been varying between that & 50 some days.

Went to Greenwich & made a drawing including part of the Hospital & Blackwall. Weather too hazy to see London & too cold to remain drawing more than 2 Hours, it was the same yesterday.

Dined at home. H Hamond & C Offley with me.

In the evening Proctor called on me to solicit my vote for his going to Rome, with the Academy allowance of £100 a year for three years, and 30 Guineas to bear his expences thither. — I promised him my vote in consequence of the very ingenious models which He had at different times made, and sent to the Exhibition. — He told me the following members had promised him their votes

Messrs. Banks
        Barry
        Fuseli
        Hodges
        P. Sandby
        Smirke
        Wheatley
        Hamilton
        Wilton
        Cosway
        Bourgeois
        Copley.

Artaud, Howard, and Joseph, are also Candidates for the appointment. —
This day the Antiquarian Society meet the first day of the season.

Friday Novr. 8th.

A Cold morning and hazy. Glass 45. Went to Greenwich and made a
drawing of Flamstead House (the Observatory).

Lysons called on me. He has been employed in Gloucestershire, in
making drawings of the floors of a Roman Villa, discovered near
Rodborough. — I called at the Shakespeare Gallery, and it was
determined by Mr. Combes, to finish the first volume of the History of the
Thames, at Teddington; that being the highest point where the Tide
reaches excepting in extraordinary instances.

This being the first day of the Royal Academy Club meeting I went
there. Twenty two members were present.

Boswell told me it was not by advice of any medical friend that Dr.
Johnson was induced to leave of drinking wine. A constant apprehension
which He had of becoming insane, made him fear the consequence of
continuing the use of it. — Yet He often declared He never had been
known to have been intoxicated, though He said He once at College drank
3 bottles at a sitting. Boswell & Humphrey proposed a small society for the
winter to meet at each others Houses, not to exceed 8 persons. — Boswell,
Humphrey, myself, George Dance, Malone, & Petre were mentioned to
begin with.

Sir Francis Bourgeois entered into a conversation with me relative to the
ensuing election of Academicians, and seemed strongly to reccomend the
claims of Hoppner.

George Dance told me that young Mr. Meyer, the Son of the late Mr.
Meyer, miniature painter, and Royal Academician, has lately destroyed
himself in Calcutta. The cause is unaccountable, as He was much
esteemed, and though very young had made 18 or £20,000.

Saturday Novr. 9th.

A fine morning. Glass 45. — Reinagle called on me to speak in favor of
Howard, a young Artist who had been his Pupil & now at Rome, who
gained the gold medal given by the Royal Academy 4 years ago. He has
been at Rome abt 3 years, and is spoken of as a very ingenious young man
& of gentlemanlike manners. His father is a Coach maker, and resided in
Wardour street, but owing to great losses from having given credit for
carriages to the Count D'Artois, Prince Condé, &c &c. of the French
nobility, has been made a Bankrupt. The Young man being thus deprived
of support, is in a state of necessity, and now applies for the annuity
allowed by the Academy to a Student. — It has been reccomended to
Reinagle to interest himself with the Academicians for a present to be
made to Howard, in case Proctor, or some other shd succeed to the

annuity. — I told Reinagle that Sir Wm. Chambers, as holding the Academy Purse, (being Treasurer) and transacting all business of the kind with the King, would be the proper Person to apply to, and that if He lent a favorable ear, there wld not be I was convinced any opposition on the side of the Academy, to such benefit as might be proposed for Howard. — Reinagle expressed himself as obliged to me & said He wld call on Sir William Chambers.

When I mentioned Proctor to Garvey yesterday, He who is just returned from Rome spoke warmly in favor of Howard, as to his ability & character. At the desire of Yenn yesterday at the Academy Club, I signed the testimonial of Mr. Stirling, Son of Sir Walter Stirling, who is desirous of becoming a member of the Antiquarian Society.

Saturday Novr. 9th[*sic*].

A fine morning. — Went to Fanhams with C Offley & Horace Hamond in a Chaise. — Changed Horses at Hambletons 12 miles, from thence to Fanhams 12 miles. — Two miles are saved by not going to the Inn at Waltham Cross.

Sunday 10.

A very fine day. Rode over to Hoddesdon. Will informed me that the Lascelles was taken up for Bengal on Friday last.

Monday Novr. 11th.

A fine day. Rode to Wades mill, and from thence went round by Mr. Bydes of Ware Park to Ware. Ware Park is very pleasantly situated looking over Hertford and up to Balls, Lord Leicesters.

Tuesday Novr. 12th.

A fine morning a little frosty. The leaves on the trees are less affected by the season as yet than I ever remember them at so advanced a season.

Yesterdays paper gives an acct of the Execution of Brissot and 20 other national Deputies. — Brissot, who 8 months before seemed almost to rule France.

This afternoon returned to Town from Fanham with Mrs. Farington. — The weather proved wet.

Five Chaldron of Coals were sent in on Saturday by Kitchener & Co. which the servants say are very good, — at 48 shillings a Chaldron.

Wednesday Novr. 13th. — 1793.

A fine morning, but windy. Glass above 50. Craig called on me. — Hodges came to Tea. — His Brother in Law, Fountaine, through His reccomendation is appointed Deputy Commissary at Toulon, under Mr. Erskine. — He is to receive as a Salary 15 shillings a day. — to have the rank of Major, — and to have half pay for life of 5 shillings a day. At a certainty his income will be from different causes, near £500 a year. — Probably many contingent advantages.

Beechy has 30 Guineas for a three-quarter Portrait. Romney has the same. — Beechy raised his Price ten Guineas after the last Exhibition.

Thursday Novr. 14.

A very fine day. Glass 51. — A Mr. Eliot called on me for my half years subscription of half a guinea, to the new instituted Society formed for the relief of distrest Artists, their widows & Children.

Mr. Alexander called at the desire of Mr. Boydell, to offer himself as an etcher & Colourer of Prints.

Hamilton called on Wheatleys affairs. A meeting of the Creditors was called on Saturday last who agreed to take the produce of the sale of the effects, and to receive £50 a year from Wheatley till the remainder of the debts is paid. A few only of the Creditors did not attend.

At two o'clock, I rode round by Hampstead & Kilburn wells. — The colours of the trees beautiful, and not yet extravagant in their Tones.

Mr. Bonney called to desire me to attend tomorrow at the Commissioners for paving lighting &c meeting, as it will be proposed to raise his salary from £70 to 100, on acct of increase of business.

Josiah Boydell & Mr. Coombes dined with me.

Coombes informed us of many particulars of the condition & behaviour of the Queen of France after Her condemnation. — When she was carried back from the Tribunal where she had received sentence of death, she requested that she might see her Children, which was refused. From this moment she appeared to have lost her senses, and continued in a state of insanity till her death. In the cart in which she was carried to execution, she took the executioner for the Dauphin & spoke to him as such. She recognised the Thulieries, and wondered she did not see her Children at the windows.

We ultimately settled this evening the subjects for Prints for the first volume of the Rivers. — Combes read to us that part of his History of the Thames which describes Nuneham.

Mr. Baker came in the evening.

Coombes says the Dauphin or rather infant King of France is now under the management of a man who was formerly a Shoemaker, who is directed to instruct him in everything vicious and immoral.

Mr. Baker had a French Gentleman from Valenciennes to dine with him, who expresses no apprehension that the place can be retaken as it must undergo a regular siege. He said a calculation had been made that 30,000 Frenchmen perish every month owing to the War and causes occasioned by it, and that the depopulation began to be felt. The violent resolutions to force woemen to marry was owing to this, as in so unsettled a state of Society, such union was naturally interrupted.

Friday Novr. 15th.

Fair but foggy. — Lysons called this morning at breakfast & shewed me some of the drawings He had made of the Roman floor, composed of figures in mosaick, found at Woodchester, near Rodborough, in Gloucestershire. — In Count Caylus's work published at Paris this floor is noticed, but a few partial pieces only had been discovered, when Lysons, with the aid of some neighbours, had the earth removed so as to show a considerable part of the floor of a principal room. — Further examinations will be made in the Spring. — That part which Lysons has explored is in a Church yard and the earth which covers it is abt 5 feet deep. Many Coffins & quantities of bones were removed to clear the way to the surface of the floor.

I rode to Hampstead. Horace Hamond went in the evening to Lynn. — Today Mr. Bonney had the addition of £30 a year allowed. — Batty called when I settled his Bill. — He spoke highly of the ability of Mr. Carlyle, the opponent of Mr. Moore for the place of Surgeon to the Westminster Hospital. — The Balance I gave Batty on acct of his dressing the Tumour on my Back under the direction of the late Mr. John Hunter, was £5-13.- which with his Bill for medicines made up £12.12.0.

Information came from Paris last night of the death of the Duke of Orleans, who was executed at Paris on the 6th of this month. — He dined with the Prince of Wales, at the Royal Academy a few years since, at one of the great annual Exhibition dinners, & it happened a whole length Portrait of him painted by Sir Joshua Reynolds, was placed above the seat on which He sat on the Princes right Hand. The Picture is a very fine one, a whole length in an Hussar dress, and a remarkable likeness, which every body acknowledged who then had an opportunity of comparing it with the original. — The Picture was painted for the Prince of Wales, and was placed in Carlton House, till the detestable conduct of the Duke in what related to the late King of France, caused the Prince to have it taken down, and it is now in some private appartment in Carlton House. The Prince moved about the same time to have him expelled the Je ne scai quoy Club held at the Star & Garter, which was immediately done & his name scratched out by one of the waiters. — He was 50 years of age, — born in 1743.

Saturday Novr. 16th. 1793.

A dull morning, thick atmosphere. — I rode to Hampstead from two to three o'clock. Called on Mrs. Wheatley. — John Offley dined with us.

The events which are succeeding each other in France, and which posterity will consider with Horror & almost doubt of from their atrocity, are received here as the news of the day; so habituated are we, by repetition, to the shocking accnts received, that the natural effect of a first emotion is weakened. — The situation of the people at large seems every day to become more desperate. The Complaints of want sent from the Cities of Rouen & Nantes show the distress for provisions & the sufferings of the multitude.

Yesterday I recd. a letter from the Commissioners of the Navy, relative to the view of Deptford Yard signed, J. Henslow, Geo: Marsh, Wm. Palmer.

Sunday Novr. 17th.

A dull morning with Rain, which continued through the day. — I did not go out.

In 1788 when I was at the Marquiss of Grahams, (now Duke of Montrose) he told me, when He was abroad and at Paris, He was sometimes of the late Duke of Orleans parties which He made for select number of his acquaintance and that Ladies were included. These assemblies were held at one or other of his country Houses, near Paris. — The Marquiss observed that He never saw a Man so well preserve the dignity of his rank as the Duke did in the midst of scenes of great freedom & voluptuousness.

Monday Novr. 18.

A fair day, but the Atmosphere too thick to see any distance. — In the afternoon I rode into Hyde Park.

More particulars of the death of the Duke of Orleans were this day published.

The accounts from Paris this day mention the condemnation & execution of Madam Roland, wife to Monsr. Roland the late Minister. — Also of the condemnation & execution of M. Bailly, the celebrated Mayor of Paris.

The account of the death of the Duke of Orleans is as follows.

[*A newspaper cutting, from the Courier 18 Nov. 1793, has been pasted into the diary here, and is printed below.*]

THE DUKE OF ORLEANS

The trial of this man occupied only four hours. — When the Act of Accusation was read, he said, "that the day of his Trial would be the happiest of his Life".

— He was sentenced to die at 2 o'clock in the afternoon of the 6th instant, and at four o'clock he was conveyed in a cart to the place of execution.

The eyes of the People were attentively fixed upon him:— He discovered much firmness and composure. The cart stopped by some accident upon the *Place de l'Egalite* before his palace — He surveyed it with much attention, and turned his head to look at it as long as he could. — To the exclamation of indignation and curses bestowed upon him by the People he made no reply, nor did he appear much affected by them. When the cart arrived at the Scaffold, he jumped upon it first, and immediately laid down his head to undergo that punishment to which he was sentenced.

Tuesday Novr. 19th.

A very fine day. Glass 56. — I rode to Deptford yard & called on Mr. White, in the afternoon.

The Revd. Mr. Powys called on me in my absence & left an invitation for me to dine with him at the Chaplains Table at St. James's on Friday at 4 o'clock. — Mr. Powys is Brother to Mr. Powys of Hardwick near Whitchurch in Oxfordshire.

Wednesday Novr. 20th.

Thick hazy day, but fair. — I called this morning on Mr. Heaviside, the Surgeon, in consequence of a letter He adressed to me & Mr. Baker as Executors to the late Mr. Webber. Mr. Heaviside told me He had attended Mr. Webber 9 months and performed many surgical operations, and that it would be a moderate demand if He charged for his trouble 100 Guineas; but that in consequence of the Friendship which subsisted between him & the late Mr. Webber He should only charge 50 Guineas. — I replyed that I would communicate his demand to Mr. Baker & that He should hear from us

Mr. Wm. Hardman of Manchester called on me. — The Picture of Ruth which Opie has painted for him He much admires, but having given a commission to Opie under an Idea that the Picture to be painted was not to exceed £40 Guineas He was surprised at Mr. Opies charge of 100 Guineas. — As I was acquainted with the extent of the commission at the time, He desired me to speak to Opie on the subject.

He mentioned to me a Young Man, the Son of a Cobler at or near Rochdale, who discovers such talents for drawing as to have induced Mr. Hardman to take him into his House & to give him an opportunity of practising drawing, till He can be removed to some other situation more favorable for his improvement.

In the Evening Hamilton called on Wheatleys affairs.

This morning I sent a letter to the Commissioners of the Navy in answer to their letter of Friday last.

Within a few days I had etched the plates of Hardwick & Maple Durham, — Whitchurch, — Junction of Canal & Thames, — and this day finished the etching of Garricks House at Hampton. — As I do not wish to be interrupted when I set down to painting, I advance many Plates together to be a Head of the Aqua tinters.

Thursday Novr. 21st.

A very fine day for the season. After breakfast I rode out, and passed through Highgate, by Caen wood, to Hampstead. The ride at a moderate rate in an hour and a half. — Lord Stormont is making considerable & in respect of architectural effect strange additions to the late Lord Mansfields house at Caen wood.

The trees are now generally much thinned or without leaves. Such as remain have the colours of Autumn carried to excess.

This day I begun & completed the etching of the view of Henley including Mr. Freemans. I can see to work between 8 & 9 in the morning, but in the afternoon it grows dark before 4 o'clock.

I recd. a letter today from Mr. Davenport of Court Garden, inclosing his account of that place for the use of Mr. Coombes.

Coombes also wrote to me reccomending the introduction of a view of Carfax, which He thinks necessary to explain his text. Carfax is the piece of antiquity which Lord Harcourt removed from Oxford and placed at Newnham, when a Plan of improvement of the streets of Oxford required it shd be taken down.

The Glass today 56.

Friday Novr. 22.

A fine day. — I called this morning on Fuseli relative to Mr. Hardmans picture of Falstaff in the Buck Basket painted by him. Afterwards on Opie to settle abt. the price of the picture of Ruth painted by him for Mr. Hardman. Mr. Hardman not expecting to pay so much as 100 Guineas for the Picture, Opie in consideration of a mistake in this respect only charges 90 Guineas. The Frame cost £14-17s.

When Mr. Hardman called I gave him my opinion on seeing the drawings of the young man who He is desirous of bringing forward. His age is 20 and the drawings very well considering the opportunities He has had, but trifling if compared with his age & what must be learned. — I told Mr. H. that engraving was the most certain branch. That if He was to be pushed forward in Painting the best course to pursue wd. be to place him in a Lodging at as easy an expence as possible, to get him introduced to Artists who would occasionally lend him Pictures to copy and to introduce him into the Academy as soon as He was prepared to study there. — That if He was to be an Engraver confine his views to that branch of the Art only, and not to divide his attention or expect him to change from an Engraver to be a Painter.

I dined today with the Revd. Mr. Powys & Dr. Fisher, at the Chaplains table. Three other Gentlemen were present.

The King has laid out since He first began to build what is called the Queens Lodge at Windsor, £70,000, in building and in various expences attending the making that place what it at present is. — The King, as is common enough, was led on from little to more, having begun that building with no other design than occasionally for him & the Queen to sleep at whenever He might Hunt in that neighboroud or make an excursion, and finds it too late for them conveniently to return to Kew or the Queens Palace in the evening. The King told Dr. Fisher, if he could have foreseen that Windsor would be their chosen residence He would have prepared the Castle & resided in it.

The King, before He built the Queens Lodge, offered the late Duke of Cumberland Six Thousand a year to give up the Rangership & House which He held of Windsor Park. The Duke refused this advantageous offer, which it was in point of income.

Mr. Powys was Tutor to Lord Bayham, & recd. part of his preferment from Lord Camden. — He said that Dr. Warren told him within a few days, that Lord Camden was so recovered of late & seemed to possess so much internal strength that He thought He might reasonably be expected to live three or 4 years longer.

At the Chaplains Table it is the custom to dine at 4, and to break up company abt 7, as no Tea or Coffee is provided. — I went to the Royal Academy Club to Tea.

A conversation had taken place after dinner brought on by Mr. Tyler as to the propriety of commemorating the 25th year from the institution of the Royal Academy. After Tea the subject was renewed and being supported by Mr. West etc. It concluded with a motion being made by Mr. Tyler, & seconded by Mr. Catton, that Mr. West, the President, be desired to call a general meeting of *all* the members of the Royal Academy, to meet at the Royal Academy on Tuesday Decr. 3d. to consider whether any commemoration shall be, & if resolved on, in what manner it shall be conducted. This motion was signed by

Messrs. Tyler
       Bigg
       Catton
       Marchant
       Nollekens
       F. Bourgeois
       Garvey
       Boswell
       Smirke
       Farington
       Rooker
       Richards

Messrs. Hoppner & Beechy were present but not having received their Diplomas, did not sign.

Mr. West assisted in settling the form of resolution.

Saturday — Novr. 23rd.

A fine day. Glass 55. — George Dance called & shewed me some ludicrous correspondence with George Hardinge, on the subject of his Portrait & a threatened Caricature. — Dr. Fisher called & sat with me some time.

The improvements & decorations of Windsor cathedral have cost £20,000, of which the King has paid £13,000. — For some years, 50 pounds a year has been paid from the income of each of the Canons towards carrying on these improvements. Forrester, who is now executing the stained Glass, since Jervais declined doing it, has an annuity for life of £200, settled on him by the King.

Remarks are made at Windsor that the President does not go there as usual. *He says* it is to prevent that envy which arose from seeing Him there so often & so noticed.

Wyatt designed the decorations at Frogmore for the entertainments given by the Queen. He was paid by the Queen: but the King was so well pleased with the effect of his designs that His Majesty presented Wyatt with a watch as a mark of his Royal approbation.

Yesterday & today I etched the Plates (outlines) of Bisham Abbey from Court Garden, — and the windings of the Thames below Culham.

Yesterday I recd an unfavourable acct. of the situation of D. Whittakers affairs.

Sunday Novr. 24.

Wind easterly & a bleak day. Glass 53. — Sat this morning to George Dance, who is not satisfied with the last sketch He made of me. — Rooker also sat. The likeness of him admirable; & that begun of me superior to any of those He has already done.

Mr. White, from Deptford dined with me.

The average Price of men of War cannot be estimated as formerly at £1000 a gun, which when fitted out completely for Sea, was supposed to have been the expence. If any Ships cannot [can] be supposed to come near it, 74 gun ships do. The advanced Price of stores of every kind has raised considerably the expence of building and fitting out Ships.

The *Hull* of a 74 gun Man of War costs about £30,000, the standing rigging about £16,000 more, including masts. — *Hulls* of Ships of 100 Guns are calculated at abt £50,000.

Hulls of Frigates of 36 Guns at about £9,000.

Common Shipwrights *now* in the *Merchants yards* get from 10 to 16 shillings a day, owing to the great demand for workmen, so many East & West Indiamen, Frigates &c are now building and repairing. By the end of January next it is supposed this great demand will cease.

There are about 500 Shipwrights in Deptford Yard.

In the evening I called on Fuseli.

Fuseli went from England to Italy in 1772; and returned to England in 1780. — On his return He passed through Swisserland where He remained several months.

George Steevens, Editor of Shakespeare, is now making a collection of Portraits of all Persons who have been connected with the works of Shakespeare, by Painting subjects taken from his works, or by having served in a literary capacity to illustrate or explain passages in any of his Plays.

This eving I recd. from Bulmer the Printer the 192d page of Coombes's History of the Thames.

Monday Novr. 25. 1793.

Bleak morning, wind East. Glass 50. Mr. Hardman of Manchesters new room, to serve as a music room & to arrange Pictures in, is an Oval, 44 feet long, and 24 feet wide, and 18 feet high.

Letter from Dick. — The Tea came right, above 30 pounds of it.

Opie came to Breakfast.

Boydell called, has recd a letter from Brand, with a present for each of us of his publication.

Horace Hamond returned to Town from High House.

Fuseli sent the Picture of Falstaff in the Buck Basket, for Mr. Hardman.

In the evening I went to Opies. The company consisted of Mr. Smith, Miss Beevor & two Misses Booth, daughters of Mr. Booth of the Adelphi who posesses more pictures painted by Wilson than any person I know of.

Opie has bought a three quarter picture painted by Sir Joshua Reynolds, for which He gave to the Proprietors of the Polygraphic Manufactory 60 Guineas. — The subject a Girl resting on her arms. — Opie thinks Sir Joshua was the greatest colourist that we have any knowledge of by their works, including the Italian & Flemish masters.

Tuesday Novr. 26th.

Wind continuing Easterly. Glass abt 50. Weather rather bleak & dry.

Lysons, called on me. He put up the name of George Dance at the Antiquarian Society on Thursday last. Sir Joseph Banks &c signed the Certificate.

The Town is in anxious expectation of hearing from Lord Howe, who was left last week in pursuit of a French Fleet of 6 or 7 Sail of the Line.

Smirke, Hoppner & Batty drank tea with me. Hoppner dwelt much on the general bad taste which prevails in this country. That the silly poetry of Della Crusca &c-&c the works of Angelica &c in painting have captivated the publick so as to corrupt the taste. I could not join him in the length He went on this subject. — He contemplates the works of Sir Joshua Reynolds with reverential respect. — Hoppner from his own account was born in London.

Wednesday Novr. 27 — 1793.

Wind easterly. — Glass 50. Dry weather but the aspect of it as before bleak.

I went down to the Shakespeare Gallery at one o'clock & met Coombes & George Steevens. We settled the Titles of some of the Prints of the views on the Thames, & I gave Coombes Mr. Davenports acct of Court Garden.

At 4 o'clock I dined as Dr. Fishers guest at the Chaplains Table. Mr. Powys made the third person. The Person who prepares the Table for the Chaplains informed them that Sir Francis Drake, Master of the Household, had given notice that henceforward neither Champaigne, or Burgundy, would be allowed at *any* of the Tables, except his Majestys. The Plea is the difficulty & uncertainty of obtaining it from France in the present distracted state of that Country. Claret, Hock, Madeira, & Port are still to be allowed, though it is probable Claret may soon be withdrawn.

The King has great pleasure in Prince Adolphus, and warm hopes of him. — He is spoken of very favorably.

Lady Augusta Murray daugr to the Countess of Dunmore, abt whom & Prince Augustus there has been much report is certainly returned to England, and pregnant by the Prince. The Countess followed him to different places in Italy, and when the danger & impropriety was hinted to her seemed insensible of it. Lady Augusta is 10 years older than the Prince. — The Duchess of Devonshire is said to have endeavoured to keep the Prince out of the snare, and He is generally considered as having been drawn into it. — The King was acquainted with the connexion by one of the gentlemen who travelled with the Prince, it is believed by Count Munster, who very honorably shewed the Prince the letter He had written to the King on the Subject. — The Prince is to go to Lisbon in 10 days to avoid the severity of the winter.

Today Hoppner borrowed Six drawings from me which I have made of Boats that are in use at Hastings.

Today I compleated my arrangement of subjects for first volume of Thames.

Mr. Kent, who has the management of Windsor Park under the King, says it will yield his Majesty £18000 a year. Before this Plan was adopted it was an expence to the King. — Mr. Kent devotes the first week in every month to the management of this concern. There is no Steward in the case; everything is settled personally with his Majesty.

Thursday Novr. 28th.

A very dull day: so thick the weather I could scarcely do anything. Glass 50. Susan very indifferent and confined to the Bedchamber, by a cold got on Sunday last.

Dr. Fisher breakfasted with me. I afterwards introduced him to George Dance, while Mr. Powyss was sitting.

In a conversation which Dr. Fisher heard the King hold with Mr. Wilson, one of the Canons of Windsor, who was Tutor to Mr. Pitt & Lord Chatham, the King remarked that Lord Chatham wrote in a clearer & better stile than Mr. Pitt. — Speaking of publick & private education the King mentioned them as instances of latter mode succeeding. Mr. Wilson related that the late Lord Chatham requested that his two Sons should not after the usual manner be required to make Themes. Such exercises He considered as unnecessary strains of the mind. His maxim was, store them with a variety of knowledge and leave it to their particular powers to use it as they might be able. — The King observed that the late Lord Chatham was not a competent judge of composition, and wrote but indifferently.

Mr. Hardman called on me this afternoon, and desired me to settle with Opie for the two Pictures, which I did in the evening, paying him 100 Guineas for the Pictures & £14-17 for the Frame of Ruth.

Lysons dined with me, but I did not go to the Antiquarian Society on acct. of Susans illness.

The Bishoprick of Gloucester is worth no more than £1200 a year. That of Bristol not £800 and in Dr. Wilsons time not £600.

Friday Novr. 29th. 1793.

Dull weather but dry. I continue employed in Tinting & washing up outlines of views on the Thames.

Dr. Wolcot, Opie, and Mr. Taylor the Occulist dined with me.

In a conversation on Political Constitutions the Dr. steadily maintained that A King & Lords were essential parts in a good government and less liable to corruption than the third estate, the Commons. — That the Political distinction between the Lords and the commons placed the former at a distance which causes them to be more neutral judges than it is likely they would be, or than has ever been found where equality or rather the name of it has been boasted.

Speaking of Poetical Characters, Dr. Wolcot gave his opinion in favor of Dr. Young, author of the night thoughts, as next in Poetical power to Shakespeare, that is of the Poets of this country.

Taylor mentioned Mrs. Billington the Singer. She has accumulated abt £10,000, and has settled £5000 of it, on her Husband, — She is lately gone abroad, as it is supposed to meet Mr. Bradyll.

Dr. Wolcot & Taylor went away between 9 & 10, — Opie sat with me till 12. — As the subject of Mr. Bromleys book was brought forward by him, I mentioned to him what passed between Mr. West, Bromley & myself on that subject, but I also told him I did not wish it to be made publick though I was perfectly satisfied with what I had done. — He expressed great pleasure on hearing that I had when called upon by Mr. Bromley given him my sentiments freely. — He said that Copley had applied to him on the night of the election of Associates to know if He would approve of a motion that the Book shd. not be recd into the Academy Library. Opie told Copley He would second such a motion if Copley made it. — It was postponed on act of the business of the night taking up much time.

Saturday Novr. 30th.

Glass 50. Weather dry but not clear. Wind easterly. — Employed in washing up outlines of Rivers.

Mr. Steers called & brought a Mr. Henderson of the Adelphi, a lover of the Arts. — Artaud, a candidate to go abroad with the Academy pension left his name.

This day I sent of in a case Mr. Berwicks 1, 2, 3, 4th Nos. of Shakespeare with the small Prints of Nos. 3 & 4 and the *Books* of No. 3 & 4 — also his framed Print of Lord Chatham, and Stadlers *Book* imitations. — 2 Nos. of Cities, & Lysons Nos. of antiquities of Gloucestershire. — The Shakespeare in one Portfolio, the various Prints in another. — They went by the waggon from the George, Smithfield.

Doctor Fisher told me that after the Duke of Yorks appointment to be Commander in Chief in Flanders, Mr. Pitt, waited on him, and requested to know what his Royal Highness proposed as a sum to defray the expence of his Table. The Duke mentioned £5000 a year, Mr. Pitt replied that He thought £6000 should be the sum, and that He would answer His Royal Highnesses drafts to the amount.

Horace Hamond went to High House. — Charles Offley & John called in the evening. Mrs. Offley agrees to make the Town House theirs & to consider the Country House only as belonging to her, which will be for their mutual advantage.

The People have been waiting this week in expectation of hearing from Lord Howe, whose situation with that of 6 or 7 French men of war has been known 8 or 9 days.

DECEMBER 1793

Sunday Decr. 1st.

Dirty weather with small rain. Glass 49. — Taylor of Hatton Garden called on me this morning and sat a considerable time. He brought with him some Poems written by Mrs. Robinson, one of them *on Sight* dedicated to him. He says Mrs. Robinson is abt 38 years of age. — Colonel Tarlton does not now live with her, but is very often at her House in St. James's Place.

Horne Tooke is inveterate against the French since the murder of Brissot & other members of the Convention.

Taylor is much acquainted with Mrs. Siddons. She related to him the singular behaviour of Coombes towards her when He was at Newnham in July last. — Not acknowledging her at first, and becoming suddenly at the Spinning Feast attentive to her. — I told him the first shyness of Coombes might rise from his having described her in His "Devil on two Sticks", as penurious in the extreme. That his consciousness might make him distant in his manner.

Mrs. Siddons speaking to Taylor on the subject of the attack on her as being miserly, said she could not have expected it. She shd not have been surprised if from a shyness of manner she had been called *proud*; but knew no ground on which the other accusation could be founded. — She was by education and necessity made careful, but that had never led her into meanness.

I gave Taylor according to promise a sketch of the Eagle Tower of Carnarvon Castle.

This evening Landseer, the Landscape Engraver, called on me to speak in favor of Artaud, one of the Academy Candidates to go to Rome.

Susan, after having been confined to her Room by a Cold 3 days, came down to dinner today.

Monday Decr. 2d.

A fair day, but dirty. Glass 50.

Called this morning on Steers in the Temple, and went with him to Mrs

Mortimers to raffle for the Picture painted by Mortimer, the subject Bacchanalians. The Picture I remember him to have painted & I think about the year 1770. — The Size 5 feet 6 Inches by 4 feet. The design formed after the model of Nicolo Poussin. The Price set upon it was 150 Guineas. There were 29 subscribers at 5 Guineas each. It was settled that whoever threw the highest number shd. pay Mrs. Mortimer for the remaining chance 5 Guineas, which wd make up the sum 150 Guineas. The Duke of Norfolk, a subscriber, not being present, Mrs. Pigot, wife of Counsellor Pigot, threw for him first, and the number proving 49 it carried the prize; the next highest number being 45 which I threw for Dr. Pitcairne & the 3d highest number 40, I threw for Mr. Hardman. — By desire of Mr. Hardman I threw for him, Mr. Daulby & Mr. Lee Philips. — Mortimer exhibited the Picture of the Iron Man in 1778.

Mr. Carey stated to me this afternoon a misunderstanding of Mr. Wilton with regard to his being admitted into the *Life* Academy, to which a week since, Mr. Wilton & Mr. Bartolozzi the visitor, consented. The Council directed Mr. Wilton to order the attendance of Mr. Carey upon them at the next meeting.

Mrs. Wheatley called this evening on acct of Furmage the Collector having applied to her for Taxes.

This night I delivered the washed up outlines of Whitchurch, — Mr. Garricks villa, — and Junction of Thames & Canal, to Mr. Stadler for him to proceed with.

Bulmer sent me the Proof sheet up to Page 205, of the History of the Thames.

Mr. Barroneau who I met at Mrs. Mortimers desired me to put him down as a Subscriber to the History of the Thames.

Tuesday Decr. 3d.

Weather colder & fair. Glass 44. Washing outlines. — Rode out to Hampstead.

A Summons came from the Academy for the general meeting on Tuesday next Decr. 10th. — Besides electing the Officers, a student is to be elected to go to Italy. The Candidates are

Thomas Proctor
William Artaud
Henry Howard
George Francis Joseph

In the evening Dance drank Tea with me and we went together to the Royal Academy meeting called for the purpose of considering in what manner the 25th year of the institution shall be commemorated.

Members of the Royal Academy present —

Mr. West — President.

Associates	Academicians	
Edwards	Messrs. Tyler	
Rooker	Wilton	
Bonomi	G. Dance —	
Tresham	P. Sandby	
Stothart	Copley	
Hoppner	Garvey	
Bigg	Nollekens —	
Reinagle	Burch	
Marchant	Opie	
	Northcote —	
	Cosway —	
	Banks	
	Fuseli —	
	Bacon	
	Humphry	
	Bourgeois	
	Yenn	
	Richards	
	Russell	
Associate Engravers	Hamilton	*Professors*
Hayward	Farington	Boswell
Collier		Sheldon

After the President had declared the purpose of the meeting, Mr. Tyler rose & read the motions which he proposed to make, the substance of which was Viz:

That the 25th year shall be commemorated
That it shall be commemorated in the House of the Royal Academy and the expence paid out of the fund.

Much conversation took place. It was proposed to address the King *in the Shape of a motion*, to obtain his majestys consent for the use of the Rooms & that the fund might bear the expence. — Mr. Copley observed that the mode proposed wd be witht example, that it had been customary for the Society to pass such resolutions as were approved & that as a matter of course if his majesty disapproved such resolutions He wd cancel them. That it would be dangerous to establish a precedent which would subject the Academy to difficulties whenever it may be judged necessary to appropriate any money for particular purposes. — I objected to the proposal for an "adress to his majesty desiring his permission to make use of the Rooms

of the Academy, & that the expences should be defrayed out of the Fund",
on the ground that it would be placing His Majesty in a situation not
becoming us to do, as to *directly refuse*, must appear ungracious, & that
would be the only alternative if His Majesty shd not think prudent to
sanction the proposal. — Mr. West supported the Idea of a direct adress.
Mr. Edwards against making use of the Societies money for what we were
not authorised to do. Messrs. Opie & Northcote for making use of it. —
This subject was discussed from ½ past 8 till 12 when many members
having withdrawn it was judged prudent by those remaining to take it up
again on Tuesday the 10th at the general meeting, and not to proceed
further at present.

As to the mode of comemorating, Mr. Boswell made a very good speech
on the necessity of doing it in a becoming manner, and He thought unless it
was altogether an Academical act to be recorded, to be celebrated in the
Rooms of the Academy & the expence borne by the fund, it would be little
better than a Club commemoration. — His speech was very well received.
— Mr. West declared for an Exhibition of the works of dead & living
artists, members of the Academy, and a publick breakfast. — The
difficulties & disadvantages attending this proposal struck me & many
other members.

After the meeting broke up G. Dance, Boswell, Hoppner, Hamilton, &
myself went to Holylands Coffee House.

Before the meeting I spoke to Mr. Bartolozzi & Mr. Wilton on the
subject of the complaint made by the latter of the conduct of Mr. Carey.
Mr. Bartolozzi has acted consistently. Mr. Wilton very much otherways. I
afterwds. spoke to Mr. West on the subject, who reccomended that Mr.
Carey shd attend the Council, where the matter wd. be cleared up, and it
wd. appear who was in the wrong.

Wednesday Decr. 4th.

A Cold day. Glass 42. — Fair weather. Washing outlines. — Miss Offley
called & talked with me sometime on the subject of the misunderstanding
between her Brothers & the Salisburys. — I told her my mind fully.

In the evening I drank Tea with Lysons at his Chambers.

George Steevens is the Son of the late Admiral Steevens. He is judged to
be abt. 60 years of age.

His dislike to Mrs. Siddons & Kemble is owing to their not approving
his conduct towards their Sister Miss Kemble, now Mrs. Twiss. His
behaviour was so unexplained that it was judged necessary by them to
communicate their sentiments on it. — This separated them.

Under the title of *Zoilus*, Murphy exhibited a character of Steevens,
who he discovered had wrote against his works, though they lived together
as friends.

Steevens is supposed to be the author of the following lines, on Mr.

Hayley & Miss Seward of Lichfield complimenting each other in a fulsome manner.

Epigrammatick dialogue.

She

Tuneful Poet, Britains glory,
Mr. Hayley, that is *you*;

He

Ma'am you carry all before you,
Trust me Lichfields Swan you do.

She

Ode didactic, Epic, Sonnet,
Mr. Hayley, your divine;

He

Ma'am I'll take my Oath upon it
You alone are all the nine.

Decr. 5th.

A Hazy day. Glass 43. After breakfast I rode round by Highgate, Caen wood & Hampstead.

Taylor called on me & read some Poetical Letters which He had recd. from Mrs. Robinson & Col. Tarleton. Mrs. Robinson is supposed to have an annuity from the Prince of Wales of £500 a year.

Mrs. Offley called & talked of the approaching change in her family. She proposed to give up Ormond St. to her Sons.

Today I finished washing the outlines of Bisham Abbey & Cirencester.

Decr. 6th.

Hazy day. Glass 44. — This morning I rode by Hampstead & Caen wood & Highgate. Miss Offley called.

I was employed in etching outlines.

At the Royal Academy Club I conversed with Bonomi & Hamilton relative to Marat, — Bonomi said Zucchi became acquainted with Marat at Old Slaughters Coffee House, St. Martins Lane, where many foreigners were accustomed to assemble. It was abt. the year 1767 or 68. — Marat appeared to Bonomi at that time to be about 33 years of age. He was called Doctor Marat, and never professed himself to be in any but the *Physical line*. His object appeared to be improving himself by consulting the practise in different Countries. In 1774 He went to Edinburgh and returned in 1775. He there took a degree or said He did. — He was born at

4–8 DECEMBER, 1793

109

Neufchatell. Bonomi's description of Marat exactly corresponded with that given me by Hamilton. While He resided in this Country in what related to Politicks, He was what was called a Wilkite, and was very eager in defending in conversation all opposition to government. — Marat lodged in St. Martins Lane. — Zucchi had the highest opinion of his abilities. Being a man of extensive classical reading Marat continually proposed Subjects which He had selected for Zucchi to design.

Hamilton became the Pupil of Zucchi in 1768, & remained with him some years. — He was then upwards of 16 years old & had been in Italy. Hamiltons earliest studies were in the Architectural line.

Russell this evening invited Hamilton & myself to come on Monday next, and see his drawing of the moon.

From the Club I went to Mrs. Offleys, & took leave of Miss Offley.

Saturday Decr. 7th.

A Heavy morning & wet day. — I took my outlines to G: Dances having appointed to meet Mr. Steevens & Coombes there. Dance made very like drawings of them.

Garrick made a will very much exceeding his real fortune. In estimating the value of some of his property He added all He might have laid out upon it to the first expence, & reckoned the whole together. His property might be abt £50,000 and He reckoned it at more than £100,000. Garrick had read but little.

Sunday Decr. 8th.

Hazy day. Glass 45. — Called on Dance.

Palmer, who was Comptroller of the Post Office & Pearce, one of the Secretaries of the Admiralty, called while I was there.

Palmer has now £3000 a year allowed to him from the Treasury in lieu of the appointment from which He has been removed. But He considers it not as a compensation for what was taken from him, and which government had in a manner contracted to give him if his scheme of mail Coaches fully succeeded, which it had done beyond expectation. — Mr. Palmer considers himself as having a right agreeable to the engagement to at least £5000 a year.

Palmers interest in the Corporation at Bath may probably cause him to be elected a member for that city if Lord Bayham vacates the seat.

Sheldon, the surgeon, Professor of Anatomy in the Royal Academy, came to sit for his Profile.

Parson Este, is the son of an apothecary who lived in Craven St. Strand. Este when a young man was intended to pursue the medical line, & attended the Hospital where Sheldon dissected.

In the evening Hearne & Baker called.

Monday Decr. 9th — 1793.

Heavy, loaded air. Glass 49.

I wrote to Mr. Davenport, of Court Garden, Marlow, acknowledging the receipt of his letter & acct of that place &c., and that I had delivered it to Mr. Coombe.

I called on Opie who began a three quarter Portrait of me.

In the evening the Revd. Mr. Gardner of Battersea called on me relative to a Lawsuit He is likely to have with Mr. Hatfield, a neighbour, who He sues for payment of a painted deception to be erected in Mr. H's garden. The Price Mr. Gardner charged was 12 guineas. Mr. Hatfield has paid into court 5 Guineas.

The Town was this evening alarmed by the firing of the Park & Tower guns. Everybody expecting that it was in consequence of Lord Howes having taken the French Ships He was left chacing were disappointed on finding the Guns were fired on acct of our troops in the West Indies having gained possession of part of the Island of St. Domingo. As the publick attention was not directed to that object, it was less felt on acct of Lord Howes returning unsuccessfull.

I wrote this evening to Sir William Chambers to inform him it was the intention of a few members of the academy to celebrate the completion of the 25th year of the institution of the Royal Academy, by dining together at the Bedford Coffee House, and to go from thence to the meeting at the Royal Academy.

Hamilton called on me, and we went together to Russells to Tea, and were highly gratified by seeing the different representations He has made of the appearance of the Moon. — Russell told us He had been about 7 years engaged in this undertaking, and that He could say He had during that time devoted 6 Hours out of 24 calculating an average number, in experiments, in drawing or in making calculations. He described to us manifest errors in the representations which have been given by others. That of Cassini is very incorrect, — & that of Mayer exhibits no knowledge of the librations.

Russell married the Sister of Mr. Faden, the Printseller, the corner of St. Martins Lane, in the Strand.

I etched part of the view from Whiteheads Oak at Neunham.

Tuesday — Decr. 10th.

A fine day. Glass 49. — This morning I called on Dr. Reynolds who reccomended to me to go to Bath for Six weeks. He considers the nervous complaints as owing to a debility in the stomach which those waters are likely to strengthen.

Opie proceeded with the Portrait of me.

I dined at the Bedford Coffee House with

	Messrs.	Tyler		
		P. Sandby		
		G. Dance		Rooker
Academicians		Zoffany	Associates	Lawrence
		Smirke		Westhall
		Hamilton		

Opie came after dinner.

Between 7 & 8 the Academicians went to the Royal Academy to attend the General Meeting.

Before the regular business of the evening was brought forward Copley entered on the subject of the Revd. Mr. Bromleys History of the Arts, which He condemned as unfit to be deposited in the Library of the Academy. He proposed two motions, of condemnation & expulsion of the Book. Opie seconded the motions; but after a tedious conversation which took up two Hours, the subject was adjourned till the next general meeting for the purpose of giving time to such members as are not acquainted with the contents of the Book, to read it.

The Silver medals were then adjudged.
That for a drawing of an Academy figure was given to — Durand.

That for an Architectural
drawing of Lansdowne House to } — Philips

That for the model of an
academy figure to } John Bacon son of the Sculpter aged 17

A Balot then took place to appoint a Student to go to Italy, when

Thomas Proctor had	19 votes
William Artaud	— 1
Henry Howard	— 4
George Francis Joseph	— 0

	votes
On the second Balot Proctor had	19
Howard	4
	————
majority	15

Mr. Rigaud then came forward earnestly reccomending that the Academy should grant an Annuity to Howard, as had been done once in the case of two Sculpters. The character, ingenuity & difficult circumstances of Howard merited such assistance. This Question was adjourned till the next general meeting. — Howard is now in Rome.

A Balot then took place for a President when Mr. West was unanimously elected.

5 visitors	New Council
Barry	Bourgeois
Banks	Smirke
Bacon	Loutherburgh
Smirke	Zoffany
Hamilton	

Mr. West stated that He had had an *audience* of his majesty who was graciously disposed to permit a celebration of the 25th year of the institution to be observed in such a manner as the Academy thought fit. — Barry spoke vehemently against the injudicious reference to the King, observing that such a precedent wd tie up the Society in future from passing any vote till His Majestys will shd be known, & consequently the independence of the Body would be at an end, it also appeared to him unbecoming in respect for the Academy to solicit his majesty in such manner.

Mr. West said a second meeting of all the members of the Academy would be called on Tuesday the 19th [17th] inst. when a Plan for the celebration wd. be laid before them.

The meeting at the Academy did not break up till past 12 o'clock, when Hamilton, Smirke & myself went to the Bedford Coffee House where we found Tyler, Zoffany, Rooker, Boswell, Dance, Lawrence & Westhall. We staid till 4 in the morning.

Wednesday Decr. 11th.

Wet day. Glass 49. — Recd a letter from Sir Willm Chambers expressing his concern at being prevented by indisposition from meeting our Party at the Bedford Coffee House.

Today I sat to Humphrey for a Portrait in Crayons.

The Duke of Dorset told the Revd. Mr. Humphreys that the Duchesses fortune was £140,000 & Lady Strathavens £120,000.

The Duke is now supposed not to live at a greater expence than 4 or £5000 a year, having very much curtailed his expences, though his income is encreased. He will be 48 years old in March next.

Humphrey dined with me, also young Randal from Eaton on his way to Norwich. — Mr. Baker called in the evening with the Copy of a Letter to Henry Webber on the subject of Heavisides demand.

Thursday Decr. 12.

Dull day. Glass 58. Weather mild. — Wet evening. employed in etching. Delivered to Stadler the washed outlines of Bisham Abbey, and Cirencester.

Bissell, the Apothecary, called on me, desiring me to take Tickets for a Play to be represented at the Lyceum, I took one Ticket & gave him a guinea.

George Dance & Tyler called.

Sir Joseph Banks & Lysons called, and I showed them the sketches I had made at Valenciennes. Sir Joseph had his feet inclosed in large Stuff Shoes yet stood the whole time of his stay, as He said to avoid too much indulgence. — *Accuracy* of drawing seems to be a principal reccomendation to Sir Joseph.

In the evening I went to the Antiquarian Society. Owen Salusbury Brereton in the Chair.

Among other papers one from Mr. Riddle of Glenriddle was read, on the subject of Stone Hatchets & Pike points, the arms of the savage inhabitants of this Island as of those of the New Zealanders. His description was illustrated by drawings.

From the Society I went to Lysons chambers, where after the Royal Society broke up Mr. Planta joined us.

Proctor, called on me to express his thanks for my vote & interest at his late election.

Friday Decr. 13th.

Wet morning. — Glass 59. — Day afterwards fine.

Today I began to dead colour the upright view at Bruges with the Town Hall & another High building. — The first time of setting my Pallet since I returned from Valenciennes, owing to my engagement in the views of the Rivers.

Banks called in the evening. I told him my opinion was strong against a Commemoration Exhibition. He said, when it was first proposed He was inclined to it, but that He had heard reasons urged against it which induced him to change his opinion. He brought forward the subject of the next Election of Academicians, & strongly reccomended Hoppner to be one, as to the other two, if Hoppner was supported, He was open to decide in favor of such as might be proposed to him in preference. I told him I had not yet determined how I should vote; that the list of Associates contained so many names of able Artists there could be no fear of improper persons being elected, and that little I believed had as yet been said on the subject among the Academicians; that there were names however before which I shd. certainly give a preference to Hoppner, but at present I was not prepared to bind myself to anything.

Marchant came & staid the evening. He related the origin how the permission for young British Artists who may have studied in Italy, came to possess the indulgence of bringing their works duty free into this country. The late Lord Camelford was the great mover of this business. Marchant the person who first instigated his Lordship to interest himself in it.

Saturday — Decr. 14th.

Mild weather. Glass 59.
I proceeded in dead colouring the Bruges views.

Sunday Decr. 15th.

Weather dull. Glass 55.
This morning Rigaud called on me. He strongly reccomended the Case of Howard who is now at Rome as worthy of the notice & support of the Academy. That his Fathers affairs were in a tottering state when He went to Italy, owing to disappointments in payments from France for Coaches &c which He had made for various of the French nobility before the revolution. Howard gained the Premium for Historical painting & the silver medal for an Academy figure, in the year 1788. Sir Joshua Reynolds delivered the medals to him with a particular Compliment.

I told Mr. Rigaud I would do all in my power to assist him in this business by speaking to Humphrey, Copley, & Yenn, 3 of the Council. The settlement of this business must be in the Council.

Mr Rigaud seems of opinion that a Commemoration Exhibition is not an adviseable measure.

At 12 o'clock I called on Dance. Soon after Taylor & Mrs. Robinson & Her daughter came. Dance began a drawing of Mrs. Robinson. She invited Dance & myself to Tea with her at her house in St. James's Place, on Thursday next.

Charles Offley & Minet dined with me.

Major Le Merchant, called with Carey while I was out & left his name.

Mrs. Robinson was at the Baths of St. Amand 3 months in 1787, but derived no benefit from the use of them. Out of a number of persons who made use of them at that time, she only took notice of one, an officer, who was the better for them.

Mrs. Robinson is the daughter of Captain [Darby].

Monday Decr. 16th.

Very wet night & morning. — Glass 57. — This day I *finished* the Skies of the two upright views in Bruges, in which the Town-House-Tower, is a principal object.

Hamilton drank tea with me. — Martin was the Juryman, who against 11 others by dint of perseverance, brought them to declare Grey [Gray] and Perry, Editors of the Morning Chronicle, not guilty. They were prosecuted for publishing a seditious letter written by Dr. Darwin.

Smirke came in, when we conversed on the subject of the Academy Commemoration. They are strenuously against an Exhibition, or a Speech from the President, and think it most prudent to have only a dinner of the members.

Boswell called to speak on the subject we were agitating. He said He had been with Mr. West this morning, & learnt from him that the Plan He meant to propose is to have an Exhibition, an Ode, and himself to make a speech, containing a review of what has been done in consequence of the institution & by the members. — He told Mr. West He understood many of the members of the Body were decidedly against an Exhibition, and that should this part of the Plan be adopted perhaps it would be most prudent to exhibit only the works of the deceased members. Mr. West did not approve this distinction.

Boswell said the Exhibition was a pretty thing in fancy though perhaps not practicable in the way that cd be wished. — He thought the safest proposal would be to have a dinner in the Royal Academy *confined to the members*, that an adress on the occasion should be signed & presented to his majesty, and that a medal should be engraved on the occasion. One cast to be presented to the King, another to the Queen, and one each to the Prince of Wales & Princess Royal. — The thought of the medal He said was Mr. Sewards.

The first part of Boswells scheme was similar to that we had adopted & the adress & medal we thought very proper. Perhaps the medal will be attended with too great an expence.

Mr. West proposed that on the first day of his proposed Exhibition the King & Queen should be requested to view it. A following day the nobility &c, when the ode & speech from the chair should be sung & read.

Having agreed to meet tomorrow at the Academy, Boswell & Smirke went away. Hamilton & myself talked a little about the ensuing election of 3 Academicians. He proposes voting for Lawrence, Westhall & Bonomi. I told him I had not positively determined how I shd vote but that I thought Lawrence, Westhall & Stothard, claimed a preference.

Perry & Grey, the Editors of the Morning Chronicle, are both Scotchmen. Grey was sometime an Under teacher at the Charter House. It is computed that the Paper clears £6000 a year. They paid abt £25000 last year to Government for Stamps. The Herald is said not now to sell more than 800 a day. Two or three years ago between 4 & 5000 a day were sold.

Tuesday Decr. 17th.

Fine morning. Glass 57. — I painted on one of the upright Bruges.
This morning I called on Boswell. I afterwards sat to Humphrey.

In the evening went to the Academy where 32 members were assembled.

Academicians	Associates
Messrs. West	Messrs. Rebecca
Bacon	Edwards
Burch	Bigg
Copley	Lawrence
G. Dance	Marchant
Farington	Tresham
Garvey	Westall
Hamilton	Bonomi
Hodges	
Humphry	Associate Engravers
Nollekens	
Opie	Messrs. Brown
Richards	Green
P. Sandby	Howard
Tyler	Collyer
Wilton	
Wyatt	
Zoffany	James Boswell
Smirke	Secretary for foreign
Bourgeois	correspondence.

The President opened the business of the evening by stating that He had a proposal to make for celebrating the 25th year. This He read. — The Heads of it were

That there should be an Exhibition for a fortnight of the works of dead & living members of the Academy, the profits of which He doubted not would discharge some arrears on the Academy.

That a day should be set apart for the reception of the King & Royal Family to the Exhibition.

That on the following day, there shd be an invitation to people of distinction, Gentlemen & Ladies, when an Ode shd be performed in the Room, & the President should deliver a speech enumerating what had been done by the Academy since its institution.

No conversation took place in consequence of this proposal being read.

Mr. Green then rose and read a paper which He had drawn up. The purport of it was to reccomend to the Academy, to make out a statement of the nature of the institution, of the views of the Society, of the income & expences &c &c, the whole to form a regular work for publication. Among other articles that some acct of each artist shd be given with a list of their principal works &c.

The whole of Mr. Greens proposal was foreign to the business of the evening, and it was reccomended to him to present his proposal to the Council of the Academy that it might be regularly taken into consideration.

After Mr. Green had finished no Member appearing disposed to bring forward a motion on the subject for which we were called together, I rose, and said I had a motion today before the meeting which I did not think necessary to preface with any remarks on the Plan of the President, or reccomendation of my own, as in a Society like this each member was capable of giving an opinion, witht. another presuming to dictate one to him, I shd therefore only beg to read over what I had to propose and leave it to be recd. or not as the members felt disposed.

But I must not omit that a general question had been put "whether the Academy was of opinion that the 25th year of the institution should be celebrated". This passed with only two dissentients, Nollekens and Opie. — A letter from Sir Wm Chambers to Mr. West was read. I then read my motions.

1.

"That to commemorate the 25th year of the Institution of the Royal Academy, a meeting of all the members shall be held at the Royal Academy on a day hereafter to be fixed, where a dinner &c shall be provided".

2d.

"That an humble and grateful adress to his Majesty, suitable to the occasion, shall be prepared and signed by the members assembled".

3d.

"That in commemoration, a Medal shall be cut in steel, with such device as may be thought proper. Impressions in gold to be presented to his Majesty, to the Queen, to the Prince of Wales, & to the Princess Royal".

4th.

"That an Impression in Silver of the medal shall be also given to each member of the Royal Academy, and the Die shall then be deposited in the Royal Academy".

5th.

"That a Committee of 6 Academicians shall be this evening appointed to obtain his Majestys pleasure on the above resolutions, and be empowered to act in consequence".

No material debate took place, and Mr. Wests proposal not having been put as a motion, my motions were regularly put and seconded by several, and were passed unanimously.

A committee was then appointed by scratching against the names of the Academicians as they stood on a printed list.

Farington 14	Dance —— 5	Opie —— 1
West —— 12	Fuseli —— 1	Hamilton 1
Tyler —— 12	Burch —— 1	Wyatt —— 1
Richards—12	Nollekens 1	Yenn —— 1
Copley —— 11	Northcote 1	Zoffany — 1
Hodges — 10		

14 members only remained in the room at the time of the Balot.

It was then agreed that the Committee should meet the following eving. at 7 in Mr. Richards room at the Academy.

The meeting broke up at ½ past 12 o'clock. — Dance told me Wyatt had proposed to bring forward a motion for medals.

Wednesday Decr. 18th.

A wet morning. Glass 57.

I was employed in washing outlines.

In the forenoon Tyler called on me with a paper He had drawn up containing the substance of the resolutions I had moved, put into a different form to be laid before his majesty.

At 7 went to the Academy, where I found Mr. West, Richards & Tyler. Copley sent an apology. Hodges did not attend.

Marchant being called in gave us information relative to the proposed die and undertook to speak to Pingo on the subject.

We employed ourselves in considering the wording the Statement of the resolutions before they are laid before his majesty.

Copy of the Paper to be laid before the King by Mr. West.

The |Academicians, Associates, and other members of the Royal Academy, beg leave to submit to his Majestys consideration, the unanimous proceedings of two special meetings held on the 3d & 7th instant at their apartments in Somerset Place.

That it is the earnest desire of all the members of this Society founded under his majestys immediate patronage to celebrate the present Epocha, being the 25th year of their institution, in the most respectable manner.

That in order to effect so desirable a purpose, they have deliberated on the different Ideas suggested by several of their own members and do with great submission offer the following propositions for his Majestys consideration.

That the members only, do dine together in one of the apartments of the Royal Academy on a day hereafter to be appointed.

That an adress be drawn up expressive of our loyalty & affection for his Majesty and the Royal family, our Gratitude for the foundation of this

Academy under his Majestys immediate patronage and protection, our zeal for the honor & interest of so important an institution, our strong sense of that pre-eminence we feel on being elected members of this body, which has become a permanent monument of public utility and royal munificence. This adress to be signed by all the members, and presented by the President, & the Officers of the Academy at such time as His Majesty shall please to direct.

That in order to mark with peculiar distinction, the period when the first Academy established in England, under Royal patronage, for the study of the Polite Arts, has compleated its 25th year; and to convey to posterity an indelible record of the prosperous situation of the society, and the sense the Members entertain of the advantages they derive from the institution a die shall be cut in steel, ornamented with emblematic devices appropriate to the occasion, that four gold medals be struck from the die, and that the Academy be permitted to present one to his majesty, one to the Queen, one to the Prince of Wales, & one to the Princess Royal.

That Silver medals be also struck & presented to the members of the Royal Academy only, by the President, after which the Die shall be sealed up & deposited in the Royal Academy.

We humbly hope that His Majesty will be graciously pleased to approve of these our sentiments in expressing our zeal on this particular occasion, and that we may be permitted to charge the expences on the funds of the Royal Academy.

An estimate was made of the probable expence of adopting this mode of celebration, and the following estimate was prepared to lay before his Majesty with the other Paper.

Cutting the Die	40 —
4 gold medals	— 26-5
65 silver medals	— 21 —
	87-5
Dinners &c	63 —
	150-[5]

The medals to be a third larger than the Pattern medal of the Pope, lent by Mr. Marchant.

The Committee broke up a little after 12 o'clock. Mr. West on our way home expressed himself strongly in favor of the Plan adopted & said if He could not have a favorable opportunity of speaking to the King in Town, He would follow him to Windsor. Sir William Chambers opposing letter had alarmed him, as He knew not where it *originated*, otherways He had been satisfied of the Kings good disposition to a celebration. — Bissell called & I paid him a guinea & half more for Tickets.

Thursday Decr. 19th.

A fine day. Glass 49. — Tinting Garricks House & Junction of Canal & Thames.

Called on Tyler and afterwards sent a fair copy of the resolutions to be laid before his majesty, to Mr. West.

Taylor dined with me, and at 7 o'clock Dance called & we proceeded together to Mrs. Robinsons in St. James's place, where we found a Mr. & Mrs. Hanway, — Mrs. Whittel, a sister of Sir Egerton Leighs, another Lady, a clergyman, and Col. Tarlton. Also the emigrant French Bishop of Troyes, who seems a sensible man, and speaks English very well. — We drank Tea & staid till 10 o'clock.

Friday Decr. 20.

Will breakfasted here a remarkably foggy morning & day. Glass 49. At 12 o'clock at noon I could not see the Houses across Charlotte St. — I called on Humphry, but the weather wd not allow of my setting.

Went to the Club. Seventeen members present. Before dinner Mr. West desired Mr. Tyler & Copley & myself to go into another room where He informed us that on Thursday evening He went to Sir William Chambers & that after a long conversation He had prevailed on Sir William to agree to the proposed Plan for a celebration. That Sir William and He had been this morning about nine o'clock with his majesty, when Mr. West delivered the paper of resolutions and inclosed in it the estimate. The King read the first through and then looked over the estimate, and said the Academy should not be disappointed and that the estimate of expence was very moderate.

After we had dined, before the Kings Health was drank, Mr. West related in a general way what had passed to the meeting, and the permission was received very cordially by all present.

In the course of the evening I mentioned to the members present, my wish and I knew it to be the wish of others, that a Uniform dress should be worn by the members of the Royal Academy at all their public meetings, which would give an impressive respectability to them and in a becoming way distinguish them as a body. Nollekens said He would second my motion, & all appeared disposed to concur in it. — I mentioned that formerly such an Idea had been held by Sir Joshua Reynolds &c & that they proposed that Gowns should be worn. I thought this would be carrying it too far and that a Blue Coat with some distinction of collar, Cuff & Button would be sufficient, and would subject the members to no real addition of expence as the Coat might be worn in common if the cape &c were taken of.

As no time is to be lost abt the celebration, Mr. West desired, Copley, Tyler & myself to attend at the Academy the following night on the Committee, as He proposed to call a Council & then a general meeting as soon as possible, as He thought it would be best to have the dinner during the Hollidays.

Mr. West, Tyler, Edwards & myself went from the meeting in a Coach together, I had a long conversation with Mr. West. Acct of Death of Lord Greys only Son aged 13. He died yesterday in Sackville Str.

Saturday Decr. 21st.

A fine day. Glass 49. Between 11 & 12 Mrs. Offley called & took Susan who has been confined to the House 3 weeks, to Fanhams.

Charles Offley called & reminded me of the Picture of Carnarvon Castle being intended for him.

Today I delivered to Mr. Stadler the washed outlines of the windings of the Thames, view of Culham, Fawley Court & Henley, and [blank], also the etching of view from Whiteheads Oak — I was employed in etching outlines. Dined with Charles Offley, and in the evening went to the Committee at the Academy. — Present Messrs West, Richards, Tyler, Hodges, Copley, Farington. We determined that the day of Meeting for the celebration shd be on the 31st of this month, that it might be within the year. That a meeting of Council shd be held on Monday evening at 6 o'clock to receive the report of the Committee, in order that the whole proceeding might be regularly recorded in the Journals of the Academy that the meeting of Council being broken up after receiving the report, should pro forma, be again immediately called to confirm the minutes of the preceding meeting. The whole proceedings then to be carried before a *general meeting* summoned to assemble the same evening at 8 o'clock, for the sake of dispatch. — The next object of the committee was to consider of an adress to his majesty, when to avoid a reference to persons unconnected with the Academy it was resolved that each of the members should prepare an adress agreeable to his own Ideas, and produce it the following evening, when the committee should again assemble.

We did not break up till past 12 o'clock.

Sunday Decr. 22d.

A very dull day. Glass 49. — In the forenoon I prepared the following adress to lay before the Committee.

May it please your Majesty.

"Animated with the warmest feelings of loyalty and affection, The President and Council, with the rest of the Academicians and Associates, beg permission to declare their inviolable attachment to your Majesty and the Royal family.

The Period is now arrived when the Royal Academy has completed the 25th year from its foundation. On this occasion, the Members of this Society are moved by duty and by gratitude to come forward to express to their gracious Founder & Patron, the full sense they entertain of the benefits derived from this institution: where rising merit that required encouragement has received support; the Public taste been improved; and the distinction conferred on the members of the Academy has advanced the Polite Arts in dignity.

While reviewing the important advantages which have been received, it is our most ardent desire to perpetuate this Epocha by an indellible record.

Thus shall posterity judge of our sentiments and veneration for a Monarch under whose auspicious patronage & protection, the Arts, in Britain, have flourished beyond all former example".

In the evening at 8 o'clock met the Committee at the Academy.

     Present

Messrs.	West	Tyler	Copley
	Richards	Hodges	Farington

Mr. West, our Chairman, called on the gentlemen to know who had prepared adresses or thrown their thoughts together in any way on the subject. He had written something for the purpose. Mr. Tyler produced a paper, Mr. Hodges, one & I mine. Mr. Copley & Mr. Richards said they had not prepared anything.

Mr. West then read his paper. Mr. Tyler followed with his, then I read mine and lastly Hodges.

Mr. Wests paper was rather a digression on the benefits derived from his majestys protection of the Polite Arts, & touched on the commercial advantages gained by the improvement of taste. It was much too long for an adress. — That of Tyler too long also, and that of Hodges too long & not sufficiently formed. As is likely to be the [case] when different persons write on a subject in a Committee, it will be difficult without seeming indelicacy, to give a preference to any particular one. After much conversation, and no decision, the Committee broke up, Mr. Copley reccomending another meeting on the following evening, before which time each person should reconsider what He had written & produce it with the alterations.

Mr. West, Tyler & myself went home in a Coach together, & conversing on the difficulty of coming to any determination when assembled together, Mr. West strongly reccomended to me and Mr. Tyler to meet together on the following day, and after comparing our proposed adresses to compleat one, and He would support it.

Mr. West mentioned to me that He understood there were likely to be some dissentient voices against the whole proceeding of celebration. — I understood He alluded to Barry & Northcote.

Monday Decr. 23d.

Fine day. Glass 49. — This morning I delivered to Mr. Stadler the etching of Chertsey from Wooburn.

In the forenoon I called on Tyler, and He agreed to proceed agreeable to Mr. Wests reccomendation, and on reading again *my* adress, He thought with a few alterations it would answer the purpose fully. We then considered it and having settled the alterations, we went together to the Freemasons Tavern & spoke to Richold, about the Dinner to be prepared for the celebration. — The great Annual Exhibition dinner is charged at half a guinea a head, the desert included, but on account of this being a much dearer season He proposed that half a crown each should be allowed for the desert making the whole thirteen shillings a head. If 54 persons dine on that day He thinks the whole expence of the entertainment will be abt 60 guineas. Champaigne is become very dear & scarce since the French troubles began, but as it has been customary we ordered it shd be served once round.

From Freemasons tavern we went to Copleys who agreed to the adress with a slight alteration or two. I went to Hodges to dinner who agreed to the adress as it now stood. I therefore made a fair Copy of it and sent it to Mr. West at the Royal Academy, to be laid before the Council & General meeting which He has called for this evening.

The adress to his majesty is as follows —

May it please your Majesty.

Animated with the warmest feelings of loyalty and affection, The President and Council, with the rest of the Academicians & Associates, of the Royal Academy, humbly request your Majestys permission to declare their inviolable attachment to your Majesty, and the Royal family.

The Period is now arrived when the Royal Academy has completed the 25th year from its foundation. On this occasion, impressed by motives of duty and gratitude, the members of this body presume humbly to acknowledge to their gracious Founder and Patron, the benefits derived from the institution: where rising merit has received encouragement, the Public taste been improved; and the distinction conferred on the constituent members of this Academy has advanced the dignity of the Polite Arts, throughout your majestys dominions.

While reviewing these important advantages resulting from your Majestys institution, it is our most ardent desire to perpetuate this Epocha by an indellible record.

Thus shall we express to posterity our sentiments and veneration for a Monarch, in whose reign and under whose patronage, the Arts have flourished beyond all former example in Britain.

At 8 o'clock I went with Hodges to the Academy, where a difficulty arose about the President taking the Chair in the general meeting as a sufficient number of the Council had not attended to form a meeting. After some time it occurred to me to state to the President that He might take the Chair and the intended business be brought forward and *when passed*, be reccomended to the consideration of the Council. This would be perfectly regular. The President accordingly took the Chair.

Present at the general meeting.

Mr. West

Tyler	Fuseli	Wyatt
Bacon	Opie	Hodges
Russell	Nollekens	Hamilton
Garvey	Rigaud	Bourgeois
Catton	Banks	Tyler
Richards	Wilton	

Mr. West read to the meeting the Paper which had been drawn up by the Committee and laid before his majesty. — Opie objected to its not having the word *resolutions* instead of *Propositions*, but Wyatt &c &c called for the motion which was instantly passed by all hands but Opies. He did not hold his hand against it. — The meeting broke up at Eleven. — Nollekens mentioned to me that Barry had objected to want of formality in the first meeting which was not Academical. Bourgeois told me some He believed would not attend the dinner.

Tuesday Decr. 24th.

Tolerable day. Glass 49. — At 10 o'clock I called on Admiral Gardner at the Admiralty. I mentioned to him that my Brother Will having been twice at the Mauritius, could give him some information that might be useful. He recd. this information with great pleasure and I appointed Monday next for Will to call on him. I spoke to him abt Bissell who is confined in the Marshalsea. He observed it would be difficult to get him restored in the Navy after such misdemeanour. — On my telling him that one of the Captains Bissell has sailed [with] had said He would take him again, the Admiral thought that might be in his favor.

When I returned home I wrote a note to Bissell in the Marshalsea mentioning that it might be for his advantage if He would inform me before Monday, of the name of His Captain who had declared in his favor, as I had seen Admiral Gardner, and should again on that day.

I wrote to Mr. West. reccomending to him, as one of the Committee, that it would be most convenient for him if He called a Council some day this week, to do the business of the Commemoration instead of having the whole to do on the day of celebration. — If He called a meeting I requested him to settle the business of Mr. Carey.

Smirke called on me & as He had not attended the meeting, I related to

him what had passed about celebration which met his full concurrence.
At 12 o'clock I left Town with Charles & John Offley and went to
Fanhams. I called at Hoddesdon and desired Will to prepare for Admiral
Gardner.

Wednesday. Decr. 25. Christmas Day.

Weather fair, but cold though not frosty. — At Fanhams, — Mrs. Offley,
Susan, Charles & John Offley and Minet came to dinner. Employed in
etching, on Windsor from Clewer, — Windsor from Coopers Hill, — and
view from Oatlands which 3 Plates I Brought down.

Thursday Decr. 26th.

Weather as yesterday. — Minet went to Town. — Recd. Gazette with acct
of General O'Hara being taken prisoner. Lord Hoods letter a strong one
on the occasion, wherein He says, "General O'Hara *promised not* to
accompany the sortie, but unfortunately *did not keep his word*".
Employed in etching.

Friday Decr. 27th.

Weather as yesterday.
Employed in etching.

Saturday, Decr. 28th.

Weather the same.
Employed in etching.

Sunday Decr. 29th.

Fine day. Returned to Town with John & C. Offley. Dined at the Percy
Coffee House. Will came to Town. Evening at home. Barry & Bartolozzi
had called on me while I was at Fanhams.

Monday, Decr. 30.

Very foggy morning. Glass 41. Frosty. Went with Will to breakfast at the
Admiralty with Admiral Gardner, when Will communicated to him many
particulars relative to the Island of Mauritius. — When I returned home
found a note from Mr. West, earnestly desiring to see me today. He had
called on me 3 times when I was out. I immediately went to him, and found
it was on the subject of having several eminent musical performers at our
celebration dinner. I told him I could not give my consent but in a
Committee where the opinion of each member might be taken & advised
him to call the Committee together at ½ past 8 this evening; which He
agreed to do. He shewed me a design He had made for the medal. On one
side the Kings Head, on the other Painting, Sculpture & Architecture,
represented by three figures. — He also shewed me an adress which Copley

had brought to him, since the one agreed upon, had been left in his hands to deliver to Tomkins. He told Copley it was to late to receive his as Tomkins had barely time to finish that now in his hands. Copleys adress was more diffuse, and unconnected, and unconnected, and contained no new Idea.

Dined with C & J Offley and in the evening went to the Academy to the Committee.

The Committee to night consisted

of Messrs. West — Hodges
Tyler — Farington
Richards

Copley wrote an apology being engaged. A difficulty arose about inviting the musical Performers who had offered their services, as we had bound ourselves only to invite the members of the Academy, but this objection was got over, by its being observed that the Stewards appointed to carry the celebration into execution were justified in introducing such as came only to add to the entertainment. Accordingly it was agreed to issue the invitation. Mr. West left us to call on Mr. Cramer. — In determining what Toasts should be drank I mentioned that Sir Wm Chambers shd be particularly noticed having so greatly contributed to the foundation by his influence with the King at that period; and I requested Mr. Richards to shew me the Minutes of the first meetings of the Academicians. I there found, That in the *first meeting* Sir Joshua Reynolds, the President adressed the meeting, and the first motion that was made was "Thanks to Mr. Chambers for his able and active conduct in planning and forming the Royal Academy".

This resolution I proposed to adopt into the Toast with the addition of "under his majestys gracious patronage & protection", this was agreed to. Mr. Tomkins brought the adress in which the word Conferred was wrong spelt, He took it back to alter. The meeting then broke up. I should before have observed that the members who had been in the early part of this business a Committee were now appointed by the Council Stewards for conducting the entertainment.

Tuesday Decr. 31st.

Fine day. Glass 41. — This morning I called on Mr. West to deliver to him the list of Toasts, which were as follows.

The King, our Founder & Patron — 3 cheers.
The Queen
The Prince of Wales.
The Princess Royal and the rest of the Royal family.
The Duke of York, & the Army
The Duke of Clarence & the Navy.

Prosperity to the Royal Academy — 3 cheers

Sir William Chambers, for his able and active conduct in planning & forming the Royal Academy, under his Majestys gracious patronage & protection.

Success to the next Exhibition.

The President of the Royal Academy (given by Mr. Tyler.) Thanks to Mr. Cramer & the other gentlemen whose musical abilities have so greatly contributed to the celebration of this day, in the Royal Academy.

Patrons of Arts &c &c.

Mr. West sent to Mr. Cramer for a list of the musical gentlemen who proposed to attend

The List

Instrumental	Mr. Cramer Borghi, Dusseck, Cramer Junr., Smith.	Harrison, Knivett & His two Sons	Vocal

In conversation Mr. West told me Peters wrote to him for his interest and reccomendation to Bowyer &c the day after the dinner we had at the Freemasons Tavern with Messrs. J. Boydell, Coombes, & Peters.

I this day finished the last of the etchings for the first volume of the Rivers, and delivered the Plates of Oatlands, Windsor from Clewer, and Windsor from Coopers Hill, to Mr. Stadler to be bit in.

Dr. Woolcot (Peter Pindar) this day published an Ode on the Royal Academy celebration. The Printer sent Printed notes to myself & several others to the Royal Academy.

At 3 o'clock I called on Tyler and we proceeded to the Royal Academy and signed the adress which had undergone (in Mr. Wests hands) a few alterations of words, which I have marked with Black lead pencil in the last of those I have written.

Members not at the dinner

Academicians	Associates	Associate Engravers
Cosway indisposed	Tresham —	
Wheatley — in the Country	Nixon — in the Country	Mayer
P. Sandby — indisposed at Windsor Lodge	Hone — in Ireland	Brown — signed did not stay
	Zucchi — at Rome	
Newton — in the Country	Elmer — at Farnham	
Angelica Kauffman	Stubbs —	
Mary Loyd (Moser)	Elias Martin	
	George James	

and three vacancies — viz: Hoare — Webber — Serres.

Present at the Commemoration dinner at the Royal Academy Decr. 31st.
1793.

Academicians	Associates	Associate Engravers	
	Messrs. Rooker		
Mr. West — President	Edwards	Valentine Green	
Sir Wm. Chambers — Treasurer	Bigg		Haywa
Mr. Wilton — Keeper	Lawrence		Collye
Richards — Secretary	Westhall	James	Heath
Barry — Professor	Stothard		
Tyler	Bonomi		
Zoffany	Hoppner		
G. Dance	Beechy		
Nollekens	Marchant		
Wyatt	Rebecca		
Banks			
Rigaud			
Bartolozzi			
Hamilton			
Loutherburgh			
Farington			
Bacon			
Northcote	Professors		
Opie			
Fuseli	Sheldon — Professor		
Russell	of Anatomy		
Burch	Boswell, Secretary		
Catton	for foreign		
Hodges	Correspondence		
Yenn			
Humphrey			
Smirke	Musicians		
Sir F. Bourgeois			
P. Sandby	Instrumental	Vocal	
Garvey	Cramer	Harrison	
Copley	Cramer Jnr	Knivett	
	Shield	Do. Junr.	
	Dusseck	Do. Junr.	
	Borghi	Bartleman	
	Smith		

As the resolutions which had been passed relative to the celebration
were resolved on at an Extra meeting of *all* the members of the Royal

Academy, though they were carried unanimously, yet not being brought forward in the Council, of course were not regular, it became necessary for them to pass two Councils & a general meeting that they might be entered on the minutes of the Academy. — Mr. West on Saturday last called a Council which passed the resolutions, as reccomended to them by the general meeting of Monday the 23d inst. — and the Council having broke up were pro forma summoned again by Mr. Richards the Secretary, and assembled in half an hour afterwards and confirmed the minutes of the preceding meeting. It now therefore remained to compleat the regularity that the President should assemble the Academicians to receive the reports of the Council, and to confirm them. Accordingly abt half past 3 o'clock a great number of Academicians being come, the President took the Chair in the *Library*, and the members having entered their names, the business of the Council was brought forward and a motion being made and seconded, that it should be confirmed, it passed unanimously. N.B. — Barry, — Opie, Fuseli, — and Northcote, were at this time present.

Thanks were then moved by Mr. Tyler, to Mr. West, for his ready concurrence with the wishes of the 12 members who first moved on the subject of the celebration at the Academy Club, and for his activity since in what related to it.

Mr. West mentioned to me this morning the propriety of thanks being given to the President as above, and also to the Committee which had been appointed for their services.

Mr. Tyler in consequence of my reporting this to him made the motion. But no person having had it suggested to him, the second motion was not made. — George Dance brought an account of the evacuation of Toulon.

The Dinner was placed on the table at about ¼ past five, & consisted of two Courses and a desert admirably served. Woodcocks &c in the second course, and in the desert, Grapes and Asparagus. Of all these plenty. Excellent Champaigne was served once round between the Courses.

After dinner the Kings Health being given the instrumental musicians, agreeable to what had been settled with Mr. West, rose for the purpose of playing a Concerto. — This was attended with an unpleasant necessity. There being no room on the outside of the tables for the admission of the Harpsichord, it was brought into the center between the tables, which obliged many members to leave their seats. — From this time it became rather a Concert with intervals, than a meeting where conversation could have any share. — Boswell and others disliked it much. — But Opie, Fuseli, & Northcote, were most conspicuous in their non attendance to it.

At half past-nine Tea & Coffee were brought in, and the Members were in promiscuous conversation till about Eleven when the President called us up to him & we formed still a numerous Company. Several Healths were drank & much festivity. Wilton, G. Dance & West, the three original Members making pleasant speeches. — at 12 we sat down at one of the

The Table

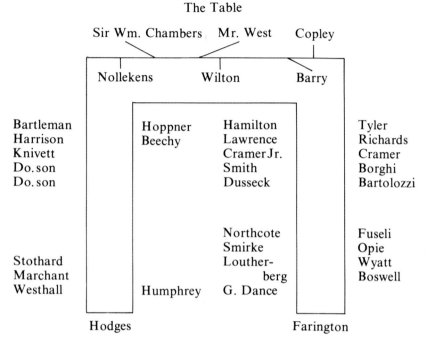

long tables to a well set out supper. After which Shields sung a song & told a story & Boswell exerted himself. At half past one I went away with Smirke, Stothard, & Hoppner, leaving the President & many others behind. — When the clock struck 12 I moved to drink the New Year standing which was done with 3 cheers. The whole entertainment did great credit to Richold & Mollard.

Bartolozzi & Richards told me this evening, that the business of Mr. Carey was this day brought before the Council by Mr. West, before the annual accounts were audited, and it appearing that no complaint ought to have been brought against him, the resolution on it was ordered to be erased from the minutes, and that He should proceed in the Life Academy.

JANUARY 1794

A fine morning. — I called on Tyler in consequence of Mr. West having desired me to mention to him the propriety of inserting an acct. of the celebration in the Public papers. Mr. West proposed to have the toasts &c introduced. We thought they shd. be omitted as it would appear too much like a common Tavern report. Accordingly Tyler drew up a concise account which was sent to Mr. West for his consideration & to be forwarded by him to Richards.

I called on Hamilton to fix about going to the Revd. Mr. Gardners at Battersea on Sunday next, on acct. of his ensuing Lawsuit. He is to send a Glass Coach for Richards, Hamilton, Malton & myself.

At one oClock I left London with C & J Offley & got to Fanhams to dinner at 5. Before I left town I wrote to Admiral Gardner abt. Bissell — also wrote to Bissell advising him to apply to Admiral Cotton for a situation.

Thursday; Jany. 2d.

Frosty weather, very cold. — employed in washing outlines.

Friday. 2d [3rd].

Frosty weather, — employed in washing outlines.

Saturday 3d [4th].

Frosty & Foggy — employed as yesterday.

Having got cold with pains in my limbs, I sent a letter by the Coach to Hamilton, desiring him to excuse me to Mr. Gardner tomorrow.

Will sent me a note from Hoddesdon in which He mentioned the deaths of Rolles Leigh, of Adlington, and Tom Parker of Cuerden.

Sunday. Jan. 4th [5th].

Frosty weather. — Minet came down. Newspapers filled these days with French accounts of evacuation of Toulon.

List of Original Members of the Royal Academy appointed by His Majesty Decr. 10th. 1768 — In all 36 *appointed.*

		died
	Joshua Reynolds	President February 23. 1792 aged 68
Portrait or History and Portrait Painters	Francis Cotes	———— 1770 aged 44
	P. Toms	
	E. Penny	Novr. 15. 1791 aged 77
	N. Hone	Aug. 14 1784 aged 70
	Thos. Gainsborough	Augst. 1788 aged 61
	Mason Chamberlain	Jany. 26. 1787 aged 60
	Nathaniel Dance	resigned 1791
	Francis Milner Newton	————
Historical Painters	Benjn. West	
	Angelica Kauffman	
	F. Bartolozzi	
	Frank Hayman	born 1708 died 1776
	G. B. Cipriani	Novr. — 1785 aged 59
	Samuel Wale	Feby. 6th. 1786 aged 73
Landscape Painters	Richard Wilson	May 11. 1782 aged 68
	George Barrett	March 6th. 1784 aged 53
	F. Zuccarelli	November 1788 aged 91
	John Richards	
	Paul Sandby	
Sculptors	G. M. Moser	January 1783 aged 70
	Agostino Carlini	———— 1790 Augst. 16th. aged 72
	B. Yeo	Decr. 3d. — 1779
	Joseph Wilton	
	William Tyler	

Architects	William Chambers Thomas Sandby John Gwynn George Dance	March 1786 aged 70 –
Marine Painter	Dominick Serres	– Nov. 4. 1793 aged 73
Miniature	J. Meyer	January 1789 aged 54
Flowers	B. Baker Mary Moser	
Animals	Charles Catton	
Portrait Painters	Johann Zoffany William Hoare died Dec. 1792 aged 84	added after the 10th of December – not by election, but by Command of His Majesty

Original Members living at the Commemoration of the 25th. year Decr. 31st., 1793.

	Ages in 1793
Benjamin West – President.	55
Sir William Chambers	70
Joseph Wilton	73
Thomas Sandby	70
Paul Sandby	63
George Dance, born April 1st. 1741.	53
John Richards	62
William Tyler	64
Francis Milner Newton, died August 7th. 1794.	65
Francis Bartolozzi	63
Charles Catton	65
Angelica Kauffman	48
Mary Moser, now Mrs. Loyd	47
John Zoffany	62
Nathaniel Dance, resigned his seat in the Academy 1789.	59

List of *Elected* Members of the Royal Academy between the year of the foundation Decr. 10th. 1768 and Decr. 10th. 1793 – including Twenty five years.

	Academicians	When elected Associates	When Academicians
Portrait & History	Copley Opie Northcote Wheatley Peters – resigned 1790	November November 1786 November 1786 November 1790 November	 Feb. 10th.–1787 Feb. 10th.–1787 Feb. 10th.–1791
Historical Painters	Barry Smirke Hamilton Fuseli Rigaud	November November 1791 November 1784 November 1788 November 17	 Feb. 10th. 1793 Feb. 10th. 1789 Feb. 10 1790 Feb. 10 – 1784
Landscape Painters	Webber died April 29th. 1793. aged 41 Loutherburgh Farington Hodges Garvey Bourgeois	November 1786 November 17 November 1783 November 1786 November November 1787	Feb. 10th. 1791 Feb. 10th. 1785 Feb. 10th. 1787 Feb. 10th. 1782 Feb. 10th. 1793
Portrait in Crayons	Russell Humphry	November 17 November 178	Feb. 10th.–1788 Feb. 10th.–1791
Sculptors	Banks Bacon Nollekens Burch	November 17 November 17 Novr. 17 Novr.	Feb. 10th. 1785 Feb. 10 –
Miniature	Cosway	Novr.	
Architects	Wyatt Yenn	Novr. 17 Novr. 17	Feb. 10th. 1785 Feb. 10th. 1791

List of Associates of the Royal Academy elected before the Year 1794 & not at that period elected Academicians.

Ages
in
1793.

—	Edward Steevens	elected	died at Rome.
—	John Mortimer	November 1779	died 1779 aged 39
—	— Dahl	elected 1770	died February 3d.
—	William Pars	November 17	died in Rome October 1782 aged 39
—	George James		
—	Elias Martin		
—	William Tomkins		died January 1st. aged 60 — 1792.
70	Antonio Zucchi		
38	Horace Hone		
51	James Nixon	Novr. 1779	
—	Stephen Elmer		
58	Biagio Rebecca		
70	George Stubbs		
55	Edward Edwards	Novr. — 177	
47	Michl. Angelo Rooker	Novr.–177	
—	William Parry	Novr.–1776	died in London Feb. 19. 1791. aged 48
—	Philip Reinagle	Novr.–1787	
—	William R. Bigg	Novr.–1787	
54	Joseph Bonomi	Novr.–1789	
24	Thomas Lawrence	Novr.–1791	
—	Thomas Stothard	Novr.–1791	
51	Nathaniel Marchant	Novr.–1791	
46	Henry Tresham	Novr.–1791	
29 Jan. 1794	Richard Westhall	Novr.–1792	
—	William Beechy	Novr.–1793.	
—	John Hoppner	Novr.–1793.	

The Royal Academy consisted on Decr. 10th. 1768 of Thirty four
Members, two more were added by the Kings Command making the
whole number *appointed*   36
Before January 1st. 1794 — The number of Members elected was   25
                                                                    ——
                                                                    61
Three vacancies were then open in the room of Hoare — Webber — and
Serres.

In 1783, Wright of Derby, through pique at Garvey in 1782 being elected
before him, declined the diploma, — and Stubbs did not receive his as He
had not lodged a Picture.

Professors, *not Artists*, in the Royal Academy elected before the year
1794.

		elected.	died.
Anatomy	William Hunter		178
	John Sheldon		
Ancient Literature	Samuel Johnson DL		1784
	Bennet Langton		
Ancient History	Oliver Goldsmith DL		17
	Edmund Gibbon		January 17th — 1794

at his apartments in St. James's Street

Secretary for foreign Correspondence	Joseph Baretti		17
	James Boswell	1791	

Chaplains	Franklin DD		March 15. 1784
	William Peters		resigned 179
	Barnard		
	Bishop of Killaloe	1791	

Associate Engravers

Thomas Major	Valentine Green
John Brown	Collyer
Francis Ravenet	
Francis Hayward	James Heath

Academicians of the Royal Academy January 1st. 1794

	Ages	
Benjamin West — President	55	
Sir William Chambers	70	
Joseph Wilton	73	
John Richards	62	
George Dance	53	born April 1st. 1741.
Francisco Bartolozzi	64	
Thos. Sandby	70	
Paul Sandby	63	
William Tyler	64	
Francis Milner Newton	65	
Charles Catton	65	born Septr. 1728.
Angelica Kauffman	48	
Mary Loyd — (Moser)	47	
Johan Zoffany	62	
E Burch	65	
Richd. Cosway	53	born in 1741
Joseph Nollekens	55	
John Singleton Copley	55	
James Barry	55	
John Bacon	54	
J.P de Loutherburgh	54	born in 1740
Edmund Garvey	54	
John Francis Rigaud	50	
Joseph Farington	45	
James Wyatt	46	born August 3d. 1747.
Thomas Banks	54	
John Opie	33	
James Northcote	48	
William Hodges	49	
John Russell	49	
William Hamilton	42	
Henry Fuseli	52	
John Yenn	41	
Francis Wheatley	47	
Ozias Humphry	50	
Robert Smirke	38	
Sir Francis Bourgeois	36	

(left brace bracketing names from Benjamin West to Johan Zoffany: "original members")

. Three
. Vacancies

Monday January 6th. 1794.

Frosty weather — washing outlines. — The 3 Miss Adams dined with us at Fanhams — this being 12th. day.

Tuesday 7th.

Frosty weather and bright morning. Left Fanham at ½ past 12 and got to Town at 4. — Called at Hoddesdon — dined with C & J. Offley. Found a letter from the Revd. Mr. Gardner thanking me for my intention of coming to Battersea to see the painting which is the subject of the Lawsuit.

Boswell called on me to know how the Club days now stand.

During my absence Messrs. Westall, — Marchant, — Hardman, Revd. Dr. Breedon, Mr. Baker, Edwards, — Steers, — and Revd. Dr. Gretton called on me.

Wednesday Jany 8th.

Frosty weather, glass 38. — Boydell called on me this morning. — Recd. the Picture of Gadshill from Smirke.

I called on Westall, to return his two visits during my absence. He mentioned the ensuing election which led to a conversation upon it. Hodges had advised him to call on some of the Academicians; I gave him my opinion that it wd. not be prudent, and that his friends (Academicians) might render him more service by their exertions. — I recommended to him to be at the Queens Birth Day dinner, and at the Club, as it was attended with advantage to mix with the Members on an occasion like this. — He told me Hodges & myself were the only Academicians He could speak to on the subject. — He said Bacon had at the Commemoration dinner adressed him which He thought promised in his favor. He reckoned upon Nollekens and hoped for Bartolozzi.

He said that He had never heard a remark made of the distant manner of one of his acquaintance of which some had complained.

Coombes has read some parts of the History of the Rivers to him which He admires much.

He makes his drawings on Cartridge paper, and finds both the tint & the surface of it answer admirably. He does not use Chalk, and hatches either with a Pen or a Camel Hair pencil.

He had called on me to know if I concurred in opinion with Hodges abt. his calling on Academicians.

Horace Hamond dined with me, at home. We passed the evening. with C & J Offley.

Thursday, Jany. 9th.

Frosty weather. Glass 36. The coldest weather we have had this season. — Employ'd washing outlines. — Edwards called on me, on the subject of the approaching election. He has called on West, — Sir Wm. Chambers, — Bacon, Dance, Burch, Tyler &c — He principally dwells upon the propriety of electing him that the *Professorship* of Perspective may no longer remain open. I gave him no answer of encouragement.

Edwards told me that Mr. Shipley who founded the drawing School in the Strand, where several Artists of reputation recd. their first instructions, is still living, and is about 84 years of age. — He is Brother to the late Bishop of St. Asaph and was a Portrait Painter.

Nixon has wrote to Edwards, and is doing very well at Newcastle upon Tyne.

Edwards has been in Kent giving instructions in perspective to Mr. Oxenden only son of Sir George Oxenden. Mr. Oxenden is abt. 38 years of age and married Miss Graham sister to Lady Knatchbull.

Boydell told me yesterday that Mr. Knight of Whitehall has discontinued his subscription to the Shakespeare. He only subscribed to the small set, and complained of the alteration from the first plan which was for the small prints to be the same subjects as the large ones.

Miss Gardner, only daughter of the Admiral was married on Tuesday last to Mr. Cornwall Junr. of Portland Place.

The Revd. Dr. Breedon called on me today.

J. Offley & H. Hamond dined with me. The eving. with them & C. Offley.

Friday, [10th].

Frosty weather. Glass 33. Coldest weather of this season dark days and very foggy mornings. Ewen pasted 6 of the Outlines River Views for washing.

Mr. Hardman & Joe Hardman called on me. — He had been at Opies and was much struck with the Head of the Boy a Study by Opie, and wished me to learn the Price.

Charles Offley dined with me. Marchant came to tea & staid the eving. with me alone.

He speaks highly of some designs made lately by Lady Spencer. He was at Althorpe at Christmas.

He leant a good deal to the subject of the election of Academicians, and said Opie & Northcote promised him their votes at the celebration voluntarily. I told him I did not know how five members of the Academy would vote & that 18 wd be required for a majority. He did not ask me for my vote & I did not in any degree lean to promise him.

Saturday Jany. 11th.

A dark & dirty day — Glass 36 — A little rain.

Bissell, who left the Marshalsea yesterday called on me. I told him what had passed between Admiral Gardner & me relative to him. That the

Admiral had removed all difficulties I believed at the Admiralty, and thought the best step He could take would be to get some one of his former Commanders to take him. He said He had wrote twice to Admiral Cotton at Plymouth, but had recd. no answer. — He does not seem to like again going on board a Ship unless He has a conditional promise of promotion to a Lieutenancy. I said in his situation to be restored to the Service is the first object, and that it could hardly be expected He should be promoted immediately on coming from his late situation. He said He should like to go on board a Ship in the River for a month or two to have his name borne, & to preserve appearances, — In short He does not seem to feel his real situation as it appears to me. I asked him how He under such circumstances could expect preferment, when His Brother against whom no objection had been made could not obtain it. — The conversation concluded with my telling him I wd. write to Captain Boyles who is with Admiral Kingsmill, in the Swiftsure, on the Coast of Ireland, for his advice & assistance.

Marchi called. Lord & Lady Inchiquin came to Town on Monday for a fortnight. — The sale of Sir Joshuas pictures is to be the beginning of March.

Philips of Pallmall called. Fryer comes to Town for good on the 28th. inst.

Notice came to me from the Academy of the Election of 3 Academicians in the room of William Hoare, John Webber, and Dominick Serres Esqrs. — The Election to be on Monday Febry. 10th. — List of the Associates.

George James

Elias Martin

Antonio Zucchi

Michl. Angelo Rooker

Biagio Rebecca

Stephen Elmer

Edward Edwards

James Nixon

Horace Hone

George Stubbs

Philip Reinagle

William Redmore Bigg

Joseph Bonomi

Thos. Lawrence, not eligible by age

Thos. Stothard

Nathl. Marchant

Henry Tresham

Richd. Westall

William Beechy

John Hoppner

The weather during the last three or four days has been so dark, that it has been impossible to apply more than three hours in each day.

Humphry & Yenn are Stewards for the Queens Birth day on Saturday the 18th. — inst.

Dined at Offleys. Messrs. Evans, H. Hamond, & Harris there. First day of their giving a dinner since Mrs. Offley gave up the House.

Sunday Jany. 12.

Dark weather, Frosty, Glass 39.

Hamilton called. — The Person with whom Mr. Gardner has the Suit depending refused to let Messrs. P Sandby, Hamilton & Malton see the painting in dispute.

In consequence of *"not eligible by age"* being put against the name of Lawrence in the Associates list, He went last night to Mr. West, and pointed out to him that *"25 years of age"* in the first resolution of the Institution is limited to *Admission* and not to *election*, therefore He cannot be excluded by it, as he will be 25 years of age in April next which is long before the Diplomas can be granted. — Mr. West admitted the distinction and gave him a letter to Mr. Richards, who is to send about new lists.

Mr. West lately called on Hamilton and talked of Copleys intended motion relative to Bromleys Book. Mr. West hinted that Books perhaps could not be displaced when once received being the Kings property.

Bonomis wish is not for the Professorship of Perspective but of Architecture in case of vacancy.

I gave Hamilton a short acct. of what passed between Bromley and me & Mr. West relative to Bromleys Book.

I dined today at the Chaplains table, St. James's, with Dr. Gretton. The Company consisted of a Mr. Turner of Lincolnshire, — Mr. Williams who married a natural daugr of Lord Pembroke, — the Revd. Mr. Freind, nephew to the Primate of Ireland, Mr. Walton. — Mr. Turner is much acquainted with Mr. Walpole, the resident at Munich.

Lord Pembroke is abt. 60 years of age, has always lived temperate as to eating and drinking. — Copleys Son is likely to be first or second wrangler at Cambridge this year.

Walton says, Lord Lansdowne has £30,000 a year, — Lord Wycombe is very deaf: excells in conversation.

Lord Pembroke gave Mrs. Williams £3000.

Went to Tea at Hodges.

Wyatt lately shewed Hodges a set of designs for a Palace to be built at Kew, which the King has a serious intention of doing, — Kew is private property of the King which He may dispose of as He pleases —

The Bishop of Peterborough is abt. 63 years of Age. It is some months since He was first attacked by Paralytick symptoms.

Langley, who offered to furnish matter for the History of the Thames, left Dr. Gretton in June last.

Monday January 13th.

Fine morning, Glass 39. — Weather rather milder. — Washing outlines of Rivers.

Lysons called on me. He was assiduously employed at Woodchester near Stroud during the Hollidays, in tracing & making drawings of the floor of a Roman Villa of which He proposes to treat in a publication, with Prints.

Mr. Hardman called and desired me to engage for the Picture of a Boy,

Half length, painted by Opie. The price Opie demands is 30 Guineas. —
Lord & Lady Grey [de Wilton] came to Town in consequence of the illness of Master Egerton. His disorder was a fever in consequence of some cold or accident got at School. — Lord Grey had just before been in Town settling matters preparatory to Lord Belgrave marrying Miss Egerton.

I called on Opie, who told me [he] was just returned from Woodmason, who proposes to open an Exhibition of His Pictures painted of subjects in Shakespeare, That He meant to limit the number of Subscribers to 500, and that all the impressions after that number were taken of should be the property of the subscribers, Himself having no claim upon them, — and that it was his intention to give the greatest number of the remaining subjects to Northcote & Opie. — He has 26 pictures already painted, and proposes to have in all abt. 70.

Mr. Gardner of Battersea called on me relative to his Law Suit, which He is advised by His Attorney to terminate without bringing it into Court. — This He may do advantageously as his Opponent has paid 5 guineas into Court, of course must pay all costs. — Hamilton & Malton have signed a declaration that understanding the painting at Mr. Hatfields is similar to one fixed up in Mr. Gardners garden, they think it might be charged at 20 guineas. Mr. Gardner desired me to sign the papers in which I declined & desired to see Mr. Hamilton, before I determined.

Mrs. Marson, the Keeper of the Marshalsea this day sent to me for the last payment for William Bissells lodgings there, which I engaged to pay for. The whole Sum I have paid is £15.12.0.

I wrote to Mr. Byrne today relative to our Accounts. Mr. Baker is to assist in settling Mr. Hearnes — after which ours are to be completed.

Tuesday Jany 14th.

Fine morning, Frosty, Glass 40. — washing outlines of Rivers.

I sat to Opie this morning for drapery. I have only sat twice for the Head. Opie has written to Wilton relative to the introduction of a Young Man into the Plaister Academy. — When the young man first applied to Wilton He said He could not admit him without a recommendation from an Academician. Opie gave a recommendation. Wilton then refused to admit as He said the Young Man cd. not draw well enough. Opies letter to Wilton was a sharp one.

Copley is determined to bring forward the subject of Bromleys Book. If the Book is not thrown out of the Library of the Academy, Copley will not belong to the Body. — At least He hints as much.

I dined in Ormond St. with J. Offley, Hamond & Harris. — Charles at the Whig Club.

Wednesday Jany 15th.

Dull morning. — Glass 43. — I called on Hamilton and represented to him that I could not sign the paper brought by Mr. Gardner. He thought I was right in declining. Mr. Gardner came in when I told him a paper might be drawn up which wd. equally answer his purpose & which I would sign. Accordingly it was stated "that having been refused admittance at Mr. Hadfields, we being informed that it was a Copy of the painted deception at Mr. Gardners own house, adjudged and declared that for his time and trouble in executing it in charging 12 guineas Mr. Gardner had been moderate" — This Hamilton & I signed, and Mr. Gardner well satisfied said He wd. take it to P. Sandby & Malton.

I was employed today in tinting Webbers Outlines for Boydell and in washing outlines of Rivers.

G. Dance called. He has been at Lord Camdens & Lord Bayhams. — The Prince of Wales has got the drawing of Miss Vanneck.

C. Offley called. Only Mr. Byng of *the superiors*, was at the Whig Club yesterday. It is reported that the Duke of Portland is on some friendly terms with administration.

William Bissell called. He is to dine on Sunday with Wilbraham Bootle, who has promised to present his case to the Admiralty — and to assist him with recommendation. — He has also been with Lord Falmouth, whose first interest will be made for Austin Bissell.

I called on Tyler who is confined by a complaint in his Leg. We talked abt. collecting Biographical Anecdotes of dead & living artists. I am to send him a Book in which He is to insert what He can remember.

I dined today with Mr. Evans, of Hatton Garden. The Company consisted of Mr. John Warre, Mr. Barroneau, Charles & John Offley, Hamond, Thomas & Harris.

Mr. Warre brought an acct. of Sir Sidney Smiths arrival with dispatches from Lord Hood with acct of the evacuation of Toulon.

Notwithstanding the extent of the destruction caused by Lord Hood, [14] sail of the Line, and the Great Arsenal, the public seem to be less gratified than one would expect. The loss of the place though held at great expence, and of no specific advantage to this country, supersedes other considerations. Had Lord Hood committed equal destruction under different circumstances, it wd. have been celebrated as a capital victory.

Warre is abt. 45 years of age. Mr. Barroneau 54. — Mr. Barroneau detected the forgery of Lyons, and is to give evidence at the Old Bailey tomorrow.

Passed the eving. in Ormond st. with C & J Offley & H. Hamond.

Thursday, Jany 16th.

Fine clear day, Glass 45. — Washing outlines of Rivers.

This day died Edward Gibbon Esqr., Professor of Ancient History in the Royal Academy. He was in his 57th. year.

Called on Tyler who has begun to put down in writing such anecdotes as He is acquainted with of different Artists. — He read to me what He had written relative to Hayman & Penny.

I called at the Shakespeare Gallery. Looked over the River publication expenses. We judge the expence of the first Volume will be £18,00.

Byrne called on me today and paid me £24–15. — His second daughter has etched a plate from a picture by Meyer (a Landscape) which is an extra-ordinary instance of ingenuity as she is only now 17 years old. — The eldest daugtr. who has an equal taste in flowers is 19 years old. Mrs. Byrne, his present wife, was governess to Lord Donnegals daughter. — Byrne says engravers are not now well employed. Several ingenious men have applied to him for business.

Susan returned from Fanham quite recovered of her cough. Dined at home. Hamond with us. Marchant came in the evening.

Banks applied to West for the Librarianship of the Academy. West told him He was too late. Burch had applied for it before, & had shown him a guinea and some silver as all he had in the world.

Banks is a violent Democrat.

An ingenious Printer is now constantly employed in printing forged Assignats. Bartolozzi says He has an uncommonly delicate hand in wiping a Plate. Mr. Blackburn, member for Lancashire talking on this subject at Mr. Townleys on Sunday, expressed his disapprobation of it. — It is talked of as being done with the private knowledge of administration. Mr. Anson of Shuckburgh in Staffordshire, is engaged to be married to the second daughter of Mr. Coke of Norfolk. She is only 14 years old and is to be married next year when she is 15. Mr. Anson is about 28. — This acct. Marchant recd. from Lady Hunloke, Mr. Cokes sister, who is at Holkham. — Mr. Anson is nephew to the late Lord Anson, the circum-navigator. — He has Lady Hunloke says 22,000 a year.

Mr. Rose of the Treasury was a Scotch Schoolmaster. Afterwards Purser of a Man of war — Lord Thurlow brought him forward in a political line. They are now at variance. — Rose is towards 60 years of age. — Charles Fox seems not to stand very high in the opinions at Althorpe.

Mr. Knight told Marchant that He had rendered all the service he could to Lawrence, and introduced him to be a Member of the Dilletanti Society. He owed this for election services rendered him at Ludlow, by Old Lawrence, and His family.

Marchant returned from Italy in November 1788.

Fuseli told Lawrence a few days ago, that He would probably become President of the Royal Academy — and ironically laughing while telling it to Marchant, said "He bore it".

Friday, January 17th.

Fine clear weather, Glass 43.

This day I finished washing the outlines of the Views of Windsor from

Clewer, — Hampton court, — and Windsor from Coopers Hill. These complete the number of views for the first Volume of the River Thames.

At Dances desire I wrote to Westall to set for his profile tomorrow for the Academical collection.

Sir George Beaumont being come to Town called on me today. I was not at home. — Steers also called.

From various accts. I receive, I believe there is a considerable ferment prevailing in the minds of many people, which has a democratic tendency. Norwich is particularly mentioned as being very violent.

Today the extraordinary Gazette of the evacuation of Toulon was published. — Captn. Sir Sidney Smith, who brought the dispatches, was employed by Lord Hood to burn the Arsenal, Store Houses and Ships in the Harbour. — General David Dundass, was Governor of the Town at the time. He wrote the acct. of the *Land Service.*

Saturday Jany 18th.

Fine morning — Glass 44. — This day I began painting.

Hamond wrote to Captn. Boyle at Cork on the subject of Bissell. — I wrote to Hardman relative to the Young Man who He wishes shd. be an Engraver. Boydell says an Engraver of reputation wd. expect a Premium of from 1 to 200 guineas, & that the times are very bad for that as well as other branches of the profession. — I wrote also to Pennington of Kendal desiring him to settle his account.

Dined with the Members of the Academy at Freemasons Tavern, to celebrate the Queens Birth day. Yenn & Humphry Stewards. — Humphry in the room of Wheatley, who is in the Country confined by the Gout.

Zoffany was there and told me he did not expect His eldest daughter wd. live till morning. She has been ill near 3 weeks. Her disorder a fever of the Brain.

I sat at a table with Wyatt, G. Dance, Hamilton, Tyler & Smirke &c. — Wyatt engaged Dance, Bonomi, & myself to breakfast with him tomorrow to see a drawing of a Staircase in the inside of a palace.

Yenn, Dance, Catton, Garvey, Hoppner, Marchant, Malton & myself supped after the principal part of the Company was gone, & staid till past 2 oClock.

Wyatt told me He had promised Mr. Nares to vote for Hoppner.

Sunday Jany 19th.

Hazy day. Glass 47. Went to breakfast with Wyatt. The drawing of the Staircase is the finest Architectural drawing I ever saw. — I judge from some circumstances it is for the King, as well as two designs for the outside of a palace.

Bonomi was there, I took the opportunity to obtain from each of them some circumstances of their progress in Art, the place of their Birth &c &c.

— The whole or part of my notes will supply the Volume of Dances Academical Heads.

Wyatt mentioned the unhandsome conduct of the Adams's towards him, and the reports which had reached the Kings ear, propagated by them, of Wyatts having recd. instructions from them & obtained drawings out of their collection. The whole grossly unfounded.

Called on Sir George Beaumont.

I afterwards called on Hoppner, and told him I had spoken to Yenn of Stothard as a man of merit.

Dined in Ormond St.

Monday, Jany 20th.

Fine day, like the Spring, Glass 49.

Engaged all day in painting. In the evening I regulated the particulars which Wyatt had communicated to me of his life.

Tuesday Jany 21.

Fine day. Glass 47. — Painting.

Dined at Tylers. Dance, Richards, Hodges, Smirke, Hamilton & Catton there.

The name of the Artist who is employed by Wyatt to draw for him is Dixon. He has been with Wyatt from the time of the building the Pantheon.

Parliament met today. House of Commons sat till 5 in the morning — division 277 to 59. — Division in House of Lords 85 to 12.

Wednesday Jany 22.

Hazy morning. Middle of day fine. Glass 47. Painting. Called on Opie & spoke to him abt. inviting the Miss Booths.

I think He daily improves in his painting, and begins to render the parts with more intelligence than He has hitherto done. This I told him. He said He had lately studied very hard.

Thursday Jany 23d.

Hazy morning, day dull, Glass 46. — Painting. Lysons call'd. Mr. Berwick to set to G. Dance on Saturday.

Dined at G. Dances, with Smirke. Went with them to the Antiquarian Society, when Dance was introduced as a Member, having been elected a fortnight since. He was introduced by Sir Joseph Banks. Sir Harry Englefield in the Chair.

Steers was also introduced. They both compounded, paying each £27.6.0 instead of £5.5.0 and £2.2.0. a year.

Drank tea with Smirke & Dance at the Coffee House.

Soane the Architect was originally with Dance in a low capacity. From thence He went to Holland the Architect, who was the son of a Builder, & had been a workman under his Father.

Soane is abt. 44 or 5 years of age. — He got the premium for a drawing of a triumphal Arch abt. the year 1772 or 3 and was sent to Italy by the Academy, where He became acquainted with the late Ld. Camelford, who introduced him to Mr. Pitt.

Friday Jany 24th.

Fine clear day. Glass 47. Painting.

In the evening, employed in finishing the account of Wyatt, from the particulars He communicated to me. — Lady Inchiquin sent *Ralph* to desire I wd. call on her tomorrow or on Sunday morning.

Saturday Jany. 25.

Painting. Fine morning, windy, Glass 47. Afternoon violent wind, with sleet. — Glass 42.

Breakfasted with Dance, expected Mr. Berwick there who did not come. Lysons came & brought his drawings of the Mosaick floors at [Woodchester]. Lysons told us Ld. Orford was with Gibbon two days before He died. That at that time, He was in good spirits, and had no apprehension of his approaching end. Gibbon died of a mortification, occasioned by a Hydrocele, *of 16 years growth*, It had encreased without his noticing the apparent distension, & He noticed with surprise at last people looking towards that part, not being sensible of the size, which was equal to that of a mans head. — It became necessary to open it at last, but the parts were then in such a state as to cause a mortification.

Gibbon by Will bequeathed the whole of his fortune to a young *Swiss* man. He did not even mention in his will, Lord Sheffield, his particular friend, or any, of the few relations He left behind.

Stothard sat to Dance today, introduced by Smirke.

Sir George Beaumont called on me, & we went together to Dance, where we found Smirke & Stothard.

Sir George says the Landscape N. Dance has painted, is superior to his former picture.

He is in great apprehension abt. the times. Wyndham told him yesterday that Fox is *not* a Republican, but that in spirit, Sheridan, & Courtenay are.

I told Sir George of the illjudged appointments made in what related to Toulon. That Ld. Loughboroughs sine cures, for Sir James Erskine & his Brother were noticed by everybody.

I dined in Ormond St. J. Warre & his Brother Captn. Warre, Mr. Reid, (a Bank Director), Mr. Rankin, Hamond, Harris, were the persons invited.

Sunday Jany 26th.

Fine day, very cold, Glass 40. The change of the weather from mild to cold has been sudden — Tom Kershaw called on me.

This forenoon I called on Lady Inchiquin. She is anxious abt. the sale of Sir Joshua Reynolds Collection of Pictures. The information she has recd. from *Miss Reynolds* &c &c causes her to believe the present season very unfavourable for the sale of pictures of value. I corroborated this opinion, & gave it as mine, that if she sold part of the collection only, & bought in the *many* pictures, the expences would be so great a drawback as to leave a very small surplus. Christie I observed to her, demanded the same per centage whether the pictures were *really* disposed of or were bought in: Which on pictures of great value which might be bought in wd. amount to a large sum. In fine, I told her Ladyship, she must either make up her mind to risk a part of the collection at what price they might go, or retain the whole till a more favourable moment arrived. — This opinion of mine *was conformable to her own.* — She told me Lawrence was desirous to have the Copies of the King & Queen which Sir Joshua had provided, & Lawrence had told Her Ladyship that whatever price she set on them He wd. be glad to pay. She desired my opinion of the price. Four whole lengths were finished and two more nearly so. As the stipulated price recd. by the Kings Painter is 80 guineas, I said I thought 250 guineas would be a fair demand from her Ladyship for the Six copies. — She thought it quite sufficient.

Lady Inchiquin has given Lawrence a fine Layman, it requires being put together, but cost Sir Joshua [blank]. She offered me such pannels as Sir Joshua had bought for painting on.

At noon I called on Sir George Beaumont who shewed me the best picture He has hitherto painted. The distance is a study in the neighboroud of Dedham. Mrs. Methuen, Mander, & Hoppner were there.

In the afternoon Mr. Berwick & Captn. Wakeman called on me. — Mr. Berwick assured us that from information recd. from an American who was in the habit of running over from England to Havre & Cherbourgh He learnt that the French are there making great preparations for invading England.

I dined at Sir George Beaumonts. His mother, & Mander, the only company. We canvassed the subject of Sir Joshuas pictures & the intended sale. Sir George was fully of opinion that this is not the season to bring them forward.

Sir George told me that Cozens is paralytic to a degree that has incapacitated him.

Monday Jany 27th.

Heavy Snow — Glass 37.

Painting. Went to the sale of John Hunters Pictures. Several modern. —

Wilson, Marlow, Barrett, &c. — Met Mr. Berwick who is disposed to purchase.

Dined at Ld. Inchiquins. No Company. — Lord Inchiquin seems determined not to bring the collection of pictures forward at this season, so unfavourable for a sale. Mr. Drew, of Grays Inn, their Solicitor for recovering monies due for Portraits painted by Sir Joshua. From Lady Inchiquins description He seems very unqualified for the purpose. — Mr. Musters absolutely refuses to pay for his whole length. — I reccomended a more active proceeding as delay was increasing their difficulty.

Lord Inchiquin told me the fortune of Lady I was given in as 3 times more than was yet realised; & that in return *real* property was secured. — I shewed him that the *pictures* were real property though they cd. not prudently be yet brought to market.

Lord Inchiquin said He attended the Duke of Portlands meeting at Portland House, before the meeting of Parliament. He said that formerly, before Charles Fox divided in Politicks from the Duke of Portland He was usually the spokesman to the meeting, but on the late occasion the Duke took the Chair, and in a short but decisive speech, declared His resolution, under the present circumstances of the times, to support the Minister. Mr. Adair was the only member present who objected to a part of the Conduct of Administration, Lord Inchiquin remarked to him that this was not a moment for them to investigate the proceedings of administration but whether they shd. give their support to the war. Mr. Wyndham afterwards spoke on the same side. — The number of members present were abt. 32. — A smaller number Ld. I. said than wd. have been had the Dukes conduct last year been more decided. It could not but mark inconsistency when after the Duke had voted in the House of Peers with administration, Ld. Tichfield &c voted against him in the House of Commons.

I remarked to Lord I. that it was surprising a man in the Duke of Bedfords situation should join the Democratic party in times like the present. He said He believed it was owing to a pique between him and the Prince of Wales.

His Lordship spoke highly of the Duke of Bedford's Character, from the report of Mr. Macnamara the Dukes principal agent. His generosity to his Brothers, and kindness to others, was great, and always shewn in the most princely manner.

I staid at Lord I's till eleven at night. When the Duke of Orleans was removed from Marseilles to Paris He believed He was to have been cordially recd. there.

Tuesday, Jany 28.

Frosty weather, Glass 37. Painting. Went this morning with G. Dance to N. Dances in Mortimer St. — The Landscape the latter has painted is very ably executed, and *very clear*. He remarked on the Custom of painters obscuring the fore-ground objects in Masses of Brown. — His parts in *shade* are as much made out as those in light.

In the eving. Marchant came to Tea. — I told him that so divided are the Members of the Academy in respect of the ensuing election I cd. not form any judgment how it wd. go.

Wednesday, [29th].

Cold. Glass 39. — Tinting river views. At home all day. — In the evening Mr. Jodrell came to Tea. He has brought his two younger sons to Eaton. The eldest is soon to be entered at Queens College, Cambridge. Mr. Jodrell said He was told at Birmingham that 12000 men had entered the service since the commencement of the War. — The Poors rate has encreased there prodigiously in consequence of many wives and Children being left. Mr. Jodrell does not approve the severity of the Scotch sentences on Muir, Palmer, Margarot & Skirving. He thinks they shd. have been allowed to banish themselves to the Continent &c, but not have been sent to Botany Bay with Rogues & Pickpockets. Such a sentence He was sure wd. not have been passed in England. — Mr. Baker who had called in, said He thought their crime much greater than that of a rogue or pickpocket and approved the sentence.

Jodrell said that in consequence of some outrage at Macclesfield a calculation had been made of the number of disaffected persons, and these were reckoned abt. 36, among abt. 12000 inhabitants. — He said that Tom Walker of Manchester is indited for High Treason, and that the Inditement will not hold good. Tom had fitted up a part of his warehouse for the reception of his Democratic friends.

He said, as Tom Kershaw had mentioned before that Rolles Lee of Adlington was only 40 years old when he died — The estate is strictly entailed, and He died much in debt. He owed a Butcher between 2 & 300 pds — Rolles had a sort of nervous or paralytic affection in one of his hands long since, owing to hard living.

The mother of Rolles Lee was daughter to a Sir Richd. Davenport, who married a sister of old Mr. Lee of Adlington. She married Mr. Rolles of Kingston, & Mr. Lee settled his whole estate on her for her life, which she divided with Rolles Lee. It is from 7 to 8000 a year.

Tom Kershaw told me, Rolles Lee had given Sally Heath a Bond for £200 a year for Her Life, but it is of no value, as He has left no personalty.

Tom & Jack Orme were with him when He died. He was laid on a sopha, and was perfectly sensible. — He has left one son & one daughter. The Estate *after the Rolles*, is settled on Mr. Cross of Shaw-Hill.

Mrs. Jodrell is so well recovered as to be able to dance lately on the anniversary of their 19th. wedding day.

Mr. Baker brought me a letter from Henry Webber. Mr. Heaviside has informed him He will not take a *farthing less* than 50 guineas for attending his Brother.

Mr. Baker is desirous to see Marchant an Academician.

H. Hamond at home with us this evening. — Lady Inchiquin sent me 8 large pannels which Sir Joshua had bought — to paint upon.

Thursday Jany 30th.

a Thaw, Glass 42. — Painting.

Went on the eveing to C & J Offley and Hamond.

Friday Jany 31st.

Thaw. Glass 49. — Painting. Fuseli called on me & wishing to speak to me I call'd on him. He is anxious abt. Marchant at the election. I told him I cd. not judge how the election wd. go, so many interests have risen. I told him I shd be very glad to serve Marchant if there was a *prospect* of doing it. — I told him I wd drink tea with him on Monday next & consider the state of the Academy as far as we cd. judge of it.

The Club was very full today 23 members present. Stothard came for the first time. Hoppner talked a good deal abt. the Duke of Clarence with whom He passed a week at Petersham two or 3 Summers ago. He spoke of the Prince of Wales as exceeding beyond comparison his other Brothers in manners. The Duke of Clarence uncommonly illiterate. Hoppner said every day after they had dined, the Duke took him to walk 10 or 12 miles.

Mrs. Jordan affords very little entertainment in Company. Her thoughts seem to be engaged abt. something not present. — Very ignorant as to information, *excepting* in what relates merely to the stage.

Jack Bannister, affords entertainment by his talent for mimickry and by retailing jokes, but is in respect of understanding an ordinary man.

Tyler being in conversation with Catton, call'd me to them. It was in consequence of Catton having told him that Beechy had in the room that Afternoon said that Lawrence cd. not be elected as He was not of age. — I described to Catton the distinction between *election* & admission. I afterwards spoke to Hamilton on the subject who was much alarmed. I told Hamilton I wd. drink Tea with him tomorrow & consider what cd. be done to prevent the objection causing a disappointment.

Garvey said Sir Watkins Williams Wynne bid in a very spirited manner for Pictures at the sale of John Hunters Pictures. Marlows, St. Angelo & the Companion, (a pair), sold for 20 guineas. Wilsons for 42 guineas, (His 25 guinea size). Marlows, London Bridge, waterworks, sold for 8 guineas. — Note — Marlows Pictures fall in value; Wilsons rise.

Went from the Club to Opies, Miss Beevor, 2 Miss Booths, Miss Dawson, of Liverpool, Captn. Beevor, & Mr. Smith there. — Marchant went with me from the Club.

FEBRUARY 1794

Saturday Feby 1st.

Beautiful weather — Glass 52. Dr. Rees, the Author of the Continuation of Chambers Dictionary, a Dissenting Clergyman, sat to Dance this morning for a Profile.

He told us Dr. Chauncy left him an annuity in the French funds of 100, but that He had not recd. anything in the 2 last years, and did not suppose He shd. receive any more.

From his conversation He did not appear to hold Democratic principles. Abt. 2 oClock Lady Inchiquin sent to desire to speak with [me] immediately. I found Mr. Burke, Mr. Drew & Lord Inchiquin together. — In the Library Lady Inchiquin spoke to me alone, and was much agitated by a conversation which had a little before taken place relative to the claims for pictures. She said Mr. Drew represented the case of the pictures in such a manner to Mr. Burke as to make him of the same opinion.

I told Her Ladyship, it made no difference to me what Mr. Drew said. The Case was plain.

We went into the dining parlour where stood the whole length of the Duchess of Gordon. Mr. Burke asked me if I considered that as a picture finished in such a manner as Sir Joshua wd. have suffered to pass. I answered that I had seen many pictures of his less finished. — Mr. Burke on the whole was satisfied with my remarks & Mr. Drew made no more difficulties. Mr. Malone was now with us.

I left Lady Inchiquin well satisfied. Lord Inchiquin has this day told Christie that the sale of the collection of Old Masters shall not come forward this season. Christie endeavoured to persuade his Ldship that it was a favorable time. I remarked to Lady Inchquin & His Ld.ship, that both the last Spring & at the present time Christie only consulted His own interest or convenience.

Marchant drank with us. Cosway today voluntarily promised him a vote & said He shd vote for Stothard and Tresham. He believed Hoppner wd. have many votes.

153

In the evening I went to Hamiltons. Lawrence was there. We talked. Tyler came. We talked over what had passed in conversation with Catton in consequence of Beechy having told him at the Club that Lawrence "is not elligible by age".

I told Lawrence I could not reckon upon his being certain of more than nine votes, and that I thought Hoppner might reckon on Ten.

Sunday Feby 2d.

Very fine day. Glass 50. Bissell call'd on me. He has seen Admiral Gardner who told him of my having exerted myself in his favor. The Admiral told him he cd. not take him into the Queen 'till He had served in some other ship. That many Ships were going with him to India, and that he must endeavour to get into one of them.

I told Bissell I wd. write to Captn. Westcote to desire him to use his interest, at Portsmouth to get him a situation.

Today Lawrence sat for a profile to Dance.

C. Offley dined with me.

Marchant came in the evening. He has call'd on Garvey today and went to Kensington to Yenn, who did not give him any assurance of assistance by voting for him. Garvey was out.

Met N. Dance & Sir George Beaumont, who had called on me when I was out.

Monday Feby 3d.

Very fine day. Glass 50. — Painting.

Call'd on Bonomi, but did not see him. called on Humphry & satisfied him that Lawrence was elligible by age. Stubbs was there sitting for his portrait. I engaged him to sit for a profile to Dance.

Humphry declared he meant to vote for Stothard, Westall, Marchant, & Lawrence.

I met Lawrence and went with him to his Lodgings. I told him Hoppner is strongly supported. He shewed me a drawing he has made, a design from Milton. He has not time to paint from it for the Exhibition.

Marchant call'd on me. He has been with Burch, who votes in preference for Beechy, but gave Marchant some hope. Burch told Marchant that it was the opinion of some Academicians that *one* Artist in *their Line,* was all the Academy would receive at one time. Burch is hurt at the prospect of the Commemoration Medal being given to Marchant.

I drank tea and passed the evening with Opie at Fuselis. We had much talk abt. the election & Bromleys book. — Marchant who had drank tea at Copleys joined us. — Copley promised Marchant a vote, & desired him to tell *us* that He shd certainly bring forward a motion relative to Bromleys Book, for which He was now better prepared than when he before mentioned it.

Fuseli had invited Northcote to join us, but He did not come.

Copley told Marchant Lawrence ought not to be elected on acct. of his age which was not compleat 25 as the Law required.

Tuesday Feby 4th.

Fine day. Glass 50. — Call'd on Lady Inchiquin who desired my opinion as to the disposal this Spring of the Collection of Prints & drawings. I told her I thought there wd. not be in my opinion any risk in bringing *them* to sale, as they were articles of much less value than the Pictures.

I called at the Shakespeare Gallery and went with Boydell to Bulmers, who has Hotpressed 300 of each of 24 Subjects of the river views.

A remark has been made by Gresse that there shd have been a greater variety of *effects* & in the *tinting* the different views. — He does not know how incapable the Colourists are of executing anything difficult, and how heavy the prints come where *effects* are attempted.

George Steevens formerly observed that the Skies in general, rather represented an Italian than an English Atmosphere. — The reason above stated rendered it necessary to execute them in a simple manner.

Mr. Lodge came to the Gallery, and expressed a deep concern for the loss of two intimate friends, Mr. Brooke & Mr. Pingo of the Heralds Office, who were last night with [blank: '15 killed' added at foot of page in diary] others crushed to death at the Little Theatre in the Haymarket, by the pressure, on the first opening the doors. It was in the Pit passage. The King, Queen & Family were at the Play.

Mr. Repton was at the Gallery and shewed me some of his explanatory sketches for proposed alterations of buildings &c.

Early this morning Stothard call'd on me. — He is very anxious abt. the election. — Bacon has promised him. Russell has given him hopes. He thanked me for the voluntary intention I had expressed of assisting him. — He told me his Father kept a public House in Long acre. That He was bred in Yorkshire, His Father placed him at School that his morals might not be affected by the scenes in a public House. He was apprentice to a pattern drawer.

I reccomended to him to call on some of the Academicians, as He is not personally much known.

In the evening Lawrence called on me. He has been with Copley, who is perfectly satisfied of his being elligible by age.

Recd. a letter from Dick [Richard Farington], in which He mentions the ruinous state of Will Whittakers affairs.

Wednesday Feby 5th.

Hazy morning. Fine day, Glass 47.

Called on G. Dance to inform him Stubbs will set for his profile — I afterwards called on Stothard.

Called on Copley: Had a long conversation with him on the Academy business. He will bring forward a motion on Monday, declaring it is required that an Academician should be 25 years of age at the time of *admission.* I said I wd. second it.

He complained from having been prevented from putting down in writing the state of the Academy funds when the Council audited the accts. on new years eve. I concurred with him that it is a secrecy on the part of the Treasurer, unbecoming the freedom of the Society.

He touched on Bromleys Book. I desired we might not enter on that subject, as I wished to be able to say in the Academy that I acted from myself. He however added that Barry had been with him & would certainly oppose the Book remaining in the Library.

Copleys son was at home. He had the honour of being second wrangler at Cambridge the last term, when he took his degree. He is of Trinity College.

Mr. & Mrs. Hamilton, Mr. Tyler & Lawrence dined with us. — We talked over the subject of the ensuing election.

Fifteen persons were killed at the Haymarket Theatre on Monday night. — Hoppner called.

Thursday, Feby 6th.

Dull day. Glass 50. — Painting. Westall called on me this morning. Nollekens & Russell vote for him.

Marchant called. Northcote will vote for him.

Lawrence call'd. Cosway will vote for him & will speak to Loutherburgh. I told him that a complaint had been made of his not speaking to Monnier [Mosnier] when He met him as an instance of supercilious conduct. He said He did not know enough of Monier to speak to him unless the latter had shewn some disposition to it.

Marchant gave me his statement relative to the introduction of works of Artists duty free into England.

Copy of Mr. Marchant's Statement.

"Mr. Marchant during his residence in Rome, had often heard the British Artists make complaints respecting the heavy duties upon their studies &c when imported into England."

"Mr Marchant one day dining with Lord Camelford, & knowing His lordship's connexion with the Minister (Mr. Pitt) took an opportunity of representing to His Lordship the heavy expence the Artists were subject to in consequence of the severe duties. Lord Camelford felt for the situation of the Artists & with humane feeling, being persuaded that several of them could scarce pay the expence of sending them to England by sea, much less bear the additional expence of the duties, His Lordship took the matter up warmly — and desired Mr. Marchant would go to the English Coffee House and acquaint the Artists that if they would draw up a Memorial Lord Camelford would get it presented to the English Minister (Mr. Pitt)".

"Accordingly, Mr. Marchant mentioned His Lordships good intentions to the Artists, and after some meetings to consider the matter, a Memorial was produced by Mr. Revely, which after some alterations had been made, was delivered to Lord Camelford, who with the assistance of the Dean of Norwich (Dr. Loyd) corrected it and put it into a proper form.

Lord Camelford told Mr. Marchant that it was necessary to procure letters from foreign Artists to shew that in other countries their works were admitted duty free. — Mr. M. applied to several foreign Artists for letters and succeeded. Besides these letters Lord Camelford said it was necessary that such British Artists who had felt the weight of the Custom House duties, shd. also send letters with the memorial stating the reasons for their complaints. Several letters were accordingly sent to Lord Camelford for that purpose, One letter of which from Mr. Irwin was directed to Mr. Marchant, Mr. Irwin considering Mr. M. as an acting person in that undertaking;

"January 10th. 1788, Lord Camelford gave a dinner to the British Artists in Rome, — After dinner the Memorial was brought forward and signed by all the Artists present, in the presence of a Notary public. Mr. Jenkins & Mr. Gavin Hamilton signed their names as witnesses. Lord Belgrave soon after took the above Memorial to England".

About a twelve month afterward, Mr. Marchant returned to England, when one day being in company with Mr. Rose, (Secretary to the Treasury) Mr. Marchant prayed his support of the Memorial. Mr. Rose said he wd use his services in behalf of the Artists as it was but just He should do so. Mr. Marchant overjoyed at this success wrote to Mr. Hewetson (Sculptor at Rome). Mr. Hewetsons answer is as follows.

"The Artists here are particularly obliged to you for having so judiciously recommended our memorial. This is a Child of your own and you do right not to abandon it".

Lord Camelford soon after his arrival in England sent to Mr. Marchant and desired him to go to Mr. Long (Secretary of Treasury) and tell him Mr. Pitt approved of the Memorial, and Mr. Harding would bring on the business, and hoped Mr. Long would support it.

Mr. Marchant afterwards went to Mr. Rose on the same business. Lord Camelford desired Mr. Marchant would use his best efforts among the Members of both Houses. — Mr. Hippesley was so good to say, if necessary, he would in behalf of it use all his interest among his friends. Mr. Marchant made frequent visits to Lord Camelford previous to His Lordship going abroad. — Lord Camelford returned to England again, and sent for Mr. Marchant on the business of the Memorial and during his stay in England Mr. M. was referred to.

"The day before Lord Camelford last left England, his Lordship told Mr. M. the Memorial had met with Mr. Pitts approbation, and the only thing remaining was to settle with Mr. West, the President of the Royal Academy, what articles should be duty free &c".

Mr. Rose told Marchant that the duties on the importation of Art both antient & Modern was no object, not amounting to more than 15 or £1600 a year.

Lord Inchiquin told me that Will Burke, who has been in India, translated Brissots Pamphlet adressed to his Constituents, from which Lord Mornington on the opening of the Session quoted so many passages. Bourdeaux is seated on the Garonne, or Gironde; and being the center of a department named from that River; the appellation of Girondists was given to a Party, whose leaders were Brissot, Roland, Petion, Vergniaux, Isnard, Condorcet &c &c.

The Girondin faction were also called *federalists,* having been accused by Robespierre, Marat &c of a treasonable design to break the *republick one and indivisible,* (whose unity they contended could only be preserved by the supremacy of Paris) into a number of *Confederate* Commonwealths.

Richard Burke, Counsellor at the Bar, and Recorder of Bristol, died suddenly on Tuesday last at his Chambers in Lincolns Inn. He was Brother of Edmund Burke. — He bore a strong family likeness to his Brother.

In the course of the last winter I passed an evening in company with him — Edmd. Burke & his son, — and Mrs. Edmd. Burke, at Lord Inchiquins.

Friday Feby 7th.

Dull day with rain. Glass 48.

Westall call'd this morning. — Lawrence call'd when I was out. I sat to Humphry. Westall called in the eving. Wilton has promised him a vote.

Lawrence & Hamilton call'd in the eving. — Catton has told Tyler He votes for Lawrence, Westall & Beechy. Hamilton has been with Mrs Wheatley, who says Wheatley will not come to town on Monday.

Saturday Feby 8th.

Fine day. Glass 50. Call'd on Tyler, who went with me to Garvey, — w talked to him on the subject of the election & found him disposed to ac with us. — He has been strongly urged in favor of Hoppner.

Went with Marchant to Dance, who finish'd his profile. Hoppner wa there. He came away with me and conversed urgently abt the election.

I called on Fuseli, who wished to speak to me relative to the election. told him Marchant had a very doubtful chance.

I din'd with Dance: Stubbs there who had sat for his profile. Stubbs gav us an acct. of his progress in Arts from infancy. — I went in the evening t Hamiltons.

Sunday Feby 9th.

Fine day. Glass 50. — Breakfasted with Wyatt, who shewed me sever paintings of flowers in water colours, by the Princess Elizabeth, painte for the Queen & intended for screens. The Queen has given Wyatt a Gold watch, and the Princesses Elizabeth & Augusta a Silver Ink Stand with their Cyphers & Coronet on it.

Wyatt will give a vote to Stothard. I called on Opie — Hoppner had been with him — Opie is disposed to give a preference to others at the election.

I call'd on Copley. Hoppner was there but went away. — Copley will support the Candidates who are senior to the last elected. — Call'd on Westall & advised him to call on Opie. Dick & Eliza [Farington] came to Town to dinner. It is supposed W: Whittaker & Co. have failed for £40,000, and will not pay more than a shilling in the pound. — Mrs. Edge will lose £1000, by them. Mrs. J. Whittaker of Ardwick £2000 her all. — Mrs. Betty Boardman £60 a year, — Tom Tipping £5000.

Hamilton call'd in the evening.

Monday Feby 10th.

Fine day. Glass 49. — Breakfasted with Lawrence and recommended to him to call on Opie.

Met Russell who is disposed to vote for the senior Candidates.

Called on Cosway, and had a long conversation with him, in which I fully explained myself to him on the subject of election. He does not know how Loutherburgh votes, but Hoppner has called on him. — Coombes came & strongly supported my arguments. I told Cosway that his & Loutherburghs votes would decide the election in my opinion. On my way to the Academy I called on Garvey and renewed my arguments with success. In Tavistock St. I met Mr. & Mrs. Loutherburgh, who I joined & returned to Cosways with them. I found Loutherburgh well disposed to give a preference to the Senior Candidates. Coombes din'd at Cosways.

Fuseli & Opie dined with me. We found it was very improbable that we shd be able to bring Marchant in, therefore agreed to give a preference to Stothard, Lawrence & Westall. Dance came in & went with us to the Academy.

Members present at the Academy.

Messrs West

Chambers	Rigaud
Wilton	Wyatt
Dance	Banks
Bartolozzi	Farington
P. Sandby	Opie
Tyler	Northcote
Catton	Hodges
Zoffany	Russell
Burch	Hamilton
Cosway	Fuseli

Nollekens	Yenn
Copley	Humphry
Barry	Smirke
Bacon	Bourgeois
Loutherburgh	
Garvey	

Mr. West having taken the Chair — Copley brought forward a motion for a censure & rejection of Bromleys Book.

Balot.

In the room of Webber

1st. Balot.

Stothard	16		Stothard	16
Hoppner	8			
Bonomi	3	2d. Balot		
Marchant	1		Hoppner	13
Beechy	1			29
Reinagle	1			

In the room of Hoare

1st. Balot.

Lawrence	14		Lawrence	15
Hoppner	7			
Bonomi	3	2d. Balot		
Marchant	3			
Beechy	2		Hoppner	13
Westall	1			28

In the room of Serres

1st. Balot.

Westall	16		Westall	14
Hoppner	5			
Bonomi	4	2d. Balot		
Marchant	3		Hoppner	14
Beechy	3			28

Mr. West, gave the casting vote in favor of Westall. — He said when Artists of equal merits were so situated He considered it his duty to give a preference to seniority. Sir William Chambers went away after the Balot concerning Bromleys Book, and before the election. Wyatt went away after the first election when He voted for Stothard.

Members who voted for Stothard, Lawrence & Westall.

doubtful – Wilton	Loutherburgh	Fuseli
Dance	Garvey	Humphry
Bartolozzi	Farington	Smirke
Tyler	Opie	
doubtful ⊢ Catton	Hodges	
Cosway	Russell	
Copley	Hamilton	

For Hoppner &c.

Bourgeois	Nollekens
Yenn	Burch
Northcote	Zoffany
Banks	P. Sandby
Rigaud	
Barry	

Tuesday Feby 11th.

Wet day. Glass 50. — Call'd at Shakespears Gallery where I met Coombes, G. Steevens, & Nicol & told them of the election. — Barry came in, & spoke very loud upon Bromleys book, many of the most material passages of which He said were taken from His Lectures. He spoke also against the use of the Kings Name in the Academy by Sir Willm Chambers. In short He was much more determined in his declaration now than He was last night on Bromleys book &c.

I looked over the arrangement of the prints in the first Vol: with Coombes.

I call'd on Marchant who became well satisfied that his friends could not assist him at the election.

I call'd on Copley, who is not disposed to let the subject of Bromleys Book rest. I told him any motion to succeed must be a *moderate* one.

Wednesday, Feby 12th.

Fine day. Glass 50. Call'd on Nollekens. He & Mrs. N. are much against Bromleys book. — They are much disappointed that Hoppner was not elected.

Call'd on Northcote. His Picture of Bolingbroke & Richd. 2d. is the best painted of any He has finished. Northcote told me of his having acquainted Hoppner last night of the unhandsome manner in which the latter had spoken of him. Hoppner is much mortified at losing the election. Fuseli call'd on me in consequence of receiving a letter from Mr. Bromley.

Today Boswell, Mr. Howard, the Surgeon, G. Dance, Richards, Garvey, Tyler & Dick dined with me. They staid till past 12.

Thursday, Feby 13th.

Fine day. Glass 57.

Went with Westall to Cosways. — Afterwards call'd on Lady Inchiquin.

In the eveng drank tea with Fuseli, who sent an answer to Mr. Bromley under cover to Mr. West. Fuseli did not explain only sent paralel passages. — In the evening went with Fuseli to Hamiltons.

Friday, Feby 14th.

Very fine day. Glass 57.

Call'd on Humphry. Afterwards breakfasted at the Duke of Montroses. The Dutchess much improved in her drawing.

Met Coombes, who related to me his difficulty abt. a dedication to the King, as Boydell objected yesterday to the *"4 principal rivers"*, being mentioned in it, as the work may be stopped if not successful. — Coombes also said they were preparing ordinary blue bindings which have a coarse appearance. — I went with Coombes to the Gallery where we found Steevens & Bulmer & they concurred that it would be illjudged to have a common papered cover. — In the dedication the *"principal Rivers"* is to be inserted without numbering them.

Din'd at the Club. Nineteen present. I sat by Wyatt, who told me that on the 7th. of last June the King *voluntarily* promised him the place of Surveyor General of the Works in case he survived Sir William Chambers. A few months after [he] told Wyatt that He had declared this to Mr Pitt to prevent applications. Wyatt considers the Queen as a very warm friend to him.

In the course of our conversation I told Wyatt of the apprehension several members of the Academy were under lest the King shd give the place of treasurer of the Academy to an improper person and of our wish that something cd. be hinted to the King on this subject. — He said Lord Harcourt was the most proper man for the purpose, & I told him I wd. take any opportunity that offered to mention it to His Ldship.

Wyatt is always treated with great respect at Windsor. He always dines at the Equerries table. — He told me that Ld. Harcourt is the only Nobleman who dines with the Royal Family, and that He has dined at the Equerries table with Marquiss Salisbury &c when Ld. Harcourt has been dining with the King. — One reason has been given on the Score of etiquette, which is that the King has been the guest of Ld. Harcourt at Nuneham.

Wyatt told me that the King has an intention of doing many things at

Windsor, but defers it during the life of Sir William Chambers.

The King has seen some of Reptons books on Gardening, and seems to think them rather Coxcomical works.

The King told Wyatt that before the 7th. of June last several applications had been made to him for the Surveyorship, on the decease of Sir William, but that He had given it away: after which He added it was to Mr. Wyatt, who he considered as the first Architect of the Kingdom & most proper for it. — Wyatt bowed & expressed his gratitude.

From the Club I went to Opies.

Saturday Feby 15th.

Fine day. Glass 57. — Westall breakfasted with me. — To remove any difficulties between him & Northcote, I went with him & introduced him to Northcote who I knew wd. be pleased, as was the case.

Bob came to day and dined. I recd. a letter from Capt. Westcote, who has got Bissell a berth.

Sunday Feby 16th.

Damp day. Glass 52. Breakfasted with Dance. Shewed the Profiles to Mrs. Opie, & Miss Hadfield.

Dined at Stubbs with Dance & Cosway.

Monday Feby 17.

Breakfasted with Admiral Gardner & shewed him Captn. Westcotes letter.

Bissell dined with me and went down to Portsmouth. He is to be a Midshipman on board the Orion of 74 guns. — Dick gave Bissell [blank].

Tuesday 18th.

Call'd on Mr. Heaviside relative to the settlement of Webbers acct. — Afterwards call'd on Copley who was going to call on Fuseli, Opie, & Northcote, on acct. of the motion concerning Bromleys book.

Dined with Dick & Bob at Offleys. — Recd. by the Penny Post a *Circular* letter in verse, abusing Copley on acct. of Bromleys book, and Fuseli, Opie, & myself as abettors.

Wednesday Feby. 19th.

Mild weather.

Went with Fuseli to Hodges where we found Tyler who told us He had determined to bring forward a motion for the discontinuance of the subscription to Bromleys book. Hodges agreed to support the motion.

Tyler afterwards went with me to Cosways, who wishes a motion to be put only to caution the Council against receiving books without examining them. This we remarked only left the business where it now is, but will have no conclusive operation against a book which has given offence. Cosway came to no determination.

I afterwards called on Smirke & told him Tyler would make the motion.

Drank tea with Fuseli, Smirke there. In the eving. call'd on Opie, & went with him to Copleys.

Thursday Feby 20th.

Mild weather. — At Lady Inchiquins who expressed mortification *at no medal* being given to the family of Sir Joshua Reynolds. — Met Northcote at the Shakespeare Gallery, He was at Cosways last night, & represented strongly to Banks & Cosway, the necessity for discontinuing the subscription to Bromleys book. — His picture of Richd. 2d. & Bolingbroke put up today.

Smirke & Fuseli dined with me and we went together to the Academy. There were present.

Mr. West		
Sir Wm. Chambers	—	T. Sandby
Wilton	—	P. Sandby
Tyler	—	Newton
Burch	—	Cosway
Nollekens	—	Copley
Barry	—	Bacon
Garvey	—	Rigaud
Banks	—	Farington
Opie	—	Northcote
Hodges	—	Russell
Hamilton	—	Fuseli
Yenn	—	Humphry
Smirke	—	Bourgeois
Richards Secretary		

After the Minutes were read, Fuseli rose, & desired to adress himself to the meeting in consequence of something which had happened relative to the business of Mr. Bromleys book. — Mr. West rose & said, as President, He must resist any attempt to introduce matter different from the proper object of the Meeting viz: to consider the business of the Medal. —Sir Willm Chambers spoke to the same effect. — Mr. Copley then rose & complained of the attacks made on him in newspapers & by circular letters & said the abettors of such proceedings were as guilty as the principal mover. Hodges rose with indiscreet warmth, and a violent altercation took place. — I then addressed the meeting and said if Mr. Copley had made use of improper words, allowance shd. be made for a man injured by such attacks. Mr. Bacon requested the business of the medal might now go on which would restore peace & order. I replyed it could hardly be expected harmony shd.

prevail in a Society where an injured man was not supported by his brethren, and if Mr. Fuseli was prevented from speaking those who espoused his cause would feel for his injury. Mr Bacon finding that Mr. Fuseli had new matter to state complyed, & Mr. West understanding Mr. Fuseli had no motion to make consented to his stating what had passed between him & Mr. Bromley. — Fuseli then recapitulated the whole with comments to the satisfaction of the members.

After He had concluded Tyler rose & shortly moved that the subscription to the Revd. Mr. Bromleys history of the Arts be discontinued. He was seconded by Smirke. — Objections were started by Bacon &c as to the impropriety of refusing the 2d. Volume after having recd. the first. — I said the first Vol: had been recd. witht. the contents having been known, — being known they were disapproved — and to continue the subscription was to encourage a work which from the specimen had was likely to encrease the disatisfaction felt in the Academy. That a man who had written with so little delicacy on the works of living artists already, might be expected to describe with great partiality and ignorance in his future volumes the professional characters of the very persons then assembled.

The Members now appearing disposed to vote for the motion of discontinuance, it was again offered by Tyler but Hodges & Newton said they would only vote for it to be *reccomended* to the *Council,* to discontinue the subscription. This not coming up to the Idea of proper control which ought to belong to the body at large, Tylers motion was put when the following persons voted, — That the subscription to the Revd. Mr. Bromleys History of the Arts be ordered to be discontinued.

For the motion

Tyler	Farington
Burch	Opie
Cosway	Northcote
Nollekens	Russell
Copley	Hamilton
Barry	Fuseli
Bacon	Humphry
Garvey	Smirke
Rigaud	

against the motion

Bourgeois
Yenn
Hodges
Newton

Sir Wm. Chambers — Wilton — P. Sandby — T. Sandby — Banks — did not vote. — Hodges & Newton would have voted to reccommend the discontinuance of the subscription to the Council.

The members then proceeded on the business of the medal. I proposed a committee of 11 to be appointed including the President — they were accordingly elected by scratching lists.

Bacon	21
Fuseli —	19
Nollekens —	15
Smirke —	14
Cosway —	14
Hamilton —	14
Northcote —	10
Banks —	11
Burch —	10
Rigaud.	

Copley & Rigaud had each 9 and being *balotted* for

Rigaud had 11
Copley — 7

I then moved that a silver medal shd. be presented to the *representative* of Sir Joshua Reynolds, which was carried unanimously. Fuseli, Smirke & Opie went home with me and staid till past one oClock.

Friday, Febry 21st.

Wet day. — Call'd at Hamiltons & from thence to Shakespeare Gallery & told Coombes & Boydell what passed at Academy. — Dined at Offleys with Evans, Hodges, Humphry, Tyler, Plott, Dick & Bob.

Saturday — Febry 22d.

Mild weather. Lieut. Coll. Hewgill & his wife call'd to see the sketches of Valenciennes.

Mr. Poggi call'd on me to speak abt. disposing of Sir Joshua Reynolds collection, of drawings. — He asks 13 per cent for his trouble.

Sunday — Febry 23d.

Mild very fine weather. — Call'd on Lady Inchiquin to mention what Poggi has proposed to me. — She thinks his terms extravagant.

Call'd on Northcote, — and on Fuseli, met Copley there.

Met Hodges who said at Church today He was suddenly seized with a disposition to faint.

Dined at Mr. Bakers. — Hearne, Joe Green, Pouncy, — and Mr. Bidwell of the Secretary of States Office there.

Mr. Bidwell says the Duke of Grafton has £30,000 a year on the table.

Gresse the drawing Master died suddenly on Thursday last. Cousins is now confined under the care of Dr. Monro, who has no expectation of his recovery, as it is a total deprivation of nervous faculty.

Monday — Feby 24th.

Mild weather, Glass 56.
Breakfasted at Ld. Inchiquins, Poggi came there. He agreed to take 10 pr cent, and that the Catalogues shall be sold.

Tuesday Feby 25th.

Glass 59.
Breakfasted at Ld Inchiquins.
Mr. Jodrell, Mr. & Mrs. Hodges, Marchant, & Dick, dined with me.

Wednesday, 26th.

Glass 53. — Very fine day.
Steers called, and desired me to paint for him a small view of Kew Bridge, for which he sent me a bond.

Thursday, Feby 27th.

Glass 54. — Fine day. — Dined at Sir Alexander Hamiltons in Upper Harley St. with Dick, Eliza & Susan.

Friday 28th.

Glass 52, Cold & rainy.
Sat to Opie — Bone the Enamel painter called to desire to copy my portrait by Opie in Enamel.

Hughes, Steers, Champernowne & Captn. Newton call'd. We went together to Comyns, the Picture cleaner to see 4 Pictures by Vernet. 800 guineas is the price they are estimated at. — One of them a Sea Storm on a Coast painted in 1754 is in Vernets best manner.

This afternoon Fuseli sent me a letter which He has recd. from Bromley, demanding a meeting with him on a point of Scholarship, before Sir George Baker, Mr. Knight or Mr. Seward.

In the evening I call'd on Smirke. — A meeting was held last night on the subject of the medal.

Messr. Desenfans & Harries sent me a ticket of introduction to see their collection of Monsr. Calonnes pictures, at the room in Spring gardens.

MARCH 1794

Saturday — March 1st.

Glass 52. — Cold weather.

Dined at the Club, which was postponed from yesterday, on acct. of the General Fast.

Sunday 2d.

Glass 54.

Mr. Champernowne & another Gentleman call'd on me to see my drawings. Mr. C. fixed on two with Asphaltum Outlines washed with India Ink.

Monday 3rd.

Glass 59. A wet day.

Dined with Mr. Champernowne at the Blenheim Coffee House, Messrs. Steers, Henderson of the Adelphi, Froude, & another gentleman there.

Fuseli sent an answer to Bromleys letter this day, which He shewed to Smirke before He sent it.

Lady Inchiquin sent to me today to desire I would come to Her to have my opinion on her resolution only to dispose of *part only* of Sir Joshuas collection of drawings this Spring. I told her she must take care to have the public assured that the part reserved were not superior to those brought forward. It must be a *division* & not a *selection*. This she saw the propriety of.

The Duke & Duchess of Montrose called on me, and now the Duke resolved to have *the View of Buchannan* as before intended. Dick dined at the Church & King Club at the Free Masons.

Tuesday [4th].

Glass 56.

Mr. Champernowne & Froude call'd on me. — Tyler call'd, abt. the Commemoration dinner. We could only make out that 59 dined including strangers. Richold had charged for more.

168

Humphry & Carey dined with me. Will came from Hoddesdon with a letter from Monro, the Purser relative to the Lascelles.

Wednesday, March 5th.

Glass 56, a fine day.
Lysons breakfasted with me. — Sir George Beaumont called.
I have been three days closely employed painting on Gadshill.

Thursday 6th.

Glass 54. Fair day. In the evening at the Antiquarian Society. — Sir Jos: Banks, S. Lysons & myself signed Smirkes reccomendation to be a Fellow. Sir Joseph sets off this eveng for Lincolnshire, to meet the gentlemen of the County as High Sheriff, when He will make a proposal for arming certain bodies.
Today I finished the Landscape of Gadshill.

Friday 7th.

Glass 54. Very fine day.
Breakfasted at Sir George Beaumonts. — Went to Spring gardens, to see Monsr. De Calonnes collection of pictures, mortgaged to Desenfans & Herries. They admit professional Artists — but no others, at present, notwithstanding many applications.
Mr. Champernowne, Steers, John Offley, H. Hamond, and Dick dined with me. — George Dance, & Mr. Jodrell came to Tea.

Saturday, March 8th.

Glass 52. Very fine day. I breakfasted with Steers. — Afterwards called on Taylor for information abt. Miss Athertons case against the Lancaster extension Canal passing through her grounds..
Dined with Dick & Eliza & Susan, at Mr. Fryers. — Mr. & Mrs. Hughes, Mrs. Watts, & Philips there.

Sunday March 9th.

Glass 52. Fair day.
Breakfasted with Sir George Beaumont. — Went with Hughes to G. Dance who made a profile drawing from him.
Harry came to town.

Monday 10.

Glass 53. Cloudy day. Hughes call'd and with Dick we went to Sir G Beaumonts at noon where we found N. Dance. — We went together to Comyns to see the pictures by Vernet. From thence to the Committee Room at the House of Commons where Mr. Rawstorne was examining on

the question of Miss Atherton's opposition to the Lancaster Canal extension Bill passing through Her grounds. — No division took place.

Mr. Dance expressed a wish to me that his Landscape should be hung
opposite to the door and not in one of the Centers. He thought it a better
situation for the great dinner day.

Tuesday, March 11th.

Glass 53. fine day.

At one oClock went to the Committee Room to hear proceedings in
Miss Athertons case. — Mr. Dance & Sir George attended. — Majority
present evidently in favor of Miss Atherton. Adjourned till Thursday.

Dined at home with Henry & Dick.

Wednesday, 12th.

Glass 52. much rain.

Finished tinting views of Oxford, Hardwick, & Maple Durham & Cirencester, which complete Forty six plates for the first volume.

G. Dance called & spoke to me abt. the place held by T. Sandby of
Deputy Ranger, of Windsor Park. — N. Dance has access to the King.

Bromleys first public letter to Fuseli appeared in the Morning Herald,
this day. — It is filled with gross falsehoods & statements calculated to
mislead.

Leave was this day given for a new Ship in the room of the Lascelles to
be built.

Thursday, March 13.

Glass 52. — Sharp weather & rainy.

Fuseli called & dined with me. He had been with Mr. Lock, who denied
having authorised Mr. Bromley to make use of his name. He said Mr.
Seward introduced Bromley to him. Accordingly Mr. Lock went to Mr.
Seward to speak to him on the liberty which Bromley had taken.

Horace Hamond din'd, Dick & Eliza din'd at Sir A. Hamiltons.

Marchant came in the evening. — Craig call'd to return me my
subscription to the Artists proposed charitable fund, the scheme being
dropped.

Friday [14th].

Glass 52. Showery weather.

The Picture of Gadshill was carried to the Shakespeare Gallery.

I went with G. Dance to the Gallery. Sir H. Englefield, there. He was at
Brookes's when Hare, Fox, &c were laughing over West's first speech, as
published in the newspapers.

Dined at the Club. I mentioned the advertisement relative to Ciprianis
monument. Nollekens promised to enquire into particulars before next
Club day.

Dance told me that Lysons has been with him and that Lady Di Beauclerk is to come to him on Sunday next.

Coombes was at the Gallery. Seward has told him that at a meeting, Knight, Lock &c. have condemned Fuseli's remarks as unfounded. — Seward was decided against the conduct of the Academy.

Boydell & Coombes shewed me the intended Title page to the first Volume of the Thames. I objected to the head of Thames, copied in a wooden print from the model of Mrs. Damer, being printed on the Title page. It is too ill executed.

Saturday — March 15th.

Glass 53. — Rainy weather.

Called on Fuseli. He was yesterday with Seward. Mr. Locke came there. Seward said He saw Bromley (who introduced himself to him) was by his conversation & manner &c vulgar & ignorant. Seward told Him, He (Seward) was not qualified to determine on the subject.

Mr. Rawstorne called on me. — Miss Athertons opposition to the Canal will prevail.

Went to Dance. Lady Susan Bathurst was sitting for a profile. — Lady Triphina Bathurst & Lady Beaumont, and Lysons were also there.

Moreton, a young man, studying under Saml. Wyatt & a relation of Mr. Godwin of Colebrooke Dale, call'd to desire me to give him my advice abt. a background to an Architectural design. — I drank tea with Dance, and reccomended to him to apply to be a Commissioner of the Lotterys; or for a fee farm rent receivership. — Saml. Wyatt came there.

Sunday March 16.

Glass 53. — Rainy weather.

Dick, Harry & Eliza went to Hoddesdon.

At one oClock I called on Dance. The Bishop of Downe, Mrs. Dixon, & Lysons came there. The Bishop sat for a Profile.

Sir G. Beaumont call'd there. N. Dance is this morning drawing a profile of C. Long of the Treasury.

Monday 17th.

Glass 53. At home all day painting. Fuseli dined with me. — He today recd. a letter from Mr. Knight disavowing the affirmations made in his name by Bromley.

Tuesday 18th.

Glass 52. Bromleys second letter to Fuseli was published in the morning Herald, in which paper the attack on Copley, and the puff of Bromleys Book had appeared.

N. Dance call'd and staid with me 3 Hours. — He read over the letters on the dispute between Fuseli & Bromley. — Fuseli whom He did not before know personally called, and related a conversation with Mr. Locke.

Dance recommended the painting Clear Skies with Ultramarine and White alone & to use Ivory Black with White for the Cloud Tints: adding in some cases a little Vermilion or naples yellow. — He said Sir Joshua Reynolds reccomended the using Black for his cloud tint, which He said would always be in harmony with the Blue & White.

We dined at Hamiltons. Tyler & Garvey & H. Hamond & Lawrence there.

Wednesday, March 18th [19th].

Glass 52. — fine day.

Fuseli met me at Opies in the evning. He had recd. a letter from Mr. Lock, disavowing any such declarations as Bromley had asserted in his first public letter to have been concurred in by the gentlemen to whom he had shown the criticism of Fuseli on his book, with his answers.

Thursday, March 19th [20th].

Glass 53. Wind easterly which it has not been for some time.

Lysons called. He goes into the country tomorrow, to complete his drawings of the Roman pavement at [Woodchester] in Gloucestershire.

Sir Alexander, & Lady Hamilton, Tyler, H. Hamond, & Harry dined with us.

Friday, 20th [21st].

Glass 52. Wind easterly, & cold.

Mr. Wyndham, Mr. Bennet Langton & another gentleman called on me to see my sketches of Valenciennes. Mr. Wyndham thought they would make very interesting prints.

I call'd on Smirke & carried to Fuseli his design for the Medal which Fuseli much approved of.

Saturday 21 March [22nd].

Glass 48. — fine day. — wind easterly.

Breakfasted with Humphry.

Recd. a note from Boydell & went to the Shakespeare Gallery with Smirke. — The Picture of Gadshill is much approved of, — but at a certain hour of the day in that room, the upper part appears rather green & Sir George Beaumont reccomended it shd be reduced. Falstaffs head is not fleshy enough they say for his body, and the figure of Prince Henry too boyish & not elegant enough.

George Dance call'd on me. George Webb [Dance] is appointed by N. Smith, the Director, a writer to Bengal. It is necessary a Bond of £1000, for his good behaviour shd. be entered into at the India House, and Dance, requested me to be a surety with him. I said I wd. N. Dance had declined but gave £100 for his outfit. — George Dance told me N. Dance had said that should He George survive him, He had left him one of his estates worth £30,000.

Smirkes design for the Medal was approved of last night by the Committee. West suggested that something shd be added to signify the relation the figure representing the Royal Academy had to the emblems of painting, Sculpture & Architecture. Smirke thought the Idea frivolous, but it was not opposed & passed.

Will, Dick & Harry dined today at Deptford with Sir A. Hamilton &c when the old Lascelles was examined. Her repairs it is supposed will amount to £5000.

Lord Harcourt call'd on me, the first time this season. I was not at home.

Sunday 22 March [23rd].

Glass 52. Wind Easterly.

Went with Smirke to the Shakespeare gallery, where I touched on the Landscape of Gadshill, — and Smirke made the head of Falstaff more fleshy & that of the Prince more manly. He also made the Head of Falstaff in the *trial* scene more fleshy, — and beautified the head of Anne Page.

Horace Hone called on me on his return from Ireland.

Will, & Harry dined with us.

Monday. 23 [24th].

Glass 52. Wind easterly. — Called at the Shakespeare gallery & spoke to J. Boydell abt. the subject He formerly proposed to me to paint of the landing of Richd. 2d. in Wales. As He has since mentioned to Loutherburgh the subject of the killing the Duke of Suffolk in Henry 6th, which is a Coast Scene, the other appears less necessary.

Tuesday March 25th.

Glass 53. Wind Easterly, fine day.

dined at C. Offleys with Susan & Eliza, Harry, Dick, Hamond & Outram, and Harris. — Call'd this forenoon on Fuseli. Sir Brook Boothby there. Bromleys 3d. letter to Fuseli appeared today in the Herald.

Wednesday 26th.

Glass 55. fine day.

George Webb [Dance] went to Portsmouth this evening to go on board the Lord Camden for Bengal.

Ogbourne, the engraver, called on me and fixed on a drawing of mine of Gipsies in a rock scene to engrave for his publication of specimens of modern Masters.

Thursday, 27th.

Glass 52. Wind easterly. fine weather.

Will call'd on me to speak abt. his affairs. After dinner Dick & Harry conversed with me thereon, Will came in the eving., when we had a general conversation on them.

Friday, March 28.

Glass 53. Wind easterly. fine weather . Lord Harcourt & N. Dance call'd on me, but I was too busy to see anybody.

Dined at the Club. — Some conversation abt. Ciprianis monument. West, Cosway & Nollekens went to the Commemoration medal committee at the Academy.

Alderman Boydell call'd on me. He read some part of his proposals for pictures to decorate the Common Council room. He had been with Rigaud who He has engaged to paint some emblematic figures in Fresco. — The Alderman is bigotted to his scheme, which seems to exclude almost every other Idea. — Boswell speaking to me of Langton said, He owed more to Industry than superior talents. — Wyndham is not a comfortable Companion, He cannot confine himself to his seat in company and has a wildness or Exentricity of thought always prevailing. Malone is respectable and gentlemanlike rather than shining. — Boswell dined a few days ago with Marquiss Townshend, who is grown so covetous, that rather than call for a second bottle of Claret He drank Port, because Boswell had joined him in the former. Boswell says He is very proud and fond of his Marquisate, yet affecting to undervalue titles.

Seven or 8 of us staid after tea & drank wine till near eleven. Hoppner in the Chair.

Saturday, March 29th.

Glass 55. Wind South West. Rainy.

Will came this morning. We had further talk of his affairs. I advised him duly to consider his situation.

I call'd on Mr. Bone, the enamel painter, who this day finished his Copy from Opies large picture of me.

N. Dance called but I was not at home.

Sunday, March 30th.

Glass 56. Fine day.

Dined at C. Offleys, with Mrs. Offley, Mrs. Lynch Salusbury, Dick, Eliza, Susan, Hamond, and Outram.

Monday, March 30th [31st].

Glass 55. Showery. Left Cards at Lord Harcourts and N. Dances.

APRIL 1794

Tuesday [April 1st].

Glass 53. Bromleys 4th. letter to Fuseli appeared.

Wednesday, April 1st [2nd].

Glass 55.
Called on N. Dance. His Landscape is improved by the use of
Asphaltum passed over parts of it — In his foreground trees, the *Dark* parts
is composed entirely of Black and light Oker or Naples yellow, & the light
part of the foliage has a little blue added to the light Oker or Naples yellow,
but there is no yellow lake used in any part of the picture. He never uses red
lake. Vermilion is the colour with which He warms his skies & distances. —
In the earthy parts of his foreground He warms by a little terra de Sienna,
added to his Black.
As his picture will not be quite hard, He desired me to apologise to Mr.
Richards for its not being sent till the next week.
Drank tea with Fuseli Mr. Lock has not recd. an answer from Bromley,
but Mr. West has told him that Bromley says He is not the person alluded
to in the printed letter. — Mrs. Wheatley brought me a letter from
Wheatley desiring my interest with Smirke that his pictures may be under
the line like Lawrences.

Thursday — April 2 [3rd].

Glass 53. — rainy weather.
Dined at the British Coffee House, with Hamond, Outram, Gerard, C &
J. Offley, & Dick.

Friday — 4th.

Glass 55. Showery Weather.
Breakfasted at Lawrences with Smirke. Lawrence is desirous to have the
whole length portrait of Lady Manners hung in the center at the head of
the room. — Smirke went to breakfast at my desire, as Lawrence had
applyd to me for my interest with him.

175

I afterwards call'd on Sir George Beaumont in consequence of his leaving a message for me yesterday. I confirmed him in a resolution to exhibit this year. — He desired me to get invitations to the dinner for Lord Beverly & Lord Mulgrave.

In the evening I went with Dick, Eliza & Susan to a dance at C. Offleys. — Tyler, Dr. & Mrs. Hewitt, Hamond & Outram. Miss Bowes, a daughter of Lady Strathmore by Mr. Bowes, came with Mrs. Ogleby of Chelsea, with whom she resides. — There were upwards of 70 persons present.

This afternoon, I went to the Shakespeare Gallery to meet Combes, who read to J. Boydell & me his intended preface to the first volume of the Thames. I proposed an alteration in that part which related to the selection of the views, and to some of the encomiastic part on my share of the undertaking. This alteration is to be made. — The preface I thought on reading once over well judged, and explanatory.

Humphry today in a conversation with me declined exhibiting my portrait this year, as Opie sends his.

I wrote a note of apology to Richards this eving. for not sending my pictures today, also a similar note in the name of Sir George Beaumont & Mr. Dance.

Saturday, April 5th.

Glass 55. A fine day.

N. Dance called on me while I was painting on the view of High St., Oxford, and told me he thought I was making the shadow side of my buildings too warm. He staid with me four Hours, during which time I went over the shadow side of University College, with tints of black & white only, thinned with Macgilp. He was satisfied with the true effect produced by the alteration.

Craig wrote me a letter requesting my interest with the arranging Committee in favor of two drawings which He has sent to the exhibition. In it He explains in a minute manner the bad effect of hanging a drawing with the shadow side towards the window.

Westall yesterday evening call'd on Smirke to remark the same thing, and to request it might be attended to in the disposal of his drawings. Dick, Eliza, & Susan, went to the Play this eveng.

Smirke call'd in the eving. The Pictures sent for exhibition were reviewed today. A greater number were refused than has been remembered. He is afraid there will be an indifferent exhibition. — Danton &c. were executed this day in Paris.

Sunday [6th].

Glass 57.

Breakfasted with Humphry.

Sir George Beaumont call'd on me to desire I wd. endeavour to get an nvitation to the Academy dinner for Mr. Long of the Treasury.

Monday [7th].

Glass 52. Weather cold. Dined in Thornhaugh St. with Dick, Outram, Hamond & C & J. Offley.

Tuesday [8th].

Glass 52. — Showery.

Bromleys 5th. letter to Fuseli. — Breakfasted at Sir G. Beaumonts. — He goes to North Aston on Thursday. Sir John Mitford, Solicitor General, is very desirous of being at the Academy dinner. Mrs. Offley, Mr. & Mrs. Salisbury, Mr. Evans C. J. & Wm. Offley dined with us.

Coombes call'd and read his corrected Preface.

Wednesday 9th.

Glass 52.

Mr. & Mrs. Paine, Mr. & Mrs. Hone & Mr. Hone of Dublin & Joe. Green dined with us. — Humphry came to tea.

Smirke came in the evening. Hoppner is likely to get most reputation by His Portraits of any in that line. — Smirke speaks of a Bachanalian picture by Pelegrini as very good. It is painted for Sir Abraham Hume. — Morland indifferent this year. Shee & Rising fallen off. — Beechy not remarkable.

Thursday 10th.

Glass 55. Showery.

Dined at Tylers, with Mr. & Mrs. Hamilton, Mr. & Mrs. Hodges, Lawrence, Dick & Eliza & Susan.

call'd at Opies this morning, and wrote a note at his desire to Smirke relative to places. H. Hamond & C & J Offley went to Massingham.

Friday, April 11th.

Glass 55.

Breakfasted with Humphry, afterwards call'd on Lawrence & wrote a note at his desire to Smirke, requesting some of his pictures may be hung in certain places.

Lawrence offered to paint my portrait for Mrs. Farington.

Dined at the Club. — We had Conversation enforcing the necessity of being circumspect in the invitation to the Dinner at the Academy.

Copley said it wd. be a good exhibition. — He spoke highly of Sir George Beaumonts landscape, which, He said, wd. have done credit to any artist of any country — also well of Dances landscape, which He said was of the Camera Obscura kind, a direct imitation.

Mr. West said the King told him last Sunday, that He thought Gainsborough Duponts portrait of him was the best likeness that had been painted.

Saturday April 12.

Glass 53. — gloomy.

Craig call'd on me to thank me for the trouble I have taken abt his drawings.

Dick, Eliza & Susan went to the Oratorio at the New Theatre of Drury Lane.

Smirke came in the evening. — They have hung my pictures at the head of the room separated from the Center of Pelegrini by two three quarters of Lawrence & Beechy.

Sunday, April 13th.

Glass 52. wind Easterly.

Breakfasted with Humphry, called on Lawrence.

Mr. Berwick called on me. I was not at home.

Monday — 14.

Glass 58. fine day.

Breakfasted with Lawrence to see his Portrait of Sir G. Eliot. Afterwards called on Northcote, who reprobated Bromley & his letters, — Bourgeois exulted in the first of them, till Northcote exposed their infamy. It shewed the opinion of those connected with Bromly.

Probably the cause of West giving up the competitorship for the design of the Commemmorative Medal was, being told by Bourgeois that Northcote said He ought not to grasp at or expect every honor; that the Academy had clothed him with a robe of velvet, but that He should not struggle for every stripe of ermine.

I wrote a note to Copley requesting his vote for inviting Lords Beverly, Grey de Wilton, & Mulgrave to the dinner, at the Academy.

Taylor of Leigh dined with us. — An account of the execution of Danton, — Camille Desmoulins, — Philipeaux, Herault &c. came today.

Tuesday, April 15th.

Glass 58. A warm day.

Went to Smirke at Holylands Coffee House, in consequence of having recd a letter from the Revd. Dr. Breedon, who desires my interest to have some of the pictures of Mr. Irwine received into the Exhibition. They have been all refused. — Smirke said some of them should be admitted, though they are so indifferent that in any situation they will make a bad appearance. — Mr. Irwine has been in Italy.

The settling the invitation list last night at the Council, went of very smoothly, without the trouble of a balot. — Seward has been invited at the instance of West & Sir Wm. Chambers. — Smirke pointed out to Bartolozzi that Mr. Smith, Mr. Pitts private secretary, did not come within the view of the Academy. He was not invited.

Lawrence told me on Monday last, that Dr. Moore, (the traveller) who is much connected with Lord Lauderdale, was in the house at the third reading of the Bill for encouraging volunteer Corps. Dr. Moore said the speech of Pitt on that occasion exceeded in eloquence, and effect, any He ever heard made, and when Fox rose to reply the Doctor was uneasy for him.

Dr. Moore has been very fortunate in the promotion of his sons, Coll. Moore in the Army, and Captn. Moore in the Navy. — Lord Chatham lately wrote to Doctor Moore expressing the pleasure He felt in having seen Captain Moores name in the list of *Post Captains.* From a First Lord of the Admiralty this was delicate.

Wednesday, April 16.

Glass 62. A very fine day. The weather very warm.

Breakfasted with Humphry.

Lords Beverly, — Grey de Wilton, Mulgrave & C. Long & — Wilberforce, are invited to the Academy dinner.

Call'd on Lawrence.

Called on Lady Inchiquin, in consequence of a message from her. She and Lord Inchiquin requested me to speak to Lawrence abt. coming to a settlement for three pair of Pictures, Viz: Kings & Queens, which have been delivered to him since the death of Sir Joshua. The price they ask is 200 guineas for the 3 pair.

I went to the Shakespeare Gallery & met Coombes, Bulmer and Boydell. — From a conversation with Boydell I find Coombes has recd. £324 on acct. of the first volume of the Rivers. The estimate He gave of this volume has in many respects far exceeded the calculation & it is doubtful to me whether we shall be reimbursed by the sale.

In the eving. I drank tea at the Academy with Smirke, Bourgeois, Wilton and Richard. I went there to enquire if Lord Inchiquin is invited to the Academy dinner as He means to attend. He is invited.

Thursday, April 17th.

Glass 60. Wind Easterly & siroccy sky.

Breakfasted with Lawrence & informed him of the Commission I had from Lord & Lady Inchiquin relative to the Pictures. — He represented to me that He had been obliged to paint near a fortnight on one pair of the pictures, & some days on another pair. On the third pair He must do the same. That Sir Joshua had paid to Roth only 20 guineas a picture and He had supposed He might have the pictures on those terms as Sir Joshua had not touched on any of them. — I went to Lord & Lady Inchiquin &

repeated the conversation I had had with Lawrence, after which they desired to have my opinion. I proposed to split the difference between 120 & 200 gs. which they agreed to.

Lady Inchiquin told me they still have great difficulties abt. the delivery of the portraits. Lord Fife has returned that of his wife, and the Duchess of Gordon having called to see hers, refused it, saying Her eyes were not green, as those in the picture were.

I went to the Shakespeare Gallery and had a conversation with Boydell & Coombes on the subject of the great expence of the first volume of the Thames, above the calculation: Coombes estimate of his claim was 100 Gs. where He has recd. 324 Gs. — I pointed out to him that the work at the price it had been put at, could hardly be expected to pay the expences. We desired him to consider for what sum He cd. undertake the 2d. Volume. After some consideration He proposed 6 gs a week for 10 months. Boydell said his first proposal was to receive 4 gns a week while carrying on the first volume, and that at 6 gns a week the lessening of expence to us wd. be scarcely any thing. — He then said He would meet us half way and take 5 gs. a week for 10 months, in which time the 2d. volume shd. be completed. — He said He wd. undertake to finish by January, if required. These terms we closed with.

In the evng went to the Antiquaries Society with G. Dance but it was postponed on acct. of passion week. — We crossed over & drank tea at the Academy with the arranging Committee. West was there.

Bromleys 6th. letter to Fuseli appeared today, and is such a composition of vulgarity & folly, as to prove the prudence of Fuseli in not entering into any public controversy with him.

Good Friday — April 18th.

Glass 60. Fine weather with a mixture of haziness.

Breakfasted with Lawrence and communicated to him what had passed at Lord Inchiquins He declared himself well satisfied with the terms settled, & that I had saved him 40 gs.

I recd. from Cheapside a Volume of the Thames half bound up, to look over.

I called today on Mrs. Playfair at her request. Poor Playfair died of a broken heart in consequence of the death of his eldest Boy.

Saturday — 19th.

Glass 63. — Fine weather.

Breakfasted at Alderman Boydells, and sorted out some sets of the prints of the Rivers.

Went to the Panorama a view of the Isle of Wight, Portsmouth &c. Badly painted but ingeniously shewn.

Bromleys 7th. letter to Fuseli appeared, including a notice to Copley that He would be attacked next.

Alderman Boydell & Richards think it will be most prudent not to offer the first volume of the Rivers alone to the Booksellers, but to continue it on the subscription Idea, till the two volumes are completed. Their reasons satisfied me.

Copley is to have £300 more from the City, out of which Alderman Boydell is to be refunded the £200 He advanced to Copley to bear his expences to Hanover.

Saunders was copying Copleys picture in the Council room.

Sunday, April 20.

Glass 66.
Went to Whitehall Chapell. Kerrick preached.

Monday — 21st.

Glass 62. Breakfasted at Alderman Boydells. Caleb Whiteford told me at the Shakespeare Gallery of Smirkes election into the Antiquarian Society. I had mistaken the day. — Recd. a letter from Sir George Beaumont at North Aston. — Lawrence wrote to me to desire me to call on him tomorrow to see his pictures finished for exhibition.

Accounts were recd. today of the taking Martinico, — and Philip Dundass told Dick that private accts. were yesterday recd. from Lord Hood which express strong hopes that Bastia will fall notwithstanding the different description given by General Dundass since his return. The latter is in an awkward situation shd. Bastia be taken. Philip also said it was hoped the great provision convoy from America to France wd. be intercepted.

This morning Bourgeois told me the Turkish Ambassador had beat Philidor at a game of Chess.

Tuesday — April 22d.

Glass 67.
Breakfasted with Lawrence. Went to the play in the evening with Dick. It was the Romance of the Forest. Opie got an order which admitted us, from Boaden the Author. — Opie cd. not go on acct. of the intelligence of Mrs. Govets death at St. Kits.

Wednesday 23d.

Glass 70. Very warm.
Breakfasted at Alderman Boydells.
This is St. George's day which I forgot & did not dine as I proposed with the Antiquarian Society.
Mr. Baker came in the evening. — Edwards the Bookseller has declined

the proposal made by Byrne of a third of the property of the Plates of Hearnes antiquities, & of the views of the Lakes. — The Antiquities, were estimated in the proposal at £1200, — the Lakes at £700. — All the prints unsold included.

Thursday — April 23d [24th].

Glass 70.

Breakfasted with Smirke at Holylands Coffee House, having before sent my pictures to exhibition. Smirke saw them placed up & gave me a favourable report of their appearance.

Afterwards went to Alderman Boydells, & from thence to the Shakespeare Gallery. — Boydell told me the story of Lady Cadogan, going of with Mr. Cooper. *His* neighbour is seen very often with Mr. Faulkner.

Humphry dined with me. Wheatley came in the eving. The first time I have seen him since October.

Fuseli call'd in the eving. He had dined at Mr. Locks, and was much mortified on finding Young Lock is not invited to the Academy dinner. I went with him to the Academy. Smirke was in the Council Chair, West being prevented from coming by a gouty complaint. The Council did not consent to invite Mr. Lock on Smirkes representation from Fuseli. — Boswell had applied in vain for a ticket for his Brother, as had Mr. Malone for his Brother Lord Sunderlin.

Friday — April 25.

Glass 67. Breakfasted with Humphry. N. Dance passed a considerable part of the forenoon with me. — He told me he had considered the effect of the Old building, the Duke of Dorsets, at Whitehall, & He thought little or no Oker is required in describing the Colour of it.

Sir George Beaumont returned today from Mr. Bowles's, I went to dine with him. — In the evening. He had notes from Lord Hardwicke & Lord Beverly to fix abt. going to the Academy tomorrow.

Saturday [26th].

Glass 71 — A beautiful day.

Breakfasted with Lawrence. At 3 went to the Academy with Opie. — Sir Joseph Banks & George Steevens were there, with whom I had some conversation.

I took places for Sir George Beaumont between Lord St. Asaph & Lord Beverly and for Lord Grey de Wilton between Lord Hardwicke & Sir Abraham Hume. I sat opposite to Charles Long, Sir Abraham & N. Dance, and between Loutherburgh & Smirke.

Hoppners portraits this year have a preference. A half length of Mrs. Parkyns & a ¾ of Lady Charlotte Legge in particular.

Sir George Beaumont, Lord Inchiquin, — Mr. Campbell, Lord Fife, —

Bourgeois, — Opie, — Northcote, — Fuseli, — Cosway, — N. Dance, — Loutherburgh — complimented me on my pictures. I think the High St. Oxford has the preference.

At 10 o'Clock West quitted the Chair, and at ½ past I went to Holylands Coffee House to Tea with Smirke, — Hoppner, — Bourgeois & Northcote. We found Seward there.

Seward this afternoon had applied to me for a vote for Dr. Gillies to succeed Mr. Gibbon as professor of ancient history. Boswell spoke violently against the pretensions of Gillies, and in favour of Mr. Mitford.

Cosway afterwards spoke as violently to me in favour of Gillies. The Company at the Academy Dinner today were [blank].

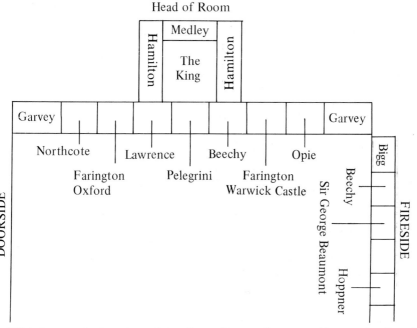

[*This key to the hanging of the Great Room, Somerset House, the Royal Academy Exhibition, appears on a separate page and without related|text.*]

Sunday — April 27th, 1794.

Glass 69. Breakfasted at Sir Georges. Lady B. wishing to see His Picture in the exhibition, she called on Susan at 3 oClock, and afterward met me at the exhibition room. Sir George came before with Lord Mulgrave. Smirke & his son & daugtr. went down with me.

Mrs. West, Mrs. Brouncker, and other Ladies were there, and

Nollekens came. — Nollekens is angry that some Busts which He desired to exhibit were refused to be placed in the Council room, in consequence He wd. not exhibit.

Susan & I dined at Sir Georges, where we met Hearne.

Today the younger Bissell, who is confirmed a Lieutenant, called on me. — Tom Kershaw also called — and Taylor desiring me to procure him a list of names.

Monday April 28th.

Glass 68. — A windy, cloudy day. The weather for 10 days or a fortnight past has been uncommonly warm and clear. We are now without fires.

Breakfasted at the Salopian Coffee House, and called at Admiral Gardners. He is at Portsmouth. — Young Bissell call'd on me again when I advised him to call on Wilbraham Bootle to induce him to use his interest again in favor of Wm. Bissell.

Boswell call'd on me on the subject of Mitford & Gillies. He applied today and secured Hodges, — Humphry, — Garvey — & Dance. He called on Bacon who had been applied to in favor of Gillies but desired time to consider. He applied to Sir Wm. Chambers, who was rather for not filling the vacancy. I told Boswell I wd. exert myself for Mitford as I thought Gillies not a proper man. That should He be elected He might be a member of the Club which would be a strong objection with me.

Dick, Susan & Eliza were at the Exhibition: They are of opinion that the Oxford view is more attended to than the Warwick Castle.

Miss Egerton was this morning married to Lord Belgrave. Lord Grey de Wilton called & left cards for me & Dick.

Tuesday April 29th.

Glass 63. Cloudy day.

Breakfasted with Humphry who is strongly against Dr. Gillies being elected to succeed Mr. Gibbon.

Met Boswell who had called on me. We went together to Northcote who sees the impropriety of Dr. Gillies being elected. He says Cosway He supposes supports Gillies out of Compts. to Lord Hopeton to whose Children or Brothers He was tutor.

Boswell was yesterday with P. Sandby, Garvey & Nollekens & secured all their votes for Mr. Mitford. Rigaud did not promise.

I called on Lord Orford who was told on Sunday by Lord Lucan that his portrait by Dance is exhibited at which supposition He was much mortified thinking it wd. appear at his time of life an instance of vanity. I assured him of the mistake of Lord Lucan.

Lord Orford does not approve of Knights poem, either for the matter or the poetry. He thinks it destitute of imagination, uninstructive, & pedantick. Bearing the title of Didactic witht. reccomending anything.

He thinks Repton a Coxcomb.

He laughs at the systematizing plan of Knight, Townley &c who attempt to prove the lascivious designs of antiquity to be merely emblematic of the creative power.

After I left Lord Orford I met Sir Hew Dalrymple, who is come to town on acct. of the arrival of his eldest son from St. Amand where he has been very ill of the Sweating fever. He is in the Guards & only 20 years of age.

Sir Hew walked home with me. I shewed him the pictures begun for him of Tantallon Castle. He desired me to finish the three.

We called together on Boswell who was not at home.

Sir Hew says the riot at the playhouse in Edinburgh was caused by some disaffected American & Irish Students.

Muir who is sent to Botany Bay was born at Glasgow, of low parents.

Miss Dalrymples expences at Mrs. Davis' School for the last year amounted to £284. — Sir Hew allows Captn. Dalrymple £400 a year.

Wednesday April 30th.

Glass 62.

News today of a Victory over the French, near Cambray.

Called at the Shakespeare Gallery. — Boydell had been to the exhibition — My view in Oxford he was much struck with., free from the objection of hardness of outline. In the view of Warwick Castle the buildings he likes best but the trees are handled too much, too much made out. It has been remarked to him that the picture of Gadshill is more free from this defect than any of my pictures where trees are introduced.

Jones, Hearne & Marchi dined with me. — The general opinion is that Lawrence this year is inferior to Hoppner.

Jones & Hearne think the handling in Dances Landscape poor & thorny: that the colouring has too much sameness: and that the greens are not of a true color. Jones particularly objected to it. They both said how much the subject would gain by being differently coloured.

MAY 1794

Thursday, May 1st.

Glass 62. Dined at Alderman Boydells with J. Boydell & his family, & Mr. & Mrs. Broderip — evening rainy with easterly wind.

Friday [May 2nd].

Glass 58, wind easterly.
Sir Hew Dalrymple, Captn. Dalrymple, — & Carey dined with us.

Saturday, May 3d.

Glass 62.
Boswell called on me. Bourgeois has obtained the votes of Russell & Burch for Mr. Mitford. Boswell now reckons upon 18 votes.
Carey today recd. a letter from Major Le Merchant at Famars with some particulars of the engagement of the 26th last.
Jack Sedgwick dined with us. — Marchant came in the evening.

Sunday 4th.

Glass 62 — fine day.
Kershaw call'd on me. I took him & Lysons to the Exhibition. He was much pleased with the small pictures of Rathbone, views on Derwentwater &c.

Monday 5th.

Glass 60. — This morning I sat to Singleton for my Portrait in his Academy picture.
Willis of Kennington call'd on me to solicit my vote for Dr. Gillies. He declared Gillies not to maintain Democratic principles and that Mr. West is his friend.

Tuesday, May 6th.

Glass 60.
Recd. an invitation from Lord & Lady Beverly to dine with them on Sunday next.

Boydell call'd. Had been with the King this morning an Hour & a half while the family were at breakfast and, with the Alderman presented the first volume of the River Thames. The King placed it on his knee and turned over *every* leaf. He expressed his approbation of the work. — He asked Boydell who wrote the Historical part. B. said Mr. Coombes: who was the Author of the letter from a country gentleman &c. — The King enquired further abt. his publications till B. told His Majesty that C. wrote the Diaboliad. — The King said He was a clever man.

Boydell solicited my vote for Dr. Gillies in consequence of having been applied to by Mr. Perry, one of the editors of the Morning Chronicle. Perry declared to B. that Gillies does not hold Democratic principles. The Revd. Mr. Burn of Hampstead had also applied to Boydell for his interest with me.

Today I called on Byrne, & find Edwards of Pallmall has declined purchasing any share of the Antiquities or views of the Lakes.

Wednesday May 7th.

Glass 60. This morning I sat to Lawrence when He drew in my portrait with black chalk on the Canvass, which employed him near 2 Hours. He did not use colour today. — This is his mode of beginning. — Lawrence is against Gillies.

Lysons called on me today in favor of Dr. Gillies — afterwards Boswell.

Fuseli drank tea with me. He has promised his vote in favor of Gillies to Hamilton, who applied to him.

In the evening I called on Smirke who is decided against Gillies. — Batty had applied to him.

Thursday. 8th.

Called with Boydell today on Lord Orford & carried to him the first volume of the Thames.

Selected sets of the work at the Gallery. — Mr. Grey came and afterwards the Duchess of Devonshire with him, and looked at the volume.

Today last Academy Club. West ill of the Gout. Tyler in the chair.

Friday, May 9th.

Breakfasted this morning with Alderman Boydell and arranged some sets of the Thames.

Called at the gallery and selected some sets for particular persons. — Spoke to Coombes abt. Gillies, whose History He understands to be inferior to that of Mitford.

Saturday 10th.

Breakfasted with G. Dance. Mr. N. Smith died worth £80,000. His fortune nearly equal between one son and 3 daugrs.

Dance called with me on Boswell — afterwards on Wyatt, who is acquainted with Col. Mitford & wrote strong letters of recommendation of him to Rigaud & Yenn. — Dance called on Rigaud & thinks he is secure, and afterwards on Barry, with whom Dr. Gillies has been, and Barry seems to be in an undecided state. Gillies spoke with great contempt of Boswell.

Lysons dined with me, and desired I wd. breakfast with Sir Joseph Banks on Monday morning, on acct. of Gillies business. Lysons has explained my statement of the matter to Sir Joseph.

Lord Orford remarked to Lysons that the style of Coombes's Thames is too flowery.

Sunday, May 11th.

Called this morning on Fuseli and shewed him the first volume of the Thames, and desired He would manage to have it decently treated in the Analytical review. — He said He would review it himself.

Mr. Rawstorne called here.

Went to the Exhibition at one, and met Lord & Lady Beverly, & Lady Charlotte Percy, Sir George & Lady Beaumont, Mr. & Mrs. & Miss Bennet.

Dined at Lord Beverlys with Sir George & Lady Beaumont at ½ past 5. Staid there till past 12.

Lady Charlotte was *presented* a few days ago. Lord Beverly lamented the effect irregular, fashionable hours would have upon her.

Monday [12th].

Breakfasted this morning with Lysons at Sir Joseph Banks's, Mrs. & Miss Banks, Mr. Dryander, Batty, and a Secretary there.

Sir Joseph had a long conversation on the subject of the proposed election of a Professor of ancient history. — Mr. West called on him and asked his opinion of Dr. Gillies to be elected in that capacity. Sir J's answer was favorable to the Dr. — who being in the room Mr. West applied to him. — This was the origin as far as Sir J. knew, of the business. — Mr. West afterwards communicated to Dr. Gillies a list of persons in the Academy to whom He shd apply, if he cd. get their votes, others over whom they had an influence wd. follow. — Sir Joseph at the request of Dr. G. applied to Russell, Zoffany & Catton.

I told Sir Joseph the mode in which such elections had been formerly conducted, and that it wd. be little honor to any man to be elected in consequence of having canvassed. — He agreed in opinion & said He had already said as much to Dr. G. in consequence of what Lysons had repeated to him. — He declared He wd. write to those to whom He adressed letters, and recall the applications.

He told me He plainly saw that Mr. West had applied to him on Dr. G's acct. to curry favor with him, but that His mind was made up on the subject of Mr. West and had been since the times when his conduct on political matters was manifested.

Before I came away Sir Joseph presented me with a Card of invitation to his Conversations, which are held at his house on Sunday evenings during the meetings of the Royal Society. — I met Boswell & proposed to him to suspend the election at present out of delicacy. Mr. & Mrs. Mansell dined with us, also Hearne, Baker & Marchant.

The first volume of the History of the Thames was published today.

Tuesday, May 13.

Breakfasted at Sir George Beaumonts.

Sat to Lawrence & afterwards went with him & Dick to the House of Commons. A critique by a Mr. Williams assuming the name of Antony Pasquin came out.

Wednesday,. May 14.

Breakfasted with George Dance. — Called on Hamilton and mentioned some of the circumstances which passed at Sir Joseph Banks. He is very willing to suspend the election.

Boydell agreed with Edwards the Bookseller to let him have a volume of the Rivers for £4-10-0.

Joe Green called in the eveng. Churton also called.

Thursday [15th].

Glass 70. — Bromley published his first letter to Copley, in which I am attacked.

dined at G. Dances. He and Soane went to Mrs Playfairs. — Went to the Antiquarian Society with Smirke who was introduced to Sir Joseph — Ld. Leicester in the Chair.

Sir Joseph told me he had written letters as He declared He wd. and wd. shew me a copy. — He introduced *us* into the Royal Society.

Drank tea at Holylands Coffee House, when Smirke informed me of his having been at Wests on Sunday last, where my conduct in the Academy was described by West.

Friday. May 16th.

Fuseli drank tea with me when I informed him of what Smirke had told me, — and that I shd. write to West on the subject.

Saturday [17th].

Called this morning on Sir F. Bourgeois. Smirke was with me. We had a full conversation on what passed at Wests on Sunday last. — He acknowledged that He was obliged to believe that Mr. West had supplied

Bromley with materials for his letters. He said Bromley had told him a falsehood, for He had declared that Fuseli was not an object of his criticism in any part of his history, and since that had in a letter adressed to Fuseli declared the contrary. Sir Francis said in my situation He would write fully to West.

Went to the House of Commons with Dick & Carey. The 3d. reading of the Habeas Corpus suspension Bill for 6 months. The speakers were.

For the suspension	*against it.*
Canning	Grey
Serjeant Walker	Lambton
Dundass	Jekyll
Wyndham	Courtnay
Pitt	Sheridan
	Fox

majority against adjournment.

$$\begin{array}{r} 183 \\ \text{to} \quad 33 \\ \hline 150 \end{array}$$

Came away at ½ past 2 & left the House sitting. — Ld. Mulgrave introduced me.

Sunday, May 18th.

Fuseli called on me when I shewed him my letter to West which He approved. — I also shewed it to Smirke & G. Dance who approved it. I sent it this day at noon to his House by James.

Copy of the letter.Sir, Mr. Smirke has informed me [page blank in diary]

Called on Tyler who has been confined by a Fever on the brain and sore throat.

Monday, May 19th.

Went to the House of Lords with Dick — Got an order from Ld. Beverly. — Duke of Montrose told me there that there wd. be no debate, as a Committee of Secrecy wd. be appointed. Lord Grey brought Rawstorne. — I had some conversation with Lord Harcourt over the rail.

In the evening Sir Francis Bourgeois called on me. He had seen my letter to West, who is desirous of an interview with me, Smirke & Sir Francis. — I shewed Sir Francis the letters of Mr. Locke & Mr. Knight & proved the falsehood of Bromley by comparing them with his assertions. — Sir Francis has told West his opinion of Bromley fully.

Tuesday — May 20.

Sir F. Bourgeois called on me & repeated Wests wish for an interview. I told him it was a question of character and I did not think I shd. agree to an interview, as Mr. West from his acct. only seemed desirous of it, that He might disclaim all collusion with Bromley. That did not affect me but in a second degree, my charge was for what He said of me. — Sir F. said Smirke seemed inclined to an interview but thought West ought to write & not propose one verbally by message.

Sir Francis said West told him he ought to have been acquainted with Bromleys character sooner if his *friends* thought Bromley unworthy. — Sir Francis told West that Bromley had said to him that while writing his history He never thought of Fuseli, which He proved to be false by declaring in one of his letters that He did mean to mark him.

Wednesday — May 21.

Recd. a letter from Mr. West of which the following is a copy. — [blank page in diary]

Boswell called on me. He dined yesterday with Dilly in the Poultry, where He accidentally met Dr. Gillies. They disputed on the subject of the Academy Professorship. — Gillies said He had a majority and was advised by his friends to proceed.

Thursday, May 22.

Went to the House of Lords with Dick and Carey, — and staid till eleven oClock, Dick remained till 2. — It was on the report of the secret committee. The Speakers I heard were.

for government.	against.
Lord Grenville	Lord Stanhope
— Spencer	— Lauderdale
— Kinnoul	
— Thurlow	
— Barrington	

This day I answered Mr. Wests letter. The following is a copy. [blank]

After I had written my letter to Mr. West, I shewed it to Smirke who approved it.

Friday — May 23.

Went to Greenwoods to see Sir Thomas Dundass's collection of Pictures.

Called on Lord Orford. Sir John Blagden & Mr. Churchill Senr. & the Revd. Mr. Beloe there.

Lord Orford said some persons thought the skies of the prints of the

Rivers were too blue. — I told him Mrs. Damers head of Thames was not introduced on acct. of its having been very badly executed. — He reccomended it to be printed on a sheet to be delivered loose with the 2d. vol that it might be inserted in the first if people chose it.

Saturday — 24th.

Breakfasted with Steers — called on Lysons who told me Dr. Gillies meant to call on me — J. Boydell called on me this forenoon and overlooked my accts. of the Rivers and appointed me to meet him in Cheapside on Monday.

Sunday — May 25th.

Breakfasted with George Dance. Mr. Hoole Senr. there, — Dance approves of my last letter to West. — Afterwards called on Tyler, who being sufficiently recovered, I related to him what had passed with West, and read him the letters which He approves of.

Lysons dined with me. — Went with him and Dance in the eving to Sir Joseph Banks's. — Nicol at Dr. Gillies's desire introduced him to me when He requested He might call on me as He had something to say to me. I told him I shd. be at home on Tuesday at 12 oClock.

Monday — May 26.

Bromleys 2d. letter to Copley appeared today.

I went to Cheapside this morning where I met J. Boydell & Stadler. The accts. of the Rivers were examined. — Coombes acct. for the first Vol is £364. He estimated it £100 a little under or over. — It appears the Volumes finished in the present manner will amount to abt. £2100 each.

In the evening called on Fuseli — Dick & Eliza went to Hoddesdon.

This day Poggi opened His sale of Sir Joshua Reynolds collection of drawings by Old Masters.

Tuesday May 28 [27th].

Dr. Gillies called on me today at 12 & staid till 2 oClock. — He related at large what had passed on the subject of his being proposed for Professor of Ancient History in the Academy. — He said Mr. West spoke to him at Sir. J. Banks's soon after Mr. Gibbons death, and told him that some of his (Mr. Wests) literary friends had pointed out Dr. Gillies as a proper person to succeed to that office. — That Mr. West spoke to Sir Joseph Banks after He had mentioned the subject to Dr. Gillies.

Dr. G. mentioned His History of Greece as having passed through many editions, whereas Mr. Mitfords had not. This might be a criterion from which the Academy though not a literary body might form a judgment of the respective estimation in which the works stood. He thought Mr. Mitford having been of Christ Church might cause Dr. Barnard to be attached particularly to him. He laid great stress on the place having been offered to Him by the President and other members as far as they had power to support him, whereas He understood Mr. Mitford does not now know of the wishes of some in his favor. He also laid great stress on the injury He shd suffer if not elected, as it must be supposed owing to a suspicion of his holding democratic principles, as had been asserted by Mr. Boswell, who is now convinced from a conversation at Dilly's that there is no foundation for the report.

I told Dr. Gillies that Boswell mentioned Mr. Mitfords name to me soon after Mr. Gibbons death, but that I had not heard of his till Mr. Seward canvassed me in the Royal Academy; & that it was after that time that Boswell was active, and shewed me Dr. Barnards letter.

I said I had told Sir Joseph Banks my opinion that it would be most becoming the gravity of the Academy and most delicate to the gentlemen whose names had been brought forward to suspend for the present filling the vacancy. — The Dr. said His friends wished to bring it on in order to do away any suspicion of his character.

I told him Mr. West had not judged well in not consulting members of the Academy before He spoke to Dr. Gillies. — The Dr. said Mr. West should have avowed, He thought, his wishes in the Drs. favor when Boswell spoke to West at the dinner of the Royal Academy which He did not.

In the evening I called on Smirke & told him Dr. Gillies had called on me, and disavowed Democratic principles &c.

Wednesday — May 28th.

Recd. a long letter from Dr. Gillies recapitulating what had passed in the conversation we have had together. — G. Nicol told me He though[t] we had best keep the place open. — Wrote a note to Yenn relative to his Volumes of the River Thames & recd. his answer.

Dined at C. Offleys. Mrs. Offley, — Mrs. Hamond, — Mr. & Mrs. Campion, Outram, — Arbouin, — Harris, — Dick, Eliza dined there.

Went to Ranelagh with Dick, Eliza, Susan, C. Offley & Outram.

Thursday May 29th.

Mrs. Rawstorne & 3 Miss Athertons called on us.

Boswell called. He declares against Gillies as before. His Democratic principles are not the original cause. Dr. Gillies is [not] a desireable man for the situation. — Sir William Scott told Boswell yesterday He thought not. — Dr. Douglas, Bishop of Salisbury, thinks the same. — Boswell will resign if Gillies is elected. — He is ready to put a letter in the papers on the subject or to write to West. I reccomended to him to do neither at least at present.

Marchant called in the eving. Mr. Windham told him today He saw me in the Gallery of the House of commons on the Habeas Bill, He supposed I was a Democrat. Marchant said He was quite mistaken for I was a violent aristocrat.

Dick went to night to hear the Banti. Her benefit.

Friday — May 30th.

I called this morning on Mr. & Mrs. Rawstorne & Miss Athertons.

Mr. John Spedding called on me & mentioned the strange acct. of Miss Lawson, who is now in town and allowed by her father *£600 a year* for life. — Spedding at the desire of the Duke of Norfolk is going into the West riding Yorkshire Militia.

Joe Green brought me a letter for Commissioner Proby for Mr. Rawstorne.

Dr. Reynolds called to meet Mrs. Myers. He recommends Harrowgate & condemns all outward applications to her face, which Mr. White has been using.

Saturday — May 31st.

Called on Singleton left Mr. West there who came in.

Called & gave Miss Atherton the letter of introduction to Commissioner Proby.

Steers called — He desires the picture of Kew Bridge may be 9 inches not exceeding 10 high, by any length which may suit the subject.

Called in at Sir Thomas Dundass's sale. Very crowded. Some pictures sold very well.

Joe Green dined with us. Marchant came in the evening. — Mr. Uvedale Price sent me his Essay on the Picturesque.

JUNE 1794

Sunday — June 1.

Went to the exhibition to meet Sir George Beaumont & Mr. Bowles. — The Speaker of the House of Commons & Sir John Mitford were to have come but did not.

Dined at Sir Georges with Dick, — Mr. Bowles, Miss Bowles, Mr. & Mrs. Palmer, — Mr. Mander & Mr. Hearne there.

Monday — June 2d.

Dry Easterly winds for several day past.

Called at Mr. Berwicks Lodgings in Norfolk St. — Met Lord Harcourt who asked me if He should not see me at Newnham this summer.

Tuesday, June 3d.

Sat this morning to Singleton for Academy picture. He says Proctor is not yet gone to Rome but goes in a week.

Went into Sir Wm. Chambers Box and heard Burke speak against Hastings; this is the 3d. day of his reply. Windham read for him. — Grey in the Box part of the time, no other managers came. Francis sat at the end of the Managers Box. — Mr. Hastings was writing or reading the whole time, and appeared to pay no direct attention to Burke. Markham was in the Councils Box, & He was much alluded to as being the agent on the station where the abuse was committed. — But few Commoners attended and only abt. 23 or 4 Lords. — The Galleries were well filled. — Several relaxations in dress since the beginning of the trial. Grey came into the Managers Box in Boots & Spurs. Several peers came upon the throne *behind the Chancellor* witht. Robes. Lord Albemarle in Boots.

Wednesday, June 4th.

Dick & Eliza left Town this morning. — Met Repton at the Shakespeare Gallery who told me the Monthly review had been severe on Knight for the criticisms on him.

Dined at the Freemasons Tavern. — Tyler, Smirke, Wyatt, Fuseli, Humphry, our party sitting together.

Crosdill played 3 quartettos. Bowden sung very well, so did Incledon. Cramer, Shields &c &c were there. West left the Chair before 10 oClock. Nobody took it after. The meeting was thin, and not convivial. "God save the King", was sung by Incledon & Bowden.

Wyatt said a good deal to me abt. Mr. Beckford of Fonthill — He thinks him a man of extraordinary abilities. — Of unbounded expence. His income from Jamaica for the three last years has not been less than 120,000 a year. Wyatt believes that the greatest part of this enormous sum he expends. Beckford is easy to professional Men, but of consummate pride to people in higher situations.

About a month before Beckford was talked of Wyatt went to Fonthill with him. Beckford shewed him a copy of a Patent of Peerage then making out for him to be Lord Beckford of Fonthill. — This was abt. the beginning of Pitts Administration. The Peerage was quashed in consequence of the rumour.

Thursday, June 5th.

Cookson calld on me. He was with the King yesterday morning in company with many others at the Queens House, to compliment on the Birth day. He thinks the King the best tempered man living.

C. Cookson who had grown to a size weighing 21 stone, consulted Physicians at Edinburgh on his condition and was reccomended to a diet which has reduced to abt. 15 stone. — dined at Mr. Mansells who is indisposed and did not appear. — Mr. Willm. Barrett & his wife & a Mr. Cooke were there.

Boswell called on me, He proposes going to Scotland in a fortnight and is very anxious that a suspension of election shd. take place rather than Dr. Gillies shall be elected.

Academicians present at the Birth day yesterday.

West	Farington	Associates
Wilton	Russell	Hone
Richards	Fuseli	Rooker
P. Sandby	Yenn	Bigg
Tyler	Humphry	Tresham
Catton	Smirke	Beechy
Burch	Bourgeois	Hoppner
Wyatt	Westhall, elect.	
Banks		

Tyler and Catton were the Stewards. They nominated for the next year P. Sandby and Bartolozzi.

Friday June 6th.

The Royal Family went this morning to the Exhibition abt. 10 oClock. I took Mrs. Hamond & Susan to Mr. Wiltons apartments to see them pass. Lord Harcourt & Lady Charlotte Finch attended. West, Wilton & Richards were there. Sir Wm. Chambers being indisposed did not attend.

Called on Lysons. He was yesterday morning at Lord Orfords. Beloe was there and spoke on the Volume of Rivers. He mentioned having been told I had made my drawings in a Camera, as if that was a merit. He mentioned the flowery stile of Coombes. On the whole He gave no favorable opinion of the work. — Lord Orford & Lysons did not countenance him in it.

Lysons says most people wd. have preferred the prints being done in Brown, and that the stile of Coombes is considered as flowery, that He has dwelt too much on Newnham, and in general made up his books from other Books rather than from observation.

He told me my pictures were generally admired. The Bishop of Down wished he cd. afford to have a set of my paintings of views in Oxford.

Hughes call'd on me. He bespoke the Rivers for Mr. Fryer. I went with him & Cookson to the Exhibition at one oClock after the Royal family had left the place. West & Mrs. West & another Lady came there. *I* had no conversation with them.

Hughes & Cookson dined with me. Hughes staid all night. The King paid Cookson a high compliment on Wednesday last on his manner of reading the service at Windsor.

Saturday [7th].

The Easterly Winds which have continued a week have blighted much. I have suffered with others rheumatic pains. — Met the Bishop of Downe who invited me to his House near Belfast.

Mr. Scott of Danesfield call'd. I told him I did not come to his House last year as I supposed it wd. be inconvenient to him.

This day I finished the picture of Deptford yard.

Sunday — June 8th.

Breakfasted with Wyatt, who afterwards sat to Singleton for his Portrait in the Academy picture. — The King means to repair the ruined end of St. George's Chapel at Windsor and to make it a burying place for the Royal family. Room for one only is left in the burying place in Westminster Abbey.

The King would have fitted up and lived in Windsor Castle but was told it could not be made comfortably habitable, which caused him to build the Queens Lodge. He still thinks of making the Castle the Royal residence. — Wyatt says the Castle might be made complete agreeable to the original Idea. It would invade something upon the court yard.

Wyatt shewed me a picture, a Landscape, painted by Rosalba. She derided Zuccarelli & Wilson for becoming Landscape painters & as a proof in how low esteem she held this branch of art desired Zucarrelli to lend her [a] picture to look at for the mere practise, and painted that which Wyatt has, the only one she ever did paint. — On seeing the picture I doubted the fact of its being the *only* one.

When the King communicates his intentions, or wishes, to persons employed by him, it is through the Equerries & Pages. The former write to Gentlemen, the latter to others.

A Fire happened at Oatlands yesterday which damaged some of the out buildings. The King had been there, and brought back a little dog belonging to the Duchess of York, who seemed more anxious abt. her animals than abt. the House. She has 18 dogs. The King observed that affection must rest on something. Where there were no children Animals were the objects of it.

Called on Smirke. Bowyer is very uneasy abt. the threatening letter signed Anti-Dauber in the Morning Herald and thinks of writing to Bate Dudley — He was in danger of being hurt by an attack in the St. James's Chronicle, some persons hesitating to advance money upon the work in consequence of these remarks. — The late Bond Hopkins was the friend of Bowyer in respect of advancing money.

I told Smirke I wd. not reccomend applying to Dudley but wd. wait for the next attack: That I thought it a revenge of Bromley intended for particular characters, & the Shakespeare gallery the real object though affecting to begin with the Historic gallery.

Went with Susan to dinner at Boydells at West end. Mrs. Kent came to Tea. We walked home. Young Nicol told us Mr. Knight was desirous of selling the Copy right of his poem, but at his proposed price cd. not find a purchaser.

Reptons father was proprietor of stage coaches & waggons at Norwich, and left him abt. £600 a year all of which he dissipated except what was settled on his wife. — He charges 5 guineas a day to those who employ him besides his expences.

Monday, June 9th.

Breakfasted with Lysons, afterwards called at Mr. Berwicks lodgings. Mr. Berwick & Mrs. Lechmere at home.

Fuseli call'd and read his introduction to the Analytical review. (Thames.)

Tuesday 10th.

Call'd with Boydell on Beloe, to speak to him upon his question to me abt. having made my sketches of views for the Thames Volume in a Camera. I explained to him. — He expressed his satisfaction in favor of the work &

6. P. J. de Louterbourg R.A. *The Grand Attack on Valenciennes*. 1793—4. Lady Hesketh.

7. P. J. de Loutherbourg R.A. *The Battle of the Glorious First of June, 1794.* National Maritime Museum, Greenwich.

said an Artist had spoken favorably of it to him. I told him fidelity was the principal consideration and to keep up a regular succession of views. — He had before said to me the description of the flower garden at Nuneham was too *flowery*. Nothing was now said on the merits of the writing part.

Boydell told me privately that Nicol said to him today that Beloe had spoken slightly of the views & call'd them "gumboaged things".

Fuseli drank tea with me. — Marchant came in the eving.

Wednesday June 11th.

Last night Sir Roger Curtis arrived at the Admiralty from Ld. Howe, announcing a great Victory gained over the French Fleet of 26 sail of the line, by the British fleet of 25. The Battle was fought on Sunday June 1st. — 6 Ships were taken and two sunk, witht. the loss of one British ship. — The Revolutionaire of 110 guns which had parted from the Fleet before afterwards sunk, making in all 9 ships taken & sunk. — The papers this morning reported the news. Nothing could exceed the publick agitation and joy, on this occasion. — I went to the Shakespeare Gallery. Lord Pomfret & Caleb Whiteford came in. His Lordship was overjoyed.

This was the 5th. day of Burkes reply against Hastings.

At 2 oClock in the morning we were knocked up to put out lights. Many windows were broke. The illuminations became general. Lord Stanhopes windows were smashed to pieces.

Thursday — 12th.

Mrs. Offley, Mrs. Hamond, Marchant, J. Boydell, Mrs. Boydell & John & Wm. Offley dined with us.

Fuseli came to me and continued his remarks, and afterwards dined with me, & we walked out to see the illuminations which tonight were general and began early. The streets undisturbed by mobs and no windows broke. — We found Barry at his door. He came with us to Charlotte St. and took some supper. He spoke of Dr. Gillies, and gave his opinion for a suspension as to filling up Mr. Gibbons vacancy. He was violent against West and said *He* proposed the Oath before Wests election, knowing the Academy wd not under such an obligation have given West the preference. He was violent against Bromley, but said had He been attacked He would have looked to West for satisfaction.

Friday, June 13th.

Ogburn the engraver called on me, He has got the picture of Bridgnorth Bridge from Steers to engrave for his collection of specimens of British Artists.

Tom Paine lived with Sharp the engraver, abt. 6 weeks. He seemed a fellow of a discontented temper, fond of gin & water.

Illuminations were again general this evening — the third night.

Saturday — June 14.

At Hastings trial with Boswell. Burke was very dull and tedious.

Boswell has had conversation with Sir Wm. Chambers on the subject of filling Mr. Gibbons vacancy. The King told Sir Wm. that unless the election was unanimous He wd. not sanction it. That He never approved of these appointments in the first instance and wd not allow such a question to divide the Academy.

Burke was abusive witht. wit or entertainment. No Manager in the Box except Wyndham who read the extracts for Burke. Francis sat in one corner of the Box. — But few Lords. — Duke of Gloucester, — Leeds, — Marquiss Townshend &c.

Mrs. Playfair called on me, being desirous of Dances advice abt. the disposing Her late Husbands Drawings &c. She has a mistaken notion of their value, which makes one uneasy.

Sunday 15.

Mr. White from Deptford came to breakfast. I shewed him the picture of Deptford yd. with which He declares himself much pleased. Sir John Henslow has not for many months said anything to him abt. the picture not being finished. Mr. Binmer is very partial to my pictures.

The new designed floating battery was launched yesterday. Her Hull costs £6000, — built of Fir, which makes Her light. She draws abt. 6 feet water with her guns in. She carries 26 guns in all, 32 pounders. also 2 mortars on her main deck, under which there are bags of cotton to ease the pressure when they are fired. — at the head 8 guns and 4 guns. abaft 4 guns.

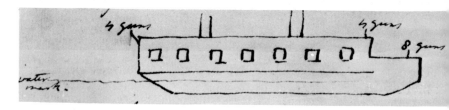

Went to Boydells to dinner with G. Dance, Fuseli, & Marchant. Mr. Mrs. & Miss Kent there, also Mr. & Mrs. Broderip & Mr. Broderip of the Temple, Mr. [blank], Mr. Kents partner, Alderman Boydell & Mrs. Loyd.

Monday — June 16.

Sent the picture of Deptford yd. to the Navy Office, — and recd. my pictures from the Exhibition — sent a Vol: of the Thames to Mr. Johnsons.

Went with G. Dance to the conclusion of Mr. Hastings trial: Burke spoke & read abt. 2 hours & 10 minutes, very uninteresting & dull, but his adress of 10 minutes was beautifully composed and admirably delivered.

Humphry, Lysons and Taylor of Hatton Garden were in the Box. Humphry & Dance afterwards dined with me.

In the eving. I went to the Committee at the Percy Coffee House, assembled to consider Mr. Dundass letter on the subject of arming each parish. Mr. Dundass seems to recommend Cavalry.

Only 10 or 11 were present, nothing was determined and the meeting adjourned to Tuesday next.

Tuesday June 17th.

Called at the Shakespeare Gallery where Caleb Whiteford introduced Mr. Stewart a young miniature painter from Edinburgh to me. He was bred to Landscape under Nasmith.

Stadler came to tea. I spoke to him abt. finishing the plates of the Rivers in Brown. He says the etched outline will stand and He cd. on that plate work them up to any effect.

G. Dance told me an intimate friend of Ld. Chatham had spoken to him on the inconvenience attending his laying in bed till the day is advanced, as Officers &c were kept waiting. Ld. Chatham said it did not signify it was an indulgence He cd. not give up. This friend told Dance.

Wednesday June 18.

Called at Mr. Bootles on Bissells acct. to get him a Lieutenancy. — Mr. Bootle went to Latham house for the Summer on Friday 6th.

Thursday, 19.

Easterly wind, and so blighting and dark at noon I cd. scarcely see to paint. Rheumatic weather.

wrote to Admiral Gardner at Portsmouth in favor of Wm. Bissell who was in the Orion in the late engagement.

Opie sent my Portrait home, which He has given me. — Marchi called. Lord & Lady Inchiquin went to Ireland abt. 6 weeks ago 4 days on their passage.

Poggi has sold drawings to the amount of £600.

G. Dance remarked that contrary to usual correctness of pronunciation Wm. Pitt always pronounces the word further, furder.

Burke pronounces the word [foither?].

Marchant call'd in the evening. He says it is mentioned in a newspaper Banks the Statuary, has been before the Privy Council.

Boswell told me the other day that Mr. Hastings frequently had remarked to him on the speeches of the Managers, to which He had attended to consider how far their speeches were well composed, and that He occassionally pointed out passages to show their defects in wanting point &c.

Friday, June 20th.

Called at the Shakespeare Gallery. While talking with G. Dance & Boydell, Mr. Cawthorne came up and confirmed the news that the Dutch have defeated the French near Charleroi, with a loss of 7000 men on the side of the French. Cawthorne said He was going to the House to oppose the thanks to the Managers on Hastings trial. He thought Burke had exceeded the authority He recd. from the House of Commons, and had introduced the subject of the Rohilla war though the House had refused to allow that to be a charge.

He said He doubted whether on some point the Lords would not contrive to find Hastings guilty. I said I concluded they wd. not for the sake of party commit themselves improperly. He was afraid Ld. Loughborough was not favorable to Mr. Hastings, but He wd. be certain of Ld. Thurlow, Kenyon, Mansfield, Stanhope &c &c. — While we were talking the Duke of Clarence passing said to Cawthorne, "Well the Dutch have saved their credit at last".

There is a strong report in Town that Captn. Molloy behaved ill in the late engagement.

Fuseli drank tea and shewed me his remarks printed, the proof sheet.

Saturday, June 21st.

Recd. a letter from Admiral Gardner who promises to speak to Lord Chatham in favor of Bissell, and recommends to write to Mr. Bootle for a letter from him to Lord Chatham. By this days Post I wrote to Mr. Bootle at Latham House, & to Bissell on board the Orion at Plymouth to inform him what I have done.

Recd. a letter from Dick who is appointed Steward for the next Manchester Races, along with Mr. Clifton of Lytham. — Will Boardmans affairs likely to turn out very indifferent.

Marchi cleaned the sky &c of my view of Malvern Abbey, with salt & water, and in some places using spirits of wine.

Yesterday the Managers on Hastings Trial recd. the Thanks of the House of Commons on a division of 21 to 50. Much remark was made on Burkes abuse, which indeed had been most profligate and unauthorized.

Sunday [22nd].

Called this morning at Sir George Beaumonts. He went to Cheltenham on Thursday last, by advice of Dr. Pitcairne.

Lord Howes letter relating the transactions of the Fleet on the days preceding the first of June — and naming the Commanding Officers, who from the reports of the Flag Officers & Captains particularly distinguished themselves.

The Admirals	*The Captains*
Sir A Hood	Lord Hugh Conway
Bowyer	Pakenham
Gardner	Berkeley
Graves	Gambier
Paisley	J Harvey
	J Payne
	Parker
	H. Harvey
	Pringle
	Duckworth
	Elphinstone

Captain Nichols of Admiral Graves's ship, Captn. W. Hope of Admiral Paisley's also 1st Lieutenant Monckton of Captn. Berklys ship, 1st. Lieutenant Donnelly of Captn. Montagues The Officers not named are

Admiral	*Captains*
Caldwell	Schomburgh of the Culloden

	Ships	{	Thunderer	— A. Bertie	}	Captains
			Alfred	— Bazely		
			Caesar	— Molloy		
			Tremendous	— Pigott		
			Gibraltar	— T. Mackenzie		
			Majestic	— C. Cotton		

The Caesar is the only ship Lord Howe specifies as not having done what He expected.

Called on Hearne. A subscription for Cozens has been raised sufficient to support him for at least a year, witht. applying to professional men. Mr. Knight & Sir George Beaumont have been the principals in effecting it. The money has been paid to Dr. Monro.

Dined at C. Offleys with Mrs. Hamond & Susan. In the evening went to Sir Joseph Banks's. Much talk abt. Lord Howe's engagement and Major Reynell described on paper their manner of maneuvring.

The Duke of Leeds	Mr. Marsden
Lord Morton	Mr. Parsons
Sir Richd. Kaye	Mr. Dalrymple &c &c were there.
Mr. Peachy	
Sir J. Blagdon	

Monday — June 23.

Called at Shakespeare Gallery. An acct. was circulated that Ypres has been evacuated by the garrison.

Sir John Sinclair called there to see the frontispiece to the publication of the Agricultural Society. He is in person very tall and appears to be abt. 35 years of age.

Mr. Repton is not satisfied to have his Prints executed in the same manner as those of the Thames. He will have them done more in the manner of the Swiss views, which are almost finished as highly as tinted drawings. — This will take up more of Stadlers time. Accordingly I sent for him when He calculated that He shd. be able to finish Reptons work, & Sir John Blaquiere's plates in 6 weeks from this day, which will be the 4th. of August.

Dance & Soane met today to arrange the business for Mrs. Playfair.

Tuesday, 24th.

Very warm weather. Glass in my painting room 74. — Mrs. Baker, wife to the Member for Hertfordshire & Her Son, a youth of 14, called with letters for me from William Bissell. Young Baker had served on board the Orion in the late engagement.

Bissells letter to me contained a Certificate of his good behaviour from Captain Duckworth, which I inclosed in a letter to Admiral Gardner at Portsmouth. — Bissell sent me a letter directed to Lord Chatham, which I do not forward as it is not a proper one. Neither is that to Mr. Bootle, — at the present crisis.

I wrote this day to Mr. Uvedale Price at Foxley, near Hereford, thanking him for his book, "An Essay on Picturesque Beauty".

An acct. came today from Paris, stating Barreres report to the Convention of the Arrival of the victualling fleet from America consisting of 116 sail, which entirely removes all apprehension of famine from France. — He also gave an acct. of the late Naval engagement, which He called glorious for France. That the English had 14 Sail of the Line more than the French, yet left the scene of Action to them. That the French had 7 Sail dismasted, which He fears are *lost*. — But the English had Ten dismasted, which wd have been taken but for the cowardice of certain French Captains, which are sent to Paris for trial. — *So much for a specimen of French representation as a Republic.*

Bissell in his letter seems to hint as if all Commanders had not done their duty.

Marchant came in the evening.

Wednesday June 25th.

At 6 this morning Susan went in the Lynn Coach from the Saracens head,

Snow Hill, in company with the Revd. Mr. Beloe, Mrs. Beloe, & their daughter. — Mr. Beloe told me he last night sent his remarks.

I breakfasted with Lysons. He says Captn. Bligh is fully prepared to answer any reflexions on his conduct which may be published by the friends of Christian, and wishes it may come to that issue. — The attacks on his character are partly imputed to Heywood and his connexions — as at present that young man, though pardoned, cannot have any promotion. I understand Captn. Bligh is the only person that can contribute to remove the obstacle, which the behaviour of Heywood will prevent him from doing. — It seems Admiral Paisley married a sister or cousin of Heywoods.

Sir Joseph Banks's Conversaziones commence the first Sunday in Michelmas term, which begins Novr. 6th. They end the last Sunday in Trinity Term. On Two Sundays at Christmas, — Two at Easter, — and Two at Whitsuntide, — there are no meetings.

Thursday — June 26th.

Rose at a ¼ before 6 — did not call on anybody today.

Mrs. Bonney, by a note, solicited me to attend the Board of Commissioners for Paving &c, to take into consideration a letter from Her Husband, in the Tower, soliciting that his Brother in Law, may act for him as Clerk to the Commissioners till his Trial is over.

Friday — 27th.

Rose at ½ past 7. — Went to Mr. Bonneys to the Meeting of the Commisioners. Mr. Perrott &c. spoke in favor of allowing Mr. Hague, to act for Mr. Bonney during the pleasure of the Board, — which passed unanimously. — A great number of Commissioners attended.

Called at the Shakespeare Gallery. Boydell said the Volume of the Rivers was called for but slowly. I told him the Town was now empty, which might be a reason. — He said Coombes had applied to him to know when He was to begin, for that at present He was idle. — Boydell said the paper was ordered.

Dined at C. Offleys. Mr. Evans & Mrs. Hamond there.

Saturday. June 28th.

Went early this morning to Alderman Boydells to settle my old acct. which Richards has to take over but He is out of Town. — Saw Rigauds designs for the ceiling of the Common Council room which He has begun. He told G. Dance it wd take him 3 months to compleat them.

Drank tea with G. Dance. Mr. Chamberlain, the Solicitor, is the person to whom the late Mr. Dummer bequeathed his great property an estate of 6 or 7000 a year, besides about £100,000 in the hands of the Accomptant general, after the death of Mrs. Dummer, (now Mrs. Dance). N. Dance gave £30,000 for his estate near Dorchester in Oxfordshire, and £12,000 for an estate in Wiltshire. He has already saved near £50,000. Mrs. Dance is now abt. 50 years of age. The late Mr. Dummer was a very weak man, and did not appear to have any partiality for Mr. Chamberlain. — Mr. Chamberlain drew up the will, and minute circumstances of furniture &c. were attended to, so as to secure them to him in reversion. — Chamberlain was formerly a Common Council man of the Corporation of London, He is now Solicitor to the Treasury.

While N. Dance continued to paint portraits, He applied very diligently, frequently rising at 4 oClock in the morning.

Accounts came today of the French having got possession of Ghent & Bruges.

Sunday — June 29th.

Rose at ½ past 7. — Dined today at C. Offleys. — Mrs. Hamond & Minet there.

Mrs. Curtis who formerly appeared at Dr. Grahams strange lectures, is sister to Mrs. Siddons.

Yesterday I recd. a list of persons offering to serve as special constables in case of emergency.

Monday 30th.

Rose ¼ before 7. — Breakfasted with Hearne and told him G. Dance will draw his profile on Saturday next. — Mr. Henderson, of the Adelphi, brought an etching on soft ground, the first he has done from a sketch by Hearne, very free & well.

Painting & sorting Prints & papers. — Young Baker wrote me a note inclosing a letter from Willm. Bissell.

JULY 1794

Tuesday — July 1st. — 1794.

Rose at 7. — Mr. Baker called on me. Mr. Trumbull, the Artist, is arrived from America — and comes in the capacity of Secretary to Mr. Jay, the Ambassador, to settle the differences which have arisen between the two countries lately. — Mr. Trumbull said everything seemed to promise fair for a settlement. He said the prudence of Mr. Washington, prevented resolutions from being passed in America of such a nature as would have produced a War between the two Countries. — He spoke of Tom Paine with aversion. His temporary pamphlet entitled Common Sense gave Tom for a while credit in America, but He was at last seen through, to be a man disposed by nature to disturb the peace & order of society.

The Arts are likely to be well encouraged in America. Stuart is now at New York and well employed. His prices are not so great as He had in England, but his expenses are proportionably more reasonable.

America thrives rapidly, Towns increase in size, and people grow rich.

Very bad accts. were recd. today from Flanders. — The French have defeated the Prince of Saxe Cobourgh, and Charleroi surrendered in consequence. Brussels, it is said, is also in their possession. — The Duke of Yorks army of British & Hanoverians, seems to be in a dangerous situation in the neighboroud of Tournay. It is said to consist of 12,000 men, almost surrounded by the French.

G. Dance told me this eving. — that Ld. Camden had informed him that young Ld. Waldegrave abt. 10 years old, was drowned in the Thames on Sunday last & that Mr. Stewart, a son of Ld. Londonderrys, nearly shared the same fate in attempting to save him. — He was son to one of the daugrs of Sir Edwd. Walpole.

Wednesday — July 2nd.

Rose at ½ past 6.

Met Byrne who told me his sister who has been a nun 28 or 9 years in an English Convent at Bruges, is, with the Lady Abbess, and the other nuns,

207

abt. 34 or 5 in all, coming to England to reside together somewhere in the country, a house having been taken for them for that purpose. Fortunately they have so managed their property as to have a sufficiency to maintain them. Their money is under the management of Mr. Wright the Banker.

In the evening Banks called on me to solicit my signature to an adress from Mr. Roberts, Brother in Law to Poor Cozens, which is to be delivered to the President & Council of the Royal Academy. The object of it is to obtain some assistance from the Body towards subsisting Cozens who is under the care of Dr. Monro witht. a prospect of recovery, Cosway, Northcote & Hodges had signed it.

It seems Cozens married some years ago and has two children, one 5 or 6 years old. His marriage was not generally known. — Mr. Roberts who married his sister, has a place in the Exchequer.

Cozens disorder is described to be a total decay of the nervous system. He appeared formerly to be of a silent, hesitating disposition, and of grave manners. Sometime since a total change took place, He became childishly noisy & talkative on trifles. He is described to be in his present state very cheerful.

The news of this day, is a Duel on Moulsey Hurst between the Earl of Tankerville, and Mr. Edward Bouverie, in which the latter was wounded. — Their seconds Col. Bennet and [Charles Nassau Thomas] published a short account.

The accounts from Flanders are of the worst description. It appears the Allies are retreating from the French in every quarter. The Inhabitants of Tournay expressed great concern when the British passed through that place.

Smirke called on me: Rossi the Sculptor is desirous of making a Model for the monument to be erected to the memory of Captn. Montague. — I told him I thought Wyatt, (having the King's ear) would be the best person to apply to for his interest. He thought Wyatt might wish to move in favor of a young man now abroad (Westmacot) whose Father has been recommended to much business by Wyatt. However He said He wd call on him. Nollekens, He says expresses no desire to have it, and some political circumstances put Banks out of the question. — I told him I thought Bacon must have moved for such a Commission before this time. Rossi is to make his Model at Smirkes House.

Copy of the advertisement published by the Seconds of Lord Tankerville & Mr. Bouverie. 'Yesterday morning, in consequence of a previous appointment, the Earl of Tankerville & the Honble. Edward Bouverie met on Moulsey Hurst, and took their places at the distance of Twelve paces when upon Mr. Bouveries declining to fire, Lord T. by direction of us, who were seconds to the parties, fired, and wounded Mr. B. but we are happy to find not so dangerously as was apprehended. We cannot omit our testimony of the coolness and good conduct displayed by both. signed Cha. Nassau Thomas, H. Bennett, Lieut. Col. first guards'

Thursday — July 3d.

Rose at ½ past 5.

Called on Smirke this morning and agreed for his three finished sketches of 'Falstaff exhorting the Prince', — 'Falstaff rising after the death of Hotspur', — and 'Ann Page inviting in Master Slender'. — These sketches are exquisite in respect of the truth of the expressions in the different characters represented.

Dined today at West end with J. Boydell — the Company consisted of Alderman Boydell, — Isaac Reid, Mr. Bowles, who wrote against Foxs Libel Bill, for which Lord Thurlow made him a Commissioner of Bankrupts, — Mr. Westhall, Mr. Pope, the Actor, — and Mr. Nicol.

On Tuesday Mr. Bouverie died of the wound He recd. from Lord Tankerville. This report was not true. [*This sentence has been added later by J.F.*] The cause of the duel was, it is said, owing to Mr. Bouverie having paid such an attention to one of the daughters of Lord Tankerville, as was unbecoming in Mr. Bouverie, a married man.

I came home with the Alderman who told me Whatman now makes printing paper equal in quality to French paper, and has an advantage from being manufactured more neatly. He does not think that in case of Peace we should again apply to France for the article of paper.

Mr. Reid said that Doctor Brocklesby had told him Mr. Burke had certainly given notice of quitting parliament.

The Alderman told me on our way, that He now finds a difference in his constitutional powers in this respect, that if He rises at 5 in the morning He is obliged to lay on a couch for an Hour in the course of the day. — He said He had always been an early riser and a moderate eater. — He said he drank milk in a morning, which agreed with him & He thought did him more service than anything. He takes common milk delivered at the door. Cold water in the morning He had drank for some time, but in the winter it was too cold for his stomach.

Friday — July 4th.

Rose at ½ past 6.

Called on Mr. Heaviside and paid him 50 guineas, His charge for attending poor Webber.

Hearne & Baker dined with me. They are going on Monday to Oxford to pass a week there, from thence Hearne goes to Che[l]tenham, to Sir G. Beaumont, and they are to make the Tour of the Wye together. — Hearne is also to go to Glastonbury Abbey & to Wells.

George Dance came in the evening. He heard the Banti, at the Opera last night and does not think her equal to Mara. She has a very fine voice & a good ear but has no knowledge of musick. — He thinks Her action, which has been much extolled, very indifferent.

It seems Mr. Bouverie, who is married to a daughter of Sir Chaloner Ogle, (sister to Mrs. Wilmot and Lady Asgill, who models Horses beautifully), took a House near Ld. Tankervilles & paid such attention to one of His Lordships daughters, as produced a letter requiring from Mr. B. a discontinuance of such attention. This being disregarded produced a challenge from Ld. T.

Mr. Hearne told me that Mr. Knight gave him written directions for the designs which are introduced into his picturesque essay on gardening as examples.

Saturday July 5th.

Rose at 7.

Called on Batty who has been very indifferent of a feverish complaint.

Fuseli & Smirke drank tea with me. Nothing was done by the Committee which [met] on the subject of the Medal last night. West was not there. It was adjourned till Monday next.

Hearne does not set to Dance today. The latter is to pass the day at Lord Eardleys, at Belvedere.

Mr. Gostling, of Bedford Square, & who owns the principal grounds at Whitton, is desirous that I shd. go there as He thinks that place is near enough to the Thames to be introduced into the second Volume as a feature. — I promised to let him know when I made an excursion into that neighberoud.

Sunday — July 6th.

Last meeting at Sir Joseph Banks's. — Called on Hearne. — Pouncy is making one set of *finished* etchings from his designs. The specimen is worked up to the effect of Vivares prints, retaining a great portion of the freedom of a loose etching. Baker, suggested this scheme to them from the specimen of etching in Knights poem on picturesque Landscape.

Dined at C. Offleys, Mr. & Mrs. Harris, Miss Harris, Mr. Arbouin, the Revd. Mr. Lawton — there. — Mr. Lawton resides near Daventry in Northamptonshire. — Althorp is abt. 7 miles distant. — Ld. Spencer is considered as living very retired, as to his neighbours, in the country. He has withdrawn all political views on the Town of Northampton, & never interferes in their elections. — The late Ld. Spencer supported a Charity School for 40 poor children. This is not now maintained. The Northampton people regret the Spencer family having forsaken them. — Lord Spencer is much respectd. Lady S. loves her ease, and is attached to her amusements.

The Northampton family is recovering a little from the ruinous state in which their affairs were. Ld. N. having long resided in Switzerland had been enabled to do this.

At the Council last Thursday the petition in favor of Cozens was presented, when Ten Guineas was voted for his relief.

The Revd. Mr. Lawton told me that S. Ireland had been making drawings in Northamptonshire of Catesby House &c.

Monday, July 7th.

Rose at ½ past 6. — This evening went to Drury Lane Play House with Opie. The entertainments were Lodoiska, and the first of June in honor of Lord Howes victory. — The Burning the Castle in Lodoiska is admirably managed. — The first of June is heavy & ill suited I think to work on the people properly, it dwells too much on the consequences of war.

Drury Lane Theatre is an instance of the worst taste I ever saw in a large building, — disproportioned in the design and frippery in the execution. — The seats in the Boxes are convenient.

Sir F. Bourgeois was there. He told me He had for 3 or 4 years past purchased a Ticket for the season for which He paid 6 guineas and was free of every part of the House. It is not transferable.

He seemed to have apprehensions from some conversation with Trumbull, of the question with America being amicably settled.

He told me the King had much noticed my view of High St. Oxford, & remembered all the buildings.

Tuesday, July 8th.

Rose at ½ past 7.

Smirke informed me this morning that at the meeting of the Commemoration medal Committee last night, His design was adopted. — I drank tea with Hamilton who has a touch of the Gout in his feet for the first time. He communicated the particulars of what passed at the Committee last night some circumstances having much surprised him.

The members present were

    Mr. West

Mr. Bacon	— Fuseli	*absent*
Banks	— Smirke	Cosway
Nollekens	— Hamilton	Northcote
Burch	— Rigaud	

Much altercation passed. Bacon said on consideration He had changed his mind relative to Mr. Smirkes design, He now thought instead of a group it shd. be only a single figure and produced a design suitable. In this He was supported by others. Hamilton proposed to determine this question by Balot which was accordingly done. Four were for a single

figure, & four for a group — Mr. West gave the casting vote for a group. —
On this being determined, Bacon produced a design of two figures, slightly
sketched, of Britannia embracing Minerva. Strange to tell though a very
poor design & very indifferently expressed, it was immediately adopted
with preference to Cosways, Wests, &c. — for when according to
agreement the Committee scratched for the different designs which were
offered, Smirke had 3, — Bacon 3, — Rigaud 1, — Cosway 1.

It then came to a balot in the Box, when there appeared for Bacon 4, —
for Smirke 4. Mr. West gave his Casting Vote for Smirke. Smirke then rose
& declared that owing to a mistake He had voted for Bacon & not for
himself as He intended.

The next business was to determine abt. modelling the design. It was
agreed to be done abt. a foot high. Smirke requested that He might be
permitted to superintend the modelling, as otherways his Idea might not
be expressed as He wished it shd. be. To this Bacon objected, & said if he
were to model it He must take the liberty to make certain alterations &c. —
Smirke surprised them by requesting that He might *himself* model it. No
objection was made to this, but Bacon said He expected Smirke shd.
declare it to be his own work. — Thus narrowly did He continue to
proceed on the business, mentioning as a reason that it shd. be entirely
executed by a Member of the Academy.

Hamilton, who receives his information from Mr. Dryander, says that
Sir Joseph Banks's Botanical work which has been carrying on many
years, and for which 1500 plates are engraved, is not likely to be published
as was expected. Some think that Sir Joseph does not choose to encounter
the opinion of the world on the merits of it, and, indeed, it is probable ill
disposed cricks wd. not be wanting.

Wednesday, July 9th.

Bromleys 3d. letter to Copley appeared.

Fuseli drank tea with me. His Father was a painter: but He was intended
to profit by literary studies. He came to England in 1766. He travelled with
Ld. Chewton, the late Ld. Waldgrave, in 1769 twelve months in France.

Thursday — 10th.

Called on Dance to desire him to speak to Soane abt. concluding Mrs.
Playfairs business.

Dined at Offleys with Smirke & Batty.

Friday 11th.

Breakfasted with Lysons. — Called on Alderman Boydell who gave me a
Volume of his own works.

Called on Walker. My visit to Croydon is postponed till the Autumn. —
When Miers's affairs are settled, Mrs. Miers will probably have 1200 a

year, besides the disposal of £5000. — Will Boardmans estate is not likely to pay more than 12 shillings in the pound. — His debt to Walkers House is from his having become security for Will Whittaker for £1500.

Dined at Offleys with Mr. Evans, Porter, Carlton, Brother to the Mayor of Dublin, — and another gentleman.

Hamilton Rowan is certainly the person who was at the Warrington Academy. — His friend who assisted to get him out of the Kingdom, in rowing the boat with too much exertion, broke a Blood Vessel & died.

Went from Offleys to Dance, where I met Soane on Mrs. Playfairs business.

Saturday, July 12.

Went to the Navy Office & was directed by Mr. Margetson, the Secretary to write to the Board to desire them to order payment for the picture of Deptford Yard. — I accordingly wrote.

Smirke spoke to me abt. a design He had made on the subject of Ld. Howes Victory. Emblematical with Heads of the Admirals. — I strongly recommended to him to have *portraits* of them, & not medalions, as people would understand them better, also to add the Captains.

Went in the evening with C & J Offley to Fanhams.

Sunday, July 13.

At Fanhams. — Minet there.

Monday, 14th.

Went with Mrs. Offley, Charles & John to look at a House near Welling in Herts, called St John Lodge, which is to be disposed of. — Dined at Welling, and returned to Fanhams in the eving.

Tuesday, July 15th.

Came to town early with C & J Offley.

Mr. Careys Brother, who formerly was with Sir Robt. Herries called on me. He came up from Southampton. Mr. Carey Senr. does not come to Town. — He desired to see the pictures which his Brother had painted. I showed them to him and told him that his Brother had greatly improved lately: that He comprehended the principles of his art: and that though it was impossible to say to what degree of excellence an Artist might arrive, I could assert that He promised very fair. That I shd. be glad to render him any service in my power though our engagements had ceased having been well satisfied with his conduct in every respect.

Dance & Soane called and we went together to Mrs. Playfairs. They wrote to Mr. Gordon.

Met Major Gardner, who told me the Admiral is in town. The Majors first wife died abt. 3 years & half ago. — He married Mrs. Thurston, formerly Miss Alworthy, abt. a year ago.

Dined at C. Offleys, no company.

In the evening Lysons called on me. Ld. Orford proposed asking me to dinner at Strawberry-Hill, to meet George Nicol and Chamberlain, — Lysons supposing it would be as agreeable to me, said He & I proposed coming together to Strawberry Hill in a short time.

This day I recd. a letter from Sir George Beaumont at Cheltenham desiring me to purchase a picture by Wilson, belonging to Ld. Thanet, now on sale at Vanderguchts. — I called on Vandergucht, who demanded 100 guineas for the picture. I agreed with him for *100 pounds.*

This picture was begun in Italy, and finished in England.

Lord Thanet hd also sent for sale a large picture by Barrett, which was considered a masterpiece at the time it was painted. For this He only asked 40 guineas.

Vandergucht told me the pictures of Wilson are getting into great request at comparatively high prices. — The Pictures of Barrett fall in value, there being few who collect them. Dr. Monro has collected a few. — He also told me the pictures of Gainsborough are decreasing in value. The raging fashion of collecting them subsiding fast.

Vandergucht told me he sold a Claude to Sir Peter Burrell for 1500 guineas, and had sold him pictures to the amount of £8000.

Wednesday July 16.

Breakfasted with Admiral Gardner. A Gentleman was there who brought the dispatches announcing the capture of Port au prince, in St. Domingo. — Admiral Gardners second son, not 22 years of age, was made Post, into the Iphigene frigate of 32 guns, two days before the surrender of the place, by which He will gain between 3 & 4000 pounds. — I talked to the Admiral abt. Wm. Bissell. He does not believe Mr. Bootle has written to Ld. Chatham, but He has put Bissells name down and gave me every encouragement to hope He wd. be promoted.

I mentioned to the Admiral Smirke & Bowyers proposal to publish a Print on the subject of the late engagement, and desired His portrait. This he readily granted, and assisted me in making out a list of the Captains with their directions, in order to get their portraits.

Serres came there with some designs to represent the naval engagement, Viz: The Ships breaking the line; and the state of the Fleet, including prizes after the engagement.

Mrs. Gardner told me she was on board the Queen Charlotte (being invited by Lady Howe) when the King & Queen came on board. Lord Howe recd. the King with his Hat on, — The King made a Gracious Speech to Lord Howe, and presented Him a Sword. Lord Howe, then taking off his *Hat*, kneeled, and kissed the Kings Hand.

Captain Hutt of the Queen, was not in a good state of health before the engagement. He was thought to be doing well, but a fever seized him, which carried him of. He pulse beat for four days before He died 136. — He was delirious the last 2 days.

Captn. Harvey was so far recovered as to be pronounced out of danger. Lady Howe visited Him, as he sat up in His chair, & was very chearful. — A contusion on his back was supposed to be the cause of his death.

I called on Smirke after I had been with Adml. Gardner — Smirke told me Bowyer was so pleased with the Picture of Gadshill in the Shakespeare Gallery, that He wished we wd. paint a picture *in conjunction*, for the History of England.

Dined at Offleys with J. Boydell.

Thursday, July 17th.

Called this morning on Bowyer, and went to breakfast at Admiral Gardners. introduced Bowyer to him, — to compare Stuarts portrait with the Admiral. — I afterwards explained George Dances scheme of Portraits of distinguished Characters of the present Age, & solicited the Admiral to set to him, which He engaged to do tomorrow.

Called at the Navy Office and spoke to Mr. Margetson abt. payment for the picture. He said the minute of the agreed price had not been presented to the Board — but He wd. mention it again. I told him the price agreed for was 60 guineas.

Recd. a letter from Sir George Beaumont at Cheltenham, desiring me to meet him at Ross, & go down the Wye with him, this I answered I cd. not do on acct. of my engagements to finish things before I left Town.

I wrote to Wm. Bissell giving him hopes of promotion, and mentioning that I understood that Mr. Bootle has not written to Lord Chatham.

In the eving. I met Bowyer at Smirkes. Bowyer has applied to Sr. Alexander Hood &c. & has met with due encouragement.

I called on Dance and fixed him to meet Admiral Gardner at my House tomorrow morning to breakfast, as His House is now repairing. — Dance is happy to have this line of professional men opened to him.

When I called on Vandergucht today I found He had delivered the picture I have purchased for Sir George Beaumont to a Young Man to Copy, the same size as the original.

Fresilicque called on me yesterday & today, but I was not at home.

The late Bond Hopkins supplied Bowyer with money to carry on his History of England, for which He was to have a certain share of the profits. Since his death the Executors have behaved handsomely to Bowyer in giving up claims of profits, and allowing him time to repay the money advanced. Bowyer, is afraid of employing Romney, on acct. of the unpopularity of his Tempest picture in the Shakespeare gallery. — He is also afraid to employ Fuseli on acct. of the great inequality of his works.

Friday, July 18th.

This morning Admiral Gardner & G. Dance breakfasted with me, and the Admiral afterwards sat to Dance for a Profile.

Lord Howe had reason to expect the Garter which was given to the Duke of Portland. Indeed the new arrangement of an Administration being afterwards settled Ld. Howe was applied to to give it up, which He did, to suit the convenience of the political parties. — What an instance of his moderation. — Lady Howe told the Admiral that a Marquisate was no object to them as Lord Howe had rank enough, and they had no Son.

The Admiral said Lord Howe had been much hurt at the attacks on him daily in the publick prints, before the late engagement, expressing his belief that He might be injured in the minds of the Seamen. He talked of throwing up his command which the Admiral most strongly urged against.

The French fleet went out to Sea full 500 miles from Brest, having as it appeared certain intelligence of the return of their convoy from America. The certainty with which Lord Howe followed their track caused Admiral Gardner to suppose He must have had certain information of their scheme, but Ld. Howe assured him He gained his intelligence only from the ships the Fleet casually met with. — Many French merchantmen &c. were taken, but so determined was Lord Howe not to weaken his ships by putting Seamen into his prizes, that He burnt them every one, though some of them were of considerable value. What a proof of his little regard to property when compared with a sense of publick duty.

When they first saw the French Fleet the Admiral thought the French did not know them, but took them for the Convoy. — The French bore down & the English proceeded towards them witht. altering a sail.

On the first of June, Lord Howes ship did not fire but a *single shot* before the Queen Charlotte, had passed through the French Line. That Shot was fired by a man after whom Lord Howe went with his sword drawn. — Mr. Bowen — Lord Howes master, told His Lordship He did not see how He cd. get between their ships; Lord Howe told him to direct the Queen Charlotte against the Bowsprit of one of them, which being done the French ship was obliged to give way to avoid the consequence. By this He shewed the folly of the French decree against breaking the line.

The Queen Charlotte suffered considerably before she got into action. So did the Queen. — The French firing incessantly while the English ships generally speaking reserved their fire.

I asked him if He thought the French fought better on this than on any former occasion. He said He thought they seemed less desirous than He has before seen them, to avoid an action; but their comparative inferiority in *close action* was still the same. He is convinced they will not stand to their guns as the English do.

The French Admirals ship went of in apparently very good condition.

Her masts and sails having suffered little. Many of the prisoners expressed great disatisfaction at the Admirals conduct.

Many of the prisoners were loyalists, but being in the requisition were obliged to go on board, or the guillotine wd. have been the consequence. — They had been told that great numbers of emigrant French were on board our Ships.

Speaking of the quantity of Shot fired on the occasion, the Admiral said it had been calculated that 60 ton of shot had been fired by the Queen in the three days. — Two shot are put into every charge and He believes they even sometime put in three. But two are recommended by the Ordnance.

Speaking of personal fear, He said Lord Howes Chaplain, who had been recommended by the Bishop of London, was so overcome by his fears during the action as to be totally unmanned. He quitted the Ship immediately on her coming to Portsmouth, of course lost the opportunity of preaching before & being noticed by the King.

The Admiral dined with the King twice. The 2d. time abt. 26 were present. — The King sat at the Head of the table and helped fish &c. and nothing cd. exceed the ease, and good humour which prevailed. The King speaking familiarly and the officers conversing with each other.

When Admiral Bowyer who lost a Leg, was carried to the Cockpit, a Tournicot was applied to stop the bleeding. This being done the Admiral insisted on those Sailors being first dressed who had been wounded before him. One of them who had lost a Leg (a Taylor belonging to the Land forces aboard the Barfleur) swore He wd. not be dressed before the Admiral, that his life was of less value, and He wd. wait. — This Mr. Davis, the Chaplain of the Barfleur, told Admiral Gardner.

I introduced Smirke to the Admiral, who was much pleased with a Sketch of the intended print.

Called on Serres, who shewed me his 4 sketches, one of the action & one after it, on the first of June, — one the Royal Salute at Spithead, — and the launching the Prince of 90 Guns. — He has applied by letter to Admiral Gardner to get him a commission from the Admiralty to paint them, or for their *sanction* that He may make Prints of them.

I told him I wd. speak my opinion to the Admiral of his sketches, which I much approved of, and would learn if I could, whether either of his requests cd. be complied with.

He said His pictures were so placed in the last Exhibition as to be a great disadvantage to him.

Lysons dined with me.

Saturday — July 19th.

Admiral Gardner & G. Dance, breakfasted with me.

The Admiral was born April 12th. 1742. — Mrs. Dixon is abt. 61. — He promised to speak to Lord Howe to set to Dance.

Artaud called to solicit my vote to go to Rome as travelling Student in the place of Proctor, who died in England a few days ago. — I promised him my vote, and that I wd. speak to Mr. Dance, who afterwards promised me.

The Admiral told me Lord Chatham is an earlier riser than is reported. The Letters are regularly sent to him abt. ½ past eleven oClock. — His habit is to sup at home about Twelve oClock and go to bed abt. two. — He seems but of a middling constitution as to strength, frequently ailing. The Fatigue He underwent while attending the King at Portsmouth almost overcame him.

Freslicque dined with me, also C & J Offley — We subscribed to his Sermon preached on board the Belerophon. — He described the conduct of Captn. Molloy, as being cowardly, in the opinion of the crew of the Belerophon. His signal for close engagement was flying near an Hour.

Sunday — July 20.

Went to Fanhams, with C & J Offley, Breakfasted at Hoddesdon. — Will & George went to dinner at Fanhams. — Mrs. Lynch Salusbury there.

Monday 21.

At Fanhams.

Tuesday 22.

Returned to Town, — found a letter from Admiral Gardner acquainting me that Wm. Bissell is made a Lieutenant, and will be appointed first Lieutenant of the Trompeuse, sloop of war. — I wrote to Bissell, on board the Orion, at Portsmouth to acquaint him of his promotion, and recommending to him to write a letter of thanks to Admiral Gardner.

Smirke called on me and told me Admiral Gardner sat to Bowyer yesterday, and had subscribed to his History of England. Bowyer went to Portsmouth last night. They have already above 100 Subscribers to the Commemoration Print.

Dined at Offleys.

Poor Proctor is supposed to have been overcome by anxiety of mind on acct. of his circumstances being deranged. — so Rossi told Smirke. — I afterwards learnt that He broke a Blood Vessel in the night, and only lived a few hours.

Wednesday 23d.

Breakfasted with Admiral Gardner. He sat yesterday to Hickel for the picture of the House of Commons. — They think the Portrait like.

Bissell is made 5th Lieutenant of the Gibraltar, Captn. Pakenham. Another Officer is appointed to the Trompeuse.

At two o'Clock I went to the Navy Office. Sir John Henslow told me the picture of Deptford Yd. is not so well approved of as that of Chatham. I said the subject of it was not so favorable. We had a long conversation, in the board room. — He made many objections while comparing it with the Chatham picture.

Lysons dined with me.

Marchant called in the eving. and we went together to Fuselis. He is not inclined to vote for Artaud.

This day we have had many showers, after fair weather for 5 or 6 weeks.

Thursday, June 24.

Called on Margetson at Navy Office. Payment for the Dock Yd. is ordered, but must pass the Board twice.

Downman called on me to solicit my vote to be an associate. He told me He had heard I Had mentioned his name for which He expressed his acknowledgements. — I told him He shd. have a vote from me, & recommended Him to desire any of his friends in the Academy to interest theirselves with their academical friends in his favor. He said He knew Mr. West, Sir Wm. Chambers, & Humphry, & had spoken to Mr. Wilton, but had few acquaintances among the members.

At the request of Bowyer who is at Portsmouth, I wrote today a letter of introduction for him to Captn. Westcote.

The Revd. Dr. Steevens, wrote to offer me the two Wilsons back at the price He gave me, which I accepted. — Wrote to Wm. Bissell — Dined at C Offleys with Minet.

Friday July 25th.

Breakfasted at Admiral Gardners and shewed Mrs. Gardner some of Dances profiles & that of the Admiral, which she thinks very like. — Molloy is to have a Court Martial. — I told the Admiral what Fresilicque had said. — I mentioned the reputation Molloy formerly bore for bravery. He said He certainly had been much respected on that account.

I called on Hickel, in Russell St. — He has made a great many Portraits of Members of the House of Commons. There are to be two pictures. The Majority being conspicuous in one with Pitt, speaking. — The Minority in the other with Fox, speaking.

Hickel was 4 days with Fox at St. Anns Hill. — Burke insisted on being placed on the opposition side and of its being filled as before the late change of political sentiment.

J. Boydell looked over some of the River subjects today for the 2d. Volume of Thames.

In the evening I spoke to Stadler abt. Manskerk drawing in some of my River Subjects on Canvass for me.

Revd. Dr. Steevens returned my two pictures by Wilson, and I paid him back forty pounds which He had paid me for them. — He had them January. 16th. 1793.

July 26th.

Called at Poggis today for the first time. His contrivances for containing the Portfolios of Sir Joshuas collection of drawings are very good. — The sale room is furnished with various drawings in water colours by P. Sandby — the price from 26 guineas to two or 3 gs. The man told me they are admired but do not sell.

At noon Mr. Dalrymple, who is distinguished by his Charts sat in my painting room to G. Dance, for a profile. — Lysons brought him, He seemed very shy in his manner. He is Brother to the late Lord Hailes — one of the Lords of Session. At Tea time Hickey, the Sculptor, called on me, on the subject of the ensuing election of Associates — I told him I had not seen a list of the Candidates, but that I supposed it could not be so strong a one as on some former occasions. He said there were few names of consequence down. — I told him I had always defended the justice of paying a proper attention to Architects, and of course shd. do the same to Sculptors, when it appeared their number shd. be encreased. I gave him not the least notice how I shd. vote.

He told me that Ld. Macartney had conditioned with the different persons who went with him to China, not to keep separate journals of what passed, but that each shd. contribute what he could to a general book which shd. be revised and published. — This information Hickey had from his Brother who went out as an Artist with Ld. Macartney.

In the eving. I called on Smirke. — Bowyer has written that *Sir Roger Curtis* himself, & other Officers, think He shd. be placed among the Flag Officers.

Smirke told me Bowyer was much pleased to find I was disposed to paint a picture in conjunction with him for the History of England.

Wm. Bissell wrote to me today from the Gibraltar, Man of War. He was sworn in 5th. Lieutenant of that Ship by Sir Charles Saxton, the Commissioner, on the 24th. — Captn. Pakenham has the Gibraltar.

Bissell sent me a Copy of his letter of thanks to Admiral Gardner. He also expresses his acknowledgements to me for having been the means of procuring him promotion. — Vandergucht sent the Mecenas Villa.

Sunday — July 27th.

Called in the morning at the Shakespeare Gallery to look out some Volumes of the Thames.

Met Fresilicque, who says dismission will be the least punishment of Molloy. — at home alone.

Monday, 28th.

Drank tea this eving. with Smirke. — He approves my selection of Charles the 2d. with the Penterells, under the Oak.

Tuesday, 29th.

Garvey called on me today to see the Mecenas's Villa. He went to Gainsborough Dupont to speak to him about the election of Associates.

I dined with C & J Offley in Ormond St.

Wednesday — 30th.

Lysons, breakfasted with me & Smirke corrected the outlines of his Roman pavement figures. — Smirke approves my design for Bowyer-figures in the print to be 3 Inches.

I dined with the Offleys & Lysons came to tea.

Went to Fuselis in the eving.

Thursday 31st.

Smirke went to Portsmouth.

Will who has been a few days at Wheelers at Hornsey, called.

At noon I went with Lysons to Lord Orfords at Strawberry Hill, — and stopped at Twickenham where we took boat & I made a drawing of Popes House, (now belonging to Welbore Ellis.)

Lysons & I dined with Lord Orford, no other company. — In the afternoon we went to Cliveden, whimsically so called from having been inhabited by the late Mrs. Clive, — Lord Orford has given it to the Miss Berrys for their joint lives. — We supped there, only the eldest Miss Berry, & Her Father at home.

At 10 o'Clock returned to Strawberry Hill. — Lord Orford usually rises between 8 & 9, and goes to bed at 12.

Lord Orford mentioned many particulars relative to the late Mr. Topham Beauclerc. — He said He was the worst tempered man He ever knew. — Lady Di passed a most miserable life with him. Lord O., out of regard to her invited them occasionally to pass a few days at Strawberry Hill. — They slept in separate beds. — Beauclerc was remarkably filthy in his person which generated vermin. — He took Laudanum regularly in vast quantities. — He seldom rose before one or two oClock. — His principal delight was in disputing on subjects that occurred, this He did acutely. — Before He died He asked pardon of Lady Di, for his ill usage of her. — He had one son & two daugrs. by Lady Di. — one married Lord Herbert, the second went abroad with her Brother, Lord Bolingbroke.

The late Lord Hertford was in his 76th. year when He died. — He was careful of his health & temperate, but drank only wine, and that Burgundy.

He left only £5000 to each of his younger children men and woemen. — The present Lord Hertford made it up £10000. — Lord Orford said He had corresponded with the late Lord Hailes, who He said was industrious but no genius.

AUGUST 1794

Friday — Augst. 1st.

Left Strawberry Hill at 7 oClock & breakfasted at Kew. Called on Zoffany & I made a drawing of Kew Bridge from his window. — He was painting on one of his Parisian subjects, — the woemen & Sans Culottes, dancing &c over the dead bodies of the Swiss Soldiers. — Zoffanys legs are much swelled by a scorbutic humour.

Dined & eving. alone.

Saturday — 2d.

Recd. a message early from Sir George Beaumont, and went to him to breakfast. — He has been down the Wye, & at Chepstow, and at Bath, where He found N. Dance. — From thence to Lord Radnors to see the Claudes. — Hearne was with him. — He speaks highly of Chepstow & Pierce field. He thinks Chepstow Castle superior to Conway.

Went with Sir George to Marchs the Dentist.

At three oClock they left Town for Dunmow, and go on Monday to Haverhill. — Sir George pressed me to come to Dedham.

In the evening Marchant & Humphry called on me.

Sunday August 3d.

Kershaw, called on me. I walked to Lambeth with him.

Went with Humphry to dinner at Paines — Marchant came there and we returned together.

Mary Paine is 17 years of age, and very ingenious. I told Mrs. Paine she might be allowed to paint in oil, as no danger wd. attend her using the colours.

Paine told me Richd. Burke, only child of Edmund, died yesterday. He had been elected member for Malton in the room of his Father 10 days since. I remember Lady Inchiquin told me last winter that his constitution was only indifferent. — Paine said His Father was afflicted beyond expression at the death of his Son.

223

Monday — Augst. 4th.

Bromleys 4th. letter to Copley appeared.
Went to the Navy Office and recd. in Mr. Davis's Office an order for the payment of £63 — the fee here 10s. 6d. — It was noted in another office, fee 5s. — I then carried it to Mr. Slade's Office, the *Pay Office*, — no fee here. The draft He gave me was on Coutts.
Called at the Shakespeare Gallery. — Boydell told me Coombe had enquired whether the Scotch Rivers were to be gone on with before the English were finished. — Boydell said nothing was settled, but that He believed the English wd. be first finished. — Coombe said He was quite of opinion that it would be best to get through them first.

Tuesday, Augst. 5th.

employed in painting Studies, did not call anywhere.
In the eving. Mrs. Hamond and the Offleys, & Opie, called while I was out. — A week I have now dedicated to painting studies on small canvasses, of various effects, from my different collections of subjects &c.
Wrote to Smirke at Portsmouth.

Wednesday, 6th.

Dined at C. Offleys. Mrs. Hamond, Mrs. Offley & Minet there.

Thursday, 7th.

Called at the Shakespeare Gallery. Nicol told me Mrs. Davis, widow of Tom Davis, the Bookseller, and author of the life of Garrick, is now abt. 70 years of age, and in very indigent circumstances, — she had £20 a year allowed Her by Cadell, while He continued Printer to the Royal Academy, which office having been taken from him this year, she loses that advantage. I told Nicol I wd. speak to Sir William Chambers on the subject. — Met Trumbull, who said if matters are accomodated with America He may stay some time.
Drank tea at Jacks Coffee House, Plott there.

Friday — Augst. 8th.

This morning met Sir John Henslow near Somerset place, & conversed with him on the subject of the Deptford yd. picture. It concluded with my offering to make any alteration for the advantage of the effect, and He said He wd. call on me when I had the picture again in my possession.
Called on Wheatley, & invited him to dine with me tomorrow.
Dined with C. Offleys. — Messrs. Campion, Evans, and Harris, there. Mr. Kingston came in the evening, and Lysons called on me, to propose going on Sunday to Richmond Gardens & to dine at Shene.
Walter King wrote the eulogium on Young Burke, published in the papers.

Saturday — Augst. 9th.

Called on G. Dance who has seen the Engraver that proposes to publish portraits of the Members of the Royal Academy. Dance has no objection to his doing what He pleases as far as it affects his own future resolutions.

Called on Poggi and had a long conversation with him on the subject of Lady Inchiquins Prints & drawings. — He desired me to give him an introduction to Admiral Gardner, that He might shew him Cleveleys designs — accordingly I gave him a letter on his informing me the Admiral is still in town.

Marchi called on me with a message from Lord & Lady Inchiquin, desiring to see me at Taplow. They came from Ireland a day or two since.

Marchi said the grief of Burke on the loss of his Son was excessive. He cd. not be kept from the room in which the Corpse lay, and after viewing threw himself on the bed in agonies, and was so weakened by his grief He cou'd scarcely stand. — Burkes servants thought the journey and business of the election in Yorkshire had hastened his end. He had sicknesses in the night which He desired his servant to conceal from his father. He was 36 years old.

Tassaerts Son is dead of the yellow fever in the West Indies. He was lately made a Purser by Sir John Jervais, & promoted in other respects.

Called on Mrs. Hone. H. Hone is at Buxton and is solicited to go to Liverpool, Manchester & Sheffield.

Fuseli, Opie, Humphry, Wheatley, — Charles & John Offley, Marchant and Taylor of Hatton Garden dined with me of Venison sent by Mrs. Smith.

Taylor, strongly recommended Hickey the Sculptor, to me to be an Associate. — He said Mrs. Siddons is about 42 years of age. — This happen'd to be Taylors birthday who is 39.

Sunday — Augst. 10th.

Breakfasted with Lysons — and went with him to Richmond gardens, to look at Sion House. — dined at the Revd. Mr. Peach's at East Shene, who gave us excellent Port wine 19 years old. — He said Dr. Cadogan had told him that after any accidental excess, He was accustomed to take as much Rhubarb as would lay on a shilling, — an equal quantity of ginger, & of magnesia, in peppermint water, which counteracted the effects of the excess.

Mr. Peach always receives benefit from the Bath waters.

The Company at dinner were Mrs. Knight, Miss Ricard, — Mr. Townson, Mrs. Townson, — Miss Peach & S. Lysons. D. Lysons came to Tea & Bicknel Coney.

Walked to Putney with D & S. Lysons, by Mortlake & Barnes Common.

S. Lysons talked yesterday with Bearcroft the Council on the subject of the ensuing trials of the persons committed for seditious purposes. Bearcroft seemed of the opinion that some of them would be found guilty.

Mr. Peach said that not more than 6 weeks ago the Duke of Portland said He wd. never make part of an administration unless Fox was of the number. — Fox would not believe till it was absolutely settled that the Duke &c. would join the Administration.

Monday — Augst. 11th.

Went to Lord Fifes to examine the view from his House. — Will, came up with George from Hoddesdon, to carry him to School.

Dined at C. Offleys. Only Mrs. Hamond, Mrs. Ball & the family.

This evening Reynolds the Engraver left His proposals for publishing Portraits of the Members of the Royal Academy.

G. Dance went to Lymington.

Tuesday — August 12.

Called on Alderman Boydell this morning and settled the Old Print account between us. The balance against me was £30 which I allowed him out of the payment due to me for the Shakespeare picture of Gadshill.

Went to Guildhall with the Alderman, where in the Common Council room Rigaud was painting in Fresco.

Afterwards I made a drawing of the Tower. — for the River views. — C. Offley dined with me. Marchant tea & eving.

Wednesday — Augst. 13th.

Called Lord Inchiquins, they were out.

At the Shakespeare Gallery. — J. Boydell suggested the advantage of introducing a Birds eye view of London from the top of Lambeth Church, to occupy a double leaf. — I thought another also from Flamstead House would be interesting.

A Gentleman called on me from Mr. Erskine of Mar, to desire to know when the drawings for him would be finished. — I told him they were forwarded, and hoped would be finished in the course of the Autumn.

Dined with C. Offley.

Thursday, August 14th.

At 8 this morning went with C. Offley to the Green man, Blackheath. After breakfast went to the Observatory where on my mentioning Mr. Dowsins's name, Dr. Maskeyline shewed me the Camera at the top of the Observatory. Finding it wd. answer to me to trace the outline of the view of London from it, I procured the Doctors leave. Mr. Frazer assisted me in managing the Camera.

I employed myself till Dinner time, when Mr. Frazer dined with us. He lives at No 10 Ryder St., St. James's Square.

Mr. Newton late Secretary to the Academy died.

Friday, Augst 15.

Went this morning to the Observatory and employed myself the whole morning in making out the view.

Saturday, 16.

Went again to the Observatory. Dr. Maskeyline who had been at London came to me. He informed me the *circumference* of the view as reflected on the Plaister of Paris, is 63 feet. — The Diameter of the field of Plaister of Paris is 3 feet. The view commencing with Deptford Church, including *London* and ending on the right with Greenwich Hospital is [blank] feet.

C. Offley joined us and informed us of the death of Robespierre. — In the eving. returned to London. — Mr. Baker & Lysons called.

Sunday, Augst. 17th — 1794.

Breakfasted with Hearne, who shewed me his sketches of Rayland Castle, on the Wye, — of Tintern Abbey & Chepstow.

Went to the top of Lambeth Steeple to look at the view of London.

Dined at Mr. Bakers, with Messrs. Hearne & Henderson.

Monday — 18th.

Went this morning to Lambeth and from the top of the Steeple begun a view of London.

Smirke returned from Portsmouth. Captn. Pakenham told Captn. Molloy when He was disposed to speak abt. the affair of June 1st. to say little abt. the business.

Westcott is thought to be situated with a man not very active. — A Bertie's conduct was thought rather shy. — Recd. a letter from Mr. Berwick with a draft for £100.

Tuesday — 19th.

Breakfasted with Lysons.

Called at the Shakespeare Gallery. J. Boydell told me his Uncle said on Monday He thought the *Rivers* would not answer.

Rigaud is to have £300 for the four Fresco paintings in the Common Council room.

Hamilton had £200 each for two of the Shakespeare pictures which He painted of the size 9 feet by 7, — but the Alderman thought it too much and expected Smirke wd. only expect 150 for the Hearnes Oak & Gadshill. — In the evening I communicated to Smirke the above, & he was satisfied to settle the matter on terms satisfactory to the Alderman, but the picture of Sly cost him much trouble & I said He was entitled to £200 for that.

Marchant called in the evening.

Wednesday, Augst. 20.

Breakfasted at Lysons with Smirke who corrected and made out the figures for the Roman pavement.

Bowyer wrote to Smirke expressing a wish that Heath should undertake the plate of Charles the 2d. in the Forest. — I said it could not be better executed by anybody.

I shewed Smirke the dead colour of the Charles 2d. picture which He approved of entirely.

Recd. a letter from Susan informing me of her having been very ill. I left London in the Mail Coach in consequence in the evening.

Thursday. Augst 21.

Got to Lynn at eleven this morning and went to Sandringham. — Found Susan better; no company there.

Friday 22d.

H. Henley called; — and Mr. Middleton the Apothecary from Lynn.

Saturday 23d.

At Sandringham, no company.

Sunday 24th.

Rode to Massingham with H. Henley. — Met H Hamond & returned to Darsingham to dinner, and in the evening to Sandringham — found Mr. Middleton there.

Monday 25th.

H. Hamond left Sandringham early. — Mr. & Mrs. Henley the Revd. Mr. Davy and Mr. Austin Davy, dined at Sandringham.

Tuesday 26.

Dined at Mr. Henleys at Darsingham with Mrs. Smyth, Susan, the Revd. Mr. Davy & Doctor Martin Davy.

Wednesday 27.

After dinner went to Lynn with Mrs. Smyth & Susan. Drank tea and supped with Mrs. Richd. Hamond, Mr. Jas. Case, Messrs. Thomas & Willm. Bagge, Mrs. Bagge, & the two Misses Bagges there. — Mrs. Smyth & Susan returned to Sandringham. — I slept at the Crown Inn.

Thursday, Augst. 28th.

Left Lynn at 5 this morning in the Post Coach, breakfasted at Brandon, & dined at Harlowe, and arrived in London at 8 oClock. — The fare of the Coach £1. 10. 0. — Mr. Upwood, the surgeon, came in the Coach to Bou[r]n — Bridge.

Friday 29th.

Breakfasted with Steers in the Temple. — He has made a tour in Scotland. He is particularly delighted with the falls of the Clyde at Bonniton, — and with the striking singularity and variety which Edinburgh presents to the eye.

Saturday 30th.

Dr. Mathews called today but I did not see him. He left me an Asphaltum Box. I wrote to him through Mr. Pocock at the Salopian Coffee House inviting him to breakfast tomorrow morning.

Carey dined with me. I told him He should be welcome to the use of his room as usual, for some months after his return from the Country.

Sunday — Augst. 31.

Dr. Mathews and his son who He has brought to London for advice breakfasted with me. — He recommends making two Volumes of the Severn & Wye. — He mentioned Coombes, who married in the year 1776, the year in which Dr. Mathews went to Edinburgh. — He thinks the style of the History of the Thames too flowery, and that incidental compliments to individual persons in a work of such a nature is injudicious.

Dr. Mathews thinks Mr. Prices book is written with information & spirit. — He thinks very moderately of Mr. Knights, which is a Didactic poem only in title.

The Doctor esteems Smirke as the Artist who perfectly feels Shakespeare, — and that the works of some of the Artists should have been omitted by Messrs. Boydells.

I went to dinner with Batty, to Smirkes House at Craven Hill, for which He pays £40 a year. It is made a very convenient residence. — Bowyer has informed Smirke that Molloy has sat for his portrait. Mrs. Molloy called first, under a different pretence.

Batty was at Lincoln with Sir Joseph Banks, the High Sheriff, during the races. — On Mr. Pelham (Lord Yarborough) giving notice that his Seat for the County wd. be vacant an offer was made of it to Sir Joseph, who declined it. He recommends young Mr. Viner, — the other person proposed was Sir Gilbert Heathcote.

SEPTEMBER 1794

Monday Septr. 1st. 1794.

Stadler drank tea with me. — The Park & Tower guns fired for the taking of Calvi. — Accts. also are come that the French are advancing in 7 Columns against Breda.

Tuesday. 2d

Dined with C & J Offley, — eving. at home.

Wednesday 3d.

Went into the City with Smirke to settle abt. the Gadshill picture &c. but the Alderman was gone to Sydenham to dinner.

Called at Shakespears Gallery & went with J. Boydell to Bulmers, who is out of Town, but his principal manager shewed us a Sheet of Copy for the 2d. Volume of Thames recd. from Coombes who is gone to Oxford but is to be in town next week, & will in the mean time send more copy from Oxford. The first Sheet includes Popes House, at Twickenham. — Bulmers manager says the whole Volume may [be] printed at the rate of 3 sheets a week if they have Copy in time. — In the course of printing the last volume He said they often waited for Mr. Coombes, who supplied them from the spot which He was describing. — Boydell & He made it out that they might compleat printing the 2d. vol: so as to publish early in June.

Smirke dined with me. In the eving. Stadler came & I shewed them my drawings for the 2d. Vol: They approved Boydells idea of two general views of London.

I told Smirke this eving. the nature of my engagement with Boydells relative to the Rivers. — That I presented my stock of designs *gratis*, and that they were to supply money as might be required for carrying on the undertaking. — This day I called at Walkers the Banker with Smirke. He did not mention a visit to Croydon.

230

Thursday, Septr. 4th.

Called on Hearne who cannot accompany me to Sir George Beaumonts as He is engaged to go into Wiltshire.

C & J Offley dined with me. C. Offley went this evening to Mr. Barroneaus, to accompany him to Buxton.

Friday — 5th.

At 7 this morning left London in the Blue Ipswich Coach, from the Spread Eagle, Grace-church Street — Breakfasted at Ingatestone at ½ past 10, — stopped at Colchester for the dinner hour, and got to Dedham at ½ past 4. — Lady Beaumont did not dine till 5. — Sir George & Lady B. the only company there.

Saturday, Septr. 6th.

Rose this morning at 7, — Breakfasted a little past 8. — The weather rainy, employed myself in washing my river views, while Sir George was painting. — Dined at 4, drank tea between 6 & 7, — and went to bed at ½ past 10. These are the usual Hours of the family which is very comfortable.

Lord Beverly has taken the house on the Ipswich River, late Lord Orwells. He is to leave Hitchin abt. the 10th. of October. That place will feel the loss of his family as He is supposed to have expended £5000 a year in that Town.

Lord Beverly went to Piercefield near Chepstow, but did not find the House large enough for his family, and had other objections to it as a residence.

The proportion of Sir George's Canvass recommended by Mr. West is 4 feet 8 inches by 3 feet 4, and I think it a very agreeable proportion.

Sunday — 7th.

The weather continues very wet.

Monday 8th.

The weather still very wet. I employed on my River subjects. Sir George painting the Sky of Chepstow composition. Lady Beaumont drawing.

Lord Beverly has £12,000 a year. Nine thousands in estate & £60,000 in money. — He expends his whole income. The establishment of servants is very expensive.

As an instance of the liberality of the late Duke of Northumberland towards Lord Beverly, when on his travels, He one year paid £40,000 drawn for by Lord B. On Lord B's return he apologized to the Duke for the largeness of his expence. The Duke only answered did you pass yr. time agreeably.

Lady Jersey has at last accomplished her ardent desire to be admitted to the Queens Parties at Windsor. — It is understood to have been accomplished by the Prince of Wales. — The Princess Royal told Lady Beverly before the last entertainment given at Windsor, that the wish of Lady Jersey was known at Court, but that it would not [be] complied with. — When Lady B went there she was surprised to see Lady Jersey in conversation with the Prince of Wales.

While matters were arranging for a separation between the Prince of Wales and Mrs. Fitzherbert, she said to him that she hoped the matter wd. be properly explained to her family, He replied "who are your family? such is the effect of connexion with Princes.

Sir Peter Burrell has abt. £18,000 a year, yet is distressed. His table is supposed to be the best & most expensive of any mans in town.

Lord Cholmondeley has abt. £8000 a year. Lady C. had £30000. He offered to her about 6 or 8 years before she accepted him.

Lady Beverly has written to Lady B. and mentioned that Pitt is very angry with the contribution levied by Sir C. Grey & Sir John Jervais, on the Islands. He has ordered them to be stopped, and the two Commanders are to return home. — The Command was offered to General Lake who declined it.

On Mr. Price's essay on picturesque Beauty being published, Mr. Knight wrote to him a strong letter, which caused Mr. P. to call on him when the difficulties were explained away. The fact is Mr. Knight very likely forseeing the subject when first mentioned to him by Mr. Price was likely to be popular, pushed for the reputation of it, and Mr. Prices preface shews that He has only adopted the Ideas of Mr. P.

Tuesday — Septr. 9th.

Mr. Coombes began to receive 5 guineas a week on acct. of 2d. Vol: of Thames this day. 40 weeks makes 200 guineas, about the 3rd. of June.

The Rainy weather still continues. — I employed myself as before on the River subjects. — Wrote to G. Nicol, by desire of Sir George, who sends five guineas by me to Mrs. Davis.

Wednesday — 10.

The weather tolerable. The Revd. Mr. Morley, a Roman Catholic priest dined with us. He is resident at Giffard Hall, abt. 5 miles distant.

Thursday — Septr. 11th.

A fine day, employed drawing as before, and rode out with Sir George.

Friday, 12th.

Fine weather. — employed as before and rode out with Sir George.

Saturday, 13th.

employed as before. Recd. a letter from Mr. Daulby of Liverpool, who has been in Scotland, and at the Lakes. He saw Haws-water, for the first time, and thinks there are two fine views of it.

Sunday — 14th.

Fine day. — Took a long walk with Sir George — In the afternoon went to Dedham Church.

Monday — 15th.

Fine day. — After breakfast walked with Sir George, and made a sketch of Dedham Vale from the grounds above the Revd. Mr. Hurlochs, — afterwards went towards Langham and made sketches — we then went in the Carriage to Mistley, and the village of Thorn, and crossing a Bridge returned through Bergholt and Stratford.

The country about Dedham presents a rich English Landscape, the distance towards Harwich particularly beautiful.

Lady B. recd. a letter today from Mrs. Carter, who expresses herself in a very strong manner in favour of the "*Mysteries of Udolpho*", and of the talents of Mrs. Radcliffe the Author.

Sir George Beaumont in now 40 years of age. — We first met at Houghton Sunday September 27th. — 1773. — The following is a Copy of a list preserved by the Revd. Mr. Davy of the party then assembled.

Sir George Beaumont
Mr. Thomson
Mr. Patterson — now in the East Indies
Rev. Mr. Prysse — deceased
Mr. Thomas Coke
Mr. Wilkinson
Mr. J. Farington
Mr. G[eorge] Farington — deceased
Mr. Josiah Boydell
Revd. Mr. French
Mr. Cook — Engraver —

Tuesday, Septr. 16th.

Fine day. — at ½ past 8 this morning left Dedham, in the Ipswich Coach, and got to London at ¼ before 7.

A passenger from Ipswich told me Sir John D'Oyley had expended in electioneering there more than £20,000, — that his interest now was not so strong as that of Mr. Cricket who carried the Bailif election, and it is very probable Sir John will not succeed at the next election. Mr. Middleton is expected to stand again. There are abt. 700 voters for Ipswich, — Sons of Freemen, & apprentices of freemen — become Freemen.

Mr. Middleton & Mr Cricket lost their popularity at Ipswich for a time, by voting for the repeal of the Test Act.

I went this evening to Tea at Holylands, Coffee House, to H. Hamond & J. Offley. Hamond sleeps at the Saracens Head, as He leaves Town tomorrow.

Wednesday, Septr. 17th.

Called on Nicol and paid him Sir George Beaumonts gift of 5 guineas for Mrs. Davis.

Met Mr. Coombes at the Shakespeare Gallery. — He told me He had not the least occasion to go on the River Medway with me, that He had been from Tunbridge to Rochester, — and had recd. from a friend a sufficient acct. of the Country adjacent to the River below Chatham to Sheerness. That it wd. be encreasing the expence for no purpose. — That He must treat the Medway in a more slight manner than He originally intended so much of his space wd. be occupied by London, and other circumstances on the Thames. — I delivered to him a list of my intended subjects, which He approved of highly — and of the proposal to have 3 or 4 general views of an encreased size. — He said the work wd. not wait for him & that He shd. have been ready in June.

I called on Bulmer who told me it wd. be a great exertion to get the volume printed by May next. He wd. do all in his power. — The paper was only delivered to him this day. — He has printed two *proof sheets* in all 8 pages, which are with Coombes to correct.

John Offley dined with me. Stadler to Tea I delivered to him the finished drawings of The Tower, view from Temple Gardens, and Popes House. —

Carey came from Southampton.

Coombes told me Mrs. Cosway is certainly returning to England. Cosway is to give a person 130 guineas for bringing her from Genoa. She declares Her resolution to live quite private and to make the education of her Child Her sole object.

Recd. a letter from William at Hoddesdon. He arrived from China in the Exeter on Thursday last.

Thursday Septr. 18th.

Alderman Boydell mentioned to me at the Shakespeare gallery his intention of having a picture painted for the Common Council room to illustrate the happy effects of industry, — He thought it not a proper subject for Westhall. — I mentioned what He had said to J. Boydell observing that if such a picture was to be painted it might as well be given to me & Smirke. Boydell expressed his indignation at his Uncles conduct, and said He wd. exert himself to put a stop to his wild schemes, but that shd. such a picture be painted He would rather it was given to us than to others.

Marchant passed the evening with me and told He had lately passed two days at St. Annes Hill with Mr. Fox and Mrs. Armstead. — Their manner of living is, to breakfast at 9, — dine at 4, Coffee and Tea soon after 6, then walk, then Cards, a slight Supper at 9, and to bed at 10.

Their table plain. — A little girl a daugr. of Mr. Fox, but not by Mrs. Armstead was there.

Mr. Fox spoke of the Arts and said Commerce must support them. He entertains the highest opinion of Sir Joshua Reynolds, — and thinks very favorably of Northcote & Opie. — Of West he spoke with contempt & thinks slightly of the works of Fuseli.

Marchant shewed him his intaglio of the portrait of Wyndham — He said it was like but bid him take it away.

Marchant has seen Copley since Bromley published a 5th. letter to him. Copley says West is at the bottom, and that the allusion in a former letter to the picture of the Squirrel cd. only originate with West.

Lord Berwick encourages the Artists at Rome.

Miss Carr of Newcastle, who is lately returned from Rome, He says excells all the Ladies in practise that are at present distinguished.

Marchant told me of the melancholy event of the death of Poor Vandergucht, the picture dealer, who was drowned in crossing the Thames at Chiswick on Tuesday last by the Boat being overset by a Barge. — He has left a widow & Eleven Children. — Marchant said Copley and Hodges w'd. not allow *Reynolds* their portraits.

[*The following entries for 19 to 28 Sept. 1794 are recorded in a separate travel diary. They are much fuller than the brief entries in the main journal.*]

Sept. 19th.

Left London at 9. — finished small outline of view from Blackheath Point. — walked to Woolwich — on way made a view of Greenwich Hospital & London from the open ground before Vanbrugh House. — looked into the grounds of Mr. Petre adjoining, — then into those of Mr. Angerstein. a succession of bold, undulating ground from Greenwich to Woolwich. — with a flat bottom towards the Thames. — no views for me at Mr. Petre's, Mr. Angerstein's or at Charlton, though very pleasant. The objects do not combine so as to make subjects for picture. — made a view of Woolwich from the high ground before the entrance. — dined at the Ship Tavern at 5, — good accommodation, slept there.

Saturday [20th].

Morning showery and windy at 11 the weather being more favourable, took a chaise to Belvedere, Lord Eardley's. Passed through the Hamlet or village of [blank] — at Lord Eardley's a servant walked with us through the pleasure grounds, which are more extensive than I expected to have found them,& with only a few peeps or open views. At the end of the walk towards Erith, a Tower is erected from whence is a beautiful & extensive prospect of the winding of the river as far as Gravesend. Erith, with its Church, are seen over the foreground trees. — on the left of the first reach of the river is Purfleet, on the right over Erith, Greenhithe with Long Reach stretching before it. In the distance the village of Grays, and still further an indication of Gravesend. I made a drawing of this view. — on examining the situation of Belvedere, I could not find a point where I could combine a view of the House with the river so as to shew the situation, and I did not think it wd. answer to make a mere view of the House. — After Belvedere went through Dartford to Greenhithe, which the driver told me was reckoned 12 miles. Greenhithe is a mean village facing Longreach, in which several Indiamen lay. — The chalk rock here at first seemed to promise something romantic, but I cd. not find a point to make a picturesque subject of them. — Ingress, formerly Mr. Calcrafts, now Mr. Roebucks, joins to the village. It is a very pleasant spot. The House is placed pretty high on the ground which slopes from the chalk rocks to the river. Mr. R is making considerable additions and when finished it will be apparently a large mansion. I was here equally unfortunate as at Belvedere, being unable to find a point whence I could unite the House with the river so as to shew its real situation. — I ascended to the top of the rocks, which rise among well-grown trees planted in abundance. A walk runs along the line of the precipice, & from a summer house, I made a drawing looking up the river which makes a reverse to the view from Belvedere, that place being the principal feature in the distance on the left, and Purfleet on the right. — The character of the Landscape abt. the rocks put me in mind of some of the compositions of Gaspar Poussin.

At ½ past 5 went to Gravesend in a chaise which I had sent for, none being kept at Greenhithe, at which place the accommodations are of the Wapping description.

— dined and slept at Gravesend.

Sunday — Septr. 21.

a fine morning. went to the windmill behind the town which serves as a Landmark to navigators & commands very extensive prospects looking both up and down the river, — and across the water of Tilbury Fort and the Essex coast. Of this view I made a drawing, and had the advantage of a fine ground in the Ruysdael stile of broken ground with a road. I made another view looking up the river. Belvedere & Purfleet appeared in the distance, and before them North Fleet on the left of the river and Grays on the right. — The windmills & cottage with broken ground composed a rich front for the distance.

I walked round the Town, endeavouring to find other views, but none of them were favourable.

At 1 o'clock left Gravesend and went to the Crown Inn near the Bridge at Rochester. I stopped the Chaise before we descended the Hill above Stroud and went into the garden of a small Ale house from whence there is a very fine view of Rochester & Stroud. Chatham & Brompton, unite happily with the other features of the Landscape — the whole being condensed within the compass of a single view. — At 4 we dined at an inn.

The distance from Gravesend to Rochester is charged 8 miles. They charge at the former place for their Chaise 14d. a mile, and I am told the same is charged at Margate, Deal & Dover, under pretence that as their Horses are only worked one way, their business is more uncertain.

We were well accommodated at the White Hart at Gravesend, and the Bill was more moderate than at Woolwich. — The waiter an intelligent man, told us, that before the war broke out there were 700 watermen & fishermen at Gravesend.

Monday, Septr. 22nd.

The morning hazy and more rain. Enquired at Chatham for a Boat to go to Sheerness. Three sailing Boats go every tide, backwards and forwards. They have cabbins. The fare is only 6d. each person. — They sail like the Gravesend Boats, at High water, and the wind being now South west, and blowing a little, we were told would sail to Sheerness, which is 18 or 20 miles distant, in two Hours and a half. If a Passenger desires to return with the next tide, he may remain at Sheerness 3 or 4 Hours to dine and see the place. — After breakfast I walked over the Bridge & up the Hill on the road to Dartford, and stopping at the House from whence I admired the view on Sunday, made a drawing of Rochester, Chatham, Brompton etc. The weather was so unpromising till after high water mark that I gave up my intention of going to Sheerness today.

I next walked through Frinsbury Church yd. from whence are delightful views of Rochester, the Bridge etc up the river, to Upnor Castle. The weather was now clear, and from a Hill above Upnor the view of the windings of the Medway from Chatham to Sheerness was so descriptive of the state of the view & of the high ground from Upnor were so advantageous that I was tempted to make a drawing from this point, Sheerness is from its distance but a small object, but its situation being completely shown, I think may be a more satisfactory view than a near one, which would shew particular parts but afford no distinct idea of how it is situated.

At 4 returned to the inn to dinner. — In the evening went to Galley, the stationers Library, where Newspapers are subscribed for, and strangers admitted free to read them.

The Castle of Rochester is 110 feet high.

Rochester Bridge, is now receiving a considerable addition to its width.

The length of the Bridge about 75 feet —. Great inconvenience has been suffered from the narrowness of the passageway, which was irregular in its width and not more than 15 feet. According to the Plan now carrying into execution the passage will be of an equal width 27 feet. — as the Arches of the Bridge as it now stands vary in their width it will not be possible with the alterations to make the face of it regular, but the arches in the new design correspond as nearly as they can be made to do. The additions are made with Portland & Purbeck stone. The Parapet and ornamental parts with the former, the piers etc. with the latter. — This expensive alteration is paid for out of estates belonging to the Bridge. I was told they were bequeathed to support the Bridge by a Lord Cobham, and Sir Francis Knollys the founders of the bridge several hundred years ago. They are vested in trust for the above purpose in a committee of gentlemen who elect in case of vacancy. Lord Aylesford, Lord Romney, are of the number. — Two arches are nearly completed, and the workmen have been employed more than a year. It was calculated that the whole wd. be finished in six years which the owner told me He did not believe wd. be the case. — Only a certain number of workmen are employed as it seems to be intended to expend a limited sum annually.

The tide rises at Rochester Bridge 17 to 20 feet in spring tides, so low sometimes as 8 feet in neap tides.

The bridge has eleven arches. — The length of the Bridge from end arch to end arch inclusive is 529 feet.

Tuesday — Septr. 23.

This morning proving very wet, I gave up my scheme of going to Sheerness, and applied myself in washing an outline. At one o'clock the weather became fine but windy. — I went to a station on the Bank on the other side the river below Bridge, and made a drawing of the Bridge & Castle. — This view is from the North west.

At 4 o'clock returned to our Inn to dinner, and in the evening went to the Library to read the papers, in one of which the death of Robinson Stoney Bowes, Husband to Lady Strathmore is inserted. He died on Sunday last in the King's Bench prison aged 58.

Wednesday Septr. 24.

This morning the weather showery. I determined to proceed today to Sheerness and take the occasional interval of fair weather to do what might be necessary there; accordingly, at ½ of 1 we went to one of the Passage boats, and leaving Chatham at 2 o'clock got to Sheerness at four. — The wind was south west which serves either for going to or returning from Sheerness. — These Boats are as convenient as the Gravesend boats, the fare only 6d. each person or a Boat may be hired for half a guinea for a passage. — Below Chatham the Medway intersects and has formed different channels through a wide waste of marshland which when viewed from the neighbouring heights has the appearance of a vast morass. These channels have formed one or more Islands in forcing their way. Some parts of these marshes have cattle turned upon occasionally, as I was told by a passenger, but I saw none, and suppose it is only in such parts as are contiguous to the fertile country.

This wide waste is bordered on each side by a line of elevated country very richly cultivated as far as the eye can judge at a distance.

A mile below Chatham the village of Gillingham very pleasantly situated and commanding a prospect of the course of the Medway to Sheerness. On the opposite side the water Upnor Castle but situated near the water's edge makes a rich background of trees over which rise steep and high banks well covered with trees. This line of high ground continues uninterruptedly till opposite to Sheerness it sinks and shoots out a long point forming with the point on which Sheerness stands the mouth of the Medway.

On approaching Sheerness between the points described the view is terminated by a long line of the Essex coast, which appears to be low and uniform. The width of the Thames here is 8 or 9 miles. Southend, in Essex is distinctly seen.

One of the Boatmen told me that young oysters are brought from particular places on the Essex coast and sunk in various parts of the Medway where they lay to grow and fatten, and are taken up when required. A man is employed to guard them so that they may not be dragged up by Boatmen passing.

Sheerness from its being situated on a point of flat land makes no striking figure when viewed from the water. There are no buildings of heigth or size sufficient to become striking pictures. Its importance is signified more by the number, variety, & size of the Ships which are crowded near to the place, forming a busy scene.

One feature on approaching the place appears singular if not picturesque. Three or 4 old men of war of 75 guns have been put on shore where they lay, and are appropriated for the use of the workmen & their families belonging to the Dockyard. These persons as occasion required have made such additions to their several lots of space by attaching cabbins etc to the sides of the ships that they are nearly covered with these odd contrivances producing altogether a whimsical effect. — From a Vessel which lay off from the shore a little way I made a sketch of them with what I could see of the yard & garrison.

We went to the Marlborough Head which was recommended as one of the two best inns. Worse accommodation we could scarcely find. Our dinner badly dressed, to that inattention owing as it seemed not so much from want of civility as from bad management, the charge notwithstanding as high as if things had been better. — The master of this inn has a

concern in the Passage boats. — At half past 6 we again entered a Passage
boat and left Sheerness with a fair wind and arrived at Chatham at a ¼ past
9, heartily rejoiced that the excursion was so soon terminated.

In the Dockyard and in the ship which I went on board there seemed to
be a sufficient jealousy to prevent persons from making sketches without
permission from the Master Builder.

Thursday — Septr. 25th.

The weather fair and pleasant. At noon left Rochester, to go to Maidstone
9 miles distant. The road passes over Bexley Hill from whence are very
extensive views across the vale through which the Medway passes, but that
River is not so well distinguished in this comprehensive landscape as I
expected it would be from the breadth and rapidity at Rochester. It
appears only of the size of a common stream, and except in a few parts, is
perceived only occasionally. Indeed the course it pursues is at a
considerable distance from Bexley Hill. — The Traveller is to take notice
that the celebrated views from Bexley Hill commence soon after He passes
the Upper Bell, a small Inn, abt. 4 miles from Rochester, and by quitting
his Chaise, and following the track of the old road on the right of the new
one He will be sufficiently interested till He arrives at the Lower Bell at the
foot of the Hill. — At less than half a mile before He approaches this
second Inn, He will see below him on the right the Druidical remains, as it
appears to be called *Kets Coity House*. Of this monument of antiquity I
made a drawing.

To speak of the extensive landscape which we have surveyed in a general
way it must be allowed to have that effect on the mind which vast space
always produces in a greater or less degree but as in this place there are no
striking features to fix the attention, no very strong impression is left on
the mind. I felt disappointed as I had reckoned on being able to describe
with the pencil the stile of this country but vain would be the attempt to
discriminate where there is no one leading feature.

When we entered Maidstone, it appeared to be a common & dirty
looking indifferently built Town. We put up at the Bell a decent Inn, and
walked downwards the river to see what its vicinity might afford past the
church & old conventual building called the College, we had not gone far
before we came to a point from whence Maidstone appeared with a very
different character. The College, the Church and a line of buildings rising
from the margins of the river, were terminated by the old bridge
background by thick trees. Not more of the common part of the Town
appeared than was required to gain some Idea of its size, over which the
country rose in a beautiful manner. This view I immediately resolved on
for my collection.

Thursday is market day at Maidstone, and as this is the conclusion of the Hop season, many Bags were standing in the streets. I was amused with observing a man cutting out of the Bags, and Pockets, samples to send to the London market, he forces a long and broad knife into the center of the Bag and cuts out a piece abt. 6 inches square, which He wraps in paper & marks to correspond with that fixed on the Bag. — They judge of the quality of the Hops by the colour & smell. These were all very fragrant, so much so that my fingers from touching them retained some of it. Variations in the prices of Hops in different seasons are prodigious. This year a Pocket will sell for 5 guineas, that holds a hundred and half weight. In a scarce year the Hops have sold for Eleven guineas a Hund.

Friday — Septr. 26th.

This morning the weather fine but cold. I made a drawing of the view I determined upon yesterday.

The Hop pickers were hard at work near me. They told me Michaelmas Day is the usual season for their picking.

At one o'clock we left Maidstone. The Bill at our Inn was more extravagant than any we had paid since leaving London, and the wine worse.

On our way to Tonbridge we passed through a rich well-wooded country for some miles. At 4 miles particularly so, Here Lady Bouverie as they call her, has a Handsome mansion called Testen, near a village of the same name. The Medway here passes between high ground well clothed with trees. — Testen Bridge makes an agreeable feature in the landscape. A little before we approached Testen, on the left is a House of Mr. Amhurst well situated.

At 7 miles on the left is Mereworth, a seat of Lord Despencer with apparently extensive grounds belonging to it well wooded.

At 8 miles on the right is Packham, Mr. Masters.

The country now becomes more flat, and quite un[picturesque?] till we arrived at Tonbridge, 14 miles from Maidstone.

On our way we passed many Hop plantations and the fragrance issuing from was sensibly felt in passing on the road.

We put up at the Rose & Crown at Tonbridge. Our first object here was to visit the castle to which we found attached a modern building and before it a small lawn, surrounded by a gravel walk & shrubbery. Nothing can exceed the bad taste of the whole, yet it is clean and I daresay very comfortable to the Possessors Mr. & Mrs. Woodgate. The Castle, House, and ground contiguous, was lately purchased from Mr. Hooker, by Mr. Woodgate of Summer Hill near this town, father of the present inhabitant.

I could not find a point near the castle from which I could make a view witht. attaching to it many unpicturesque circumstances. — The situation I chose was across the river & below the Bridge, from whence both unite happily enough in the composition with the castle and surrounding objects.

The Medway is not navigable above Tonbridge, and from hence to Maidstone the stream in what relates to navigation is the property of certain Individuals. A committee of Gentlemen superintend this concern, and under their direction proper care is taken of the Locks etc. — including a Lock at Maidstone and one here, there are 14 Locks on this River. There is no Lock below Maidstone, to that town it is what is called Tides-way. — A proposal has been made to erect Locks *below* Maidstone as the Tide does not always answer sufficiently up to that town, and to make a canal by a shorter cut to a certain part of the River. This proposal was opposed successfully as I was told by the Tonbridge committee.

From *Tonbridge* to *Maidstone* the Barges are towed but not below.

There are at present 13 Barges belonging to the committee. These are almost entirely employed in carrying Timber which has been purchased in the adjacent country and brought down to Tonbridge, to the Dockyards of Chatham & Sheerness.

Barges not belonging to the committee are allowed to navigate the river on paying *riverage* as it is called at so much a mile.

The Barges returning to Tonbridge usually bring back Deals and Coals.

Coals sell now at Maidstone for 33 shillings a chaldron, and at Tonbridge for 36 shillings.

Saturday, Septr. 27th.

The weather very fine but cold. — I made a drawing of the Bridge & Castle, and afterwards walked up to Summer Hill Mr. Woodgate's an ancient mansion finely situated on an eminence abt. 2 miles from Tonbridge. At a short distance from the House where two large Beech trees form a distinguished group, the view is still more extensive, a country rich as cultivation & foliage can make it. The Town of Tonbridge is a pleasing circumstance in the view, but no part of the River Medway can be seen, nor indeed does any other water appear.

Much of the landscape especially under the influence of this days atmosphere reminded me of the pictures of Artois.

I returned from this excursion abt. 12 o'clock and immediately took a Chaise to go to Sevenoaks by way of Penshurst. The direct road to Sevenoaks is 7 miles but by Penshurst 15 miles is charged. It is remarkable that 5 turnpikes are paid in this short distance. To go to Penshurst we proceeded abt. 2 miles on the Tunbridge Wells road and then turned to the right from it. The road passes over a hill from whence a very extensive view in the right is displayed. — On approaching Penshurst I was struck with the venerable appearance of that mansion so long celebrated from having been the residence of the family of Sydney. The situation is well chosen on the slope of grounds which rise considerably and from a noble

Park, as I was told 6 miles in circumference. — The Medway runs a small stream in front of the House but from the steepness of the banks is not seen. I made a sketch of the House etc. and then proceeded to the Inn at Penshurst near the Church. We found a few scattered houses only near it scarcely sufficient to be termed a village.

Having heard of the Penshurst Oak, I went into the Park to see it. It is not more than half a mile from the House. Having made a drawing of this tree I measured it, and found that at 3 feet above the ground it is 25 feet 11 inches in the general girth, *not* measured by following the *indents of the bark* — the 3 feet I took from the entrance into the Hollow of the tree. — In the Hollow is a seat which will hold three or 4 poeple & 7 or 8 may stand in the side, which is scooped like an old fashioned kitchen chimney. — I measured the longest projecting branch which measured from the trunk 36 feet. The heigth of the Tree I suppose to be [blank] feet. It is excepting of a few branches well covered with foliage. — The vulgar report here is that the tree was planted at the birth of Sir Philip Sydney, but I should suppose it to be of a much older date.

We afterwards went to the mansion. It is of an irregular form. We entered by a large gateway over which is an inscription signifying that that tower (gateway) was erected by Sir Henry Sydney, Knight of the Garter, in 1585 as a token of gratitude to the memory of Edwd. 6th., who granted the estate of *Pencester* (so it was called,) to Sir William Sydney, (father of Sir Henry) Sir William had been Chamberlaine, and Steward to King Edwd. till his coronation.

There are two principal courts in this quadrangular building. However respectable the general appearance of it is when seen externally, I do not remember to have seen any building of that date more gloomy & less desirable to choose for a residence than Penshurst. In the design of the House there are sufficient proofs of ancient hospitality: the great Hall, Kitchen with 3 vast fireplaces, servants' Hall etc.

In one wing of the house is a large picture gallery, filled with very indifferent collection. — In Houses like this one is naturally induced to dwell on the Portraits as it is probable they are authentic. Lady Dorothy Sydney *Waller's Sacharissa,* exhibits a countenance not interesting; and in a groupe of 3 children, Algernon Sydney, as a child, shows a countenance sour and discontented.

In a cabinet a very indifferent picture is shown which the Housekeeper tells you is reckoned worth 1500 guineas.

The family of Sydney has been extinct in the male line some time. — The last of the name Colonel Sydney as the housekeeper called him, and afterwards Knight of the Bath, as appears from a picture of him, had 2 daughters only, one married to Lord Shannon, the other to Mr. Perry, by whom she had several children, who all died young except one daughter who married a Mr. Shelley of Horsham in Sussex. She left children, the eldest of whom a Son, is now abt. 22 years of age, and in the army. — He has taken the name of Sydney & is now possessed of this estate.

In the Park of Penshurst Herons build their nests in the trees in great abundance.

About a mile further on our way we passed on the left the Reverend Mr. Harveys, a situation which commands an extensive & beautiful prospect.

About 3 miles before we reached Sevenoaks we began to ascend a very steep and long continued Hill. On the right is river Hill a charming situation belonging to Mr. H. Woodgate, brother to the owner of Summerhill.

Before we entered Sevenoaks we had the Duke of Dorset's park of Knowle on our right with peeps of that respectable and extensive mansion.

The White Hart an Inn is situated very pleasantly abt. a mile short of Sevenoaks, but we took up our quarter at the Royal Oak opposite Knowle Park gate.

Coals at Sevenoaks are now 38 shillings a Chaldron, they are brought from Tunbridge. It is to be observed that they are now in London 48 shillings pr. C.

We passed by an Oak in Penshurst Park which grows near the road. We thought it as large as the Sydney Oak but on measuring it found it was only 21 feet 1 Inch at 3 feet above the ground.

We were very much satisfied with our accommodation at the Royal Oak. The house is clean, but not large, and the poeple civil. — The Bill more moderate than any we have paid on this Tour.

Sunday — Sepr. 28.

A beautiful morning. We walked in the Duke of Dorset's Park which is kept in beautiful order, and contains many fine trees, Beech in particular.

On the left of the Town is Kippington a very pretty spot, which Sir Charles Farnaby Ratcliffe, has lately sold & quitted. It now belongs to Mr. Austen of Sevenoaks.

Returned to London to dinner. Carey dined with me. Susan returned from Norfolk yesterday.

Monday 29th.

Called at the Shakespeare Gallery. J. Boydell gone this morning to Norfolk. — Called on Singleton who is not yet come to Town. — Called on Smirke who has laid in the figures of the Charles 2d. picture. — He has settled with A. Boydell for the former pictures. The prices to be 150 guineas for Gadshill — 180 for Hearnes Oak, and 200 for Sly.

Will came in the evening. Is for William going into the Navy.

Tuesday Septr. 30.

Alderman Boydell has spoken to Smirke abt. the City picture He intends of the good effects of industry. — I related to Smirke what had passed on that subject.

I saw Coombes at the Shakespeare Gallery, and told him it would be necessary to make an opening for a view of Penshurst and that Maidstone contrary to his expectation made an excellent subject. — I told him these scenes wd. make a variety there being much sameness on the lower part of the Thames views. — That I cd. not make a subject at Angersteins nor at Charlton. — He approved much of the introduction of Penshurst.

He mentioned Knights shabby conduct abt. the Shakespeare. Coombes began an ironical poem on their, Price & Knight, making pictures their models for gardening, but had not time to proceed with it.

OCTOBER 1794

Breakfasted at Lord Inchiquins. Young Mr. Obrien the sailor there. Lady Inchiquin told me that Poggi had been with Her, that He had recd. £460, but that He Begged He might be allowed to postpone a settlement till February. — That He had been at great expences & had lately been subjected to great expences & to inconvenience by Mr. West having insisted on his paying a sum of money which He had lent to Poggi. — Lady Inchiquin, said, the Executors wd. be much startled by such a proposal, and their apprehensions wd. be raised for the safety of the property if they found in the first instance that He could not make his payments. — Poggi said if it was absolutely necessary He must sell out of the Funds, though as stocks are now, at great loss, and wd. pay £300. — Lady I, desired my opinion, expressing her fears abt. placing more of the Prints & Drawings in Poggis hands unless they cd. be secured from seizure in case of his Bankruptcy. I told her I knew not how to advise, but as a preliminary step, I wd. recommend a request to Dr. Lawrence to inform her if the property deposited in Poggi's hands |could, be secured from seizure in case of his distress. This she said she would do.

There appeared to me to be great discontent abt. Lord Inchiquin. Christie has said how much better it wd. have been to have disposed of things by the Hammer, and such reports have reached His Lordship. — Lady Inchiquin told me Poggi had said to her that West had undervalued the collection. I told her I had heard the same. She said He had always been the enemy of her uncle.

Lady I. desired me to speak to Lawrence abt. settling the acct. for the King's pictures, but that in part Lord Inchiquin wd. set to Lawrence for a half length. I mentioned to her that his price was 80 gs.

At one oClock I went to Poggis, where I found Captn. Mansfield. The two drawings by Clevely, of the action of June 1st. were there. Lord & Lady Inchiquin came & saw his room for the first time. I have never seen Lord Inchiquin so much out of spirits before.

Lady Inchiquin this morning described to me the death of Young Burke.

Two days only before his death he was removed to Brompton, and it was
not till then that his Father was sensible of his danger. — On the day He
died, He heard His Father so loud in his expressions of grief in the next
room, as himself to be much moved by it. He ordered his servant to dress
him & make him appear as well as He could. He then walked into the next
room to his Father & adressed him on his allowing his grief to overcome
him. — 'You unman me, Sir, by it, — recollect yourself, — come into me,
and talk to me of religion, or some other subject'. — They returned
together and being seated the Young Man said, my heart flutters. —
Hearing a noise like rain He said does it rain? His Father replied No, it is
the wind, — Again hearing it He said surely it is rain, No said the Father it
is the wind among the trees. — The son then began to repeat that part of
the morning Hymn from Milton, — beginning with, —
His praise ye winds! that from four quarters blow,
Breathe soft, or loud; and wave your tops, ye pines!
With ev'ry plant, in sign of worship wave.
Fountains! and ye that warble, as ye flow,
Melodious murmurs! Warbling tunes his praise.
  While proceeding in repeating the Hymn, He sunk forward into his
fathers arms and expired. — Mrs. Burke came in at this distressing
moment.
  Lady Inchiquin says Mrs. Burke is as well as can be expected, but that
Mr. Burke seems as far from recovery as ever. — He scarcely speaks on any
other subject than that of his Son, and when publick affairs are touched on
says, Had Richard been living He wd. have been able to have suggested
something for the publick good. — That whenever He adopted any
measure that gained him credit His Son instigated him to it. Thus far does
He carry his fondness.
  Old Hickey, the Lawyer, is dead, and but in indifferent circumstances.
— His daugtrs. have taken a House at Beaconsfield.
  Will Burke has had a slight paralytic stroke, & is gone to Bath.
  Minet came in the evening. Mrs. Offley and John are gone today to
Margate.

Thursday Octr. 2d.

Recd. a letter from Dick. Mrs. Edge was buried on Tuesday last. She died
at Jos: Mariotts of a bowel complaint. — She has left Jos: Mariott £1000,
— Mrs. Wm. Boardman, the dividend on £1300, owing by Wm.
Boardman, which may amount to £700, — and the remainder 7000 guineas
to Mrs. Rooke.
  Smirke called, having sent me a pamphlet describing the escape of
Charles 2d. something different from Humes acct. I gave it as my opinion
that we were bound to adhere to the text of Hume. — In this He agreed
with me.
  Alderman Boydell called on Smirke today, to know if He had thought

on the subject of the *industry picture*. I told Smirke I thought it might admit of being well described, & He desired me to turn my mind to the subject so as to scratch even a few lines.

Medley called and paid me Mr. Daulbys river subscription. He has been at Leigh, employed somehow by Taylor.

Bell Wakefield is married to a Quaker, a Brewer at Ipswich.

Friday — Octr. 3d.

Will went to Hoddesdon.

Battersbee called on me. He sold Beddington Lodge, yesterday by auction, to Admiral Pigot for £1500. — Battersbee is well satisfied. In all He may possibly have sunk by the Beddington concern abt. £200. — He has bought a House at Stratford upon Avon, and goes to reside in a fortnight.

Bestland, called on me. He is much concerned to find Reynolds has begun a work of the Academicians. He called this morning on West, from whom He understood that Reynolds said He knew Bestland who had no objection to the undertaking of Reynolds. Beechy went with Bestland to Wests, & to Paul Sandbys, whose head is already completed; Sandby on hearing Bestlands objections seemed sorry He had allowed his head to be engraved. — I found on the whole that Reynolds has made an improper use of the names of the Members, which indeed I suspected before, — I therefore told Bestland, that if He thought the undertaking of Reynolds wd. affect His publication I would withdraw my name. He said He wd. call on all the Academicians.

Saturday — Octr. 4th.

At Home. — No Company.

Sunday Octr. 5th.

Humphry called. — He has taken the Lodgings in Bond St. for another year.

Hoppner called, He has been sometime in the Country painting, — at Mr. Bowles, Lord Darnleys, &c &c.

He mentioned the vacancy made by Newton, and expressed his hopes of succeeding at the election in February. I told him I had not yet seen any member except Smirke, of course could not do more than express my own opinion which certainly was that He had the best chance.

He said Hodges had painted two pictures, very large, the subjects, War & Peace, expressed by exhibiting the same scene under those different circumstances. He thought the subject as it appeared *in peace* very beautiful.

A son of Dr. Harrington of Bath has written a violent encomium on the extraordinary merits of Young Barker of Bath.

The morning of this day was fine, the afternoon very wet. The weather has been much broken thick & heavy during the last week.

Monday — Octr. 6th.

At Home all day. Humphry drank tea with us. — He unites with me in opinion that Hoppner is the Associate likely to be elected to fill Newtons vacancy. — Marchant he says is very urgent.

I recd. a list of Candidates for Associate. The election to be on Monday Novr. 3rd. at 7 in the evening. The balot to be examined at a quarter before 8.

List.

Painters	Sculptor	Architects
Thomas Walmsley	J. Hickey }	
George Anthony Keenan		
Francis Towne		
John Downman	John Soane }	
Martin Shee	George Byfield	
John Graham	Thomas Malton	
Daniel Brown		
Gainsborough Dupont		
Samuel Woodforde		
Henry Spicer		
Paul Barbier		
Mather Brown		

Humphry says there are beautiful lines on Penshurst in Dodsleys collection, which were wrote by Mr. Coventry. Lord Camden has given the eldest Son of the Revd. Mr. Humphry, a Boy of fifteen, a place in the Exchequer, of £80 a year.

On the Trial of David Downie, at Edinburgh for High treason, one of the Jurymen declared to the others that He would starve rather than bring in a verdict against him unless they wd. unanimously join to recommend Downie to mercy. — This caused the recommendation.

This day the Grand Jury found Bills for High Treason against the 12 following persons.

Secretary to the London Corresponding Society — T. Hardy.

John Horne Tooke.

T. Holcroft — Author of Road to Ruin &c.

— Richter — Clerk to Sir Robt. Herries.

M. Moore,

Attorney — John Augustus Bonney   A leader in the
                                    J. Thelwall, — London Corres-
Barrister — S. Kidd.   ponding Soc.
Chaplain to ⎫
Ld. Stanhope⎭ – J. Joyce.   R. Hodson,

                                    J. Baxter.

            T. Wardel, not in
                    custody.
Hair dresser — J. Lovett,
            not found.

Tuesday — Octr. 7th.

Called on Humphry, where I found the Rev. Mr. Humphry & his Son, who He this morning brought to Town to commence his attendance in the Exchequer. — He told me He had fixed him to board & lodge at the Revd. Mr. Scotts, in Smiths Square, Westminster, at 50 guineas a year.

Sir Charles Farnaby Ratcliffes estate of Kippington is sold to Mr. Motley Austen of Sevenoaks for £34,000. — Sir Charles is of the same age as the King. He is supposed to have wasted the whole of the family property, about £2000 a year, excepting a small estate entailed on his Brother, the Colonel, who married Miss [Lennard] of Sevenoaks, with whom He had a handsome fortune. The Col. has several Children, & with legacies and savings is supposed to have £2000 a yr. He had an opportunity of obliging Mr. Pitt with some land near Holwood, in return for which Mr. Pitt made him a receiver in one of the offices. — Sir Charles, continues Member for Hythe, and it is conjectured draws his support from government. — He is grown extremely fat and cannot ride on Horseback or walk much. — Lady Farnaby has behaved through the changes of his fortune with a submission to circumstances, that proved her compliance.

The House at Seale, in which Mr. Humphry resides was presented to him by a relative of Lord Camdens who gave £500 for it, and with £700 laid out by Mr. H., it is become a very convenient dwelling.

I called on Lawrence. He was employed on the picture which He proposes to present to the Academy. — I told him the message which Lady Inchiquin desired me to deliver to him. 'Her wish that He shd. paint a Half length Portrait of Ld. Inchiquin, in part payment for the Kings pictures.' — Lawrence said Had He not better settle with her first, & then the picture might be ordered. I told him I could not see why the money shd. be paid which must be returned. I perceived He was apprehensive of the picture being ordered to cancel part of the debt, — and assured him it appeared to be Her Ladyships wish to have a portrait of his Lordship, for there seemed to be only one of him & that very ill painted. That possibly had the money not been due from Lawrence on acct. of pictures she might have hesitated abt. laying out so much, but as it now stood it was an expence that was not felt.

Lawrence asked me abt. the ensuing election. I told him the list was a weak one, when it was considered that three vacancies were to be filled. I said that two names I certainly would not vote for, Mather Brown, & Graham, and that I could not think it would be decent for the Academy to elect Malton in preference to Soane and Byfield. — He thought Soane for his respectability likely to have a good chance and mentioned Duponts name. I did not say who I shd. vote for, neither did He. — He thought Hamilton would vote for Malton.

Lawrence & Hamilton went to Sevenoaks lately, and they made studies in Knowle Park. — Those He shewed me were very good of Beech trees &c. they were made on Silk & Blue paper with black chalk, touched with white. He shewed me a very high finished drawing in Crayons, of Miss Angerstein, and another Lady with two Children. — He said He was three weeks about it.

Erskine, who is retained as Council by some of the Prisoners to be tried says, that if no more appears against them than did against the Scotch Offenders they cannot be found guilty.

Wednesday — Octr. 8th.

Called this morning on Reynolds, the Engraver, — I told him that I had been led to believe from his description, that no objection wd. be made to his undertaking by Bestland, as he described Beechy to be a warm friend to his undertaking, who was to have executed the Portraits of the Academicians for Bestland. That I had reason to believe He had mentioned the names of Academicians as being principal encouragers of his work, who in fact had taken no part in promoting it, as for instance He had mentioned *my name* to Mr. Dance, as an introduction to him, which He had no authority from me to do. — He said if anything like what I described had appeared it was witht. his *intending* it. That Mr. Opie had yesterday mentioned to him the complaints of Mr. Bestland, & that in consequence He proposed to offer terms to Mr Bestland, viz: 'to make a joint concern of the two undertakings, or even to go beyond that in favour of Mr. Bestland'. — He said the undertaking was to him a great object to which He must devote 4 years. — I replied that the situation of Mr. Bestland was much worse than his. Mr. B. had engaged Mr. Singleton at of course a large expence to paint portraits of all the Academicians, and given up all other views to devote himself to engraving from the Picture which had now been in hand a considerable time. — He said Beechy did not approve of the engraving which He had made from Paul Sandbys Portrait, which He shewed to me as in a finished state. He also shewed me a beginning of Sir Wm. Chambers portrait. — In my private opinion He is unqualified as an Artist for such an undertaking. — His prints are not sufficiently like the pictures, and are very poorly executed. I mean those of Sir F. Bourgeois and Paul Sandby. There were painted portraits of Beechy, Opie & Hoare of Bath in his room. — And the *illumination* outline by West of the King, intended as a frontispiece.

I concluded by telling him that He must consider me as suspending having anything to do with his work, while I believed Mr. Bestland had objections to it.

Called on Lady Inchiquin and had a long conversation with her abt. the Prints & drawings. She cannot reconcile the two accts. of Poggi. He told Marchi He had sold £600 worth of drawings, whereas the acct. He gave her accounts only to £460. — I told her Poggi gave it as his opinion that the best way of disposing of the Prints would be by auction, but that He hoped they wd. be sold in *his room*. That she said could not be, Christie had been promised the disposal of whatever was to be sold by auction. — She said Poggi desired to have the remainder of *the drawings*, — I was clearly of the opinion that the remainder should not be brought forward till the *present lots* had been offered through another season. — She told me she was determined they should not. — Her Lawyer has assured her that in case of derangement of Poggi's affairs, Her property cannot be seized as Poggi has it *only on trust* & not *by purchase*. — I told her the aspect of public affairs was now such that I should think it best to dispose both of the Pictures & Prints the next spring, as there was no calculating when they might be expected to be sold to better advantage. — She said it had been sometime determined to sell the pictures in the next spring.

She gave me an impression from Sir Joshuas Russian picture, and a portrait of Burke. — She desired me to cut off *the writing* which had been directed by Sir Joshua, abt. the time Burke separated from his party, but Burke objected to it from the encomium being too strong.

She invited me in the most friendly manner to visit them at Taplow.

Carey, called on me. He met an Officer a Captain of the Queens Dragoons, on his way, who was come up from Blackwall, where 32 transports, with 1500 Horses & men on board now lay waiting for orders. They were down at the Nore a fortnight from whence they were ordered back to Blackwall. — What a proof of the uncertainty of administration how to direct their force.

Secretary Dundass said the other day in the Office, such daily bad news is enough to make one sick.

I touched upon some of Careys sketches & gave him instructions.

William came up from the Exeter to dinner. — He is grown taller and more stout. — At Mackenzies Shop I saw two small Landscapes by Rathbone, lately painted, nine inches wide, on sale, at one guinea each.

Lady Inchiquin told me government has settled on Mr. Burke £1200 a year for life, to be continued to Mrs. Burke, should she be the survivor, and that His debts as Lady I. understands, are to be paid, which she believes are considerable.

Thursday, Octr. 9th.

This morning I called on Bulmer, and had a long conversation with him on the printing the second Volume of the Rivers. He told me Coombes dined with him two days ago, and said He should according to the agreement made with J. Boydell & me furnish two Sheets a week. — Bulmer says there will be 75 sheets, so that it will at that rate take 38 weeks to complete the volume. — The *second* sheet is now finishing. — We cannot therefore expect the volume to be *printed* before the 9th. of June, after which sewing up & binding will require a month. — It seems plain that we shall not be able to publish before the middle of July at soonest. — I spoke strongly to Bulmer as to our situation and how illmanaged a work of such expence had been. — He said it was Mr. J. Boydells fault in not managing about the paper in a better manner. That the paper which He now had was that which had been refused two years ago, and that in the general width *when opened* it was ½ or ¾ of an Inch narrower than that made use of for the first volume.

Bulmer told me Coombes desired to have the *Copy sheets* of the first Volume, which I said that understanding that they were of no further use, I believed I have used the whole as waste paper.

On reckoning up the time Coombes proposes to be abt. the second Vol: allowing 38 weeks at 5 guineas a week, it will amount to 190 guineas.

Friday — Octr. 10.

This morning Malton called on me, on the subject of the next election. He said he had promises from Hamilton – Nollekens

Catton – Westhall

Burch – Stothard

Wheatley – Barry

Lawrence had not promised him.

I told him that for the number of vacancies, three, the list might be considered as weak. That there were only 2 vacancies and 24 candidates, now only 16 candidates. — We concluded our conversation on this Topick with general civility on my part & nothing more. I said I had had no conversation on the subject with the Academicians.

Malton told me He had not yet been paid for what He had done at the Drury Lane Playhouse. — That there was £350 due to him on his own acct. — He said that in the 80 odd nights which that House was opened the last season upwards of £30,000, had been taken.

Nollekens gave an acct. to Malton of the cause of the death of Newton. He had dined with some Magistrates in the neigheroud of his House at Barton in Somersetshire, and was a little affected by liquor, but on coming to his carriage He found His servants much more so, which caused him to put them into the carriage and He mounted the Coach Box. — The Night was very wet & He neglected when got home to use any precautions against cold, the consequence being an immediate fever which killed him in two days.

Soane the Architect was foot Boy to George Dance, who encouraged an inclination He discovered in him for drawing. The remembrance of his former situation rendered his situation in *Dances Office* amoung the young men rather unpleasant. He removed to Holland, the Architect, and was his Clerk. He drew for the Prize Medal and Malton was his competitor, Soane obtained it and was sent to Rome by the Academy, where He secured the Patronage of Mr. Thos. Pitt, afterwards Lord Camelford, who on his return to England introduced him to Lord Chatham &c — Soane married the niece of Saml. Wyatt, who built the Albion Mills, and at whose death He came into possession of a large fortune. — Mr. Pitt obtained for him the appointment of Architect to the Bank which is a very good place. — Soane gave up a place of £300 a year in the board of works, and was the means of obtaining it for Mr. Groves, the builder.

Wheatly has been much afflicted by the gout the last summer, & is now confined. He has not been tolerably well more than 5 weeks in 3 months.

I called on Batty, and we went together to Smirke. — Smirke again spoke to me of a design for Alderman Boydells industry picture for Guildhall. — I said upon consideration I did not suppose the Alderman could be pleased unless the design described his favorite Ideas.

Smirke thinks the list of Candidates is so weak that it is highly imprudent to fill all the vacancies. I concurred with him in opinion, but said who would hold a conversation with such a [erased: President?] as we have got, who would reveal any opinion He was intrusted with & that in the most dangerous way. On whom no reliance could be placed and who would tell a falsehood as readily as speak truth. Opie call'd this evening.

Saturday Octr. 11.

Westhall called this morning. — He has finished or nearly so, his picture for the Academy. — He has promised a vote to Malton, for civilities recd. from him. He told me in the Sunday paper called the Observer there are severe strictures on the professional characters of Artists and that He has been roughly handled. They are supposed to be written by — Williams, who assumes the name of Anthony Pasquin.

Batty prescribed for me yesterday for a violent cold which I got the day I left the country.

Sunday Octr. 12th.

At home confined.

Monday. Octr. 13. ⎫
     — 14. ⎪
     — 15. ⎪
     — 16. ⎬ [*No entries*]
     — 17. ⎪
     — 18. ⎪
     — 19. ⎭

Monday — 20 Dr. Reynolds called. — This day James
     — 21 ⎫   Adam the Architect
     — 22 ⎬ [*No entries*]   died. — aged 58 or 9.
     — 23 ⎭

     — 24 ⎫ Bob & William came from Hoddesdon.
          ⎭ Boydell called. He wrote to Smirke.
     — 25 — Bob went to Oxford.
Sunday — 26 Came down into the drawing room.
     — 27 [*No entry*]

Octr. 28.

Boydell called, and informed me of letters having passed between Mrs.
B. and the Alderman. — Lysons called. He came from the Country
yesterday. Mrs. Piozzi has written to him abt. having some drawings of
mine views of London.

Marchant came in the evening. He has made a tour among his friends in
the Country. He was with Lord Pembroke at Wilton. He says there are
very few good things among the Statues &c there. He was at Sir Richd.
Hoares, at Stourhead, — and at Mr. Banks at Corfe Castle. — He was last
night at Lady Spencers, who said what Lord Spencer had done in politicks
was from a pure love of his Country.

Wednesday, Octr. 29th.

Garvey called on me. I told him He might be assured of Gainsborough
Dupont having my first Vote. He is disposed to vote for Dupont,
Downman & Soane.

Dupont called on me. He told me his Uncle Gainsborough had completed his 61st. year when He died. The Tumour in his neck, which proved
cancerous & caused his death He had been sensible of 5 or 6 years, but
when He occasionally mentioned it, He was led by others to believe it only
a swelled kernel. — A cold He caught at Hastings Trial, caused it to

inflame. He applied to Dr. Heberden who treated it lightly, and said it would pass away with the cold. He applied to John Hunter who advised salt water poultices which greatly encreased the inflammation, & a suppuration followed. There seems to have been a strange mistake or neglect both in Heberden & Hunter. — Gainsborough was ill Six months. A fortnight before his death He desired to see Sir Joshua Reynolds, who visited him. He regretted leaving the world at a time when He thought He had discovered something new in the Art. — A little jealousy of each other seemed to exist in the minds of Sir Joshua & Gainsborough. — The latter thought himself slighted by the former in some occasional advances which He made towards him. — Gainsborough proposed 2 or 3 years before his death that they shd. paint each others pictures. Sir Joshua sat once to Gainsborough, but did not seem ready to make a second appointment.

In the latter part of his life Gainsborough painted chiefly by candlelight, which became his inclination.

This evening notice came from the Secretary of the Academy that as the Academicians elect had not recd. their Diplomas there would be no election of Associates this year.

Smirke & Batty drank tea.

Thursday Octr. 30th.

Taylor of Hatton Garden called and mentioned the enquiries of Mrs. Siddons.

Hearne called on me.

Batty drank tea. — Hamilton told him that Lawrence had acquainted Mr. West that his picture was ready.

Friday Octr. 31st. — 1794.

Tyler called.

Ben, from the Academy called to acquaint me that his mother, Mrs. Malyn, Housekeeper to the Academy, died yesterday aged 76. — He is petitioning the Members that his wife may supply her place. — Humphry drank tea.

NOVEMBER 1794

Saturday, Novr. 1st.

Hodges, — Smirke & Marchi called. Batty dined with us. — Marchant came in the evening. — Zoffany — Bartolozzi, — Loutherburgh — & Stothard, have promised to vote for him.

Sunday — 2d.

Edwards called. — His Mother is now 88 years of age. — Tyler came in the evening.

Monday 3rd.

Humphry came to tea. — Daniel has brought from India 1400 drawings, including black lead pencil outlines &c. H. Hamond went to Lynn.

Tuesday 4th.

Sir F. Bourgeois called, but I was not come down.

Wednesday Novr. 5th.

This day a letter came from Will, to acquaint us that my Mother was seized with a paralytic complaint on Monday at dinner time. — Owing to a neglect of the poeple who manage the Hoddesdon Coach parcels, Wills letter of yesterday was not delivered till this day. Susan wrote to Harry, Dick & Bob. — A second letter from Will dated yesterday was brought this evening, to inform us that no material alteration had taken place in my mothers condition since Monday.

Batty dined with us — Tyler called in the evening.

Monday — Novr. 6.

Antiquarian & Royal Societies met today.

Steers called. — Jones called, He says the poeple in that part of Wales where he resides are now very quiet, and little is said abt. the rights of man.

257

Bob came from Oxford this evening. — He recd. Susans letter by the mail coach before 7 this morning.

Friday — 7th.

First Academy Club.
Bob remained in town today not being able to get a place for Hoddesdon. — In the evening William came from Deptford.
Lysons came in the evening. — He was at the Antiqarian Society yesterday evening, the meeting pretty full. Lord Leicester in the Chair.

Saturday Novr. 8th.

Steers called today. — Bob & William went to Hoddesdon.
G. Dance, & Batty drank tea, afterwards Byrne, Marchant & Stadler came. I introduced Stadler to Dance, as a proper person to undertake the printing Ogbournes engraving of Lord Camdens head.
Dance says Newgate is divided into 3 Courts, — one for the Debtors, the Middle Court for common Felons, in which is the condemned hole, — and the third court for state Prisoners or those of a superior class. — It is 50 feet square. The building is 3 stories high. The rooms for the prisoners are abt. 15 feet by 18 feet, windows glazed, walls plaistered, and a fire place in each.
Marchant told us there were only 9 Members at the Royal Academy Club yesterday. — The weather was very bad.

Sunday Novr. 9th.

Tyler drank tea. — Richards told him that the notices to the academicians of the Election of Associates being postponed were not issued by him till Wednesday the 29th. of October, when neither Westhall, Lawrence, or Stothard had delivered a picture. Lawrence & Westhall sent their pictures in the evening of that day. Stothard not yet. Richards issued the notice of his own accord as there was not time left to go through the necessary business of calling a Council, — preparing the Diplomas, — and waiting on the King.
Richards described the behaviour of Ben (Mrs. Malyns son) & his wife and family being such that on the night of the funeral He was obliged to order them to be turned out of the Academy appartments.

Monday Novr. 10.

Taylor called. Old Mr. Lawrence contradicted Taylors statement of the Academicians elect, and Westhall & his sons pictures were delivered in time.
Smirke, Batty & Hamilton drank tea. — Hamilton considers Hoppner as sure of the next election.

Tuesday, 11th.

Westall called. He is going to take a House in Upper Charlotte St. & to build a painting room.
J. Boydell called. The Alderman is induced by the Bankers to suspend his Guildhall print scheme.
Dick & Harry came in the evening from Hoddesdon.
George Dance drank tea. He yesterday walked in the City procession as Master of the Merchant Taylors Company.

Wednesday — Novr. 12th.

Steers called.
Dance, Smirke & Batty drank tea.
Dance has paid Ogbourne £30 for engraving Lord Camdens head. — He has now undertaken that of Sir Wm. Chambers, which he expects to do for £16 at most.

Thursday 13th.

Dick & Harry dined with Mr. Wells at Deptford & saw the new Lascelles on the stocks.
This day Mrs. Offley lent me her Coach & I went with Susan into Hyde park.

Friday 14th.

Mrs. Offley called & we went in her Coach to Hyde park. — G. Dance drank tea.
Holcroft is the son of a gardiner at Bath, so Lawrence told me.
Holcroft, who is indicted for High Treason, was a chorus singer some years ago. In that capacity Wm. Dance, the musician, saw him in the country and at the time Miss Harrop, (now Mrs. Bates) was of the party. — Holcroft had a Son, who He is said to have treated with great severity. The Lad ran away and went on board a ship, and being traced by his father who went to the ship, blew his brains out on his father approaching him. — Holcroft is avowedly a man of the most loose priciples with regard to religion.

Saturday Novr. 15th.

recd. from Bulmer letter press of 2d. Vol: of Thames to page 48 inclusive.
Today Dick & Harry went to Hoddesdon.
Mr. Frazer called. He proposed introducing me to Ld. Bredalbane.
As instances of the profligate charges made by the persons employed by the Prince of Wales, He said the Farriers Bill for one year was £1800 though the Prince has reduced his stud to a very small number. Dr. [blank]

the Farrier, charged 2 guineas a day for attendance, and when He went to Brighton that sum and 14 guineas for expences.

Mr. Frazer is employed by the board of Agriculture in surveying Counties. Mr. Pitt was not inclined to the establishment of the board on acct. of the expence. About £3000 a year is now allowed for all expences, which Mr. F. says is too little. — The king is favourable to the scheme.

Humphry came in the evening, and Hamilton.

Lawrence is obliged to quit his lodgings in Bond St. and is to have the late Mr. Bacons in Bruton St. for which He is to pay £300 a year. He wd. build painting rooms but cannot get a lease for more than 14 years.

Mrs. Cosway is returned from Italy, in company with young Bartolozzi and Flaxman, the Sculptor. Flaxmans drawings and sculpture are highly spoken of.

Sunday Novr. 16th.

Byrne called. His 3 daugtrs. possess extraordinary talents for drawing & etching. — The eldest. flowers, the second is now employed in painting minature, the youngest in etching. — Edwards called. He desired to see the first volume of the Thames, and expressed his approbation.

C. Offley called.

Revd. Dr. Breeden called.

Copley called. — He thinks Richards is acting very wrong in refusing to correct his own misstatement of the motion relative to Bromleys Book. — Richards has put down Hodges motion 'to recommend it to the Council to discontinue the subscription', — instead of Tylers 'that the subscription to Bromleys History of the Arts be discontinued'. — It is particularly strange that Richards should hesitate to correct his mistake as Tylers written motion is now in his Richards hands.

Monday — 17th.

Horne Tookes trial began today.

Tuesday, Novr. 18th.

Weather cold. Glass 45. — Taylor called.

Batty, recommended increasing the quantity of Valerian.

G. Dance, drank tea & eving. — Lord Camden is subpoened by Horne Tooke, and came to town yesterday. — The intention of administration is to support the war.

Dick & Harry returned from Hoddesdon and left my mother much better. She can use her left arm.

Marchant — came in the evening.

Wednesday 19th.

Weather very cold. Glass 40. Ice. Dick & Harry informed me that Wills debts amount to £650. — To discharge them there is £239 of Georges money, Bob owes £90, and Dick pays the remainder. All Wills Hoddesdon debts were discharged yesterday, and this day his debts in London are to be settled. [*At this point an almost completely successful attempt has been made to delete nineteen lines of the text. It would appear that they refer to Will Farington's financial difficulties.*]

D. Bell, called. He told me that Stone, the prisoner in Newgate for treason prevailed on a Mr. Payne, formerly partner with Bush & Masterman, to enter in to partnership with him in the Coal Trade. — This partnership had only lasted 4 months when it appeared that Stone witht. the knowledge of Payne, had raised money in their joint names to the amount of £25,000, which it is supposed He has remitted to France, or America, & that He meant in a short time to have gone abroad after having completed his fraud. — Payne is ruined. — This is another specimen of the Honor & honesty of a man who is a pleader for 'the rights of man'.

Steers, called and fixed the size of the view of Kew-bridge. The brick arches are to be left out.

Harry, dined with us. — Dick at the Captains Club. — Wilson, has got a Bombay & China voyage.

Humphry, called in the evening. — The Princess Sophia of Gloucester is to set to him.

Thursday — Novr. 20th.

Dick, Harry & William dined at Offleys, the weather was so cold Susan & I did not go.

Wilson made 9000 guineas by his freight from Bombay to China. If all turns out well He will clear £15,000 by the voyage.

Friday — 21st.

Harry & Dick left London at 9 this morning. — We finally settled our accts. before we parted. — They have settled Wills affairs.

Cosway, called and took me in his Coach to the Royal Academy Club. — nineteen members were present. — Tyler in the Chair. — Much talk today of the apparent prevarication of Mr. Pitt yesterday when He apppeared as on evidence on Horne Tookes Trial.

Nollekens said, Dalton died worth about £5000. — He married the daugtr. of a Spitafields weaver who had £500 a yr.

Lawrence told me He & Westall had sent a letter to Mr. West today, to inform him their pictures are ready, and desiring a Council may be called in order that they may receive their Diplomas on the 10th of Decr.

Marchant told me that Poggis man had informed him that Hodges means to make an Exhibition of his two Pictures of War & Peace.

Copley told me that the Plate of Lord Chathams death, had yielded no more than 2500 impressions, and was quite worn out. — He expressed great discontent abt. Bartolozzis process in that Plate. In one day 18 months work was beat out, and the Plate proved rotten from repeated erasures. — He seemed to have little desire to engage again with Bartolozzi. — I told him I now only recollected two engravers who besides Bartolozzi were fit for great undertakings, — these were Sharp & Heath. He allowed it, and particularly dwelt on Sharp. — He said the difficulties of a Painter began when his picture was finished, if an engraving from it should be his object.

Lawrence desired me to set to him on Tuesday next that he might proceed with my Portrait.

Saturday Novr. 22d.

Horne Tookes trial concluded this evening. The Jury retired at 8 oClock and were out only 10 minutes when they returned with their Verdict Not Guilty.

William came from Deptford this evening.

Sunday, Novr. 23d.

Batty, was at the trial yesterday. He complained of the Lord President (Sir Jas. Eyres) charge, as being hard on the Prisoner. — After the acquittal, Sheridan & Genl. Tarleton, came down from the Bench to congratulate Horne Tooke. — Beaufoys evidence is considered as prevaricating & contemptible. — He did not He said remember the Uniform worn by the Members of the Association though He was one. — Batty said Sir Joseph Banks declared, He had seen Beaufoy at his House in that dress many times.

Dance, drank tea. He has heard Mr. Pitts manner of giving his evidence defended.

At the last meeting of the Architects Club Holland proposed to bring forward a Motion 'that any member who might give offence to another member either in or out of the Club, should be liable to mulct, fine, censure or expulsion, as should be determined by the Club'. The members in general seemed to think the motion improper, but it stands over for the consideration of the next Club. Dance says Hollands aim is at him, on acct. of his arbitration in the dispute Holland had with Ld. Thurlow about payment.

I told Dance that if Soane desired to secure his election in November next, He must endeavour to associate with the Members of the Academy that they might have a personal knowledge of him.

Soane & Dance have settled the business between Mrs. Playfair & Mr. Gordon. The latter gave up a claim of £150 which Playfair had overdrawn him.

Baker, called in the evening. There was a very great mob abt. the Old Bailey, yesterday evening. — The Lord Mayor, (Skinner,) addressed them, saying He would only use the *civil* power when a guard was necessary, and recommended to them to retire peacably. — Erskine & Sheridan addressed them from Erskines windows.

William, returned to the Ship.

Susan, began to take Valerian.

Monday Novr. 24th.

Byrne, applied to me for my vote in favor of Mrs. Hadriel, the Printers widow, to succeed Mrs. Malyn.

Tyler called. He has completed 20 leaves of Manuscript of his proposed work of the progress of the Arts in England.

Revd. Mr. Este, called. He has been in Ireland 7 weeks, and returned on Friday last. — He says the Irish hold Ld. Westmorland in great contempt. His Ld. ship is attached to Mrs. Stratford, wife of Col. Stratford, Brother to Lord Aldborough, and daugtr. of Mr. Hamilton Brother of Sir William Hamilton. — She is abt. 45 years of age and paints white and red. Este, says the Lady Westmorland died of a broken heart, from feeling the partiality of his Lordship for Mrs. Stratford.

Este, says, republican principles prevail in Ireland. They seem to have no partiality for any set of rulers, and are as indifferent to Lord Fitzwilliam as to Lord Westmorland. — In a company of 50 he has heard a toast given 'His Highness & His *brave followers*', alluding to the Duke of York & the French.

Este rejoices in the acquittal of Horne Tooke. — He asked if the publication of the Rivers was going on, I told him Coombes was proceeding with the 2d. Vol:, He said He was surprised at that, as he understood Coombes wd. not write any more for that work, but observed that as it was the Thames, He supposed that River which was begun was not understood. — I assented to his supposition.

Este dined with Gandon, the Architect, 3 or 4 times, in Dublin, who is now building the four Courts, which will be finished in a year & a half, & will be a very magnificent pile.

Bob, wrote to me from Hoddesdon. My Mother was very indifferent on Saturday and Sunday.   •

Tuesday — Novr. 25th.

Henry Webber called and I settled with him for the Ultramarine which He left with me to dispose of. I purchased all that remained, which at an estimation amounted to £44. — I offered him £34 which He readily accepted, and it is not probable He could dispose of it to the same advantage elsewhere. The whole of the Ultramarine left by John Webber we estimated at £74.

William came from the ship, being relieved for the last time. Mrs. Hadriel called this morning. Copley first proposed to her to offer for Mrs.

Malyns place. Humphry, Bourgeois, and Burch she had seen. They had mentioned Mrs. Tomkins (widow of the late Associate) as having offered herself. — I sent Mrs. H. to Smirke, who recd. her kindly, and I then advised her to get a letter from Copley to Zoffany and to go to the latter at Strand on the Green.

Marchant, came in the evening. He said Banks & his family are to dine with Horne Tooke on Sunday next at Wimbledon. A rejoicing dinner on Tookes delivery.

Marchant was at Lord Spencers a few days ago. Lord Camden said Lawrence was fallen of in his painting, thus it is that when the word is given by one, others follow.

Wednesday — Novr. 26th.

For the first time of walking out in almost seven weeks, Lawrence, I went to this morning at ½ past ten and sat for my Portrait till 3. If a vacancy in the Academy should be made by Burch, He thinks *then* Marchant might succeed.

Erskines attack on the Lord President Eyre, after the trial of Horne Tooke, certainly was owing to his vanity being touched by the praise which the Lord President had bestowed on Mr. Gibbs' speech.

Lawrence has seen some of the designs of Flaxman for Homer, & says they are very fine and have so much of the true spirit of the antique that they appear as if they had been designed when the book was written.

Lawrence wd. have voted for Dupont, Downman & Soane. — Steers, Garvey & Bestland called while I was out.

The post today brought a most unfavourable acct. of my mothers condition from Bob which I found on my return from Lawrence.

Thursday Novr. 27th.

The accounts from Bob this morning were more favourable.

William, went to Hoddesdon.

Marchi called. — The Club He says at the Coach & Horses, in Castle Street, now consists of Hearne, Baker, Tassaert, Col. Macdonald, whose sister married Christie the Auctioneer, — Gardner, — Munden, the Actor, & Davis, — Edridge, miniature painter, — Old Lawrence, Marchi, &c &c.

They meet in a Box in the common room. Marchi, is perpetual President.

Marchi told me that Jones has made a will and settled £500 a year on each of his two daughters.

H. Webber called. He will not consent to Heaviside being paid the value of the voyage Prints, but that they shall stand as a debt. — He says Heaviside declared to him during the illness of his brother, that He only visited him as a freind — Webber mentioned to me today his intention of becoming a drawing master.

Rev. Dr. Fisher invited me to dine at the Chaplains Table on Saturday next.

Batty, called. — Hodges has mentioned to him that he proposes to exhibit his pictures of War & Peace, and has taken a room in Bond street for that purpose.

Batty says Erskines complaint against the Lord President Eyre is that His Lordship, contrary to custom, omitted both in His charge on Hardy & Tookes trial, to notice his speeches.

Friday — Novr. 28th.

Bob, wrote. His account of my mother more unfavourable than yesterday.

Saturday Novr. 29th.

Called on Dance. Mrs. Bate, (late Miss Harrop) to set to him. — On the loss of £10,000 which she had saved; and which her husband engaged in the scheme of the Albion Mills which were burnt, Lord Thurlow obtained for her a pension from the King of £500 a year. Lord Thurlow, is very fond of musick and Mr. & Mrs. Bate are frequently with him.

The Revd. Mr. Powis & Dance called on me and we went to the Chaplains dinner at St. James's. — Mr. Powis knows Barry, the miniature painter. He & the Revd.Dr. Barry are sons to an Apothecary of that name who lived at Bristol Hot wells. He married a Miss Brown, daughter to a minor Canon of Bristol, a pretty & good kind of woman. — The Revd. Dr. Barry was brought up an Apothecary and not being able to obtain orders in England, went to the Isle of Man, where He was ordained.

Marshal Conway is 73 years of age.

Dr. Fisher, Dr. Gisborne, Physician to the King, Revd. Dr. Pearce, Mr. Devaynes, the Apothecary, Revd. Mr. Fisher, & Captn. George Fisher, Captn. Hale eldest son of General Hale, Mr. Powis, Coombes, G. Dance dined.

George Fisher has made a series of drawings in Canada from which He proposes to make etched outlines and to have them Acqua-tinta'd by Edye, who is recommended by Sandby. They mean to publish them as a joint concern.

The River of Niagara, proceeds from the Lake Ontario, about a mile and half before it precipitates over the great fall the rapids commence. The declivity of the bed of the river in this distance is abt. 50 feet. Any boat that is drawn in to the rapids is irrecoverably lost. The width of the River at the great falls is 3 quarters of a mile. — The depth of the falls is 149 feet. below

[*See drawing over page.*]

the falls the water proceeds with such furious rapidity that for 10 miles out of 18, no boat can work up against the stream. — The Canadians work

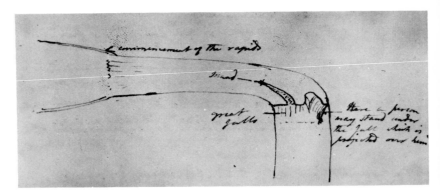

Canoes down the stream with difficulty over a bed of rocks, and the flowing of the River is similar to the fall at London bridge at low water.

Captn. Hale saw General Washington. — The new federal City of Washington, is laid out, but no buildings were erected when He was on the spot. As the lines of the streets were cut among trees, the plan might be clearly understood. They spoke of the City of Philadelphia, and do not approve of the plan of that City, all the streets of which form right angles to each other. The great streets are distinguished by Street No. 1, do. No. 2, and the short streets bear the names of trees, as Cedar street, — Pine st. &c &c.

Captain Hale is the eldest of 20 children now living. He spoke of Mr. Robinson, the present Lord Rokeby, as a very singular man, who allows his beard to grow, — eats only raw meat with some slight preparation by himself, and many other peculiarities.

Humphry, met us at tea to which Dance & I returned. Dance recommended Mrs. Hadriel to him.

Hodges frames for the pictures of War & Peace are to cost 60 guineas.

Dance will not set to Singleton, as He does not think the Architects are placed in situations such as that class of Artist should have had.

Sunday Novr. 30th.

Marchant, came in the evening. This morning Hodges took him to Ormes room where the pictures of War & Peace, are to be exhibited. The room is hired for three months, from Decr. 1st. at Six guineas a week. Mr. Thomson, the person who is to attend the room, is to have twenty five shillings a week.

Hodges told Marchant that Hayley, the poet, had first suggested to him that Landscape painting was capable of expressing moral subjects. — He began studying the subjects of War & Peace in May last.

Marchant, thinks the pictures are liable to criticism, the first scene, *peace*, exhibiting an English Country and people, — the second, *War*, the same scene under circumstances of devastation, with *Turkish* soldiers only in the front. — He also thought that the Vultures introduced as symbols relate to the *past* and not to the *present* and that where red hot balls are preparing that Bird cannot with propriety be represented.

DECEMBER 1794

Monday — Decr. 1st.

The Premiums were this day adjudged at the Royal Academy. Three Historical Pictures were offered for the Gold Medal, the subject, Cassandra coming into the Council, vide Troilus & Cressida — candidates, Philips, — pupil to West, [blank]. The Pictures being thought indifferent, it was put to the Balot whether the Medal should be given. No, by 13 to 7.

One Basso relievo, 1 only, by a son of Bacon, the subject, "Adam contemplating Eve sleeping", had the Gold Medal unanimously.

One design in Architecture for an "Exchange", — was offered for the gold medal. — Mr. Dance, expressed his opinion that it did not merit such a distinction as to receive a gold medal, and was seconded by Mr. Yenn. — It was put to the Balot, whether the Premium shd. be given, — No, 14 to 6.

Sixteen drawings of Academy figures were offered for silver medals. — It was determined by a Balot of members that *4 Medals* shd. be given. — Cardons the best.

Two geometrical elevations of Ld. Besboroughs, at Roehampton, were offered. It was determined that *two medals* should be given. — A single model of an Academy figure was offered.

This day when Mr. Richards read the minutes He acknowledged having entered the Motion relative to Bromleys Book, wrong. — He had entered Hodges's motion to "refer the discontinuing the subscription to the Council", instead of Tylers "that the subscription to Mr. Bromleys History of the Arts, be discontinued". — By direction of the meeting He corrected the mistake.

This day a Council was called to meet in the evening to receive the Pictures of Messrs. Stothard, Lawrence and Westhall.

Bonney, Joyce, Holcroft & Kidd, were this day discharged from Newgate without trial. — Fuseli & Dance drank tea with me. — Fuseli pressed much in favor of Marchant at the ensuing election. I told him I was certain Hoppner would have 20 Votes & wd. carry it. Young Cipriani has applied

268

to Fuseli, and to Hamilton, & Humphry in favor of Lowe's widow, to succeed Mrs. Malyn. She has 3 Children.

Barry told me at the Academy that the report of his having been robbed of £290, was true. About ten days ago some persons got into his House through a window and went directly to a Bureau where his money lay. — He was on the point of concluding a bargain for the lease of a House in St. Georges Row, for which He was to have paid £300.

Tuesday — Dec. 2d.

William, came from Hoddesdon this evening, & brought a letter from Bob. — my mother departed this life at 6 minutes past 8 oClock this morning. — my mother was born in March 1716.

Wednesday, Decr. 3d.

Westhall, called on me yesterday. He has taken the House in Upper Charlotte Street. — His lease is for 30 years at £70 a year.

He had heard that his & Lawrences pictures when first put in were very slight — They had their pictures back to reconsider them. Lawrence made no alteration. Westhall, changed the effect of his. The Boys head was first in shade, relieved from a light background, — He has now made the Head light, & the back ground dark.

Raphael West told him lately that his Father was busily employed at Windsor, preparing an Oration for the 10th. of December.

Tyler, called. His mother is now living with him, aged 88 years, but very infirm. — N.B. She died in January. — C. Offleys called.

Thursday Decr. 4th.

D. Bell, called and desired my opinion of the wishes of his friend Mr. Lindo, who is very desirous of improving himself in painting. He was some years since in a situation in Barclay (late Thrales) Brewhouse, and has now some concern in the Corn line, but his inclination to the Arts supersedes everything. I said it was impossible for me to give an opinion unless I saw some of his productions, and was better acquainted with him, as so much depended on the turn of mind of the party, and the probability of his applying so as to make up for lost time. — Mr. Bell is to bring him to me some morning.

Landseer, called. Bowyer has spoken to him abt. engraving from the Picture of Charles 2d. with the Peverells. — I told him I could not at present shew it to him as it had been delayed by my illness. — Artaud is 31 or 32 years of age. I dined at C. Offleys. Barroneau there, — J & William Offley only. — William returned to Hoddesdon.

Friday — Decr. 5th.

H. Webber, called and desired my opinion of His proposal to teach drawing, & modelling in Wax or Clay. I recommended an alteration which He thought was for the better.

Paine, is one of the Jury on Thelwalls trial. The Jury this day retired at 12 oClock & at 10 minutes before 2 returned with a Verdict, not guilty.

Saturday Decr. 6th.

Harry, wrote to me assigning reasons why the interment of my mother shd. be at Hoddesdon. I concurred in opinion & forwarded the letter to Bob at Hoddesdon.

Craig, called on me. He has painted a portrait of Dr. Brownrigg, who is now 85 years of age.

Craig was at Mr. Fawkes's in Yorkshire, 12 miles from Leeds when Hodges was there to make sketches for 4 pictures. The subjects were left to his choice. The Pictures abt. half lengths. Hodges charged 300 guineas for the four, besides frames. — Mr. Fawkes, is extremely discontented. He complains that the views are not made like the places, that they are slightly painted & the charge very great. The Pictures are taken down & turned to the wall, & Mr. Fawkes says He will never buy another oil picture. He is abt. 26 years old. — Smirke, drank tea. At the Council on Monday last West read a letter adressed to him by Messrs. Lawrence & Westhall, signifying their having delivered their pictures & desiring that a Council might be called and their Diplomas obtained in time that they might on Wednesday the 10th. exercise their right of voting. — The Council thought the letter dictatorial, and this not being the drawing room week, the Diplomas cannot be signed unless Messrs. West & Richards go to Windsor on purpose. This the latter said He cd. not conveniently do. It is, therefore understood that the Diplomas will not be signed till after the 10th. — West spoke to Smirke abt. the King having been informed of his holding democratic principles. He intimated that G. Nicol had told Barnard, the Librarian, who had carried it to the King. He also seemed to hint at Boydells.

Lysons, called in the evening. — He heard Pitt & the Duke of Richmond examined on Horne Tookes trial, & thought they both made poor figures. — He said the acuteness & coolness with which Tooke examined them was admirable. — He was disgusted to see Lord Lansdown, one day before the Court sat formally, — beckon to *Frost*, and talk familiarly to him over the benches.

Sunday, Decr. 7th.

C. Offley dined with us. — He adressed Miss Backhouse, eldest daugtr. of Mr. Backhouse, a merchant of Liverpool formerly partner with Tarleton. — She had a previous attachment.

Tyler came to tea. — Dumerque, the Dentist made out a Bill for attending the Royal Family at Windsor and in Town, a year and a half £3000, — He was paid £1500.

Marchant, came. — The man who attends Hodges exhibition, yesterday told him that nobody came, and that there was not a single subscriber.

Batty, told us today that Mrs. Hodges on Friday had a paralytic affection in one of her cheeks, and that Her mouth was drawn by it a little on one side. — It is not reduced. He imputes it to her bearing children too fast for her constitution.

Monday — Decr. 8th.

Revd. Mr. White, of Lichfield, wrote to me recommending Mr. Glover, a drawing master of that town, who proposes coming to London.

Westal, I called upon. — R. West told him the other day that His Father was busily employed at Windsor writing a discourse to be delivered at the Royal Academy. — He thought His Father had better have left it alone as it was out of his way. — He said He wished His Father would allow him £100 a year, with which He wd. do his best & require no more. — Being left to himself He shd. very likely apply to painting much more than He did now He was pressed to it, — which gave him the bile.

Tuesday — Decr. 9th.

H. Howard, called on me to request my Vote for his going to Italy on the Academy foundation. He told me Artaud is in tolerable circumstances having some independent income. — I said I had conceived to the contrary, and that it would certainly weigh with me in favour of a Candidate that the income granted shd. be necessary to him. — He appears to have a majority of the Academy in his favor, if the names He mentioned have promised Him their votes. — Garvey & He lodged in the same House at Rome.

Humphry & Marchant came in the evening. — Marchant gave me Durno's letter with signatures of Artists ackowledging his being the first cause of the indulgence for admitting works of Art, duty free.

Wednesday — Decr. 10th.

Garvey, I called on & told him of Howards visit to me. — He gave a very high character of Howard, & I told him in consequence I shd. make no exertion in favor of Artaud.

Fuseli, Dance & Opie drank tea with me. We went together to the Academy. — After opening the balots the Academicians went into the Great Room.

A Gold Medal was given to —

— Bacon —

4 silver medals for academy figures.
1 do. for a model of do.
2 dos. for geometrical elevations of Ld. Besboroughs.

Mr. West, began his discourse at 20 minutes before 9 and finished in 40 minutes.

Academicians present

Wilton — Catton — Barry — Farington
Richards — Zoffany — Bacon — Opie
Dance — Burch — Garvey — Northcote
P. Sandby — Nollekens — Banks — Hamilton
Wyatt — Russell — Tyler — Copley
Fuseli — Yenn — Wheatley — Smirke
Bourgeois — Humphry came to the Ballot but was not at the Lecture.

Associates

Lawrence — Rooker — Marchant — Beechy
Hone — Bigg — Tresham — Hoppner

Associate Engravers

V. Green — Collyer —

Lord Pomfret, Sir H. Englefield, Mr. Jay, the American Ambassador, — were there. Mr. Seward.

The election of a President afterwards took place in the Council room. West [22] Burch 1, — Catton 1, — Copley 1 — Mrs. Lloyd 1. — A contention took place abt. admitting the last name on the books of the Academy. Barry supported the necessity for it. It was at last agreed to be omitted, as it was evidently intended as a joke, and if seriously she was not eligible.

Four persons were then elected to be the new Council.

Farington	14	elected	4 Visitors.		
Dance	13				
Tyler	11		Wheatley	16	elected.
Bacon	8		Northcote	14	
			Fuseli	13	
Garvey	6		Rigaud	11	
Rigaud	6				
Opie	6		Opie	10	
Wyatt	5		Bourgeois	10	
Nollekens	4		Zoffany	5	
Northcote	4		Russell	5	
Cosway	4		Cosway	4	
Catton	4		Catton	4	
Banks	3		Copley	3	

Barry	3	Tyler	3
Fuseli	3	Humphry	1
Hamilton	3	Wilton	1
Russell	3	T. Sandby	1
P. Sandby	3	Hodges	1
T. Sandby	2	Garvey	1
Wilton	2	Farington	1
Yenn	1		
Wheatley	1		
Hodges	1		
Chambers	1		

No notice was taken in the Council room of the President's discourse. It seemed to be a general feeling amongst the Academicians to avoid anything that could seem to sanction it.

At Eleven the meeting broke up, and I went home in Cosways Coach with West, — Bourgeois, — and Northcote.

Bromley was at the Academy this evening and sat by V. Green. H. Hamond, came to town.

Thursday Decr. 11th.

Daniels, I went to, this morning with Smirke and saw two Portfolios of his drawings made in India.

Fuseli drank tea. — The late Lord Pomfret employed him to paint three pictures. One of them, a scene in the Rape of the Lock, the figures representing Ld. Lempster, Mr. Fermor, and Lady C. Fermor his Children. — Peter Denyss, a young man, who had been recommended by Mr. Moser, of the Royal Academy, to Ld. Pomfret was then at Easton, employed in Teaching the young people to draw. — Peter was the son of a Swiss settled in England, as a language master — Peters younger Brother was bred a musician, and his sister kept a boarding school situated on the other side of Blackfryars Bridge. — After the death of Lord Pomfret Peter married Lady C., his daugr. with the consent of her mother, & two young Brothers. She has £4000, a year in her own right. — The widow, Lady Pomfret, has something of melancholy insanity about her. — Peter is very plain in person and near sighted. — Wests, discourse on Wednesday, was evidently intended to be conciliatory, by his introducing the names of Sir Joshua, with his picture of Hercules, — R. Wilson, with his Niobe, — and Proctor, with His design of Ixion, — also Hogarths, marriage a la mode. — It concluded with a compliment to living British Artists whom He could not name as many of them were present.

Friday — Decr. 12th.

H. Webber, brought me his altered proposals for teaching drawing &

modelling. — The manager at Mr. Wedgwoods declined engaging to shew proofs of his skill in modelling, if poeple were referred thither.

We dined at C. Offleys. The Company Mrs. Offley, Messrs. Campion, Evans, H. Hamond, C, J & Wm. Offley.

Mr. Evans said Mr. Pitt had this day agreed for a loan on terms which He considered to be very advantageous to the public. — Robarts Curtis & co, — Thellussons, Solomon, are the persons who have agreed for it.

Mr. Campion mentioned the Duke of Richmonds conduct in the County of Sussex relative to the armament of Corps by subscription. — When he could not direct everything He declined acting.

Saturday Decr. 13.

Taylor, called. — He said He had written a short acct. of Wests discourse for the True Briton at Heriots request.

G. Dance called. — A quarrel between Soane & Yenn took place at the last Architects Club. Yenn accused Soane of having spoken disrespectfully of the Royal Academicians & of the Institution. Soane returned a flat denial. Soane has since written to Yenn again denying his assertion.

Lord Lansdowne said a few days ago He believed Pitt would go out. — That the Prince of Wales had given the most profuse orders for Diamonds &c in consequence of his intended marriage.

The scheme for introducing warm air into Ld. Lansdownes library is suspended, in consequence of his Lordship having been told it would spoil his Books, as the air though warm wd. cause damp.

Smirkes, I dined with. The two Daniels & Batty there. Smirke told me Alderman Boydell had called today about the Guildhall picture. — Daniels proceeded up the Country to about 1200 miles above Calcutta. They saw the nearest snowy mountains at the distance of 180 miles. The farthest mountains seen must have been still more distant.

The Ganges when the floods come down rises 30 feet above the ordinary level.

Flaxman, has got the monument of the Three Captains. Lady Spencer has contributed to procure it for him.

Sunday — Decr. 14th.

Wyatt I breakfasted with. Mrs. Wyatt was so affected by the loss of her daughter 5 years ago that she has not since been in the dining parlour, and is only lately come into the drawing room.

I talked with Wyatt on the subject of the Treasureship to the Royal Academy. He thinks West wd. be the proper person to say anything on the subject to the King.

Yenn is only employed as a Clerk of the Board of Works in preparing some rooms at Windsor. — Holland, withdrew his motion at the last meeting of the Architects Club.

West intended Major Price and Col. Greville to hear his discourse at the Royal Academy, and told the former that in it He was pursuing the Ideas of Mr. Uvedale Price in his Essay on picturesque beauty.

Holland, the Architect, is accustomed to speak disrespectfully of the Royal Academy. This is readily accounted for: He is not, nor is likely to be, a member. His motion intended against Dance at the Architects Club, He withdrew on finding a large majority wd. be against him. — Holland proposed Young Hadfield to be a member of that Club. At the last meeting in assenting to the motion Yenn said He had the satisfaction to remark that the person now proposed had derived the greatest advantage from Royal Academy. It was by the Royal Academy He was sent to Italy, after having been presented by that Body with a gold medal. — This was a proof in favour of that Institution which Mr. Holland was usually ready to decry. However He was not so much surprised at Mr. Hollands abuse as at that of a person who sat by him, Mr. Soane, who also was frequently heard reviling that Body also, to which He owed everything. It was that Body which had presented him a gold medal, had sent him to Italy, and supported him there three years, — where He formed connexions that laid the foundations of his great success in life: But what was additionally surprising He had after pouring out such abuse lately put down his name as Candidate for the rank of an Associate. — Such was the acct. of Yenns adress as given by him to Wyatt. — He added that Soane denyed having put down his name to which Yenn replyed, It was *printed* & sent to him as one of the list of Candidates. — The next day Soane wrote and sent a letter to Yenn of a very abusive kind, in which He expressed his contempt for the abilities of the latter, and how little he merited any rank in the Royal Academy.

Wyatt on being consulted, advised him not to send an answer.

Hollands prejudice against Dance, Wyatt says, is most unreasonable. Before the arbitration of Lord Thurlows business, Holland was accustomed to speak of Dances integrity and abilities in the highest terms. — Wyatt, says if He had happened to be so situated as to have interfered, He could have removed Hollands complaint against Dance beyond his power of replying.

Marchant, came in the evening. He dined today with Zoffany, who has begun two pictures, the subjects *Peace & War*. He likes the Idea but not Hodges manner of treating the subjects. — Hodges has dismissed the man whom He agreed to pay 25 shillings a week to for remaining in the room.

Monday — Decr. 15th.

Bob, came from Hoddesdon. Miss Atherton has subscribed £200 to the Lancashire fencible regiment.

Smirke, called in the eveng. — He has given some directions to Cooke, the engraver, relative to the map of the Thames.

Tuesday, Decr. 16th.

Jackson Dowsing, called. — He is lately returned from the Mediteranean as Lieutenant of one of the French prizes. — He now hoped for promotion through the Walpoles, & Sir Martin Folkes. J. Boydell, called. We talked abt. the picture ordered by the Alderman from Smirke. I said the Frame was hung up. He said that did not signify, He wd. immediately write to Smirke to counter order the picture. — Boydell told me Coombes now keeps a Horse given to him by Macreath, and a servant.

Boydell has instructed some members of the Common Council on the subject of the Aldermans dispute with Copley and they have undertaken to bring the business forward and to maintain the Aldermans claim to be reimbursed the £200 he lent Copley.

Boydell called on Heath the engraver today, who has desired that the cause of the former dispute may be forgotten. — The Plate of Major Pearson is to be finished in abt. 4 months, — it will then take nine months to print 1500 impressions.

Tyler, called. He will not vote for Marchant. — G. Dance drank tea. Major Reynell has expressed great pleasure on his profile being to be engraved. He has given Dance a set of his works.

Dance introduced *Haydn*, the Composer of Music, last night to Mr. & Mrs. Bates at their House in John St., Bedford-row. — Mrs. Bates sung some of Haydn's songs, in so admirable a manner as drew from him the warmest eulogiums. — He had never heard them sung so well. — Mrs. Bates is about 40, years of age, — Dance thinks her a very sensible woman.

Wednesday Decr. 17.

Smirke, I called on, & told him of the conversation I had with Boydell yesterday. — He has begun a sketch in oil for the picture bespoke by the Alderman.

Humphry, called and informed us that Lord Spencer this day was appointed first Lord of the Admiralty, and Lord Chatham, Lord Privy Seal. — Dr. Pitcairne told Humphry that the Income to Pitt from the Cinque Ports is abt. £1200 a year, & that He is said to be £60,000 in debt. — It is understood that Dundass, in the Cabinet, has rather, in dividing, inclined to the Portland side.

Batty, drank tea. Horne Tooke dined with the Athenian Club on Monday. He mentioned that during 13 weeks of his confinement, no person was allowed to visit him, — that He was denied the use of pen, ink & paper and of Books, — and that one of the Wardens during part of that time slept in the same room with him.

Tooke said that the following enormous fees were paid to the Law Officers on the late trials. The Lord President, — Sir Jas. Eyre £500 a day, the other Judges, *each* — £100 a day. The Council employed each £1000 except Mr. Garrow who had £800. — Sir Joseph Banks, was a member of the Athenian Club, but quitted it, because while the dispute in the Royal Society between Sir Joseph &c & Dr. Horsley &c, was carrying, Mr. Griffith the Editor of the monthly review took a neutral part in that review, where the dispute was mentioned. Mr. Griffith is a member of the Athenian Club. — Dr. Blagdon also left the Club. The Athenian Club consists of 25 members. — One Black Ball excludes. — Hoppner was elected on Monday last. He was proposed by Mr. Sharp, of Fish St. Hill. Dr. Griffith mentioned the intention of proposing J. Taylor but found He would not pass the balot.

Horne Tooke, mentioned Francis, the *member* of parliament, who on the trial of Tooke spoke as if He had only a slight knowledge of him, whereas Tooke said he had been acquainted with him 40 years. — Beaufoy, also affected to know little of Tooke, though it was to Him He applied for advice how He shd. proceed to get into parliament when he proposed quitting the vinegar business.

Lysons, called. — He is going into Gloucestershire on Monday to complete his drawings of the Roman pavement.

Hughes, wrote to me today kindly inviting me & Susan, to pass the Christmas at Wimbledon.

Thursday — Decr. 18th.

H. Hone, called, — He has been at Buxton sometime painting miniatures. — Macklin told him yesterday that Laporte is to go to Ireland next Summer to draw 50 views for him, chiefly in the county of Wicklow. Hone says, the more romantic parts of Ireland, the County of Roscommon & the Lakes, have not been sufficiently noticed.

Bestland, called. I told him that Dance had declared to me He would not set for His portrait in Singletons Academic picture, since the Architects were to be placed only in the back ground. — He said the arrangement was broken through by *Burch*, who vehemently insisted upon being placed in a front situation, as He was an officer of the Academy (librarian) besides his other pretensions.

C. Offley, settled to have the picture of Carnarvon Castle — and the drawing of Do. and desired to have a drawing of Garricks Villa at Hampton, of the same size as the Church at Stratford on Avon.

I dined at C. Offleys. Messrs. Barroneau, Arbouin, Col. Robinson, who is raising a Corps of fencibles, Major Macdonald, — Mr. Johnson, Mr. Ironside, a student in the Law, — H. Hamond, J & Wm. Offley, there.

Will & William, came from Hoddesdon preparatory to Williams going on board one of his majestys Ships.

Friday, Decr. 19th.

Singleton, I sat to for my portrait in his Academy picture. — Burch was the cause of his altering his arrangements by insisting on being introduced in the place allotted for Wyatt. — Nollekens is also disatisfied with his situation, and Mrs. N. has expressed herself warmly to Bestland on the disrespect shewn to Nollekens. — Royal Academy Club. — There were 19 members present. West in the Chair for the first time this season.

West spoke of the origin of Gothic architecture. A society of men of Lombardy first gave specimens of that species of Architecture. Freemasonry originated from the same source. They spread over Europe, but wherever stationed, they were considered as a distinct class of men. — The two most ancient specimens of Gothic Architecture in England are in Rochester Cathedral, and at Boston in Lincolnshire.

Tyler told me tonight that at his end of the table it had been suggested that it would be liberal and proper, to admit such students of the Academy as had recd. gold medals, and had been abroad at the Academy expence, to be Honorary members of the Club. — But not to be admitted but by Balot.

The American merchants a few days ago invited Mr. Jay, the American Ambassador, to a grand dinner in the City, and invited all the Cabinet ministers to meet him, excepting Lord Chatham, thus expressing their disatisfaction.

The Students of the Academy are subscribing a shilling each to pay for advertisements of thanks to Messrs. Boydells and Macklin, for the privilege granted them to go into their picture galleries witht. expence.

Saturday Decr. 20th.

C. Offley, called. He has an intention of sending William to Lisbon with a view to his becoming a Partner in the concern with Mr. Evans. — Lysons, drank tea, — and brought his Portfolio made up of the materials for his Roman floor at Woodchester. — Smirke met him and is correcting his figures. — During the Christmas Holidays Lysons proposes to dig within the Church at Woodchester, in order to explore how far the Roman foundation extended.

Sunday — Decr. 21.

Stadler, I told this morning that the print of Richmond Hill from Twickenham, will not do, and He agreed to engrave it over again if I will etch the outline.

This day I had a conversation with Will abt. his situation. I recommended to him to take George with him to such situation as He may fix upon for his family residence, on acct. of the advantage He would derive from receiving £40 a year from Bob and me on acct. of George, who might go to the nearest good school. He made no answer approving or disapproving the proposal, — and I think is not inclined to leave Hoddesdon, — where He says, Coals excepted, things are as cheap as in other places. — He also says it wd. cost £100 to repair the House at Hoddesdon for any tenants.

Baker, called on me. — Henderson has bought Hearnes sketches on the Wye.

Lawrence, I called on, and went with him to look over the House he has taken in Piccadilly. — His Landlord is the Honble. Mr. Butler. The House was built by Novosielski. It cost £5000 and the ground rent is 93 guineas a year. Lawrence has a lease for 40 years from Christmas, with liberty to quit at the expiration of each successive 7 years. — He is to pay £250 for the first 7 years, 250 guineas for 21 years, and 300 guineas a year for the remainder of the term. — The Taxes are about £80 pr annum.

G. Dance, I dined with, He has drawn a very strong likeness of Taylor of Hatton garden today. — Tyler, Garvey, & Hodges, dined. — Soane, came after dinner. — Dance says the House Lawrence has taken is ill built, and the offices below very bad and inconvenient. — Soane, told me He was sent to Rome by the Academy in 1778. He did not live upon the £60 a year, but on his return in 3 years was about £120 in debt. — Before He applied to the Academy to be sent to Rome, He waited on Sir Wm. Chambers, who He prevailed on to show some drawings which He had made to the King, which Sir William told Soane his Majesty approved, and directed that He shd. be sent to Rome by the Academy. Soane considering himself certain of the appointment gave up the situation He was then placed in. When Sir William moved the business in the Academy Sir Joshua Reynolds opposed the appointment of Soane, unless it came *regularly* by *election* of the Academicians, and carried his point after a contest with Sir William. In consequence Soane was formally called upon by letter from the Secretary as being one of those who had gained a premium and others also recd. a similar notice. — That the Academicians might be capable of comparing the respective claims, the drawings of such as offered were again brought before them. — Soane had 17 votes out of 20. — He went abroad in company with Brettingham, the Architect, who also had £60 a year allowed him by his Father. — Soane gave 2000 guineas for the Freehold of his House in Lincolns Inn-fields, and rebuilt it. — He told me He entertained a very respectable opinion of Sir Wm. Chambers notwithstanding what his friend Yenn said to the contrary. I said from what I had observed of Sir William He was a humane man.

Monday, Decr. 22d.

Batty, called and told me he dined with Horne Tooke at Wimbledon yesterday. A large party was there — Tooke told Batty, that his expences in consequence of being taken up and tried, would amount to £1000.

Tooke said He had no opinion of Talien, who notwithstanding his attack on Robespierre, had been concerned in many of the former cruelties. — Tooke thought very ill of Robespierre, but well of Barrere, who He considered as one of the most honest men of the French leaders.

Near Tookes House at Wimbledon, He and Sharp, the engraver, met Mr. Dundass, the Secretary. Sharp spoke to him as they passed, and afterwards said He was so good natured a man that it was impossible not to like him. Kidd, the Counsellor, & Pearson, a young Counsellor, also dined at Tookes. Batty thinks the latter an inflammatory young man.

William went to Portsmouth this evening, to go on board the Aquilon, Captn. Barlow.

H. Hamond and C. Offley went into Norfolk.

Sir George Staunton was an Irish Apothecary. He went to the West Indies and while there became known to Lord Macartney, who when He was appointed Governor of Madras took Mr. Staunton with him. — Since Lord Macartney returned from China, Sir George was appointed contrary to all former usage, to go as Chief Supra Cargo to Canton, to succeed Mr. Brown. The emoluments of Mr. Browns situation have been known to amount to £8500 a year. — Sir George was seized with a paralytic complaint about a month ago.

Tuesday — Decr. 23rd.

Marchant, drank tea. — Lord Bristol, invited Soane from Rome to Ireland & remitted him £30 for his expenses. Soane went, but could not agree with that capricious character. He left him & returned to England, where He found the late Lord Camelford, who He had known in Rome. To him He stated his disappointment and Lord C., recommended him to Mr. Pitt &c. Lord Spencer, paid Marchant £50 for engraving the head of Mr. Wyndham. Marchants price is £40 only — *To Artists* He only charges £30. Mr. Baker of St. Pauls Church Yd. has desired Marchant to engrave a head of Bartolozzi for him.

Decr. 24th.

Will, went to Hoddesdon.

Joe Green came to breakfast. He has been in Yorkshire at Mr. Beaumonts of Whitley, who says that had not the measures of Government alarmed the ringleaders there wd. have been an insurrection in the neighberoud of Leeds.

Bob came from Oxford. On Monday last the Principal (Bishop of Chester) and Fellows of Brazen-nose-college, unanimously agreed to raise the livings belonging to that College which were under £300 a year. — Such livings as are in London are to be raised to £350 a year, and such livings as are in the Country to £300 a year. The difficency to be made up from the Domus accumulation arising from the estates belonging to the College.

A Senior Fellowship of Brazen-nose is worth on average about £200 a year. A Junior Fellowship not above £40 a year. — Brazen-nose-College is the best endowed College in the University of Oxford.

They are possessed of an acknowledgement in the Hand writing of Charles the first of his having received a sum of money besides Plate from that College.

On Monday last, St. Thomas's Day, Bob spoke an Oration in College. The subject He chose was on the Union of Religion with Philosophy. The Bishop of Chester expressed his approbation of the composition in warm terms, both for the matter it contained and the elegance & force of the Latin, saying He had not heard it equalled in many years. He strongly recommended to Bob to stand for the Bampton Lecture-ship. — This Lectureship is paid out of an estate and is £120 a year. A Lecturer is chosen annually.

Thursday Decr. 25th. — Christmas Day

Hoppner called on me.
Offleys, we dined at. Mrs. Offley, Mrs. Salisbury, John, William, Minet, Susan, Bob and myself. — Minet, says there is so much money floating that the minister might have had double the sum He required if necessary. — much French money is now here.

Lord Beverly paid £300 a year for the House, Park, and use of the furniture at Hitchin.

Friday Decr. 26th.

Mr. & Mrs. Hamilton, Mr. & Mrs. Wheatley, Tyler, Lawrence & Batty dined with us.

Tyler agrees with me that it would be imprudent to propose advancing above 3s. 6d. a head for the Academy dinner.

Hamilton says the life Academy requires regulation: but the Plaister Academy much more. The Students act like a mob, in endeavouring to get places. The figures also are not turned so as to present different views to the students.

Saturday — Decr. 27th.

At home. — Bob says there is as yet no great reason to expect much from young Lord Temple who has been at Brazen-nose College 2 years & ½. — He is between 18 & 19, and of Boyish manners. — He does not shew any disposition to expence or dissipation.

Sunday — Decr. 28th.

Messrs. Daniels, Smirke, Marchant, & Batty dined with me.
Messrs. Daniels, attempted to make a passage up the Red Sea, and to have come through Egypt to England, in company with Major Macdonald who undertook the direction of the navigating part. In this they failed and it appeared the Major was not qualified with knowledge for the purpose. They reached Muscat & were detained there 12 days. The heat was intense.

Fahrenheits Thermometer, stood in the shade at 104. — Failing in this undertaking they sailed from Bombay, and from thence visited the Islands of Elephanti and Salcet. Both of which were within a few miles of Bombay.

At Canton Messrs. Daniels met Mr. Hickey & Mr. Alexander, the artists who went to China in Lord Macartneys suite. It appeared that little had been done by them, excepting some figures well sketched by Alexander. Alexander described the country through which they passed from their first landing in China till they reached Pekin to be as flat as the neighberoud of Canton. — When Lord Macartney went from Pekin to visit the Emperor of China, He left the two artists behind painting banners &c with the King of Englands Arms &c to decorate tents &c for a proposed shew. — Thus they were deprived of seeing a country which is said to be beautiful and romantic, particularly beyond the celebrated China Wall.

It seems that Hickey devoted more of his time to writing than to drawing or painting, and Alexander complained that Hickey refused to supply him with paper & pencils when he required them, though a large stock was laid in of which Hickey had the care.

Mr. Daniel told me that a breed of English Dogs when carried to Bengal soon degenerate. The Heats overcome them.

Monday Decr. 29.

Sir George Beaumont called. He came to town yesterday. He has painted two pictures lately which He thinks are better than those He was working upon before. As He observes His hand was not in before owing to his having been many months from painting.

Mr. Cambridge, called to see my portfolio of Webbers drawings particularly those made in the Isle of Wight. Landseer sent him to me. — He is eldest son to Mr. Cambridge of Twickenham, and has resided in the Isle of Wight.

Mr. Glover, from Lichfield, called on me with some specimens of his drawings.

G. Dance, drank tea with us. — Smirke recommends to him to write a letter to the Council of the Academy in favor of Mrs. Hadriel.

Tuesday, Decr. 30th.

Glover, called this morning, — He was born at Leicester or somewhere in that neighberoud. He has only been in London four times before this visit abt. Christmas, and came up to see two exhibitions. During those visits to the metropolis, He recd. 8 lessons in drawing from Payne, — and one lesson from Smith. — He has been well encouraged at Lichfield, when he went out to teach He had two guineas a day, or one guinea each when He went to two Houses. He has for sometime past sent drawings to Norman, a publisher in the strand, to whom He charged a price, and Norman made what He could of them. His drawings have through this Channel sold rapidly. Such as are nine Inches wide by 7. He charges a guinea & half. If larger and *less work*, He charges no more. — His process in drawing is the same with that of Smith & Payne. No outlines, He never leaves the paper unwashed for his highest lights, but makes a mixture of gumboage & lake to warm the tint of the paper. — Over the Blue part of the Sky He also washes a little lake or mixes lake with his Blue. — In preparing his drawing for tinting, He covers the middle tints and deep shadow parts, foreground included, with a flat colour, made up of various gradations of tints composed of Blue, Lake, Tierra di Sienna, and India Ink. The Highest lights He leaves *uncovered*. Thus prepared he begins to lay on his tints, which He afterwards breaks with a tint made of India Ink, Terra di Sienna, Blue & Lake. — This Tint, in a lighter gradation, He makes use of in the distances as well as foregrounds, to harmonize the whole. — He makes use of sap green as it causes the colours to bear out acting like a varnish where it is laid. — He does not use yellow oker thinking it too heavy.

He can make one of the drawings of 9 Inches wide in abt. 5 Hours.

He proposes to divide the year between London & the Country. From Christmas to June, in London, & the remainder of the year at Lichfield &c. — He proposes to ask 7 shillings a lesson for one hour. Lady Harrington, — the Curzon family, — Sir Nigel Gressley, — Revd. Dr. Vyse, &c are his Patrons.

Steers, called while Glover was with me and took his direction No. 29 Leicester fields, to give to Dr. Munro.

Steers says Dr. Munros house is like an Academy in an evening. He has young men employed in tracing outlines made by his friends &c. — Henderson, Hearne &c. lend him their outlines for this purpose.

Tyler called. So many complaints have been made of the want of regulation in the Academy, He thinks a resolution shd. be passed that when the Academy is opened after the next exhibition, an examination should be made into the merits of the students and each student approved of shd. be formally admitted but not on any former claim.

Wednesday Decr. 31st.

G. Steevens, I met at the Shakespeare Gallery. — He told me his Library consisted of abt. 5000 Volumes. He mentioned the library of Lord Spencer as being the most select in England & not worth less than £30,000. — Lord Spencer, possesses the edition of the classics collected by Compte Revinsky, who was Ambassador here. Lord Spencer was to give him an annuity as the purchase, and the Compte died after receiving one years annuity. — Steevens, mentioned the Revd. Mr. Cracherodes library as being very valuable.

Steevens brought Boydell a sheet of letterpress which He had prepared to be inserted in the European Magazine, describing a picture of Shakespeare lately brought to public notice and which has been engraved for Richardson of Castle St. Steevens, gives no credit to the statue of Rysbrack as being a likeness of Shakespeare, & spoke with disbelief of Malones recommendation of the picture from which it was taken, and from which picture Humphry made a copy for Malone. — J. Boydells approbation of the picture from which Richardson has published a print has caused Steevens to become again friendly with the Boydells, with whom He had been cool sometime, on acct. as He said of their unnecessarily hurrying him, abt their publication of Shakespeare.

Humphry dined with us. — G. Dance & Smirke to tea. — Humphry & Smirke went to the council.

	Present	Messrs. West — Smirke
Yenn attended with annual accts. for Sir Wm. Chambers		Copley — Bourgeois Bartolozzi — Zoffany Loutherburg — Burch Humphry —

Mrs. Hadriel was *unanimously* appointed to succeed Mrs. Malyn as Housekeeper. — Dance, Tyler & myself went to the Academy at nine and supped.

Present	West Humphry Smirke Bourgeois	Burch Bacon Dance Tyler	Richards Farington Yenn

Expence 8s. 6d. each. — staid till 2 oClock.

I had a long conversation with Yenn, who does not like the first Vol. — of the Rivers. — He says the Prints are not approved of particularly the colouring part, — and the History is condemned as being spun out beyond what the work required. These are opinions held by others. Willis, had read the Book and does not approve it. Yenn told me that had He known the Boydells had a share in the work He wd. not have subscribed to it. — we talked of a coolness that had subsisted between us and came to a right understanding.

Date Due